THE BRITISH SCHOOL
OF PSYCHOANALYSIS
The Independent Tradition

EDITED BY
GREGORIO KOHON

Free Association Books / London / 1986

Published in 1986 by
Free Association Books Ltd
57 Warren Street, London W1P 5PA

A CIP record for this book is available from
the British Library

ISBN 0 946960 23 2 pbk

Impression: 99 98 97   6 5 4

Printed in the EC by J.W. Arrowsmith Ltd, Bristol, England

150·195

1032

CONTENTS

[5]

Regression and the psychoanalytic situation

Female sexuality

CONTENTS

ACKNOWLEDGEMENTS

The following papers are reproduced here by kind permission of the *International Journal of Psycho-Analysis* and the *International Review of Psycho-Analysis*: 'Technical problems found in the analysis of women by a woman analyst: a contribution to the question "What does a woman want?"', by Enid Balint, *Int. J. Psycho-Anal.* (1973) 54: 195-201; 'The transformational object', by Christopher Bollas, *Int. J. Psycho-Anal.* (1979) 60: 97-107; 'Some pressures on the analyst for physical contact during the reliving of an early trauma', by Patrick J. Casement, *Int. Rev. Psycho-Anal.* (1982) 9: 279-286; 'Woman and her discontents: a reassessment of Freud's views on female sexuality', by William H. Gillespie, *Int. Rev. Psycho-Anal.* (1975) 2: 1-9; 'Premature ego development: some observations on disturbances in the first three months of life', by Martin James, *Int. J. Psycho-Anal.* (1960) 41: 288-294; 'Reflections on Dora: the case of hysteria', by Gregorio Kohon, *Int. J. Psycho-Anal.* (1984) 65: 73-84; 'Affects and the psychoanalytic situation', by Adam Limentani, *Int. J. Psycho-Anal.* (1977) 58: 171-182; 'Ego in current thinking', by John Padel, *Int. Rev. Psycho-Anal.* (1985) 12: 273-283; 'Attachment and new beginning: some links between the work of Michael Balint and John Bowlby', by J.R. Pedder, *Int. Rev. Psycho-Anal.* (1976) 3: 491-497; 'The analyst's act of freedom as agent of therapeutic change', by Neville Symington, *Int. Rev. Psycho-Anal.* (1983) 10: 283-291; 'Problems of management in the analysis of a hallucinating hysteric', by Harold Stewart, *Int. J. Psycho-Anal.* (1977) 58: 67-76. By kind permission of Mark Paterson on behalf of the Winnicott Trust: 'Fear of breakdown', by D.W. Winnicott, *Int. Rev. Psycho-Anal.* (1974) 1: 103-107. By kind permission of The Hogarth Press: 'The concept of cumulative trauma' (1963), by M. Masud R. Khan, published in *The Privacy of the Self* (1974); and 'An enquiry into the function of words in the psychoanalytical situation' (1958), by Charles Rycroft, published in

Imagination and Reality (1958). By kind permission of Jason Aronson: 'Elements of the psychoanalytic relationship and their therapeutic implications' (1976), by John Klauber, published in *Difficulties in the Analytic Encounter* (1981); and 'On basic unity (primary total undifferentiatedness)', by Margaret Little, published in *Transference Neurosis and Transference Psychosis* (1981). By kind permission of Tavistock Publications and Mrs Enid Balint-Edmonds: 'The Unobtrusive Analyst' by Michael Balint, published in *The Basic Fault* (1968). By kind permission of Pearl King, Honorary Archivist of the British Psycho-Analytical Society: the letters of Ernest Jones.

A revised version of Patrick Casement's paper has been included in: Casement, P., *On Learning from the Patient* (1985), London: Tavistock Publications. Juliet Mitchell's paper 'The question of femininity and the theory of psychoanalysis' was first published in Mitchell, J., *Women: The Longest Revolution* (1984), London: Virago Press Ltd.

I was sorry not to have been able to include, for copyright reasons, papers by Paula Heimann, Pearl King and Marion Milner.

It is an understatement to say that to edit a book is at least as difficult as to write one. This impossible task has been made feasible by many people. My gratitude to Bob Young of Free Association Books, who gave me unconditional encouragement to carry out the project for this book; to Tom Hayley, Editor of the *International Journal of Psycho-Analysis* and the *International Review of Psycho-Analysis*, for his generous support; to Ann Scott, editor at Free Association Books, for the thoroughness of her efforts; to the many people who contributed with their criticism: Iris Bigio, Christopher Bollas, Karl Figlio, John Forrester, Valli Shaio-Kohon, Juliet Mitchell Rossdale, Jason Wilson, and Bob Young; to Jill Duncan, the Library Executive Officer of the Institute of Psycho-Analysis, whose humour was always as helpful as her inspiration to find sources of information.

My gratitude also to Dr Nina Coltart and to Mrs Enid Balint-Edmonds. My debt to Dr Harold Stewart is very great.

Special thanks to Sue and Kit.

BIOGRAPHICAL NOTES

ENID BALINT: Organizer of the Citizens' Advice Bureau in London, 1944-7. She initiated the Family Discussions Bureau, later to become the Institute of Marital Studies, Tavistock Institute of Human Relations, London, where she has been a consultant since 1954. A training analyst since 1963, she has actively participated in the administration of the British Psycho-Analytical Society. She was made an Honorary Fellow of the Royal College of General Practitioners in 1980 in recognition of her extensive work as a leader of Balint Groups for GPs. She is in full-time private practice.

MICHAEL BALINT: Born in Budapest, moved to Berlin to escape anti-Semitism in Hungary, where he started his training with Hanns Sachs. Before completing his training he went back to Budapest, where he finished his training with Ferenczi in 1926. He moved with his wife, Alice, to Manchester in 1939, after the political persecution in his own country became intolerable. After Alice's death, he moved to London. In 1948 he joined the Family Discussion Bureau, whose leader, Enid, was later to become his wife.

The Balints' influence on the organization and practice of the probation services, social work in general, the work of general practitioners, and the development of brief psychotherapy in Britain has been very great. During 50 years as a psychoanalyst, Michael Balint wrote seven books and over a hundred papers. He died in 1970, during his third year as President of the British Society.

CHRISTOPHER BOLLAS: Born in the USA. He has been Honorary Non-Medical Consultant to the London Clinic of Psycho-Analysis, and, since 1978, Visiting Professor of Psychoanalysis at the Istituto di Neuropsichiatria, University of Rome. He is at present Director of Education at the Austen

Riggs Center, Inc., Massachusetts, and Visiting Professor of English Literature, University of Massachusets.

PATRICK J. CASEMENT: Having graduated from Cambridge in theology and anthropology, he worked for ten years as a social worker. Before becoming a psychoanalyst, he trained with the British Association of Psychotherapists. He is in full-time private practice in London.

NINA COLTART: Took her first degree in modern languages at Oxford, before doing her medical training. She became a training analyst in 1969, and was Director of the London Clinic of Psycho-Analysis for ten years.

WILLIAM H. GILLESPIE: Born in China in 1905, he qualified as a doctor in 1934. In 1931 he went to Vienna to study psychoanalysis and completed his training in London in 1937. He was President of the British Psycho-Analytical Society, and Vice-President and President of the International Psycho-Analytical Association. He has been Freud Memorial Visiting Professor, University College London, and was made Emeritus Physician in 1970. He is a Fellow of the Royal College of Physicians, and a Founding Fellow of the Royal College of Psychiatrists.

MARTIN JAMES: Became a physician in 1940, and a training analyst in 1953. He was Consultant Psychiatrist at the Hampstead Clinic; Consultant to the National Association of Mental Health, and to the Association of Independent Preparatory Schools. In 1984 he was Chairman of the Winnicott Trust. He is in full-time private practice in London.

M. MASUD R. KHAN: Born in Pakistan. He was Editor of the Psycho-Analytical Library, The Hogarth Press, and Associate Editor of the *International Journal of Psycho-Analysis* for many years. He is at present Coredacteur Etranger of the *Nouvelle Revue de Psychanalyse*, and Director of Sigmund Freud Copyrights Ltd.

JOHN KLAUBER: Took a history degree in 1939, obtaining his medical qualification in 1951. He started work in private practice as a psychoanalyst in 1953. At the time of his death, in 1981, he had been President of the British Society for a year and was about to take up the post of Freud Memorial Visiting Professor at University College London.

GREGORIO KOHON: Born in Argentina, he took his degree in clinical psychology at La Plata University. He is Consultant Psychologist to the London Clinic of Psycho-Analysis, and is in full-time private practice.

ADAM LIMENTANI: Born in Italy. He was President of the British Psycho-Analytical Society and of the International Psycho-Analytical Association. He is a Fellow of the Royal College of Psychiatrists, and Honorary Consultant Psychotherapist, Portman Clinic, London.

MARGARET LITTLE: Qualified as a Member of the British Psycho-Analytical Society in 1946, becoming a training analyst in the 1950s. She partially retired in 1971, but continued teaching and doing private consultations. She is a member of the Royal College of Psychiatrists.

JULIET MITCHELL ROSSDALE: Born in New Zealand, she read English at Oxford. She taught English literature at the universities of Leeds and Reading, and lectured in many countries. She is in full-time private practice as a psychoanalyst in London.

JOHN PADEL: Read Classics at Oxford, and taught Greek and Latin language and literature for thirteen years before training in medicine and psychoanalysis. He worked at the Tavistock Clinic, London, where he is a visiting lecturer, and was Deputy to the Director of the London Clinic of Psycho-Analysis for eight years. He has published a radical new edition of Shakespeare's *Sonnets*. He is in full-time private practice.

BIOGRAPHICAL NOTES

JONATHAN R. PEDDER: Studied medicine at Oxford and the Middlesex Hospital in London, and psychiatry at the Maudsley Hospital in London. He has been Chairman of the Psychotherapy Section, Royal College of Psychiatrists. He is Consultant Psychotherapist at the Maudsley Hospital, and is also in private practice.

CHARLES RYCROFT: Studied economics and history at Cambridge. Through the influence of Adrian and Karin Stephen he became interested in psychoanalysis, qualifying as an analyst in 1947. In 1978 he let his membership of the British Psycho-Analytical Society lapse, and moved away from the Society. He is a Fellow of the Royal College of Psychiatrists, and is in full-time private practice in London.

HAROLD STEWART: Qualified in medicine in 1947 at University College Hospital, London; he became a training analyst in 1967. He is a Consultant Psychotherapist in the Adult Department, Tavistock Clinic. He was elected a Fellow of the Royal College of Psychiatrists in 1978. He works in private practice.

NEVILLE SYMINGTON: Worked as a Senior Psychologist at the Tavistock Clinic before moving to Sydney, Australia, where he now lives. He is in private practice.

D.W. WINNICOTT: Qualified as a doctor at St. Bartholomew's Hospital in London, and worked for many years as a paediatrician at Paddington Green Children's Hospital. He was President of the British Psycho-Analytical Society, and practised in psychoanalysis and child psychiatry until his death in 1971. He also lectured at the Institute of Education, London University, on child development and at the London School of Economics; he gave many radio talks, designed to introduce psychoanalytic ideas about the family to a non-specialist audience.

[13]

Nobody can tell how you are to live your life,
or what you are to think,
or what language you are to speak.
Therefore, it is absolutely essential
that the individual analyst should forge for himself
the language which he knows,
which he knows how to use,
and the value of which he knows.

Wilfred R. Bion, 'Evidence'

Introduction

For Valli.
For Mariela, Silvana and Sebastián.

people (e.g., professionals, artists) across generations. The contradiction between a true need for independence of thought and a fervent wish to respect the main teachings of Freud was at the very heart of the project carried out by the pioneers of the psychoanalytic movement in Great Britain.

The Independent British analysts created and developed the theory of object relations, a term that has now been overused. It denotes so many different theories, it includes so many varied authors, that it has become meaningless for some (see Greenberg and Mitchell, 1983). This is not my opinion. In the context of this book, the term 'object relations' designates 'the subject's mode of relation to his world; this relation is the entire complex outcome of a particular organization of the personality, of an apprehension of objects that is to some extent or other phantasied, and of a certain special type of defence' (Laplanche and Pontalis, 1967). It implies a way of relating that is considered as an interrelationship: the individual affects his objects as much as his objects affect him.

The term 'theory of object relations' is used here in a strict sense, as the theory developed by the authors mentioned above, and those included in this book. The theory concerns itself with the relation of the subject to his objects, *not* simply with the relationship between the subject and the object, which is an interpersonal relationship. This subtle (but complex) and fundamental differentiation has caused much confusion, sometimes even within the British psychoanalytic movement. It is not only the real relationship with others that determines the subject's individual life, but the specific way in which the subject apprehends his relationships with his objects (both internal and external). It always implies an unconscious relationship to these objects.

Object Relations writers concentrated their attention on the internal world of the subject, exploring further what Freud had initiated. It was a logical consequence of the increased interest in the issue of transference. But the development of the theory of object relations entailed a certain revision of Freud's theory of the instincts. This development was prompted by the difficulties encountered by analysts in the treatment of severely disturbed patients. All object relations theoreticians have been 'deeply rooted in clinical work' (Sutherland, 1980); their theory emerged from clinical practice, partly characterized by a strong refusal to adhere to a rigid method of treatment.

Sandor Ferenczi was perhaps the first analyst to acknowledge and recognize the importance of object relations, in the analysis of regressed patients and in the observation that the deepest analyses included regression to primitive object relations. As the leader of the psychoanalytic movement in Hungary, he analysed Ernest Jones, Melanie Klein, and Michael Balint, all of whom later had great influence in England. Ferenczi's concept of 'early maternal deprivation', and his notion that object relations exist even in the deepest layers of the mind, were the theoretical background that allowed the ideas of Melanie Klein, Michael Balint, Ronald Fairbairn, Donald Winnicott, and others to develop. These authors concentrated their attention on the early development of the infant, rejecting the idea of an infant who does not relate to his objects from the very beginning. Michael Balint, for example, suggested that the physical and mental development of the child depended on the existence of object relations, the intense, complex libidinal involvement with the environment. He characterized the earliest relationship with the environment as a relationship to a 'passive object love', the wish to be totally loved by this object (embodied by the mother's breast). When Michael and Alice Balint moved to England in 1939, they found that the ideas developed in London had progressed along similar lines.

Fairbairn, some of whose most important contributions date from the first half of the 1940s, gave great impetus to the theory of object relations. In his account of 'the origins and growth of object love', Fairbairn conceived the development of the personality as based on the actual experiences with objects from the very start of life. Fairbairn's underestimated contributions to British psychoanalysis could be summarized as follows: the instincts are not pleasure-seeking but object-seeking; the pleasure involved in object relations has a selective and formative function, it is not the primary aim of activity; since there

[21]

are object relations from the beginning of life, this presupposes the existence of an early ego, or self; aggression is understood as a reaction to frustration in reality; the original anxiety is related to issues concerning the separation from the first, maternal object (see Sutherland, 1980). Most British analysts share these views.

The British object relations authors have been recently and acutely characterized: '[They] do not constitute a "school" by virtue of subscribing to a set of shared beliefs but, like a school of painters, by virtue of a shared set of problems and sensibilities' (Greenberg and Mitchell, 1983). A common sensibility, a shared attitude or approach to similar clinical problems, do indeed distinguish the psychoanalysts of the British School of Object Relations, beyond sometimes very serious theoretical differences.

The Independent Tradition best represents the tradition of the British Psycho-Analytical Society. This Introduction is not intended as a complete history of the psychoanalytical movement in Britain, nor is its aim to present a polished version of the theory of object relations, nor even to systematize the body of contributions from the Independent analysts. It offers an overview of some of the clinical and theoretical areas of interest, often derived from the work of Balint and Winnicott, of some of the contemporary analysts belonging to the Independent group.

First I consider the history of psychoanalysis in Britain, and focus my attention on three factors which have contributed to the distinctive characteristics of British psychoanalysis. These are: the acceptance of lay analysis; the development of the psychoanalysis of children; and the interaction with a specific cultural milieu.

These three factors grew out of particular historical contradictions. Firstly, the acceptance, the protection, and the encouragement of lay analysts coexisted with but contrasted with a suspicious, distrustful attitude towards non-medical practitioners. Secondly, the flourishing of important schools of child analysis, which revolutionized attitudes and policies in British society, occurred in a culture that was characterized (at

[22]

least, in its middle and upper classes) by a distinct and clear distance between parents and their children. Finally, psychoanalysis developed in the context of a society where individuals were not supposed to ask for psychological help; where psychotherapy was looked upon as an unnecessary indulgence, and psychoanalysis more or less ignored by the academic and professional institutions; but where, nevertheless, the tolerance shown by that same society made the growth of the psychoanalytic movement possible.

Secondly, I concentrate on countertransference, an issue that has occupied British analysts from early on. I believe that the contributions to this subject made by Independent analysts are of singular importance. I also believe that many other theoretical, clinical and technical issues crystallize around this particular notion.

I am expressing my own views, both in this Introduction and in the selection of papers. This book is not necessarily representative of the opinion and ideas of all Independent analysts; many will positively disagree with them. This is in the spirit of the Independent tradition.

Notes on the history of the psychoanalytic movement in Great Britain

The beginnings

THE HISTORY OF the British Society is a history of failed beginnings, a history of individual and institutional crises, and of a successful struggle for survival through hard and complex times.

It is difficult to imagine that Freud would have accepted an invitation to emigrate to any other country but England. It was no easy task to convince him of the need to emigrate, in spite of the evident proofs at hand (Freud, A., 1979). In March 1938 German troops occupied Austria and Hitler entered Vienna. Freud's works had already been 'consigned to the flames', and the stock of books at the International Psycho-Analytical Press in Leipzig confiscated and destroyed. The entries in Freud's abbreviated diary for March 1938 read as follows: 'Sun 13/3 Anschluss with Germany – Mon 14/3 Hitler in Vienna – Tues 15/3 Inspection (by the Gestapo) of printing press and house – Wed 16/3 Jones (Ernest) – Thurs 17/3 Princess (Marie Bonaparte) – Tues 22/3 Anna with Gestapo' (E. Freud et al., 1978). Freud wished to remain in 'his Vienna', at 'his post', but he also wanted to protect Anna. Ernest Jones finally won the argument by telling him the story of the second officer of the *Titanic* who, when asked why he had left his ship, answered: 'I never left my ship – the ship left me' (Jones, 1957). From another point of view, Freud had reasons to feel ambivalent towards England, and especially the psychoanalytic movement

[24]

in London. As early as 1921, he had expressed strong criticisms of Jones as editor of the *International Journal of Psycho-Analysis*. This was followed by severe judgements about what he believed to be Jones's involvement with Joan Riviere (when she had been Jones's patient). Finally, Freud had been very annoyed at the British Society's positive reception of Melanie Klein and her ideas while, at the same time, he was offended by the critical and personal attacks on his daughter (Brome, 1982; Steiner, 1985).

On the other hand, Freud had a very special regard for Britain from very early on in his life. He had visited close relatives in Manchester as a young man of nineteen, and had returned to England to discover London in 1908. Oliver Cromwell, William Shakespeare, and Charles Darwin always formed – for different reasons – part of his collection of highly admired figures. In 1880, he had translated what became the last (12th) volume of John Stuart Mill's collected works into German.

Right from the beginning, the publication of Freud's work in Britain produced a limited response. Frederic W.H. Myers gave an account of the 'Preliminary Communication' (Breuer and Freud, 1893) as early as three months after its publication. Michell Clarke praised the *Studies on Hysteria* (Breuer and Freud, 1895) in the well-known neurological journal *Brain* the year following its publication in German. (In fact Freud had published a paper in *Brain* in 1884, originally written in English, 'A New Histological Method for the Study of Nerve-Tracts in Brain and Spinal Cords'.) *Brain* later published 'Freud's Conception of Hysteria', a paper by Bernard Hart, a psychiatrist working in an adolescent unit, who was to participate in the foundation of the first psychoanalytic society. Hart's bibliography is truly impressive, with references to papers by Freud, Abraham, Ferenczi, Jones, Jung, Stekel, and many other authors less well-known to us today (Hart, 1911).

Myers, Michell Clarke, Havelock Ellis, and Wilfred Trotter are the first names associated with the origins of the psychoanalytic movement in the British Isles (Jones, 1959). It was Trotter, a surgeon with strong views against the medical establishment and a close friend of Ernest Jones, who first mentioned the *Studies* to Jones. Together, the two friends studied the psychological works of William James, Frederic Myers and Milne Bramwell, as well as the French medical psychologists, including Pierre Janet. Although at first impressed by Clarke's review, it was reading the 'Dora' case in the *Monatsschrift für Psychiatrie und Neurologie* that made a real impact on Jones. From then on, the history of psychoanalysis in England is completely entangled with the personal and professional history of Ernest Jones.

Jones met Freud for the first time in 1908, at the First Psycho-Analytical Congress in Salzburg. Jones presented a short paper, 'Rationalization in Everyday Life', in which he introduced the term 'rationalization' (Jones, 1908). Freud presented the case of the 'Rat Man', and in the history of the case, published the following year, Freud refers to Jones's concept, a 'typical occurrence in obsessional neuroses' (Freud, 1909). The concept caught on and remained a very important one in common psychoanalytic usage.

'England seems definitely to be stirring,' Freud writes to Jung in a letter of 3 March 1911. 'In the next few days I am expecting our most exotic supporter, Lt.-Col. Sutherland from Suagor in India, who means to spend two days here on his way to London' (ed. McGuire, 1974, p.400). W.D. Sutherland, a medical officer, was to participate two years later in the foundation of the first psychoanalytic society. Ernest Jones had meanwhile spent four years in Canada, where he had gone after troublesome times in London (for an account of this difficult period in Jones's life, see Brome, 1982; Jones, 1959). On his return to Europe in 1913, Jones spent some time in Budapest, where he had the opportunity to be briefly analysed by Sandor Ferenczi. The analysis took place twice a day, and lasted for two months. This was probably the first 'didactic analysis' (Gillespie, 1979), an analysis recommended by Freud to Jones specifically for training purposes. On his return to London Jones founded the London Psycho-Analytical Society, on 30 October 1913. It had fifteen initial members, only four of them practising psychoanalysis.[1]

The first organized psychoanalytic group survived for less

[26]

than six years. David Eder, a disciple and former pupil of Ernest Jones, had presented the first case of a neurotic patient treated by psychoanalysis to the British public in 1911. Six years later he published a book called *War Shock – The Psycho-Neuroses in War Psychology and Treatment*. But, according to Jones, Eder was unable to understand and accept the differences, by then well established, between Freud's and Jung's theories. He made life difficult for Jones because he wanted to accept members into the society who had clear Jungian sympathies. After dissolving the London Society, Jones immediately proceeded to form a new British Psycho-Analytical Society, on 20 February 1919. The group of founding members included Douglas Bryan, H. Devine, Barbara Low, Stanford Read, Eric Hiller, D. Forsyth, Robert M. Rigall, W.H.B. Stoddart, and J.C. Flugel.[2] In the next few years, the Society added to its membership people of the calibre of Joan Riviere, James and Edward Glover, Susan Isaacs, John Rickman, Sylvia Payne, James and Alix Strachey, Ella Sharpe; and David Eder who, after being analysed by Ferenczi, had returned to London to pursue a successful analytic career in the new Society.

From the day of its creation, the life of the Society developed very quickly indeed. Papers on diverse topics were presented at its Scientific Meetings, some of them predicting the subsequent interest particular to British analysts: 'The Psychology of the New-born Infant' by Forsyth was, according to the 'Minutes', the first paper discussed (15 May 1919). This was followed by 'Note-taking and Reporting of Psycho-Analytic cases', presented by Barbara Low, emphasizing the British preoccupation with the immediacy of the clinical situation (12 June 1919). The organization and publication of the *International Journal of Psycho-Analysis* (1920); the founding of the *British Journal of Medical Psychology* (through the influence of analysts participating in the British Psychological Society, in 1920); the creation of the International Psycho-Analytical Library (1921), and the association with the Hogarth Press (1924); the foundation of the Institute of Psycho-Analysis (1924); the setting up of the London Clinic of Psycho-Analysis (1926); the organization of the Eleventh International Psycho-Analytical Congress in Oxford (1929), were all projects accomplished during the first ten years of the Society's life. It was a remarkable achievement.

This flourishing of psychoanalysis went hand-in-hand with a growing opposition. In Britain, as in many other countries, the new psychoanalytic science was strongly opposed by the general public, the Church, the medical and psychiatric establishment, and the press. Jones, in particular, spent a great deal of time trying to defend psychoanalysis against ignorant protests and unjust attacks. In a letter to Freud, he writes: 'The imbecility of discussing technical matters with ill-informed pseudo professors of psychology is too self-evident from their own wild ramblings about psychoanalysis' (quoted in Brome, 1982). Freud knew about the futility of such an attempt. Jones was now discovering the same from his own experience: 'a bunch of psychologically illiterate nincompoops', he says of his audience. Given the wild accusations that were developing against psychoanalysis and the public concern as expressed in the popular press, a Special Committee was appointed by the British Medical Association at the Annual Representative Meeting that took place in Nottingham in 1926. The Committee's purpose was 'to investigate the subject of Psycho-Analysis and report on the same'. The Committee met from March 1927 to May 1929, and included among its members H. Godwin Baynes, representing the 'Jungian School of Analytical Psychology', and Ernest Jones, representing the 'Freudian School of Psycho-Analysis'. Among others, J.C. Flugel and Edward Glover gave evidence to the Committee during its proceedings.

The professional opposition was as ignorant and 'psychologically illiterate' as the public opposition. The 'Minutes of the Psycho-Analytic Committee of the British Medical Association', a copy of which is kept in the Archives of the Institute of Psycho-Analysis, show with great clarity how confused and frightened Jones's colleagues were. The 'Minutes' in the Archives also include some letters exchanged between Jones and other members of the Committee. They make fascinating reading, and one gains a dramatic picture of what

Jones had to deal with. When, towards the end of their meetings, the first drafts of the future report were under consideration, Jones wrote to Hawthorne, a physician colleague: 'I was rather in despair when I heard paeans of praise for a Report which to my mind was pretentious, tendentious and muddleheaded.' It would be better, he added, if the Committee 'refrains from adopting lofty attitudes' towards psychoanalysts (Letter, 7 February 1929). Jones must have felt quite desperate, but his chances of promoting a favourable report were improved by the Committee's decision to form a Sub-Committee of three members (including Jones) to prepare a final draft (Jones, 1957).

In its final 'Report' (published by the *British Medical Journal* in June 1929), the Committee declared that the investigation 'has enabled the Committee to get a clearer view of what psychoanalysis actually is, i.e., the technique and theory elaborated by Freud and his co-workers, and to approach some definition of the respects in which it differs from other methods of psychotherapy'. These other methods ought to be investigated as well, said the report, although at this particular time the Committee had contented itself with indicating their existence as different from the psychoanalytic method. In their Conclusions, the members of the Committee decided to respect 'the claims of Freud and his followers to the use and definition of the term' psychoanalysis, as applied to the theory (and the technique based upon it) devised by Freud, who was recognized as having been the first to use the term. The Committee also decided that 'psychoanalysis should not be held responsible for the opinions or actions of those who are not in the proper sense psychoanalysts'.

The disagreements amongst the members of the Committee were very extreme. A reference is included in their Conclusions about some members who 'do not even go as far as' accepting the existence of the unconscious as a reasonable hypothesis – even if it were called by a different name. The Committee, finally, declared itself to be incompetent to make a pronouncement on the criticisms of the theory and method of psychoanalysis, and to pass judgement on E. Jones's answer to their criticisms. The last paragraph reads: 'VI. From the nature of the case the Committee has had no opportunity of testing psychoanalysis as a therapeutic method. It is therefore not in a position to express any collective opinion either in favour of the practice or in opposition to it. The claims of the advocates and the criticisms of those who oppose it must, as in other disputed issues, be tested by time, and by discussion.'

The references in the literature concerning this report have mostly (the exception is Brome, 1982) held the view that it had drawn positive conclusions about psychoanalysis. Jones calls it 'satisfactory', and claims that it has been called 'the Psycho-Analytic Charter' (Jones, 1957); Gillespie speaks of it as the 'Magna Carta of psychoanalysis in Britain' (Gillespie, 1963); Pearl King sustains the view that it had given psychoanalysis its 'certificate of respectability' (King, 1979, 1981). The report produced very favourable *consequences* for the development of the psychoanalytic movement and for the establishment of a psychoanalytic community, but not for the reasons usually assumed. The report refused to approve, even appreciate, the claims sustained by psychoanalysis. Although it declared no opposition, it did not give psychoanalysis any credit. The Committee had declared itself ignorant to judge. It was only from this neutral point of view that its members recognized psychoanalysis as an independent science, outside their competence and their expertise. It was accepted as a method of treatment for the neuroses based on the discoveries of Freud about the unconscious. They agreed that the followers of Freud could use the term 'psychoanalysis' but this did not imply an acceptance of it. In any case, why should the acceptance of psychoanalysis as an independent discipline have been that important?

Jones acknowledged that the recognition of the British Medical Association could not make any special impression on Freud *because* it had been made by medical doctors (Jones, 1957).

The question of lay analysis

The question of whether psychoanalysis was creditable or not in the eyes of the medical establishment was interlocked with the question of lay analysis. I will extend myself on this particular question because I believe that it illustrates the conflict between an independent mind and the weight of tradition, leaving aside the rights and wrongs of both sides of the debate. Jones, then president of the British Society, was at the same time deeply involved in the work of the International Psycho-Analytical Association. Freud had very recently published *The Question of Lay Analysis* (Freud, 1926), whose sub-title, *Conversations with an Impartial Person*, referred to somebody who, in reality, could not finally be convinced. His work brought to the fore a serious difference of opinion that existed within the international psychoanalytic community, and that threatened to split up the international movement.

Given the importance of the issue, the British Society decided to appoint a Sub-Committee on Lay Analysis, on 2 February 1927. An 'Abbreviated Report', dated 26 May of the same year, was published (Jones *et al.*, 1927). The report ends on the following cautious note: '... *the British Psycho-Analytical Society is practically unanimously of the opinion that most analysts should be medical but that a proportion of lay analysts should be freely admitted provided that certain conditions are fulfilled*' (authors' italics). During that time, the American analysts, being very concerned with the proliferation of 'quacks', had managed to win State's approval in their fight against the lay analysts; in 1926 a law was passed in New York making the practice of psychoanalysis by lay practitioners illegal.[3] The question was going to be debated at the Innsbruck Congress and in preparation for it, a series of articles were pre-published in the *International Journal of Psycho-Analysis* (Jones, 1927). Those articles reveal the intensity of the feelings aroused by the question under discussion, and the profound disagreements between the different authors. Clearly, the problem extended beyond the question of lay analysis to *what was psychoanalysis all about?*

[31]

There is a remarkable opposition to Freud's view, reminiscent of the opposition to psychoanalysis in general. Brill speaks scornfully of the 'master', only to show great pleasure in rejecting (for once) 'his brilliant expositions'. Another analyst from New York, Oberndorf, compares Freud's endorsement of lay analysis – at that point in time – to a doctor who had made a premature unnecessary diagnosis (in other words, to a 'quack'). Among Freud's supporters, Hanns Sachs concentrated his attention on the difference between *analysis for therapeutic purposes* and *analysis for the purpose of training*. The papers presented by the British analysts, Jones, Glover and Rickman, are by far the most elaborate considerations of the subject (Jones, 1927). It is useful to consider Ernest Jones's paper in some detail.

Jones speaks of the British Society being 'the most friendly towards lay analysis', its membership consisting of 40 per cent non-medical people, several of them being of 'first rank'. Nevertheless, after this opening, Jones comes down very much on the side of analysts being required to be qualified as medical doctors. When speaking of the need for some kinds of procedure to eliminate the 'less satisfactory types' of individuals, Jones states: 'It is in connection with *this essential process of preliminary selection* that the question urgently arises of the attitude to be adopted towards the would-be lay analyst' (my italics).

Why, indeed, this should be the case, he does not explain, except that his statement contains a belief in a preliminary selection done by a medical school, to which the aspiring lay analyst would not be subject. Furthermore, Jones sustains the view that psychoanalysis has the 'nearest and most promising point of contact' with medicine, more so than any other branch of science; most patients in need of help came through referrals made by medical practitioners. Medicine would be, according to Jones, the best 'education' against the temptations of the 'rarefaction of the mind into intellectualization, either through religion or philosophical methods'. After making a distinction between the *prescription* of treatment, and the actual *carrying out* of treatment, he concludes that '. . . whether a lay person carries out an analysis or not, he should in no case prescribe it, i.e., he should not engage in practice independently of the medical profession'. This rule, Jones says, should be *an absolute one* (my italics). A physician should decide on the suitability of patients and their need for treatment at the hands of lay analysts. In Jones's understanding, this was assumed to be a strict rule in the British Society. Among his papers, held at the Institute of Psycho-Analysis in London, is a copy of the following letter sent to lay members on 29 November 1929, signed by Jones and Edward Glover:

> The closer knitting of the relationship between medical and lay analysts in the reorganization of the Institute would seem a suitable occasion to clear up some misunderstandings which evidently exist in the minds of some of the latter in regard to the professional obligations they have undertaken. While on their side medical analysts have undertaken to cover legally and to support in every way the therapeutic practice of their lay colleagues, the latter have equally undertaken *to refrain from independent practice*. This means that if a prospective patient wishes to consult them, to obtain their opinion, diagnosis, etc., *they explain to such a patient that they are not engaged in independent practice, have no intention of usurping the duties of the medical profession, and cannot see any such patient till he has first consulted a physician*. To get such a patient formally inspected by a physician after holding a consultation with him is contrary to the whole spirit of the undertaking. This principle, that *consultation and diagnosis are the province of the physician only, which he cannot share with anyone else*, a principle incorporated into the laws of every country, is accepted so completely by every medical analyst that we wish to convey our sense of its importance so as to leave no opening for possible misunderstandings in respect of it. (my italics)

This angry, unfriendly letter was sent to colleagues who were not medically qualified, only six months after the excruciating and painful negotiations with the British Medical Association

[33]

had ended. The pressure on Jones must have been very great, and his wish to keep psychoanalysis free from any risk of being slandered might have been one of the motives for this letter.[4]

In his 'Discussion on Lay Analysis' Jones expresses the opinion that 'it is desirable that most analysts be medically qualified, but there is no good reason why selected lay persons should not conduct analyses under certain definite conditions' (Jones, 1927). One should notice again that he speaks of selection for lay analysts, not for medical people. He goes on to state, against Freud's opinion and wishes, that psychoanalysis should be considered a special branch of medicine, not an independent profession. Jones also supported the idea that a medical education should be recommended to any non-medical candidates, and he hoped that the International Association would make this an official rule. Should this advice prove to be inexpedient (impossible, for example, for financial reasons), then a candidate could be exempted. In line with this opinion, Jones suggested to anyone who approached him for training that they take up medical studies: Karin and Adrian Stephen were two of those who followed his advice. James Strachey, on the other hand, lasted about one week in medical school. He then decided to forget Jones's advice, and wrote 'out of the blue' directly to Freud, who immediately invited him over to Vienna.

The future that Jones imagined for psychoanalysis is very relevant:

> The majority of analysts, however, would be, as now, medically qualified, so that direct continuity would exist between the psychological and physiological points of view. Psychoanalysis would be regarded as essentially a branch of clinical medicine. . . It would only be a question of time when psychiatrists also would make a regular practice of being trained in psychoanalysis, for I do not regard this expectation as in the least chimerical; the process is indeed already beginning. Once psychoanalysis had obtained a secure foothold in the more psychological departments of medicine, the rest would automatically follow: that is to say,

the gradual penetration of psychoanalytical doctrine among the ranks of the profession, and the incorporation of truly psychological, i.e., psychoanalytical, points of view into general medical education. The naturalistic and biological outlook characteristic of both disciplines could only result in their reinforcing and supplementing each other to their mutual benefit. (Jones, 1927)

Jones is well aware of Freud's position throughout his exposition. Jones insists that the medical qualification would protect the public. He claims that lay analysts have been spared the time, labour and money involved in medical training, and considers the suggestion made by some people that, because lay analysts have invested far less in training, they could afford to charge lower fees to their patients. Finally, he refers to lay analysts' 'disadvantages' and 'inferior position', which motivate them to look for compensatory behaviour (i.e., 'to have resort to artificial devices for maintaining self-respect').

Let us compare Freud's vision with that of Jones. Freud says to his imaginary interlocutor:

> Permit me to give the word 'quack' the meaning it ought to have instead of the legal one. According to the law, a quack is anyone who treats patients without possessing a state diploma to prove he is a doctor. I should prefer another definition: a quack is anyone who undertakes a treatment without possessing the knowledge and capacities necessary for it. (Freud, 1926a)

Not only was the situation very complicated then, as it is in many ways even more complex today, but one has to allow for differences in the social and cultural contexts between New York, Vienna, and London. Jones was concerned with the activities of the 'wild analysts', whose number – he believed – was greater in London than in any other place at the time. But this is not the whole story. There is a more fundamental disagreement between Freud and Jones. While the latter recommends that candidates obtain medical qualifications, the former states: '. . . in his medical school a doctor receives a training which is more or less the opposite of what he would need as a preparation for psychoanalysis.' And later on: 'It would be tolerable if medical education merely failed to give doctors any orientation in the field of the neuroses. But it does more: it gives them a false and detrimental attitude.' Freud's position is clear: '. . . I lay stress on the demand that *no-one should practise analysis who has not acquired the right to do so by a particular training*. Whether such a person is a doctor or not seems to me immaterial' (Freud's italics).

A year later, Freud is even less prepared to compromise. In his 'Postscript' (Freud, 1927) to *The Question of Lay Analysis* he writes: 'I cannot see how it is possible to dispute this. Psychoanalysis is a part of psychology,' not a specialized branch of medicine. He continues angrily: '. . . I still feel some doubts as to whether the present wooing of psychoanalysis by the doctors is based, from the point of view of the libido theory, upon the first or upon the second of Abraham's sub-stages – whether they wish to take possession of their object for the purpose of destroying or of preserving it.' Finally he adds his ironic, personal touch to the discussion:

> I became a doctor through being compelled to deviate from my original purpose; and the triumph of my life lies in my having, after a long and roundabout journey, found my way back to my earliest path. I have no knowledge of having had any craving in my early childhood to help suffering humanity. My innate sadistic disposition was not a very strong one, so that I had no need to develop this one of its derivatives. (Freud, 1927)

Jones was torn between his conviction on the need for medical training for future analysts and the convenience of the medical outlook, characterized as 'naturalistic and biological'; and Freud's ideas about the same issue, which he took seriously. More tellingly, Jones admired and respected the work of lay analysts of the stature of Melanie Klein, who had, in September 1926, started a successful treatment of Jones's children.

In those days, lay analysis was associated and confused with 'wild analysis' by the public and by the medical profession. In

English, the word lay can mean *non-professional, not learned*, although Freud intended it to mean *non-doctor*. This connotation attracted a lot of prejudice and, in some quarters, it still does. The question was further complicated by the fact that lay analysis was also associated with child analysis, which in those days was considered 'easier' to do than to practise 'proper', adult psychoanalysis. Jones was indeed concerned with the possibility of jeopardizing the growth and development of psychoanalysis in Britain, and wanted to protect the new science as much as possible. It is likely that he genuinely believed he was doing so, by wanting to turn psychoanalysis into a medical specialty.[5]

It was hard to be a creative disciple and to remain faithful to the teacher. While Jones opposed Freud's ideas, he fulfilled his teacher's wishes of keeping the doors open to lay analysts in the British Society. He had committed himself to this when, in 1926, he wrote to Freud: 'The thing I think you have settled beyond all doubt is that it would be very injurious to our movement to forbid lay analysis. There will be lay analysts, and there must be because we need them' (Letter, 23 September 1926, quoted in Jones, 1957). Jones and his early colleagues rejected the easier option of satisfying the demands of the medical establishment and the general public. Whatever he might really have thought about lay analysis, he supported and protected his lay colleagues. The maintenance of a high proportion of lay analysts in the British Society has been one of the most consistent and courageous achievements on the part of the British psychoanalysts. It has also been one of the most important factors forming the specific character of British psychoanalysis, both within and outside the British Psycho-Analytical Society. Twenty years later, the question seemed to be definitely settled. Ella Sharpe wrote, before her death:

> If psychoanalysis is a science that concerns the whole field of mental and emotional development then it follows that every psychoanalytically trained observer can be of value. Since all human problems are ultimately psycho-physical the science imperatively needs the services of the trained

[37]

medical man. It needs the biologist, physiologist, neurologist. Equally it needs the chemist and the physicist. But likewise, the historian, the anthropologist, the sociologist, the educationalist, the trained observer of infants, children, delinquents, all are indispensable for the building up of an unassailable body of truth concerning psychological development. (Sharpe, 1947)

The psychoanalysis of children

Melanie Klein, who was then living in Budapest and being analysed by Ferenczi, read her first paper, 'The Development of the Child' to the Hungarian Society in 1919. In 1921 she moved to Berlin, entered into further analysis with Abraham, and read 'The Child's Resistance to Enlightenment' to the Berlin Psycho-Analytic Society. The papers, published as one in 1921 in the journal *Imago*, give an account of her treatment of a boy named Fritz. Later, Melanie Klein came to see this case as the start of her psychoanalytic play technique (Klein, 1921).

About the same time another school of thought concerning child analysis was emerging, developed independently by Anna Freud in Vienna. By the middle of the 1920s, it had become clear that the two leading figures of child analysis, Klein and Anna Freud, had taken different paths and opposed each other in more than one way. Melanie Klein thought of her play technique as a comparable replacement for the basic rule of free association in adult analysis. Anna Freud saw the interpretation of the play of a child as mere interpretation of symbols, similar to a purely symbolic dream interpretation, and therefore inadequate and unsatisfactory. The differences in technique were the logical consequence of fundamental disagreements in their theoretical beliefs. These covered, among other things, the dating of the Oedipus complex, the emergence of the ego and of the superego, the question of the possibility of transference neurosis in children, the role of early anxieties, and indications for treatment.

Melanie Klein worked in Berlin until 1926. During that time

people like James and Edward Glover, Alix Strachey, Barbara Low, Mary Chadwick, Ella Sharpe and Sylvia Payne left London to have training analyses in Berlin. James and Edward Glover reported Klein's paper 'Early Analysis' (translated first as 'Infant Analysis', 1923) to the British Society. The first child analyst in England was Mary Chadwick, who started seeing children in therapy in 1922 (Glover, 1949). There were also other women analysts interested in child analysis in London, including Nina Searl (later to become a colleague of Klein's), and Sylvia Payne, who, although she was not seeing child patients, read a paper to the Society on child analysis. Alix Strachey – who was having her analysis with Abraham – sent a report from Berlin in 1924 on the treatment of children as developed by Melanie Klein. In July 1925 Melanie Klein, on her own initiative and suggestion, gave a series of six lectures to the members of the British Society. Soon afterwards, deprived by Karl Abraham's death of her main supporter in Berlin, Klein accepted Jones's invitation to move to London, where she quickly became involved in the scientific life of the Society. She stayed in London until her death in 1960, having become one of the most influential figures in the development of psychoanalytic theory.

Anna Freud published her book on child analysis in German in 1927 (Freud, A., 1929), and it was summarized by Barbara Low for the British Society. This was followed by a 'Symposium on Child Analysis' held on 4 and 18 May 1927 (Klein *et al.*, 1927). Melanie Klein opened the symposium with a detailed critique of Anna Freud's book, followed by presentations by Joan Riviere, Nina Searl, Ella Sharpe, Edward Glover and, finally, Ernest Jones. This provoked a true polarization between London and Vienna, as well as between London and Berlin. Freud immediately expressed his disagreements with Melanie Klein's position, and his annoyance at Jones's approval of it (Steiner, 1985). But whatever Freud thought about it, the fact remains that Melanie Klein had arrived at a terrain already fertile and receptive to her ideas. Pearl King rightly points out:

Some of the points of view and theoretical formulations put forward by Ernest Jones, and which were generally accepted in the British Society, were parallel to some of those held by Melanie Klein. Among these were the importance of pregenital and innate determinants over and above the influence of external and environmental stress, and their vital role in determining beliefs and perceptions of reality; the role of hate and aggression and their relation to morbid anxiety and guilt; and the early development of female sexuality. (King, 1981, 1983)

It was only natural that London became influenced by her teachings.

There was an initial period of harmonious honeymoon between Melanie Klein, her supporters, and the rest of the psychoanalysts of the British Society (King, 1983; Segal, 1979). The romance lasted until about 1935, when Klein presented her paper 'A Contribution to the Psychogenesis of Manic-Depressive States', in which she introduced the concept of the depressive position (Klein, 1935). Some of her followers claim that this marked the constitution of a Kleinian school of psychoanalysis, as distinct from the British (or English) school (Segal, 1979). At this time an exchange of lectures between Vienna and London was arranged, aimed at producing a better understanding between the two psychoanalytic centres. Jones went to Vienna in 1935, and Robert Waelder returned his visit. Joan Riviere followed Jones in 1936. During this same period the opposition to Melanie Klein's ideas within the British Society began to take shape, and included people like Barbara Low, Edward Glover, Melitta Schmideberg (Melanie Klein's daughter), Barbara Lantos, and Kate Friedlander. These last three were among a group of analysts who had emigrated because of the growing Nazi threat; by 1936, the British Society had opened its doors to about 36 analysts from Germany. (This generous reception was not, of course, exempt from ambivalence. Many of them were merely seen as 'old-fashioned Continental analysts' [Lantos, 1966].) The opposition to Klein was further reinforced with the arrival of the Freud family and colleagues from Vienna. Most of the parties in conflict now came together under one roof, that of the British Psycho-Analytical Society.

Members of the Society began to express their unease at the way things were developing. There were two main manifest sources of discontent: in the first place, the atmosphere of the Scientific Meetings was made 'increasingly unpleasant' by the disagreements between the different parties (King, 1979); the conflicts created a house divided against itself. At the same time, the 'monarchical' (Strachey, 1963a), undemocratic management of the institution, concentrating power in the hands of a few, created the second source of unrest. Although the Society was clearly going through a period of *Sturm und Drang*, it had by then developed enough for the rules to be changed. A new constitution set a maximum of three consecutive years for most of the high offices and, under this new rule, Sylvia Payne became the first president, elected in 1944.

The controversial discussions

As far as the theoretical disagreements were concerned, a series of meetings was arranged which is now known as the 'Controversial Discussions'. They took place between January 1943 and May 1944 during the Scientific Meetings of the Society, and consisted of a debate on four papers that had been previously circulated to all members. Three of the papers were later published as 'The Nature and Function of Phantasy' by Susan Isaacs; 'Certain Functions of Introjection and Projection in Early Infancy' by Paula Heimann; and 'Regression' by Paula Heimann and Susan Isaacs (all included in ed. Riviere, 1952). There was also a paper by Melanie Klein, 'The Emotional Life and Ego Development of the Infant with Special Reference to the Depressive Position', which remains unpublished.

The Controversial Discussions constitute the most important period in the history of the British Psycho-Analytical Society. The complexities of the arguments involved can be grasped by reading the limited literature available on the subject (Brome, 1982; Gillespie, 1963; Glover, 1949, 1966; King,

1979, 1981, 1983; Schmideberg, 1971; Segal, 1979; Steiner, 1985), as well as the official records of the discussions reproduced in the 'Scientific Bulletin' of the British Psycho-Analytical Society (1967). A considerable amount of material – letters, biographical accounts, etc. – remains unpublished. It goes well beyond the scope of this Introduction to give an account of the arguments that took place and of the issues at stake during the Discussions. Here I will make only a few points.

The purpose of the Discussions was to clarify Klein's position *vis-à-vis* the metapsychology of Sigmund Freud. The quarrelling parties in this supposed Armageddon have been presented as participating in a grave marital conflict between 'mamma', Melanie Klein, and 'papa', Sigmund Freud (see Strachey, 1963a). This row seriously threatened the unity of the psychoanalytic family, while the children were the witnesses to this war between the sexes. The fact is that the hostilities were fought out by two women – Melanie Klein and Anna Freud – not by a man and a woman (which prompted Glover to call it a 'bisexual controversy', 1966).

Anna Freud and her colleagues had developed their own specific version of Freud, quoted as much as the Kleinians quoted theirs. One aspect of their interpretation of Freud's contributions was the emphasis on the genetic aspects of the libido. Melanie Klein was not interested in the different stages of psychosexual development; she was more concerned with describing different *positions*, present throughout the life of an individual and denoting specific forms of object relations, with particular anxieties and corresponding defences.

In contrast to Melanie Klein, Anna Freud focused on the developmental view of the libido in the manner of Abraham. It must be said that Freud, who had first described the different stages of libidinal development in the *Three Essays* (1905b), was not really concerned with a genetic point of view. He constantly makes use of the concept of *Nachträglichkeit* and of *nachträglich*, translated in the *Standard Edition* as 'deferred action' and 'deferred' respectively. Laplanche and Pontalis define 'deferred action' in the following way:

Term frequently used by Freud in connection with his view
of psychical temporality and causality; experiences, impres-
sions and memory traces may be revised at a later date to fit
in with fresh experiences or with the attainment of a new
stage of development. They may in that event be endowed
not only with a new meaning but also with psychical effectiveness. (1967)

In Anna Freud's interpretation of Freud, the concept of
developmental lines is fundamental for the rest of her theories.
Nevertheless, the notion of *Nachträglichkeit* (which is not
really fully conveyed by the English translation) makes it
impossible to interpret the history of an individual as merely
the result of a linear, deterministic development, in which the
present is explained by the past.

At the same time, Melanie Klein's lack of interest in the
stages of libidinal development did not stop her from having a
genetic point of view, as could be gathered from the question of
the early Oedipus complex. It was not just a matter of the dating of the Oedipus complex. In Freud, the relationship to the
father *retrospectively* determines the relationship with the pre-
Oedipal mother; in Melanie Klein, however, the relationship
with the mother determines the relationship with the father following a linear cause-and-effect movement. For Freud, the position of the subject in relation to the castration complex determines his relationship to the first object. For Melanie Klein, the
experience of separation from the first object, the breast, determines all later experiences.

Melanie Klein refuted what her opponents always maintained: that she had departed from the main body of Freudian
psychoanalytic theories. Klein and her followers wanted to
prove that their contributions continued the theoretical lines
suggested by Freud. With hindsight, it is no surprise that a
theoretical accord between the two warring factions was never
reached. Melanie Klein was creating a different metapsychology, a different model of the mind, based on different hypotheses from those that Freud had developed. For example, the
Kleinians kept the Freudian terminology but formulated a

completely different concept of the death instinct. In changing the death instinct, they changed the rest of the theoretical construct, not just that one concept. Further changes were related to notions such as the unconscious phantasy life of the child at a pre-verbal stage; the archaic structure and sadism of the superego; the belief in the existence of object relations right from birth; the dating of the emergence of the ego; the different conception of female sexual development; the elimination of primary narcissism; the role ,of early anxieties; and so on. These interconnected changes formed a new body of meta-psychological ideas (see Bianchedi *et al.*, 1984; Mitchell, J., forthcoming).

These brief considerations give a rough idea of the intricate, complex problems involved in the Discussions. There were great differences in theoretical beliefs, in what each party saw as the aims of psychoanalytic treatment, in the relationship between theory and practice. There were profound disagreements over the question of formulating and giving transference interpretations to the patient. One should also remember the personal likes and dislikes, the loyalties and allegiances provoked by the situation of training, the weight of contrasting cultural traditions, the tendencies to political confrontations present in any institution, etc. At the end of it all, the gaps that had existed before the confrontations became greater and nastier.

The two sources of discontent mentioned above – the scientific disagreements and the structure of power – were closely interconnected. The crucial crossroads where all the interested parties met (or, with less luck, could have collided) was at the point of the training of candidates. Since the Controversial Discussions had done very little to resolve the splits, the only solution was to devise ways of allowing the rival groups to coexist. What had started as a war between two women ended up with a 'gentlemen's agreement' signed by three women: Melanie Klein, Anna Freud, and Sylvia Payne (Pearl King calls it a 'ladies' agreement', 1983). The compromise in the sphere of training was agreed by the Society in 1946, by which two parallel courses – A and B – were introduced. Both courses were the responsibility of one Training Committee, which was also in charge of the selection and qualification of students. While the leaders of the seminars in Course A were drawn from the Society at large, Miss Freud and her followers would teach the seminars and lectures on psychoanalytic technique for the students of Course B. The supervisor for the students' first training case was chosen from their own group, the second was to be elected from the group of analysts who did not identify themselves as either Kleinian or Anna Freudian. In this way, a Middle Group was created: the Society remained one, but divided into three separate groups with two training courses. This arrangement was complemented by a political compromise by which all three groups were to have representatives on the main committees of the Society. While the training has greatly changed since 1946, the political side of the agreement has been maintained to the present day.

It was another characteristic achievement of the British psychoanalysts, accomplished through their remarkable capacity for compromise. Unfortunately, the system did not quite fulfil its promise; new discontents soon emerged. After several changes, a new organization of the training was finally established. In 1973 it was decided that each candidate would be free to select his own programme of lectures and study groups from the curriculum, with the help of a senior analyst.

Although there has been peaceful coexistence between the three groups, they have remained separate. In spite of the restoration of good relations, a subtle, unorthodox individuality remains within each of them. The identity of the groups is more or less maintained by the expectation that a student will belong to the same group as his analyst. While in the Kleinian group the students are expected to be supervised by people of that same group, the students training with an Independent, or a B group analyst, have more freedom to choose. Nevertheless, it is in theoretical work that the separations are – for some analysts – tightly maintained: they would never be found quoting from colleagues of any of the rival groups.

[45]

The cultural milieu

One specific thing made possible the successful development of psychoanalysis in England. The interest and the direct or indirect support that psychoanalysis received from 'lay cultural sources' (Glover, 1949) cannot be dismissed, and although it was coloured by intense ambivalence, it was nonetheless there. Psychoanalysis drew a large number of active participants from this lay cultural establishment. This was not exclusive to England; Freud, when referring to the kind of people who had become analysts, spoke of 'people of academic education, doctors of philosophy, educationalists, together with women of great experience in life and outstanding personalities' (Freud, 1926a). There were also anthropologists, psychologists, professors of literature.

In England, some of the early psychoanalysts came from a powerful intellectual élite, sometimes connected to what has been called, in a vague, journalistic way, the 'Bloomsbury group'. This same sort of intellectual élite also contributed to formal groups, like the 17 Club, the Fabian Society, and the Labour Party. Bloomsbury itself was basically a group of friends, with a complex relationship with the psychoanalytic movement. Adrian Stephen, the brother of Virginia Woolf and Vanessa Bell, approached psychoanalysis from this lay intellectual background. The same applies to his wife, Karin Costelloe, who had been a pupil of Bertrand Russell's, had written papers on philosophical issues, and been accepted as a member of the Aristotelian Society in 1912, the same year that she married Adrian. Joan Riviere was another analyst who came from a similar background: she belonged to the Verrall family, her uncle being Arthur Verrall, a Cambridge classical scholar. The Verralls were very involved with the Society for Psychical Research, which had been started in Cambridge by F. Myers and Henry Sidgwick. This Society itself had a great impact on numerous people, and it was the only place where there was access to psychological literature. Freud himself read a paper at one of its meetings. James Strachey acknowledged in Riviere's obituary: 'We came from the same middle-class, professional,

[46]

cultured, later Victorian, box' (Strachey, 1963b). John Rickman and, more recently, Charles Rycroft, came from similar stock. In the books written by, or about, the members of the Bloomsbury group, the references to Alix Sargant Florence (later to become James's wife) are numerous.

The fact that so many psychoanalysts came from this particular background led to the acceptance of people with a certain degree of psychological disturbance, but who could be of 'outstanding personality'. In his speech at the celebration of the 50th Anniversary of the British Society, referring to the changes in the regulations qualifying a candidate for membership, and especially referring to their curriculum vitae, Strachey says:

> Documents of this kind fill me with bloodcurdling feelings of anxiety and remorse. How on earth could I fill up one of them? A discreditable academic career with the barest of B.A. degrees, no medical qualifications, no knowledge of the physical sciences, no experience of anything except third-rate journalism. The only thing in my favour was that, at the age of 30, I wrote a letter out of the blue to Freud, asking him if he would take me on as a student. For some reason he replied, almost by return of post, that he would. . . (Strachey, 1963a)

He then goes on to explain that, back in London a couple of years later, he was made an associate member: 'I can only suppose that Ernest Jones had received instructions from an even higher authority.' He ends with the following remarks: '. . . there I was, launched on the treatment of patients, with no experience, with no supervision, with nothing to help me but some two years of analysis with Freud.' He agrees with the need for 'the gradual development of systematic machinery for training candidates', but finally asks: 'Whether it is possible for it to become over-institutionalized is an open question. Is it worthwhile to leave a loophole for an occasional maverick? I don't know. . .' (Strachey, 1963a). I suspect that he did know. He uses 'maverick', a word which means someone who does not have masters, somebody who is independent. Its origin

[47]

derives from a Texan rancher who neglected to brand his calves.[6]

However, within the same cultural group there was also strong opposition to psychoanalysis. Lytton Strachey, for example, wrote a comic parody of Freud's discoveries in 1914 in an article called 'According to Freud'. Later on he apparently changed his mind, influenced by his brother James (Sherman, 1983). Leonard Woolf, who never dreamt of taking Virginia to a psychoanalyst, was publishing Freud's work at the Hogarth Press. Whether Virginia Woolf was mad or not, the fact remains that she was always treated by highly incompetent psychiatrists who were, nevertheless, successful in their profession in those days.[7] It is doubtful whether Virginia would have accepted a recommendation for analytic treatment, or even whether it might have helped her. Her prejudices at the time (1924) about psychoanalysis were clear:

> I shall be plunged in publishing affairs at once; we are publishing all Dr Freud, and I glance at the proof and read how Mr A. B. threw a bottle of red ink on the sheets of his marriage bed to excuse his impotence to the housemaid, but threw it in the wrong place, which unhinged his wife's mind – and to this day she pours claret on the dinner table. We could all go on like that for hours; and yet these Germans think it proves something – besides their own gull-like imbecility. (Letter to Molly MacCarthy, quoted in Trombley, 1977)

The early pioneers of psychoanalysis shared three basic characteristics with the members of the intellectual élite. Whether these were for or against the new science, many of them had a certain degree of psychological disturbance, which still seems to be an important element in creative thinking; they all shared an immense, greedy intellectual curiosity, without which psychoanalysis could not, and cannot, survive; and, lastly, they lacked moralistic judgements, which did not in any way exclude an ethical commitment to professional standards.[8]

Psychoanalysis was very lucky not to be accepted by the medical establishment in Great Britain, and to find that the academic psychologists, the university professors, the philosophers, had very little time for its theories. It was perceived as belonging to a different realm. Psychoanalysts and their patients were tolerated as part of a wild but harmless bunch of eccentrics in a land of eccentrics. In 1951, Rickman could still say that 'A group of people reckoned as eccentric is never given professional status, they are thought of as outsiders' (Rickman, 1951).

The Independent Group

Let us return to the history of the Society. As a result of the complicated political process that took place after the Controversial Discussions, the 'Middle' group was created. In fact at the beginning this was not a group at all; the analysts who found themselves belonging to it had merely refused to belong to either of the sectarian groups that had been formed. This was then, and still continues to be today, the attraction for many analysts. Most of its members refuse to be politically organized, or to have any one leader, or to proselytize. This, in a tough world of political life, might in the end make it disappear. In any case, the creation of the group was the result of a process of elimination: if one was neither 'Kleinian' nor 'Freudian', one was 'Middle' group. The analysts of the Middle group became a political force without wanting to be one: ironically, since they were the majority, they held the political balance in the British Society. Depending on what one thought of it, the group was seen as rather 'timid' and 'uneasy' (Glover, 1949); or as a bunch of peace-loving people who rejected participation in the intrigues conducted by extremists (Schmideberg, 1971); or, more recently, as the group of the 'non-aligned analysts' who sometimes fall into 'the special dogmatism of the self-professed eclectic' (Steiner, 1985); or, in rather less generous fashion, as the group of 'uncommitted analysts' (Segal, 1979). In the 1960s the Middle group was finally constituted as a Group and, after the reorganization of the training programme, was officially known from 1973 as the 'Independent Group'.

THE BRITISH SCHOOL OF PSYCHOANALYSIS

For all 'official' purposes, those analysts who do not belong to the B Group or to the Kleinian Group are considered as Independent. Some analysts, like Michael Balint or Donald Winnicott, always refused to be identified as belonging to any one sectarian faction. The Independent analysts only agree to constitute a group for the specific purpose of participating in the political and institutional life of the Society. The Independent position is characterized by a reluctance to be restricted by theoretical or hierarchical constraints. Some others expressed their wish to remain independent by moving away from the Society, although I am sure this was never the only reason. Still others, while participating in the life of the institution, refused to become training analysts, thus excluding themselves from the corridors of political-institutional power. At the same time, many analysts – while belonging to the Independent group – are, in their theoretical outlook as much as in their practice, more Kleinian or more Anna-Freudian than anything else.

The authors in this book are all Independent analysts; some refused to belong to any group; some others became Independent after having been trained in other groups; and one of them resigned from the Society a few years ago.

Countertransference:
an Independent view

F OR PSYCHOANALYSIS, according to Laplanche and
Pontalis (1967), transference is

> a process of actualization of unconscious wishes. Transference uses specific objects and operates in the framework of a specific relationship established with these objects. . . As a rule what psychoanalysts mean by the unqualified use of the term 'transference' is *transference during treatment*. (authors' italics)

Countertransference, on the other hand, for the same authors is 'The whole of the analyst's unconscious reactions to the individual analysand – especially to the analysand's own transference' (Laplanche and Pontalis, 1967). From the very beginning the concept of countertransference has had a double connotation: on the one hand, countertransference was to be seen as the awakening of the neurotic conflicts of the analyst through an unconscious reaction to the patient's influence on the analyst. This is the way that Freud referred to it in the first instance, in 'The Future Prospects of Psycho-Analytic Therapy', stating that 'no psychoanalyst goes further than his own complexes and internal resistances permit' (Freud, 1910). Thus he recommends adequate and continuous self-analysis. Later on, he advocates the need for a 'training analysis' ('The Dynamics of Transference', 1912a). Some 25 years later, in

'Analysis Terminable and Interminable', his recommendation becomes a suggestion that the analyst returns to analysis from time to time, specifically to deal with problems that he might eventually find in himself.

In the analysis of his patients (Freud, 1937a), counter-transference, simply put, was considered at this stage a resis-tance on the part of the analyst. In this line of thinking we can include later authors like Fliess (1953), A. Reich (1951), Hoffer (1956), and Tower (1956); and Winnicott, who described countertransference as the analyst's neurosis spoiling his capacity to sustain a professional attitude (1960c).

On the other hand, Freud also suggested that the analyst's unconscious should be like a 'receptive organ', a 'telephone receiver'. It is through his own unconscious that the analyst will be able to reconstruct the unconscious of the patient ('Re-commendations to Physicians Practising Psycho-Analysis', 1912b). Freud was not referring here to countertransference, and although he never came to see countertransference as an important tool for the analyst, his considerations opened up the possibility of turning countertransference into something that could be used to gain insight into the patient's predica-ment.

This double quality of the countertransference, as resistance and as a useful tool, has marked two different technical approaches that Kernberg has described in a rather simplified way as the 'classical' and the 'totalistic' (Kernberg, 1965). They are not only different views of the countertransference, of *what* and *when* the analyst should interpret, but also different views of the position of the analyst in the treatment, and of treatment itself.

Countertransference is a concept that members of the British School should, and probably do, feel proud of having developed. The influence of Melanie Klein has been decisive in this respect. It was through her inspiration that Paula Heimann came to write the paper on countertransference which became a turning point in the history of psychoanalytic technique (Heimann, 1950). The time was obviously ripe for such a con-tribution. Winnicott had, for example, written his paper 'Hate in the Countertransference' in 1949. It has been through contributions from Ella Sharpe (1930, 1947), James Strachey (1934), Barbara Low (1935), Michael Balint (1933, 1949), Alice and Michael Balint (1939), Donald Winnicott (1949c), Margaret Little (1951, 1957), Charles Rycroft (1956b), and again Paula Heimann (1960), that the Independent analysts' work and thoughts on countertransference were developed and expanded.

The Object Relations view is that the psychoanalytic situation is always created and developed from the specific and unique interaction between the patient and the analyst. The analyst is never an 'outsider'; he is part and parcel of the transference situation. In fact, one could argue that the transference is as much a function of the countertransference as the countertransference is a result of the transference. Klauber, in the paper included in this book, stresses what he considers to be the most neglected aspect of the psychoanalytic encounter: that it is a relationship. Almost provocatively, he states that 'Patient and analyst need one another.' They form a private, intimate, secret relationship. Klauber acknowledges that there is always 'an element of a tease in psychoanalytic therapy since emotions are constantly aroused which the analyst will never satisfy.' Hopefully, the analyst will be more interested in analysing his patient than in satisfying his own, or his patient's, instinctual needs. But Klauber reminds us of something that psychoanalysts have sometimes tried to forget: the recognition by Freud that some aspects of the patient's love for the analyst are 'genuine'. What about the analyst's feelings for his patients?

One thing is certain: it is impossible for the analyst to share the experience of this peculiar relationship with anybody else. The analyst, I believe, is always betraying or being unfaithful to somebody else in his involvement with his patients. Love and hate will develop in the context of the analytic encounter, and this will put a certain amount of strain on the relationship. Klauber does not play down its consequences, and he asks: 'What elements of the transference can reasonably be expected to be resolved?'

[53]

Limentani, in his paper, refers to the *unique atmosphere* an analyst will create for his patients, and describes some of the ambiguities present in the analytic situation in the following manner:

> . . . at the outset, we invite the patient to enter into a relationship which offers a mixture of satisfaction and frustrations, and with a demand for utter trust which he can hardly experience towards a total stranger. We stipulate that words shall be the method of communication, knowing full well that most affects cannot be adequately described in words. We assure the analysand that both of us will be able to work better if we are not to stare at each other, yet we know how difficult it is for an infant in the first months of life to take his eyes off his mother. . . It should cause little surprise if certain patients may wish from time to time to use every means at their disposal to express their feelings and to create unforeseen situations which can exercise the analyst's emotional responses as well as his technical skills.

One characteristic of the British Independent analysts has been the importance they have always given to 'the analyst's emotional responses', not only to 'his technical skills'. Given the emphasis on this interrelation between patient and analyst, countertransference has developed as the source of the most important clues for the formulation of transference interpretations. But this, to my mind, has become a mixed blessing. Nowadays, the concept of countertransference is sometimes used and misused to hide the prejudices, at other times the mistakes, very frequently the lack of information, the ignorance, even the simple stupidity on the part of the analyst (a point made by Jacques Lacan) in his relationship to his patients.

Not all Independent analysts would agree, I suspect, with Michael Balint's notion of the countertransference as comprising the totality of the analyst's attitudes, feelings and behaviour towards his patients. Most would probably agree, however, that it is the quality of the analytic relationship that matters for the outcome of the analysis. Although the only thing that the analyst is supposed to do, and does do most of the time, is to interpret, it is the nature of the relationship, formed through the interpretative work, that really matters for the end result. Masud Khan (1960a), Pearl King (1962, 1978), Enid Balint (1968), John Klauber (1972), Dennis G. Brown (1977), and Christopher Bollas (1982, 1983) are all British Independent analysts who have made direct or indirect contributions to the theory and the clinical uses of countertransference. One should also add to this list the papers included in this book by Adam Limentani, Harold Stewart, Christopher Bollas, Patrick Casement, Jonathan Pedder, Nina Coltart, and Neville Symington.

In her 1950 paper Paula Heimann uses the term countertransference to cover all the feelings that the analyst experiences towards the patient; these feelings, she says, represent 'one of the most important tools for his work. The analyst's countertransference is an instrument of research into the patient's unconscious.' She specifically emphasized the fact that the analytic situation is a relationship between two people. 'Our basic assumption,' she says, 'is that the analyst's unconscious understands that of his patient. This rapport on a deep level comes to the surface in the form of feelings which the analyst notices in response to his patient, in his "countertransference"' (Heimann, 1950).

This view, which was revolutionary at the time, became extremely influential, and is today part of our common psychoanalytic heritage. But I think, in the same way that there has been an 'overextension' of the concept of transference (Sandler *et al.*, 1969), that something similar has occurred with the concept of countertransference. This 'overextension' has resulted from the very same ideas emanating from Heimann's paper. At the end of the paper she says that the analyst's countertransference is 'the patient's *creation*, it is part of the patient's personality'. Thus in the same way that it came to be believed that everything created or produced by the patient was 'transference', everything created or produced in the analyst came to be considered 'countertransference'. I believe these two 'overextensions' of the terms in fact go together, and are the result of an overemphasis on, and a certain abuse of, the concept of projective identification.

[55]

For many colleagues, especially Kleinians, projective identification has become the most important mechanism in the
analytic situation. For example, Brenman Pick, in a recently
published good paper, writes that 'Constant projecting by the
patient into the analyst is the essence of analysis. . .' (Brenman
Pick, 1985). Another Kleinian analyst states:

> What should be at the centre of the interpretation . . . is the
> immediate relationship between analyst and patient, with its
> verbal and non-verbal expressions. This means that the
> knowledge of "projective identification" is central to the
> understanding of the analytical material. Projective identifi-
> cation is an unconscious fantasy through which the person
> projects parts of himself into his object, which is then per-
> ceived as affected by that which was projected. (Riesenberg
> Malcom, 1985)

The assumption contained in both of these views is that all
aspects of the patient's relationship to the analyst are exclusively repetitions of past relationships, and they were in fact
described as such by Melanie Klein (Klein, 1932). The task of
the analyst would then be to decode these projections that have
been put into him, which is where the value of the countertransference is seen to reside. We all know that this does happen in any psychoanalytic treatment; the question remains as
to whether this is the *only* thing that happens. Basing all
interpretations on countertransference feelings, understood
only as a result of projective identification, denies what the
patient has to say. The analysis is now based more on the discourse of the analyst, not on that of the patient.

The theory of the countertransference has come to be used as
a defence against the impact of the analytic relationship, a
defence that belongs to the analyst, not to the patient. I agree
with the way Sandler *et al.* pose the question of transference
(and I would extend it here to include countertransference).
They argue that transference – and countertransference – are
multi-dimensional phenomena. They are clinical rather than
metapsychological concepts, and include a whole variety of
different elements that enter into object relations. These ele-

ments are facilitated in the special conditions of the analytic situation. Thus the important question, they say, is 'not what is and what is not transference' (and, I would add, counter-transference) 'in the analytic situation, but rather *what dimension of relationships enters into the special and artificial analytic situation, and how are these involved in the process of treatment?*' (Sandler *et al.*, 1969, authors' italics).

Contributions by Independent analysts to the theory of countertransference

I would now like to refer in some detail to four papers by members of the Independent Group of the British Psycho-Analytical Society which I see as important contributions to the theory of countertransference. (Two of these papers are included in the present book.) I will start with Enid Balint's paper on the analyst as a mirror or receiver (Balint, E., 1968), which followed another excellent paper, 'On Being Empty of Oneself' (Balint, E., 1963). The opaque mirror technique suggested by Freud (1912b) – by which the analyst should show to his patients only what is shown to him – is understood by Balint as 'a biphasic attitude in which the analyst first identifies with the patient and then, by his interpretation, shows what the patient's thoughts and ideas "look like" to him. . . This assumes a high degree of identification by the analyst and a minimum of projection.' This metaphor of Freud's has been widely criticized (not least by some of the authors represented in this book), but Balint's re-evaluation of it is a very refreshing one. She retranslates Freud's position as follows: 'Freud's intention was to make it clear that the analyst's personality and opinions should not be shown to the patient, nor should he give advice, sympathy or consolation. *His job was just to reflect back to the patient what he was able to understand*' (my italics).

Although acknowledging, as Freud himself did, that the analyst responds with his total being, Enid Balint – disagreeing here with quite a number of colleagues – argues that the patient will not perceive the analyst as he really is. 'We will be seen,' she says, 'in at least as many different ways as we have patients.' This would seem to confirm the view, quoted above, of the analysis as a constant process of projection by the patient into the analyst. But Enid Balint takes this further, into another problem. She questions an overemphasis that had been put on the personality of the analyst, and of its effect on the treatment. This point is a fundamental one. It somehow put right something that had formed the basis for a misunderstanding dating back to James Strachey's classical paper on the function of interpretation (Strachey, 1934).

Strachey's paper is still a source of ideas and inspirations. His concept of the function of mutative interpretations, his view of the therapeutic action of analysis as a process affecting analyst as much as patient, have been crucial in our understanding of psychoanalytic treatment. But the misunderstanding is related to his statement about the patient's internalization of the analyst as a substitute, 'auxiliary' superego. When Strachey makes this proposition he is trying to criticize Sandor Radó's concept of a 'parasitic superego', the internalization of the superego of the hypnotizer by the person being hypnotized. Although Strachey argues that in psychoanalysis this process is different, in that there is an internal change in the nature of the patient's superego itself, I do not find the distinction convincing. We are still talking here about a process of suggestion: the substitution of the superego of the analyst for the superego of the patient.

It is ironic that that which was put forward by Freud as a psychoanalytic explanation for hypnosis ends up being used as an explanation for psychoanalysis (Miller, 1979). This conception has supported the idea of 'the goal of analysis' in terms of a successful internalization of the analyst as a 'good object', or a 'benign figure'. It has contributed to the idealization of the analyst as an object.

Enid Balint has something different in mind, and her position makes the outcome of analysis a more problematic, uncertain process. She suggests that our patients might be quite grateful to us for our adhering to the mirror model: it is, she says, the analyst who more frequently wishes to deviate from that model. Consequently, she also claims, she has not found that 'an analyst needs to express sympathy except when things go wrong in the conduct of the analysis itself.' At this point Enid Balint introduces a very simple but fruitful idea: she refers to the *distance* of the analyst from the patient. She states: 'In my opinion, the mirror model enables the analyst to be neither distant nor close, but just there. . .'

I would like to link this notion of being *just there* to the concept of the transitional object, in order to understand the dynamics of the transference-countertransference process. What is transitional is not the object, says Winnicott, but the use that one makes of it. The analyst occupies that transitional space where the objects are not quite internal, nor are they quite external. Like a transitional object, the analyst *is* and *is not*. This paradoxical quality of *being* and *not being* does not take away any reality from the psychoanalytic encounter. We are, as analysts, as important to our patients as teddy bears are to children. As objects, we have been created by the patient, very much like the teddy bear is created by the child. Patients do not get better by internalizing the good images that we can offer them. We do not, in fact, 'offer' anything 'good' or 'bad'; what we offer them is very little, and as Enid Balint suggested, patients know very little about the reality of our 'goodness' or 'badness'. Hopefully, what they get from us is what I would call our *progressive absence*. (The idea for this is taken from Pontalis (1978), who talks of the mother's progressive constitution as *absence*.) We are just there, although the situation of the transference makes us excessively 'present'. The working through of the transference should make us become more and more absent, and not more and more present.

This idea of a progressive absence is just the opposite of what Strachey's notions suggested. The success of the analysis is not achieved through the identification with, or the incorporation of, the analyst into the patient's inner world. The dissolution of the transference is, to my mind, one and the same thing as the dissolution of the figure of the analyst, whether as 'good' or 'bad'. A good-enough mother is also somebody who becomes more and more absent: she is not the one who loves us alone, but the one who has somebody else to love and be loved by. Her narcissism does not depend entirely on the child; or to be more precise, her narcissism depends progressively less and less on the child. In this sense, she will turn more and more into an absence. The same applies to the analyst. Our health could be said to be based on the possibility of having a good relationship inside ourselves with that absence, which will form, in the way described by Winnicott, the basis of our capacity to be alone.

This is what is created and re-created in the process of an analysis: the fact that the analyst is *just there* confronts the analysand with the fact that the space occupied by the analyst will always be defined as absence. It is in this contradiction – that the analyst is there to announce an absence – that the status of the primary object resides. The analysand will have to reconcile himself with the fact that the primary object will never be found again. It is not an object, in the sense that our keys are objects: one loses the keys to one's house only to discover later on that one's children have been playing with them. The primary object is an object which will never be found again. The misfortunes of the subject did not start 'the day the breast was withdrawn from his lips' (Masotta, 1976); it is the very process of being lost forever that counts. A cure conceived along the lines of a replacement of 'bad' by 'good' by definition maintains the illusory implications of the patient's transference. The notion that Enid Balint proposes, that of *just being there*, is not the same as suggesting that 'good' should replace 'bad'. If it were, we would be confirming the analysand's hopes that he could – if only he tried hard enough – find a 'better' mother than his own, 'real', 'bad' mother.

I will leave this question here, and move on to Nina Coltart's paper presented to the English-Speaking Conference of Psychoanalysts in 1982 (this volume). '"Slouching Towards Bethlehem. . ." or Thinking the Unthinkable in Psychoanalysis' provoked a certain amount of hostility among members of the British Society who were in the audience: not only did the then director of the London Clinic of Psycho-Analysis shout at one of her patients, but she was transforming her ignorance into a virtue, into an ideology. I found the paper an important contribution: it brought to everybody's attention characteristics of the psychoanalytic stance that belong to the best of the Independent tradition. 'It is of the essence of our impossible profession,' Coltart says, 'that in a very singular way we do not know what we are doing.' In spite of our training, our literature, our experience, however much we gain confidence, or refine our technique, each hour spent with a patient, claims Coltart, is an act of faith. This faith is mainly concerned with what she calls 'the sheer *unconsciousness* of the unconscious'.

This declaration of belief in the power of the unconscious results in a clear attempt to cut the supposed power of the analyst down to size. What Coltart reaffirms for us is the unconditional trust that we, as analysts, need to have in order to believe that whatever else happens in the analysis, IT will continue working. . . We do not always know what is going on with the patient, we rarely know what is going on *inside* the patient, and this limitation of our knowledge makes reference to the vicissitudes of the transference. What Nina Coltart adds to this is that we do not always know what is going on with the analyst; in fact we know very little of what is going on *inside* the analyst, and this is a reference to the vicissitudes of the countertransference.

A patient tells me of his objections to circumcision, and the barbarism of its practice; he then follows this with his complaints about baptism in the Christian religion, or how – he says – this religious ritual puts a limit, right from birth, on the freedom of the individual. He then moves on to the practice of medicine in the USA, the lack of clear political definitions about the problem of nuclear disarmament in a certain political party, his dissatisfaction with a professor in the postgraduate course that he is attending. We are now getting closer and closer to the *here and now*, and I can see the monster of the transference emerging, moving slowly, growing faster, getting to the target. Far from being psychotic, this patient is in fact a pervert, fighting, struggling with himself in a battle I have no certainty he is going to win.

A few hours later another patient, this time a fairly disturbed one, tells me about his aspirations to belong to the upper classes, to have lots and lots of money, his wish to be a millionaire so he could have his shoes handmade to order by some famous shoemaker who is becoming old and is in the process of retiring. In the middle of this, he says: 'Suddenly, this song came to my head: *"I fought against the Law, and the Law defeated me. . ."*'

There is not much to these stories. While the first patient awakens in me a certain impatience, which nevertheless does not exclude my sympathy and the possibility of working together, the second patient forces me to smile. With the first one I would like to argue, although all I will do is interpret; with the second one I would like to know more about the song, and although I feel free to ask, I decide to remain silent. To speak of 'a decision' here is mystifying: IT decides, I would say. Our own analysis and our own training, plus our experiences, our reading, our learning, have taught us to accept certain rules. They are fairly rigid rules, which in our daily practice become habits: we greet our patients in a certain manner, we state our interpretations in a certain way. Once habits, they come to form a style, and this style, instead of putting rigid limits to our work, forms the background to our spontaneous acts. Interpretations will come to us, against this background, as a novelty. They will impose themselves on us, will burst into light coming from an area within ourselves that we know little about.

Israël (1972) refers to a painting of René Magritte's entitled *The Therapist*, in which a man is sitting on a sand dune with a leather bag by his side. The upper part of his body is made like an open cage; there is a pigeon in the cage, and another one outside the cage. The cage is partially covered by a blanket, and on top of it there is a hat. Interpretations must have been made of this painting; it is too tempting not to do so, but part of the attraction of this wonderful picture is the mystery in it, a certain obscurity present in most Surrealist paintings: something is being suggested, but not quite said. In fact, it is not clear that anything could be said. We live with this contradiction most of the time: the feeling that what I say to the patient is completely useless and has no meaning, together with the knowledge, the conviction, the belief that for the patient there is nothing more serious in the world. The therapist in that picture is a surrealistic object himself: like the patient, the analyst also escapes a certain objective understanding.

This is different from 'encouraging ignorance as a virtue'. We are faced every day, in our work with our patients, with the true limits of our knowledge: the question is not how much we are learning, but how little we know. In her paper Coltart is far from supporting a mystical or religious attitude, where the 'Beyond Words' (the title of the conference at which the paper was presented) would form the realm of reality. Just the opposite: language is the only possible realm of psychoanalysis. One can only be preoccupied with silence, as Coltart is, if one believes at the same time that words restore a certain existence, they give birth to that which needs to be named. What makes our profession impossible is that however much we name it, IT is never finished; however much we think we know it, IT remains obscure; however much we can grasp it, IT escapes us.

Coltart reacted with passion to her patient. There is always this sneaky feeling that when we talk of countertransference, we are putting ourselves above the confusing world of passions. Eric Brenman, a Kleinian analyst, referred to this in a paper read to the Society: 'To eat from the Tree of Knowledge,' he said, 'carries with it the danger of attempting to become God' (Brenman, 1978). Not that we take ourselves to be God – since we are too clever to do that – but more that, like him, we are *beyond passions* (Leclaire, 1975). If passion were not present in the analyst's life, why would we need so many measures to deal with our own feelings? Why otherwise would 'supervision' be called 'control'?

Lévi-Strauss has demonstrated how belief systems, myths and mythical stories are in fact preoccupied with the problems of boundaries. Our own psychoanalytical mythologies fulfil the same purpose. The idealization of a possible 'right' kind of technique that is proposed by some colleagues, the idealization of a particular theory, like the negative of a photograph, show that which is being repressed. Freud said that 'the formation of

[63]

an ideal heightens the demands of the ego and is the most powerful factor favouring repression' (1914b). Coltart's reaction
to her patient is not an act of repression but a creative act: her
faith in the unconscious gives meaning to the patient's desola-
tion, despair, and loneliness.

The third paper I will make reference to is Neville
Symington's 'The Analyst's Act of Freedom as Agent of
Therapeutic Change' (1983, this volume). In it Symington
describes what he calls an 'x-phenomenon'. The very fact that
he calls it by this name suggests how little we might know
about it. Symington's basic assumption is that

> at one level the analyst and patient together make a single
> system. Together they form an entity which we might call a
> corporate personality. From the moment that patient and
> analyst engage in what we call an analysis the two are
> together part of an illusory system. Both are caught into
> it. . . The analyst is lassoed into the patient's illusory world.
> He is more involved in it, more victim to it than the average
> social contact. As the analytical work proceeds the analyst
> slowly disengages himself from it. In this way transference
> and countertransference are two parts of a single system;
> together they form a unity. They are the shared illusions
> which the work of analysis slowly undoes.

The illusions or delusions are shared; they belong to both
patient and analyst. This implies a radical change of view as
regards resistance: the resistances that we traditionally place
on the side of the patient belong to the analyst as well. It might
happen that sometimes they belong more to the analyst than to
the patient. But the main point put forward by Symington is
that the resistances belong to the process. Patient and analyst
are locked into it, and both of them need to be freed from it.
The 'x-phenomenon' is then that inner act of freedom on the
part of the analyst by which he frees himself from some of the
illusion, and it is this which causes a shift, a therapeutic change
in both participants of the analytic interaction.

Symington takes good care to distinguish the process of
mutual involvement between analysand and analyst from the

process of projective identification, by which the patient ends up being blamed for what the analyst feels: 'The analyst's feelings are *his* feelings even though they may have been stirred up by the patient.' The psychoanalytic process, in this view, as in Enid Balint's and Coltart's views, is a humble process. The limitations intrinsic to the interaction between analysand and analyst do not make it any less painful, less powerful, or I dare say less mysterious.

Symington argues that the shared illusions are located in the superego. I would like to add that the illusions relate to the ego-ideal, perhaps as a specific structure within the superego. These two concepts are sometimes considered synonymous but I find it useful to differentiate between them. Lagache (1966) introduced a distinction whereby the superego corresponds to *authority*, while the ego-ideal corresponds to *the way the subject should behave* in order to respond to the authority's expectations. The distinction is subtle but relevant to the work of the analyst, whose individual ego-ideal might interfere with his work by its adherence to the institutional superego. (For a thoughtful consideration of the concept of the ego-ideal, see Chasseguet-Smirgel, 1975.)

The fact that the 'x-phenomenon' is defined as an act of freedom goes against any notion that there is a 'right' kind of technique, or a 'right' kind of interpretation. Cookery books never made good cooks. Of course we need cookery books and recipes, but we also need a certain amount of creativity when the sauce is being made: it is then that one sees the real skill of the cook. The notion that there is only one 'right' kind of technique, or recipe for deciphering the unconscious of the patient, might account for a certain sterility in the productions of psychoanalytic writers; something that has been justly acknowledged both inside and outside psychoanalytical societies.

I see the 'x-phenomenon', the act of freedom on the part of the analyst as described by Symington, as an act of commitment. Whether I make a mistake or not, an interpretation – in fact any intervention on my part – is always something that will come from a personal, though hopefully, professional stance: it

[65]

is never 'impersonal', out of the boundaries of my responsibility, something for which I could blame the patient. The very fact that it is a matter of freedom on the part of the analyst makes it clear that it is an ethical concern: not so much related to what we 'should' do according to some absolute knowledge, but simply to do what we can in the best possible way.

The fourth and last paper by an Independent analyst that I shall mention is Christopher Bollas's 'Expressive Uses of the Countertransference – Notes to the Patient from Oneself' (Bollas, 1983). The titles of the different sections of this paper give a fair flavour of its content: 'Countertransference readiness', 'Analyst as patient to himself', 'The analyst's use of the subjective', 'Self relating in the analyst', 'Sensing', 'From indirect to direct use of the countertransference'. Like others, Bollas's assumption is that the analytic situation involves two subjectivities in mutual interrelating and experiencing. He speaks of the establishment by the patient of an *environment* through which the patient's internal world is conveyed, and in which both patient and analyst live a 'life' together. The analyst becomes what Bollas had called in a previous paper a *transformational object*, not so much an object in fact as a process of alteration of self experience (Bollas, this volume). Bollas believes that it is possible for the analyst

> to report selected subjective states to his patients for mutual observation and analysis. By disclosing certain subjective states of mind the analyst makes available to the patient certain freely associated states within himself, feelings or positions that he knows to be sponsored by some part of the patient.

The analyst might find himself in the position of not quite knowing what the meaning of his subjective state of mind could be, but he can share this with his patient 'as long as it is clear to the analysand that such disclosures are in the nature of reports from within the analyst, in the overall interests of the psychoanalysis.'

Bollas distinguishes between indirect and direct uses of the countertransference. By indirect use he means 'those occasions when the analyst becomes witness to his own feeling state and may in the presence of the patient offer this feeling state for consideration.' By doing so, Bollas clearly redefines the subjectivity of the analyst, establishing it as a 'useful and consistent source of material in the psychoanalytic situation'. By direct use of the countertransference, Bollas is referring to 'that quite rare occasion, but one which may be of exceptional value to the effectiveness of the analysis, when the analyst describes his experience as the object.' The analyst could, let us say, sense something about the patient; the use of this 'sensing' would be an indirect use of the countertransference. When the analyst describes to the patient how he feels in terms of being the patient's object, the analyst would be using the countertransference in a direct way.

As Symington does, and as Balint and Coltart imply in their respective papers, Bollas also objects to the characterization of the countertransference as based solely on the process of projective identification. (I gather that most Independent analysts would agree that the concept of projective identification is an extremely useful one: a certain tendency on our part to make jokes about it admittedly represents a caricature parallel to a caricatured version of its use.) If the freedom postulated by Symington confronts us with our need for commitment, Bollas's conception restores a certain responsibility to the position occupied by the analyst. The place of the analyst is a very privileged one but his experiences, his feelings, his ideas are certainly not: they do not constitute, for example, the 'official' version of what the truth about the patient's unconscious could be. Everything the analyst puts forward can only be considered as interpretation, that is to say as hypotheses to be investigated by patient and analyst. These hypotheses can no doubt be changed, turned around, turned upside down, can frequently contradict each other, be confirmed, disproved, or, as Bollas himself says: 'kicked around, mulled over, torn to pieces'. What we create in one interpretation might be destroyed by the next, and reappear again in the following one.

This is not to say that we have a careless attitude as regards the interpretations we make. Interpretations are like the

swings, the slide, the climbing frame, the sandpit in the play-
ground – a word used by Freud to refer to the transference situation – in which analysand and analyst are playing. Interpretations are not the dice in a game, but at the same time they cannot be considered statements of fact. Interpretations are
formed by real words but they constitute an imaginary story.
The story is a fiction that takes place in a world created by the
mutual working influence of analyst and analysand, with
characters borrowed from reality. When we interpret we try to
explain, we attempt to elucidate, we would like to make something clear; but we also give our own interpretation, as one
does in interpreting a composition in music, a landscape in
painting, or a drama in the theatre. In our daily work we give
our own interpretations of the melody we hear coming from
the couch, but we are not the creators of that melody. We interpret but that does not give us the right to believe we have understood: the proof of this is that probably any other analyst playing the same melody coming from the couch would give it a different interpretation. Not all the Independent analysts would
agree with the choice of words that Bollas uses with his
patients, but the description given by Bollas of this 'open struggle' to put into words something 'beyond words' validates a
way of working that most Independent analysts do share. The
analyst is not the spokesman of some hidden truth about the
patient. Such a way of working embodies an attitude which is
the opposite of one that could be characterized as interpretative fervour, or 'militant interpreting' (Bollas, Personal communication, 1984). The attitude of militant interpreting
assumes that the analyst not only should understand everything, but should also interpret everything he thinks he has
understood. For those analysts who think they have understood it is very difficult to admit the possibility that something
different, something *new* might be happening.

The work of the analyst as described by Bollas echoes Winnicott's provocative statement that one of the reasons for making interpretations in a session, paradoxically, is 'not to give
the impression to the patient that he, the analyst, understands
everything' (Winnicott, 1962). The analyst in this picture does

[68]

not occupy the place of an omnipotent superego demanding obedience, forcing the patient to identify himself with the superego of the analyst; does not submerge or drown the words of the patient in the discourse of the analyst. There are no early, premature interpretations, no room for quick, sharp understanding of the patient's predicament, no overdoses of symbolic meaning.

This analyst I go to suddenly went deaf. He diagnoses hysteria and is working on it but it's a blow to his purse as well as his pride. Meanwhile, those of his patients who don't feel defrauded by the thought of a deaf psychoanalyst are trying to adjust to his altered patterns of behaviour. There's about a dozen of us left – the hardcore sons of his fatherfigurehood.

. . . He still thinks he's going to get his hearing back but I'm far from encouraging.

'Mac', I say to him, 'the only way to get back your hearing is give up being an analyst. It's your drums rejecting all this garbage you provoke – a defence mechanism!' He smiles benignly and shakes his head. He can't hear me. . .

Anthony Edkins, 'Why I Like Ess'

I believe, with Masotta, that the only serious thing about human beings is that we are structured like a joke (Masotta, 1976). Like dreams, like symptoms, like artistic creations, like slips of the tongue, we also are the products of condensation and displacement. One of the most wonderful jokes in psychoanalysis is that Freud discovered psychoanalysis through his relationship with Fliess. We all consider that remarkable relationship between Freud and Fliess as the first transference situation, the first, original analysis. Now, this man Fliess was a very tense, mad scientist, with a mad and delirious scientific mind. Freud makes him the object of his idealizations, turns him into the father figure of his preoccupa-

[69]

tions, his master and friend. Freud could have chosen other, more important figures of his time: Brücke, von Fleischl-Marxow, Helmholtz, Charcot, Breuer, etc. In fact they all became his heroes but Freud, nevertheless, follows what his transference dictates, and the great surprise is that it gets him somewhere. To use an image offered by Freud himself: Fliess made him 'summon up a spirit from the underworld by cunning spells'. We have been lucky enough that Freud did not 'send him down again without having asked him a single question' (Freud, 1914a). What a misunderstanding! Fliess expected something from Freud, and Freud expected to find knowledge in Fliess. Is this what happens between patient and analyst? What kind of knowledge is this psychoanalytic knowledge?

Transference is an illusion. In this sense, though, it is no more or less of an illusion than any other relationship. As soon as love and hate develop in a relationship, illusions, and sometimes delusions, take shape and develop. In the *commedia dell'arte* all characters wore masks, except for the lovers: not because love shows the truth but because it is in itself enough to hide the lovers' gestures (García, 1980). In a Valentine's Day postcard by the cartoonist Mel Calman all we can see is a blind man with his walking stick and a pair of sunglasses: he does not look particularly happy or unhappy; the only thing that makes him so distinguishable – and yet so universal – is the shape of the frames of his glasses: that of two small hearts. Love is blind, yet very real. Breuer escaped from the consequences of the transference, but then he did not discover the Oedipus complex. The analysand knows very well who we are; we do not need to tell him that we are not his father, mother, brother, or sister, although this is what we try to show him a lot of the time during an analysis.

The very notion of a psychoanalytic type of knowledge implies the recognition that there is a certain part of ourselves that will never be reachable, never become clear. If we continue with our self-analysis, and sometimes with further analysis, it is not only because there are parts of ourselves that remain obscure to our knowledge, but also because there are parts of ourselves that will always be in the process of being re-created.

This accounts, in part, for the fact that the same person can have such different analyses when he happens to have more than one. For that process of re-creation, what the patient has to learn is not something about the unconscious – it is more than that: it is something about love and hate, in which the unconscious has a place, and fulfils a function (Mannoni, 1980).

A patient comes in a very damaged state to the analysis; one could say that the task of the analysis is to help him to repair his damaged internal objects. This is part of the process, and in fact we all refer to it more or less in those terms. But at the same time a patient does not come to us in the way that a car goes to the garage to be repaired after a crash. In a sense, for the patient nothing can be repaired. What he will have to be faced with, in the end, is not the damage, or the lost happiness, or the lack of happiness in the past, but rather the sheer narcissistic hurt that forces him to accept the impossibility of that happiness. In other words, the primary object is not some object that was lost somewhere along the line of development but an object that is structured by its own loss. There is something about the nature of the object itself that makes it not-available. I think this is the real meaning of the depression that Melanie Klein refers to as happening at the end of every analysis. Or, in Freud's terms, the real bedrock of castration that the subject will have to face.

The same applies to the analyst. What gives me my status as a psychoanalyst is not my having become a member of the Institute of Psycho-Analysis. What turns me into an analyst is that precise moment in which a patient shows signs that I have become an object in his imaginary world: he is now interested in me, he attributes to me a knowledge, expects something special from me. My work as an analyst can now start, it is the time when the analysis can begin. It will entail, will imply a narcissistic hurt for me as much as for the patient, in the sense that I will also be faced with the impossibility of being either close to or distant from him. I will be *just there*, not in a state of inactivity or passivity, but the opposite, usually working quite hard, and perhaps sharing, with some luck, the impossibility of our relationship.

[71]

Independent analysts question any notion of the psychoanalytic process as exclusively one of projection and projective identification. This does not mean that they do not use these concepts for the understanding of the psychoanalytic situation (see, for example, the careful consideration of his patient's projective process that Patrick Casement makes in the paper included here). The belief that whatever happens in the psychoanalytic process is a result of something emanating from the patient, which is then projected into the analyst, has contributed to the creation of a distinctively stagnant psychoanalytic product: the 'you-mean-me' interpretations (Coltart, Personal communication, 1977). 'You-mean-me' interpretations automatically refer everything that the patient says to a comment about the analyst. Such comments are then said to be 'transference' interpretations. In fact they represent a certain paranoid position on the part of the analyst, systematized and presented under the useful disguise of good, 'depressive', 'maternal' work.

Independent analysts put forward a different conception of what they understand psychoanalysis, and the place of the analyst, to be. One hears sometimes that the Independent Group is not a 'middle' group but a 'muddled' group. There is some truth in this. The Independent analysts are 'muddled', in one sense, for example, since they start from a point of *theoretical* uncertainty with their patients. But what other people might see as their handicap is in fact the Independents' strength. What they have to offer is primarily but not exclusively a professional stance, a *professional attitude* (this term comes from Sandler *et al.*, 1973): this is what allows the necessary distance of the analyst from the patient.

Attitude is for some a bland word but I think it is the adequate term. The word originated in the arts, with which I think we have a lot in common. It refers to a position of the body as much as to a frame of mind; it describes a kind of habitual behaviour as well as a certain readiness, fitness, and disposition. Charles Rycroft, in the paper included here, defines the analyst's attitudes as a *sentiment*, 'an organized, enduring disposition of emotional tendencies, which is maintained more or less consistently'. Our psychoanalytic attitude could be defined by the respect that our theory shows for the complications, subtleties, and variations of human relationships, evident on the patient's side as much as on the analyst's. 'To say that the analyst,' says Ella Sharpe, 'will still have complexes, blind spots, limitations is only to say that he remains a human being. When he ceases to be an ordinary human being he ceases to be a good analyst' (Sharpe, 1947).

The patient comes to analysis, and all he wants at the beginning is for a lullaby to be sung to him. It is a very vulnerable, though understandable, position to be in. Sometimes we hear of some truly mad lullabies being sung to patients. What can the patient do? A lullaby, however mad, is after all better than none; and all the more so if it is sung with an 'air of undue certainty' (Kernberg, 1965), and the analyst singing it does not seem to present any doubts. By contrast, the Independent authors referred to in this Introduction, and those included in this book, show great care in describing how the analyst should avoid putting alien feelings into the analysand's heart, and foreign words into the analysand's mouth.

Concluding remarks

MOST OF THE AUTHORS of the object relations school have certainly moved away from the classical, Freudian frame of reference, but this does not make them non-Freudians. I believe that what characterizes British psychoanalysts above anything else is an extremely astute clinical sense, which surpasses a simple opposition between theoretical and clinical practice. The British insistence on the clinical aspects of psychoanalytic practice does not exclude a capacity to use and create theory, or to exercise speculative abilities: without these abilities the writings of Fairbairn, Michael Balint, Winnicott would not have been possible.

What brings the authors of this 'school of painters' together, and what so far has kept them together, is their firm belief in the Freudian unconscious, and in the essential need to listen to the patient. It was from his patients that Freud learned psychoanalysis.

Psychoanalysis itself militates against any possibility of a single theory that would be definitive, unitary, free from contradictions. This tendency helps to explain the theoretical differences between the diverse authors who belong to the British school. Freud opposed the illusion of religion (to believe in something through ignorance), and the illusion of philosophy (the search for systems that develop into a need for some kind of final unity). He only kept his sympathy for the illusion of the aesthetic experience. We can study the works of the 'painters' of the British school, but we could never codify or systematize them. Any attempt to do so deforms and changes their creations. Their writings constitute what I would call a 'literature of excess'. Psychoanalysis has always been a literature of excess: it exceeded custom and reason, it overstepped acceptable scientific limits, it courageously explored beyond the prescribed authorities of modern thought. The excesses of an immigrant new science flourished and did very well in a country of moderation and restraint, which was able to contain other creative and cultural forms of excess. If one removes excess from psychoanalysis, we have no work of art left.

The contributions made by the Independent analysts emphasized the interrelations between the analysand's and the analyst's subjective experience. This emphasis on subjectivity caused the creation, development, and re-evaluation of theoretical concepts and clinical notions like: *countertransference*, as something of clinical relevance, not just a psychopathological interference; *acting out*, as a means of communicating something significant emerging from the history of the individual; the revision of the *criteria for the selection of cases*, enlarging the spectrum of patients considered suitable for analysis; a demand for *modifications in technique*, in order to adapt the technique to the patient, not the patient to the technique; the consideration of the *influence of the early environment* in the creation of an illness, including the study of the dynamics of the mother/baby relationship; and the positive *uses of regression*, and the creation of a *facilitating environment* in the context of the psychoanalytic treatment (James, 1980).

The papers that follow are grouped in four different sections:

1. Early Environment: Success and Failure;
2. The Psychoanalytic Encounter: Transference and Countertransference;
3. Regression and the Psychoanalytic Situation;
4. Female Sexuality.

The attention centred on the influence of the early environment in the development of the individual was a specific result of the theory of object relations. Different authors, more or less at the same time, developed similar notions resulting from the interest in the relationship between mother and baby. They attempted to describe particular characteristics found in the treatment of disturbed patients: premature ego development; cumulative trauma; basic unity; true and false self; basic fault. They all try to account for 'something missing' in the patient's life: it is not a conflict to be resolved, or a trauma to be unco-vered; it is a 'fault', something wrong in the mind, a kind of deficiency which must be put right (Balint, M., 1968).

The papers by Martin James, Masud Khan, and Margaret Little deal with this area of experience. Christopher Bollas's paper also addresses itself to the question of the early relation-ship between mother and baby. His concept of the 'transforma-tional object' identifies the first object – the mother – not so much as an object but as a *process* of alteration of self experi-ence. The object is not 'known' through a representational knowing; it is a 'symbiotic' type of knowledge. Winnicott's thoughts concerning the *fear of breakdown* are one of his major contributions to psychoanalysis. The idea that the fear of breakdown is 'the fear of a breakdown that has already been experienced' is of great clinical importance; he speaks of an agony that is 'unthinkable', and therefore not 'interpretable'. Attempts to interpret this might create a situation in the analysis which could be experienced by the patient as 'tantaliz-ing' – 'perhaps the worst thing that can happen to a human baby'. Following the theory of object relations, the develop-ment of the individual from the very beginning is based on the vicissitudes of the relationships with objects (and not from the vicissitudes of the instincts) and implies the mediation of some kind of self, or ego, present from very early on in life. John Padel's paper concerns itself with the notion of ego in current psychoanalytic thinking.

The treatment of very ill and psychotic patients created the need for new clinical and *practical* approaches. Michael Balint asks: 'how much of the two therapeutic agents – interpretation and object-relationship – should be used in any one case; when, in what proportion, and in what succession should they be used?' His paper gives a clear, concise picture of the task of *the unobtrusive analyst* in the treatment of regressed patients. This also gave rise to the consideration of the question of physical contact in the context of psychoanalytic treatment. Patrick Casement's and Jonathan Pedder's papers refer to this issue. Finally, Harold Stewart's paper on the treatment of a hysterical depressive woman with hallucinating episodes deals with problems of management, and the introduction of parameters that could be used in the analysis of regressed patients.

Female sexuality has always been an important subject in the history of psychoanalysis in Great Britain. William Gillespie's paper summarizes some of the thoughts regarding this subject, and presents certain theoretical problems for consideration. Enid Balint's contribution to the Freudian question, 'What does a woman want?', deals with technical problems she encountered in analysing women patients whose mothers were depressed or withdrawn. She puts forward the idea of a 'state of primitive concern' in relation to the mother that is used in mature object-relationships. Kohon's and Mitchell's papers take up a critical position in relation to the traditional object relations approach to female sexuality. Kohon's paper relates hysteria to femininity, suggesting that there is a hysterical stage in the development of women. Mitchell's work does not deal with the question of the different theories of femininity; but with how the question of femininity is at the heart of the development of psychoanalytic thinking.

I believe that only people properly trained as psychoanalysts should practise psychoanalysis. I also believe that those involved in clinical practice are the ones in a position to develop psychoanalytic theory. We need this theory as much as we need our practice. No amount of clinical experience, by itself, is going to solve our theoretical problems. All psychoanalytic theories, like the hysteric, suffer from reminiscences. There is no possibility of a psychoanalytic theory that is not created by the desire of the theoretician. The conditions for the existence of a theory, like those for a work of art, are that it should be different from a symptom; we could compare the creation of a symptom to the creation of a work of art or a theory, but they are not the same.

Like art, psychoanalysis is a discipline of contradictions: the task of the analyst, as much as of the patient, is to accept them. The revolution provoked by psychoanalysis has to do with the way in which it turned our own relationship to knowledge upside down, by revealing our libidinal involvement with knowledge. Given the proliferation of other psychotherapies, the variety of trainings now offered in the market, and the watering-down of psychoanalytic findings, I suspect that we are – ironically – back to the early days of the psychoanalytic pioneers. In spite of the apparent acceptance of psychoanalysis, we are again in a position of having to show real courage to believe in psychoanalysis.

Psychoanalysis continues to be full of contradictions and ambiguities. In the end, these only reflect our human condition.

NOTES

1. Brome quotes a letter from Jones to Freud, 29 November 1913, where he speaks of 'a membership of nine'. The figure stated by Jones (1959) and in all later accounts (including Brome's) is fifteen. The original list of members as published in the *Internationale Zeitschrift für Psychoanalyse* (1914) 2 411 included fifteen names, six of them with addresses outside London: in Scotland, Ireland, Canada, India and Syria. It is this fact that probably accounts for the difference.

2. Bryan, Devine and Forsyth had participated in the foundation of the London Psycho-Analytical Society together with Jones. Owen Berkeley-Hill and Lt.-Col. Sutherland had been members of the previously dissolved Society and were soon to become members of the new one.

3. Half a century later, the American analysts, concerned with the sterility of their productions and their creativity, are beginning to reconsider opening the doors of their Institutes to non-medical candidates (see eds Joseph and Widlöcher, 1983). It is clear, in any

case, that the 'law of the country' in the USA does not seem to prohibit the practice of psychoanalysis by non-medical practitioners (See Eissler, 1965).

4. At present the rule concerning practice by lay psychoanalysts of the British Psycho-Analytical Society establishes that a medical practitioner should take medical responsibility for the treatment of a patient. This implies that a patient should be seen by a medical practitioner before the treatment is begun.

5. I would like to make another more complex point concerning the issue of lay analysis. Through the considerations presented by Jones on the practical question of lay analysis, one can see how his 'naturalistic and biological outlook' also determined his theoretical conceptions. His paper 'The Early Development of Female Sexuality' was published in 1927, at the same time that lay analysis was being discussed. In presenting his ideas about female sexuality, Jones adopts a biological, naturalistic perspective (Kohon, 1984 [this volume – Ed.]; Mitchell, 1982). His support for psychoanalysis is perfectly concordant with his theoretical conclusions: the body he has in mind when he writes about female sexuality is the same body that belongs to the medical sciences. The body implicit in Freud's practical and theoretical positions is not a biological body but a sexualized one; it is a body where sexual desire lives, or better still, where it hides, only betraying its existence through symptoms. Jones's body can be investigated, can be known, can be cured. The only thing that we know for sure about Freud's body is its fundamental fragmentation, its basic split. Being a sexualized body, we can only suspect that we are all afraid of its desires. Freud always saw the movement against lay analysis as another form of resistance. I believe that it was the biological implication of his theories that made Jones, right from the beginning and throughout the years, feel closer to Melanie Klein, with whom he agreed on a number of theoretical issues. The development of female sexuality, for example, was one; another was the importance of innate determinants in the development of the individual. Melanie Klein, by the same token, found affinities in Jones's ideas, and this must have helped her to make the decision to leave Berlin – where she was opposed and disliked, except by her own analyst, Abraham, and a few of her other colleagues.

6. In their procedures of selection, psychoanalysts have been aware of this 'need for a maverick', but I suspect that even this aspect is now

under threat of becoming institutionalized: candidates *must show* a certain amount of neurosis to be accepted. Revolutionary movements seem to share similar destinies. The psychoanalytic movement, since its creation, has been under a particular threat: instead of being a challenging institution, where the aim is to further new studies, debate new ideas, provide intellectual stimulus for its members, it is in danger of being just an institution aimed at forming professionals, to protect their careers.

7. Henry Head, who held 'enlightened and sympathetic views', was perhaps the only exception, but Virginia only met him once, and treatment was never pursued (Trombley, 1981).

8. This lack of moralistic implications has probably changed. It has been most noticeable in the changes concerning the view of sexuality, the latter being greatly influenced by a particular reading of the implications of the depressive position, introduced by Melanie Klein: that which in Freud was an ethical concern (between a person and his own self) became a moral concern (between him and others).

Early environment:
success and failure

The transformational object

CHRISTOPHER BOLLAS

W̲E KNOW THAT because of the considerable pre-
maturity of human birth the infant depends on the mother for
survival. By serving as a supplementary ego (Heimann, 1956)
or a facilitating environment (Winnicott, 1963a)[1] she both sustains the baby's[2] life and transmits to the infant, through her
own particular idiom of mothering, an aesthetic of being that
becomes a feature of the infant's self. The mother's way of
holding the infant, of responding, of selecting objects, of perceiving the infant's internal needs, constitutes the 'culture' she
creates for herself and her baby, a private culture that can only
be inhabited by the two – mother and child – composed of a
language of highly idiomatic syntaxes of gestures, sound, pattern and mood that ensures its privacy, and emphasizes the
sequestered ambience of this first relation. In his unparalleled
work on the mother-child relation, Winnicott (1960b) stresses
what we might call its stillness: the mother provides a continuity of being, she 'holds' the infant in an environment of her
making that facilitates his growth. And yet, against this recip-
rocally enhancing stillness, there is an active exchange between
mother and child, a constant process of negotiated moments
that cohere around the rituals of psychosomatic needs: i.e.,
feeding, diapering, sleeping, holding. It is undeniable, I think,
that as the infant's 'other' self, the mother continually *trans-*

forms the infant's internal and external environment. Writes
Edith Jacobson:

> when a mother turns the infant on his belly, takes him out of
> his crib, diapers him, sits him up in her arms and on her lap,
> rocks him, strokes him, kisses him, feeds him, smiles at him,
> talks and sings to him, she offers him not only all kinds of
> libidinal gratifications but simultaneously stimulates and
> prepares the child's sitting, standing, crawling, walking,
> talking, and on and on, i.e., the development of functional
> ego activity. (1965, p. 37)

Winnicott (1963c) terms this comprehensive function of the
mother, the 'environment' mother, because he wants to
acknowledge that, for the infant, the mother is not yet another;
far more, she is the total environment. To this I would add that
the mother is less identifiable as an object than as a *process* that
is identified with cumulative internal and external gratifications. Because my paper will be about the *trace* in adult life of
this early object relation, I want to identify the first object as a
transformational object. By that I mean an object that is experientially identified by the infant with the process of the alteration of self experience; an identification that emerges from
symbiotic relating, where the first object is 'known' not by cog-
nizing it into an object representation, but known as a recurrent experience of being – a kind of existential, as opposed to
representational, knowing. As the mother integrates the
infant's being (instinctual, cognitive, affective, environmental)
the rhythms of this process, from unintegration(s) to integra-
tion(s), informs the nature of this 'object' relation rather than
the qualities of the object *qua* object. The mother is not yet
identified as an object but is experienced as a process of transformation, and this feature remains in the trace of this object-
seeking in adult life, where I believe the object is sought for its
function as signifier of the process of transformation of being.
Thus, in adult life, the quest is not to possess the object; it is
sought in order to surrender to it as a process that alters the self,
where the subject-as-supplicant now feels himself to be the
recipient of enviro-somatic caring, identified with metamorph-

oses of the self. As it is an identification that begins before the mother is cognized as an object, it is not an object relation that emerges from desire, but from a kind of proto-perceptual identification of the object with its active feature – the object as enviro-somatic transformer of the subject – and manifests itself in the person's search for an object (a person, place, event, ideology) that promises to transform the self. I shall outline the features of this early object tie, provide a clinical example that hyperbolizes one pathological variant of it, and finally, argues that this relation not only emerges in the transference of many patients, but is unconsciously acted out by psychoanalysts, as, I will argue, the analytic ecology enacts what Freud excluded: the early object relation of mother and child.

The experience of the mother as transformation is supported from several directions. In the first place, the mother assumes the function of the transformational object; she constantly alters the infant's environment to meet his needs. That the infant identifies the mother with transformation of being, through his symbiotic knowing, is not a delusion, but a fact; the mother actually transforms the infant's world. In the second place, the infant's own emergent ego capacities – of perception, motility, integration – also transform his world. The acquisition of language is perhaps the most obvious such transformation, but learning to handle an object, to differentiate objects, to remember objects that are not present, are transformative achievements: they result in ego change that alters the nature of the infant's object world. It is not surprising that the infant identifies these ego achievements with the presence of an object, as the failure of the mother to maintain provision of the facilitating environment, through prolonged absence or bad handling, can bring about ego collapse and psychic pain. With the infant's creation of the transitional object, the transformational process is displaced from the mother-environment (where it originated) into countless subjective-objects, so that this transitional phase is heir to the transformational phase, as the infant evolves from experience of the process to articulation of the experience. With the transitional object, the infant can play with the illusion of his own omnipotence (lessening

[85]

the loss of the environment-mother with generative and phasic delusions of self and other creation), he can entertain the idea of the object being got rid of, yet surviving his ruthlessness; he can find in this transitional experience the freedom of metaphor: what was an actual process can be displaced into symbolic equations that, if supported by the mother, mitigate the loss of the original environment-mother. In a sense, the use of a transitional object is the infant's first creative act, an event that does not just display an ego capacity – such as grasping – but which indicates the infant's first proto-subjective experience of such capacities.

The search for the transformational object in adult life

It is in adult life that I think we have failed to take notice of the wide-ranging collective search for an object that is identified with the metamorphosis of the self. In many religious faiths, for example, the subject believes in the deity's actual potential to transform the total environment, thus sustaining the terms of the earliest object tie within a mythic structure – where knowledge remains symbiotic (i.e., the wisdom of faith) – that coexists alongside other forms of knowing. In secular worlds, we can see how the hope invested in many objects (a new job, a move to another country, a vacation, a change of relationship) may be both a request for a transformational experience, and, at the same time, a continual 'relationship' to an object that signifies the experience of transformation. We know that the advertising world makes its living on the *trace* of this object; as the advertised product usually promises to alter the subject's external environment and thus change internal mood.

In adult life, the search for such an experience may generate hope, even a sense of confidence and vision, but though it seems to be grounded in the future tense, in finding something in the future to transform the present, it is an object-seeking that recurrently enacts a pre-verbal ego memory. It is usually on the occasion of the aesthetic moment (Bollas, 1978) that an individual feels a deep subjective rapport with an object – a painting, a poem, during an opera or symphony, before a landscape when the person experiences an uncanny fusion with the object, an event that recalls the kind of ego experience which constituted his earliest experiences. But such occasions, as meaningful as they might be, are less noteworthy as transformational accomplishments than they are for their uncanny quality: the sense of being reminded of something never cognitively apprehended, but existentially known, the memory of the ontogenetic process, rather than thought or fantasies that occur once the self is established. That is, such aesthetic moments do not sponsor memories of a specific event or relationship, they evoke a total psychosomatic sense of fusion – an ego experience – that is the subject's recollection of the transformational object. This anticipation of being transformed by an object – itself an ego memory of the ontogenetic process – inspires the subject with a reverential attitude toward the object, so that, even as the transformation of the self will not take place on the scale it did during early life, the adult subject tends to nominate the objects as sacred.

In adult life, therefore, to seek the transformational object is really to recollect an early object experience, to remember not cognitively, but existentially through intense affective experience, a relationship that was identified with cumulative transformational experiences of the self. Its intensity as an object relation is not due to the fact that the object was desired, but because the object is identified with such considerable metamorphoses of being. In the aesthetic moment, the subject briefly re-experiences through ego fusion with the aesthetic object, the sense of the subjective attitude towards the transformational object, but such experiences are only memories, not actual recreations. The search, however, for such symbolic equations of the transformational object and the experience with which it is identified continues in adult life. Man develops faith in a deity whose absence, ironically, is held to be as important a test of man's being as his presence. We go to the theatre, to the museum, to the landscapes of our choice, where we search for aesthetic experiences. We may *imagine* the self as the transformational facilitator, and we may invest ourselves with capacities to alter the environment that are not only impossible but downright embarrassing on reflection. In such daydreams the self as transformational object lies somewhere in the future tense, and even ruminative planning about the future (what to do, where to go, etc.) however it may yield practical plans, is often a kind of psychic prayer for the arrival of the transformational object: a secular second coming of an object relation experienced in the earliest life.

It should not be surprising that varied psychopathologies emerge from failure, as Winnicott put it, to be disillusioned from this relationship. The gambler, who invests his game with the certainty of a transformational object that is only just about to metamorphose his entire internal and external world, is one example. This goes for much criminality, for, again as Winnicott (1956a) has pointed out, the delinquent is adamant that the environment must make something up to him. In my concept, he relates to the environment as if he can through the perfect crime discover the perfect object, a crime that will transform the self, internally (repairing ego defects and fulfilling id needs) and externally (bringing wealth and happiness). Indeed, different forms of erotomania may be efforts to establish the other as the transformational object. I do not think that the search for the perfect crime or the perfect woman is only an idealized split; it is also some recognition in the subject of a deficiency in ego experience and a recurrent reliving of the area of what Michael Balint (1968) called the 'basic fault'. The search to commit the complete crime, the planned seduction of the perfect woman, however they serve to split the bad self experience away from the subject's cognitive knowledge, are nonetheless semiological acts that signify the person's search for a particular object relation that is associated with ego transformation and repair.

Clinical example

I think that one of the most common psychopathologies of the transformational object relation occurs with what we have called the schizoid self: the patient who may have a wealth of ego strengths (intelligence, talent, accomplishment, success) but who is personally bereft and sad without being clinically depressed. I have written about Peter before in another paper, (Bollas, 1976).

Peter is a 28-year-old single male whose sad expressions, dishevelled appearance, and colourless apparel are only mildly relieved by a sardonic sense of humour which brings him no relief, and an intelligence and education which he uses for the sake of others, but never for himself. He was referred by his general practitioner for depression, but his problem was more of an inexorable sadness and personal loneliness. Since his break-up with a girlfriend he had lived alone in a flat, dispersing himself during the day into multiple odd jobs. Though his days were a flurry of arranged activity he went through them in a style of agitated passivity as if he were being aggressively handled by his own work arrangement. Once home he would collapse into the slovenly comfort of his flat where he would prop himself before the TV, eat a scanty meal of packaged food, masturbate and, above all, ruminate obsessively about the future and bemoan his current 'bad luck'.

Every week, without failure, he would go home to see his mother. He felt she lived in order to talk about him and thus he must be seen by her in order to keep her content.

Reconstruction of the earliest years of Peter's life yielded the following. Peter was born in a working-class home during the war. While father was defending the country the home was occupied by numerous in-laws, all middle-European who were holding on to their lost culture by speaking constantly about local folklore and disclosing regional and familial curses, hexes and signs. Peter was the first child born in the family and he was lavishly idolized, particularly by his mother who spoke constantly to her relatives about how Peter would undo their misery through great deeds. An inveterate dreamer about golden days to come, mother's true depression showed up in the lifeless manner in which she cared for Peter, investing all her liveliness towards him as mythical object rather than actual infant. Soon after Peter's therapy began it became clear to me that he knew himself to be primarily inside a myth he shared with mother; indeed, he knew that she did not actually attend to the real him but to the object of her dreams which happened to be him. As *her* mythical object he felt his life to be suspended and, indeed, this was the way he lived. He seemed to be preserving himself, attending to somatic needs, waiting for the day when he would fulfil mother's dream. But because it was mother's myth, he could do nothing, only wait for something to happen. He seemed compulsively to empty himself of his true self needs in order to create an internal empty space to receive mother's dream thoughts. Each visit to the home was curiously like a mother giving her son a narrative feeding. So he would empty himself of personal desire and need in order to fulfil mother's desire and he would preserve himself in a state of suspension from life, waiting for the myth to call him into a transformed reality. Because mother has transmitted to him his crucial function as her mythic object, Peter does not experience his internal psychic space as his own. Inner space exists for the other, so that in reporting inner states of being Peter does so through a depersonalized narrative as this region is not the 'from me' but the 'for her'. There is a notable absence in Peter of any sense of self, no quality of an 'I', nor even of a 'me'. Instead his self representation bears more the nature of an 'it' on an existential plane. Being an 'it' means for him being dormant, suspended, inert. Free associations with Peter are more like *logs* of 'it'-states: ruminative reports on the happenings of his body as depersonalized object. As mother's primary concern was for him to remain in good health in order to fulfil her dreams for him, he was consequently obsessed with any somatic problem, which he reported with almost clinical detachment.

Gradually I recognized that the mythic structure (existing in a narrative rather than existential reality) masked the secret discourse of the lost culture of Peter's earliest relation to his mother. His ego-states were an utterance to mother who used them as the vocabulary of myth. If he was feeling like a casualty because of ego defects and the failure of id needs, it was because he was her knight errant who had fought battles for her and must rest for future missions. If he felt depleted by his personal relations it was because he was a cherished god who could not expect to mix successfully with the masses. If he spoke to his mother with a sigh she responded not by discovering the source of the sigh, but by telling him not to worry, that soon he would make money, become famous, go on TV, and bring to the family all the wealth that they deserved. His existential despair was continually flung into mythic narrative: a symbolic order where the real is used to populate the fantastic. On the few occasions when he tried to elicit from his mother some actual attendance to his internal life she flew into a rage and yelled that his misery threatened their lives, as only he could deliver them. He must remain the golden larva, the unborn hero, who, if he does not shatter mythic function with personal needs, will soon be delivered into a world of riches and fame beyond his imagination.

In the transference Peter spoke of himself as an object in need of care: 'my stomach hurts', 'I have a pain in my neck', 'I have a cold', 'I don't feel well'. He spoke to me in the language of sighs, groans, and a haunting laughter which served his need to empty out agitated desire and to elicit my acute attention. He rubbed his hands, looked at his fingers, flopped his body around as if it were a sack. As I came to realize that this was not obsessive rumination which served as a resistance, but was, in fact, a secret discourse recalled from the culture of his earliest relations to mother, he found my attention to his discourse an immense relief. I felt that he was trying to share a secret with me, within the transference, but it was a secret utterance that was prior to language and masked by its enigmatic quality. I could only enter this sequestered culture by speaking to him in its language: to be attentive to all groans, sighs, remarks about his body, etc. Above all, I was to learn that what he wanted from me was the sound of my voice which I gradually understood to be the need for a good maternal sound which framed his experience with me and eventually transformed our relationship. My interpretations were appreciated less for their content, and more for their function as structuring experiences. He rarely recalled the content of an interpretation. What he appreciated was the sense of relief brought to him through my words.

Peter's sense of fatedness, as a potential transformational object to the other, suggests that not only does the infant require separation and disillusion from the mother's apparent function as the sole agent of transformation, but equally, the mother must suffer some generative depressive experience after the birth of her infant, a 'let-down', brought on by the real needs of the infant, which mitigates the mother's unconscious wish for an infant to be her transformational object. Peter's mother continually refused to recognize and attend to him as a real person, though admittedly, there was a quality of what we might call covetous mothering about her care: she possessed him as if she was an alchemist guarding dross that was her potential treasure. His real needs went unmet, as mother insisted that Peter fulfil her sense that destiny would bring her a deliverer-child.

Discussion

Now this is an obvious example of the psychopathology of the transformational object relation, and our work with narcissistic patients (who function with the illusion of self as transformational object, but who exhibit the forlorn depressive features of one who is forever failed in self-provision), and with schizoid persons, hyperbolizes the features of this particular object situation. I believe, however, that the search for the transformational object, in both the narcissistic and schizoid character, is in fact an internal recognition of the need for ego repair and, as such, is a somewhat manic search for health. To be sure, one of the features of such patients is their comparative unavailability for relating to the actual other – their obtuseness or excessive withdrawnness – but I think such characteristics, reflective of psychodevelopmental arrests, also point towards the patient's need to assert the region of illness as a plea for the arrival of the regressive object relation that is identified with basic ego repair. In analysis this can result in the patient's almost total inability to relate to the analyst as a real person, while at the same time maintaining an intense relation to the analyst as a transformational object. What is the patient trying to establish? It seems to me, as I have written about Peter, and as other authors have pointed out (Smith, 1977), that such patients seek to live within a special ambience with the analyst, where the analyst's interpretations are far less important for their content, and more significant for what is experienced as a maternal sound – a kind of verbal humming. Indeed, so-called analytic neutrality of expression – ostensibly to mitigate the hysterical or obsessional patient's dread of feeling criticized and to facilitate the analysand's freedom of association – actually works in a different way for narcissistic or schizoid patients; they become *enchanted* by it, and can appear oblivious to the actual content of the interpretation so long as the song of the analytic voice remains constant. Now, we may look upon this as a complication in the path of analysability, or we may recognize that the analytic space (the provision of the holding environment) facilitates a process in such patients that leads to the evocation of a deeply regressed state which may be a part of this patient's necessary path to cure. Indeed, my experience with such patients is that a regression to this form of object-relating takes place often in the *first* session of therapy, and that the ecology of the analytic room (analyst, analyst's interpretations, couch, the rest) becomes a kind of sacred space for the patient. As I view it, the patient is regressed to what Balint has called the level of the basic fault, but as each regression points to the region of illness within the person, it also suggests the requirement of a cure, and in such patients I believe what is needed is a prolonged experience of successive ego transformations that are identified with the analyst and the analytic ecology. In such moments, the patient experiences interpretations primarily for their capacity to *match* his internal mood, or feeling, or thought, and such moments of rapport lead the patient to 're-experience' the transformational object relation. Such patients appreciate the analyst's fundamental unintrusiveness (particularly the analyst's not demanding compliance) not because it leads to freedom of association, but because it feels like the kind of relating that is needed to become well. Now some analysts might regard this perception of the patient only as a resistance, but if so, I think we overlook the undeniably unique atmosphere we create for relating. We know that the very offer of treatment invites regressive longings in many patients. We know that placing the patient on the couch induces a sense of anxious expectation and dependency. Our reliability, our unintrusiveness, our use of empathic thought to meet the requirements of the patient, is often far more of a maternal ambience for the patient than the actual mother provided. And in such moments, the patient's identification with the analyst as the transformational object is not dissimilar to the infant's identification of the mother with such processes. Indeed, just as the infant's identification of ego transformations with the mother is a perceptual identification – and not a desire – so, too, the patient's identification does not seem to reflect the patient's desire for us to be transformational, but his adamant perceptual identification of the analyst as transformational object. In the treatment of the narcissistic, borderline and schizoid characters, this phase of the analysis is both necessary and inevitable.

This stage of treatment is very difficult for the therapist, as in a sense there is as yet no *analysis* of the patient taking place, and interpretive remarks made may be met with a gamut of refusals: from polite contempt to rage. One such patient would often nod politely, say that yes he did see what I meant, indeed was impressed with how accurate my remark was, but invariably he would end by saying: 'But of course, you know what you have said is only technically correct. It doesn't help me with life experiences, so, as such, as correct as it is I don't see what you think I can do with such a remark.' He was convinced I knew how to take care of him, and even if it was only for an hour a day, he wanted me to soothe him. Analysis proper was regarded as an intellectual intrusion into his tranquil experience of me, and I was for him a kind of advanced computer storing his information, processing his needs into my memory banks, all this towards an eventual session when I would suddenly emerge with the proper solution for him and in an instant remedy his life. I have come to regard this part of his analysis as that kind of regression which is a re-enactment of the earliest object experience, and I think it is folly for a therapist to deny that the culture of the analytic space does indeed facilitate such recollections. If such regressions are a resistance to the analysis of the self, they are resistances only in the sense that the patient *must* resist analytic investigation *as it is experienced as a precocious overachievement of the patient's psychic position*, and in the transference – which is as much to the analytic space and process as it is to the person of the analyst – the patient's regression is to the level of relating to the transformational object, that is, experiencing the analyst as the environment-mother, a pre-verbal memory that cannot be cognized into speech that recalls the experience, but only speech that demands its terms be met: unintrusiveness, 'holding', 'provision', insistence on a kind of symbiotic or telepathic knowing, facilitation from thought to thought, or from affect to thought, that means many of these sessions are in the form of *clarifications* which the patient experiences as transformative events. Interpretations which require reflective thought, or which analyse the self, are felt to be precocious demands on the patient's psychic capacity, and such patients may react with acute rage or express a sudden sense of futility.

Perhaps because so much of psychoanalytic theory evolved from work with the hysterical patient (who interpreted the analytic ecology as a seduction) or the obsessional patient (who adopted it willingly as another personal ritual) we have tended to regard regressive reactions to the analytic space as resistances to the working alliance or the analytic process. And yet, perhaps the hysteric's sexualization of the transference, and the obsessional's ritualization of the analytic process (free dissociation?) were themselves defences against the very 'invitation' of the analytic space and process towards regression. Thus, in the analyses of such patients, psychic material was readily forthcoming and one could be relatively pleased that there was considerable grist for the analytic mill, but treatment often continued endlessly with no apparent character change, or was suddenly intruded upon by archaic or primitive material. In such cases I believe the analyst was unaware that the failure of the patient to experience the analytic situation as a regressive invitation was – if we will – a resistance; indeed, the analytic process, with premium on the mechanics of free association and interpretation of the patient's defences, could often result in denial of the very object relation that was 'offered' to the patient. If the analyst cannot acknowledge that in fact he is offering a regressive space to the patient (that is, a space that encourages the patient to relive his infantile life in the transference), if he insists that in the face of the 'invitation' *work* must be carried out, it is not surprising that in such analyses patient and analyst may either carry on in a kind of mutual dissociation that leads nowhere (obsessional collusion), or in a sudden blow-up on the part of the patient, often termed 'acting out'.

As I view it, then, the analyst functions as an evocative mnemic trace of the transformational object, as the situation will either induce a patient's regressive recollection of this early object relation, or the variations of resistance to it: i.e., either denial by sexualization, or obsessional ritualization. Indeed, the transference, from this point of view, is first and foremost a transference reaction to this primary object relation and will help us to see how the patient remembers his own experience of this early object situation. There may be a deep regression to a demand that the analyst fulfil the promise of the invitation and function in a magically transformative manner, or the patient may have enough health to be able to report his experience of the situation, and to have enough insight into regressive recollections, to carry on with subsequent work in the analysis, and yet do so while remaining in touch with more archaic aspects of the self. Indeed, I believe that much of the time a patient's passivity, or wordlessness, or expectation that the analyst either knows what to do or should do something is not a resistance to any particular conscious or preconscious thought, but is a recollection of the early pre-verbal world of the infant being with mother. Unless we recognize that psychoanalysts share in the construction of this pre-verbal world, through the analyst's silence, the total absence of didactic instruction, and empathic thought, we are being unfair to the patient and he may have reason to be perplexed and irritated.

I have taken this diversion into (hopefully) excusable over-simplification of clinical issues, in order to clarify my belief that the transference relation rests on the paradigm of the first-transformational-object relation. Freud tacitly recognized this when he set up the analytic space and process and, though there is comparatively little about the mother-child relation within Freud's theory, we might say that Freud acted out his non-verbal and unconscious recognition of it in the creation of the analytic ecology. Indeed, the construction of the psychoanalytic process rests itself on the memory of this primary relation, and the psychoanalyst's collective unconscious re-enactment (a professional countertransference) is to recollect by enactment the transformational object situation. What Freud could not analyse in himself – his relation to his own mother – was acted out in his choice of the ecology of psychoanalytic technique. And unless we can grasp that as psychoanalysts we *are* enacting this early paradigm, we continue to act out in the counter-transference Freud's one, and eminently excusable, area of blindness.

Though the search for transformations and for the transformational objects is perhaps the most pervasive archaic object relation, it bears restressing that the search is not out of desire for the object *per se*, nor *primarily* out of craving or longing, but derives from an insistent perceptual identification with the object of transformations of the self. To be sure, the entire range of human feeling may be elicited in the search for the object – euphoria if felt to be found, despondency if felt to be non-existent – but the search for the object is out of certainty that it will transform the subject. Of course this may lead to the object's achieving a secondary idealization – as in the legend of Christ – but making the object sacred occurs only after the object's transformational potential has been declared. In each instance, I believe, the reason for the isolated affect of adamant certainty that the object will deliver transformation is based on the object's nominated capacity to resuscitate the memory of early ego transformation. In arguing this, I am maintaining that though no cognitive memory of the infant's experience of the mother is available, the search for the transformational object, its nomination as the deliverer of environmental transformation, is an ego memory. In a curious way, it is solely the ego's object, and may, indeed, be to the utter shock or indifference of the person's subjective experience of their own desire. A gambler is compelled to gamble: subjectively, he may wish he did not gamble, and this internal identification with the perfect moment may indeed cause personal misery. In Melville's novel *Moby-Dick* Ahab feels compelled to seek the whale, even though he feels alienated from the source of his own internal compulsion. He says:

> 'What is it, what nameless, inscrutable, unearthly thing is it; what cozening, hidden lord and master, and cruel, remorseless emperor commands me; then against all natural lovings and longings, I so keep pushing, and crowding, and jamming myself on all the time; recklessly making me ready to do what in my own proper, natural heart, I durst not so much as dare? Is Ahab, Ahab? Is it I, God, or who, that lifts this arm?' (1851, pp. 444-5)

There is something *impersonal and ruthless* about the search for the whale, and all objects nominated as transformational. Once early ego memories are identified with an object that is contemporary, the subject's relation to the object can become fanatical, and I think many extremist political movements indicate a collective certainty that their revolutionary ideology will effect a total environmental transformation that will deliver everyone from the gamut of basic faults: personal, familial, economic, social, and moral. Again, it is not the revolutionary's desire for change, or the extremist's longing for change, but his *certainty* that the object (in this case the revolutionary ideology) will bring about change that is striking to the observer.

Conclusions

In work with certain kinds of patients (schizoid and narcissistic) who hyperbolize a particular object-seeking, and in our analysis of certain features of culture, I think we can isolate the *trace* in the adult of the earliest experience of the object: the experience of an object that transforms the subject's internal

[98]

and external world. I have called this first object the transformational object, as I want to identify it with *the object as process*, thus linking the first object with the infant's experience of it. Before the mother is personalized to the infant as a whole object, she has functioned as a region or source of transformation, and as the infant's own nascent subjectivity is almost completely the experience of the ego's integrations (cognitive, libidinal, affective) the first object is identified with the alterations of the ego's state. With the infant's growth and increasing self-reliance, the relation to the mother changes from the mother as the other who alters the self, to a *person* who has her own life and her own needs. As Winnicott says, the mother disillusions the infant from the experience of mother as the sole preserver of his world, a process that occurs as the infant is increasingly able to meet his own needs and requirements; but the ego experience of being transformed by the other remains as a memory that may be re-enacted either in the subject's search for aesthetic experiences, in a wide range of culturally-dreamed-of transformational objects, such as new cars, homes, jobs, vacations, that promise total change of internal and external environment, or in the varied psychopathological manifestations of this memory: in the gambler's relation to his object, in the extremist's relation to his ideological object. I have argued that the ecology of the psychoanalytic space, outfitted with a silent and empathic analyst, a couch to 'hold' the patient, the release from socialization, and the emphasis on fantasizing to the analyst, etc., often leads to the identification of the analyst with the transformational object. This occurs *because* the analytic ecology sponsors such a regressive relating, and because the idiom of the analytic relation bears considerable psychic resemblance to the mother's attendance to the infant. As such, the patient's insistence that the analyst is the transformational object is not necessarily a resistance to the work of analysis, but is a memory resuscitated by the analytic process itself, and it behoves the analytic profession to analyse more thoroughly the unconscious communication of the analytic ecology. I have argued that we continue to *act out* in what is now the ritual idiom of the analytic technique a lacuna in

Freud's self-analysis: his own relation to his mother. Recollected aspects of this relation, I suggest, are reproduced in the analytic technique, though psychoanalysts, having inherited Freud's insights, have also inherited his blindness in not recognizing how psychoanalytic technique both enacts and elicits memories of the earliest object relation. We might call this a professional unconscious countertransference, as we offer a patient one kind of relationship (the regressive re-experience of infant to mother) which still revives not only ego memories but expectations and, on the other hand, we insist, at least in more classical formulations, on proceeding to analytic 'work'. Such work cannot take place, I maintain, until the analyst has a thorough understanding of his own profession as a countertransference enactment of an early object setting and relation. Until we cognize this non-verbal enactment of our own, we cannot successfully facilitate our patients through their own recognition of it. Finally, we can see, perhaps, how in the aesthetic moment, when the person engages in deep subjective rapport with an object, the culture finds in the arts varied symbolic equivalents of the search for transformation, as in the *quest* for a deep subjective experience of an object, the artist both remembers for us and provides us with occasions for the experience of ego memories of transformation. In a way, the experience of the aesthetic moment is neither social nor moral; it is curiously impersonal and in a way ruthless, as the object is sought for only as a deliverer of an experience. The aesthetic space allows for an appropriate enactment of the search for this object relation, and we might say the culture engages in memories of ego experiences that are now profoundly radical experiences, as the culture cannot possibly meet the needs of the subject as the mother met the needs of the infant, but in the arts we have a location for such occasional recollections, intense ego memories of the process of self-transformation.

Premature ego development some observations on disturbances in the first three months of life

MARTIN JAMES

ANYBODY TRAINING to be a psychoanalyst in the British Society from 1939 was forced to consider the divisions which were present in the Society. This was certainly so for someone like myself in analysis with Anna Freud. These divisions were both political and formal: political when they involved voting and office but also, more important to me, formal in the sense of intellectual scruple.

I wrote this paper on premature ego development soon after I qualified in 1949 and it was an intellectual response to how I thought theory should develop. The paper was generally recommended by Anna Freud, but the difficulty it met in acceptance by other members of the B Group contributed eventually to my moving to the Middle Group. The Kleinians too did not understand it, which made me feel like Michael Balint who always drew fire from both sides.

Melanie Klein herself very kindly discussed the paper when I read it to the Society, but her objections disturbed me about her stance generally. The point I remember her making is that no newborn baby can be expected literally, or in principle, to receive 'almost 100 per cent cathexis' from the mothering person. I felt that whatever Mrs Klein might know about babies she didn't know about the ordinary devoted mother and her newborn. I expect she had a nanny.

I was in the event thus faced with two leaders in my world

[101]

with whom I had come to difference. Klein, the mother of two or three children, unsound about what for me was then and remains a first principle of mothering: primary maternal preoccupation. Anna Freud had told me, 'We take a good-enough infancy for granted.' Now I know that in saying this she was talking of cases that we should select for treatment. It was for her a typically pragmatic notion, but I sensed that it was also a judgement which she would apply to development as well. This attitude may be welcome for an analyst who is disposed to ego restriction, but it is hard for less worldly-wise or less judicious or less canny analysts.

Reduced to essentials, the premature ego paper is about the question of the extent to which mothering affects the infant. Klein, with her strict adherence to the concept of the death instinct, denied the infant's dependency on the environment. For her, self and object were separate (and subject to projection-introjection) in utero. So that for Klein, ego is not only inevitable from the start, it cannot be premature.

Anna Freud, while not discounting the importance of learned experiences in infancy, preferred to exclude consideration of them in analysis. This meant that she neither wanted to stress the importance of handling (mothering) in infancy nor in any way to consider its preventive possibilities. Both Klein and Anna Freud were thus structuralists in the sense that they knew the merit of the analytic principle of taking 'the material for the day' as the text for that day. Neither of them wished to become involved with prevention.

Anna Freud was largely not scientifically interested in infancy, first because Freud was not, second, she was too scrupulous to guess in symbolic interpretation; and third, she couldn't, in her blood, have a feeling for psychotic concrete thinking and direct bypassing of defence. As a political animal her constituency was the well-endowed, educated public, and she held close to what they could accept and not fight.

Klein's description of the depressive position must rank with Freud's description of the Oedipus complex in our esteem. Her Achilles heel, for all her splendid achievements, is exposed by Frances Tustin in work on autism (1972, 1981). Tustin, long in analysis with Bion, has laid an axe to the root of the tree. She establishes definitively that separation of self and object, too early, produces autism. Ego *can* be premature.

Author's Preface, 1985

In this paper I am reporting observations made on a full-term infant and followed for seven years. These observations relate to neural patterning which seems to result from premature stimulation in the first three months of life. They suggest that a more or less irreversible and what may rightly therefore be called a *constitutional* influence can be exerted by the early *environment*.

Greenacre (1953) raised, in effect, the question of environmental contributions to constitutional equipment. She discusses the organization of prenatal and immediate post-natal narcissism, the influence of birth upon it and upon the predisposition to anxiety. She suggests that experiences in these earliest days of life 'leave some individual and unique *somatic* memory traces which amalgamate with later experiences and may thereby increase later psychological pressures.' She goes on: 'It is in fact extremely difficult to say exactly at what time the human organism develops from a biological to a psycho-biological organization.'

Schur (1959) in a definitive series of papers shows processes at work in the change from biological to psychological organization. He discusses the relation between neural-biological patterning and the psychological affect of anxiety. He also adds a new concept when he refers to ethological analogies in the neural patterning. He concludes: 'When children show an innate or early acquired homœostatic instability, both maturation and ego control are jeopardized, resulting in imperfect and unstable desomatization. . . . Such children show predisposition to severe anxiety and to severe pathology, specifically also to psychosomatic disorders.'

From psychoanalytical reconstruction it is assumed that environmental factors in the narcissistic phase of libido organization contribute to the origin of a wide variety of conditions

[103]

such as addictions, fetishism and perversion, psychosomatic disease, pre-psychotic, psychotic and other disorders. Reconstructions along such lines are familiar from the time of Freud's original proposition that the fixation point for dementia praecox lay at the stage of primary narcissism. Observations of what the fixating experience in infancy would look like, however, are not common.

Mahler (1953, 1955) in her studies of autistic children *reconstructs* such a fixation point, but the youngest child on whom she reports *observations* is eighteen months old. She refers to a clinical syndrome observable in infancy which she calls by the name 'organismic distress'. Anna Freud describes how early somatic upsets may pattern later psychosomatic responses.

The study most relevant to the present case is that of Bergman and Escalona (1949) who in a direct observation on full-term infants describe a syndrome of 'unusual sensitivity' around six months. These are infants who are at first so precocious as to seem budding geniuses. They also show, however, very much the quality of tenseness and characteristic jumpiness which I shall describe. Like Goldstein's idiots savants (1959) the precocity and alertness proved in follow-up to be associated with weakness and vulnerability, so much so that in their later development they showed reactions of psychosis, traumatic neurosis, and feeble-mindedness. They in fact show first precocious ego development and then a later failure of ego development, both of which the authors relate to the 'unusual sensitivity'.

My observation is a description of the response to handling of Bergman and Escalona's type of infant. It is also the sort of experience in infancy which psychoanalysis at a later stage might reconstruct when a trauma is assumed in the phase of primary narcissism. I draw conclusions about dynamics and metapsychology, but there is an applied aspect to the case, for I suggest that neural-biological patterning is reversible only at the time of the trauma and is not itself directly accessible to later psychoanalytic interpretation, since it is not symbolic. In this way the observation reported underlines and defines the prophylactic importance of environmental homoeostasis (i.e., successful mothering) for the normal infant.

The infant I shall describe was in a state of tension due to hunger for about three months. It was born hungry, and after birth a monthly nurse fed it not to satiety but on a rigid schedule. Although it gained weight steadily it was never satisfied, and so it was always tense, alert and jumpy. The mother, being preoccupied after the death of a brother, was prevented from acting in the skilled and experienced way of which she had before and later proved herself capable. But this is not relevant, for her failure in mothering was mediated to the infant by a failure of need-satisfying function, and the infant's reaction to chronic slight hunger was the result. In fact feeding was done by a nurse for six weeks.

Of interest from the point of view of early neural patterning is the fact that the child still has a wool fetish as transitional object or comforter and that the observer predicted this would happen during this first month. It seemed to arise in the following way: the nurse tied the infant's hands before feeds in a napkin. The infant in its chronically restless and hungry state sucked and mouthed this. The tying only happened for one month, but nevertheless she still, at eight years old, picks a jersey while sucking her thumbs, and tickles her nose and upper lip with the wool she has picked. This could be an accident, but it might also be regarded as a permanent biological pattern of discharging tension which originated at this point; a sort of permanent conditioning or neural patterning such as is described by Greenacre on the one hand or the ethologists on the other.

I emphasize that different varieties of patterning are part of such a general syndrome that individual outcomes are not an issue. The fate of early ego nuclei to some extent depends upon subsequent experience, and so the question whether such a reaction-potential disappears in a split-off uncathected ego-remainder or enters fatefully into all subsequent ego considerations depends upon our well-established principles of psychoanalytic child development.

It seems to me only a question of dosage of tension and style

[105]

of impact that governs what form of patterning is established. For example, in this case a premature ego development with some pre-psychotic type of verbal and motor qualities appears, but if instead of hypercathexis of attention there had been vomiting and diarrhoea or more prominent somatic discharge phenomena, then these would have attracted cathexis and instead of a premature ego development a psychosomatic development would have taken place.

The reaction by neural techniques that did occur seemed largely to bypass motility. Since motility is the first agent of reality testing, may this not offer a prodromal encouragement to later pathological traits that muscular techniques would not? Freud speaks of muscle sadism as directed in a primary way to objects. Could techniques of neural or mental control act as prodromal states for a cerebral analogy to muscle control? Such accidental experiments happen all the time and can be watched in a proportion of new babies.

The infant which I shall describe could be seen to lack the normal instinct barrier (the *Reizschutz*, described by Freud in *Beyond the Pleasure Principle*). It showed the 'unusual sensitivity' described by Bergman and Escalona and for example at two weeks, although it lived in deep rural quiet, it would, unlike an ordinary baby, be roused from sleep even by a distant backfire, by a dog's bark, by the noise of a far-off aeroplane, a door slamming, or footsteps close at hand.

Even during the first fourteen days the infant was not only excessively wakeful owing to this perceptive acuity which, as Sandler (1960) points out, is in itself an activity, but also reacted by means of such motor response as is available to a full-term infant. What should be stressed is that this fourteen-day infant in turning its head and eyes and reaching *gave the impression of a much older baby* apparently forced by its instinctive need to act as though focusing and purposive, certainly anticipating and therefore *forced to tolerate delay*. I would contrast this with the situation of an infant whose mother provides an instinct-barrier. Only the mothering person can arrange this, for an infant cannot arrange an instinct-barrier for itself beyond a certain point. Such a barrier was only provided from three months old when this infant was fed to satiety for the first time.

The function of the mother as guardian of the instinct-barrier has been made actual for us in Winnicott's (1958) writings. The mother, by her devotion (which is mediated to the infant by her continuous presence and resulting special empathy with its needs) can anticipate and divert almost all stimulation reaching her baby or ration it so that it is enough but not too much. In this way she sets up what Winnicott has called 'a good-enough holding environment'. The mother who provides this acts as an auxiliary ego and saves the baby from both under- and overstimulation and from premature development of its own resources.

The situation is different by the end of the first year, for as the months go by the mother gradually passes her functions over to her baby. During the reign of primary narcissism, as Hoffer (1949) stresses, the mother is the whole environment: a healthy infant can so to speak 'assume' this and so take no responsibility for itself until the mother judges it possible. *Premature ego development would imply that the infant, during the phase of primary narcissism, took over functions from the mother in actuality, or started as though to do so. This would not be phase-adequate behaviour under three months.*

Consistent failure to guard the instinct-barrier happens when, for reasons either of her situation or of her personality, the mother cathects other things than her baby and, as we say, 'has something else on her mind'. In either case she is compelled, whether it is by circumstances or by her nature. Her interest is drained away from the task which for these few earliest months Winnicott properly defines as 'almost 100 per cent adaptation'. Incidentally, to fulfil her function of total concern for her baby and not to have preoccupations and distractions she, too, needs an auxiliary ego, and under modern conditions this is often the husband's role. In this case the nurse's training prevented full need satisfaction.

The infant I am describing showed by the age of three months to an observer, and also in photographs, a facies which to an onlooker expressed something between bewilderment, discouragement, and depression. This was a quiescent state which alternated with a hyper-reactive tendency and hypersensitivity to stimulation affecting all perceptive channels. Nevertheless by eight months this baby had overtaken its early difficulties and had won a prize in a baby show, and indeed was rather overweight. This gain in weight was certainly connected with a capacity to drink large quantities more rapidly than usual. Having charming colouring she was a natural prizewinner. This has since become her public personality. She is accepted as unusually attractive and successful and this impression remains, however vulnerable or potentially depersonalized she may be.

In spite of these compensatory favourable elements this infant, as she grew, began at later ages to show in her character classical oral traits which would normally be lost sight of by being absorbed and sublimated during the course of development. At eight months her very appealingness, which we might also call object hunger, and also her later sympathetic quality were, I suggested, pseudo-sublimations of an impaired sense of identity and of a fluidity of identification. This seems to be related to her responses of mental alertness and liveliness from earliest weeks which, when compared to the phase-adequate response, are relatively pathological in that they represent blocking of age-adequate instinct. This pathological aspect is not altered by the fact that they are later exploited in the service of ego-development proper.

To give an example: early reactivity to the environment and facility for identification had the effect at later ages that if there was a period of contact with other children for example on a holiday, there was likely to be, to a quite different degree from other children, an obdurate acquisition of their mannerisms, accents, postures, and interests. This particular child's character at five was full of 'attributions'. Being with her, if one knew the quotations, was like listening, to a musical pot-pourri. Socially this passed as deliberate and to some was even an attraction. I think it should make us uneasy if we consider it a narcissistic process of identification and as such a substitute for true object relations.

In psychoanalytic terms, then, instead of a phase-adequate access to instinct and physical function, so to say a body ego relish leading through need satisfaction to object relations, this infant cathected and developed a narcissistic 'thought action' which also fulfilled a need satisfaction, but in a different way. On the one hand such infants miss something, and on the other they acquire a quality that others do without. That is, they develop non-muscular and symbolic aspects of themselves which are yet active responses. This is a special kind of ego development with its own potential advantages, no doubt, as well as disadvantages. We should only evaluate reluctantly. They may even come to have survival value in later life.

To give an example of the reciprocity of mental and motor reactions in the basic constitution. In follow-up, this child from the time of first walking and expressive gesturing showed a subtle disorder of motility which seemed to be linked with her unusual mental plasticity and activity. She was always 'falling over herself', partly out of impulsive haste and partly out of 'clumsiness'. Her ideas ran away with her, and if she thought of a thing she was liable to act as though (by magic) it had already happened. Simple actions, such as reaching for a potato at a meal, thus led to upsetting the water or banging herself. The intermediate steps seemed to be lost in a magical elision: only the potato mattered, as it were, and the glass and chair did not exist for her. It seemed natural that magic proper later became important to her and she was often spoken of as a witch because she was preoccupied with magical influences which never occur to less 'imaginative' children. This also showed in her punning and neologisms and in her idiosyncratic and distinctive way of using words. A variety of constitutional traits, not only of oral character, but also schizoid mechanisms and characteristic motility and body habits, were related to the particular sensorimotor balance which this infant developed. This includes also the later-developed characteristic mannerisms with the arms and the willowy way of running and walking which could have a magical and symbolic significance giving them affinity with the organ speech of developed schizoid processes.

[109]

As an example of how the fate and outcome of such tendencies may be influenced by handling, I will describe a successful attempt at prophylaxis in this case. Her older sibling went to morning nursery school at three and a half. The two-year-old, in her wish to keep up, began efforts at further inappropriate ego development; that is, she began to learn letters and to pretend to read and write and gave her parents the impression that she would make great strides in intellectual development. I do not think that any amount of talk could have dealt with this. Intellectual lopsidedness could only be prevented, and a phase-adequate development ensured, by means of what was really an enforced regression.

This calculated regression took the form of systematically offering a more age-adequate gratification at the very time each day when the mother was preoccupied getting the older sibling off to school. It was nothing to do with verbalization, but purely a matter of handling. The mother being busy, the father gave up some work and devoted himself to his child for an hour in mutually sharable and enjoyable activity: swings, shopping, and walking to do things with Daddy, but with emphasis on the child's need.

This two-year-old child's clumsiness, I suggest, had symbolic implications. To enjoy ordinary reality-adapted motor activities became therefore therapeutic. Words could never produce this, and indeed would only have aggravated the tendency to use symbols. With two-year-olds actions are more phase-adequate than words, which means that in the hierarchy of development actions are regressive rather than progressive dynamically speaking. This handling enabled the child to look forward to a phase-adequate alternative to going to school which she came to value equally. It successfully reduced the intellectual precocity and the symbolization and delibidinization of objects which this threatened to enhance. It reinforced her reality testing, her control of her body and realistic mutuality with her father and got rid of her wish to go to school and all that it stands for in a mental way.

In passing we may say that it is important to note how hard it may be for parents to resist the pressure and seduction of one-sidedness in favour of all-round development. It is easy for the parent to take credit for having a 'forward' child, and not to notice at the time the loss of later ego-integration from narcissistic developments not achieved through object relations. This would be an example of the kind of choice before parents which so subtly enters into the ego-ideal and superego of a two-year-old. It is interesting too for the study of early predispositions that in the phallic phase compensation of the pre-patterning led to the development of special skill in running, climbing, and jumping in identification with boys. This must have been partly reactive and defensive in terms of the earliest experiences and in some degree therefore depersonalized in terms of affect. Gradually the motor features of the earliest times, as other compensating areas of ego developed, came to show only in revealing moments of stress.

Metapsychology

My case, while in no way psychotic in outcome in terms of Kanner's cases, can be understood as having been started by environmental experiences in the first three months down the road to atypical development. I am suggesting that as a result of chronic tension through continual physical hunger in the first three months, we can much later observe the effect of a constitutional tendency to a state of regression within the infant's mental apparatus from the motor to the sensory end as described by Freud in chapter 7 of *The Interpretation of Dreams*. In this chapter Freud gives a diagram showing the passage of stimuli in a progressive direction from perception, via memory-storing agencies, to unconscious, preconscious, and conscious areas of the mind. In dream formation this direction is reversed, the logical relationships of the dream thoughts disappear, and 'the fabric of the organized dream-thoughts is resolved into its raw materials'. Freud speaks of this as a regression towards the perception end of the apparatus.

In the mental apparatus of the very young infant we do not think of thoughts in an organized sense. In the cases I am describing the capacity for delay has to be developed; in this particular case progressing from two weeks old. Capacity for delay is the distinguishing feature between reflex activity and more organized activity in the central nervous system. In this type of infant there is an economic flooding and hypercathexis of the perceptual and memory-storing end of the mental apparatus in the absence of any 'progressive' means of discharge. This is not the result of a dynamic regression from secondary to primary process, as in dream formation or psychosis, but of traumatic overstimulation of the sensory apparatus. My picture is of a physiological 'organ compliance' brought about by memory agencies flooded with memory traces, the whole balance of the process from perception to motility becoming then disturbed by what physiologists call 'facilitation' of this part of the mental apparatus. To state it differently: this is not the dream mechanism: thoughts dissolving into images threatening to organize into thoughts. This at a time when secondary process is not, certainly, phase-adequate nor, to my mind, probably even possible. Some motor activities, however, are possible. These together with the activity of perception will help to act as discharge systems.

Mahler perhaps has this in mind when she discusses the effect of a shift of cathexis from proprio- and interoceptive perceptions, which are the phase-adequate neurological arrangements of this age, to external perception. The shift, she argues, leads to diminished cathexis of the infant's own body and so also of the mother's body in order to cathect what is to become 'the peripheral rind of the ego', as Freud calls perceptual consciousness. This would involve a sort of secondary 'organ compliance' within the nervous system. The significance of this shift is as follows: at a certain point ideas become possible in the course of normal development; with this, pre-patterned bias manipulation of a sensory imago takes place instead of manipulation of reality. If this underlying prodromal pattern is reinforced by usage and habit, then the stage is set so that in due time intrapsychic events can come to be treated as realities, ideas as though they had substantial existence, words as things.

In developed forms these are mechanisms characteristic of atypical cases, as also is the complementary peculiarity of magical organ speech shown in motor expressions such as the style of walking, posture, and gesturing. The characteristic 'willowy' or 'fey' manneristic quality, of which the 'schizoid grin' is the best-known example, is of course then not only descriptively but metapsychologically diagnostic of an early narcissistic trauma. The movements represent not only a retreat from reality testing (effected by altering reality through motor manipulation) but also, in correspondence with this, a tendency to use magic perceptual and thought techniques instead. This may be chronic, that is, organized and a character trait, or it may be a split-off part of the ego showing only transitorily in moments of stress and regression. In either case it may be found associated with an otherwise stable ego; depending upon later development. Happening as it does in the predominantly biological phase of infancy such patterning must be conceived as being as much part of the constitution as, for example, the effects of premature birth or physical birth injury.

The word constitution, following Freud's comments in *An Outline of Psycho-Analysis* and 'Analysis Terminable and Interminable', and following greater acceptance of Hartmann's concept of autonomous ego functions, has come to require a stricter definition. Nowadays it seems often to be used by psychoanalysts as automatically meaning 'hereditary'; 'part of the germ plasm'. But this is only one of its meanings. Psychoanalysts were the first to recognize systematically that character traits which descriptive psychiatrists and general usage would consider 'constitutional' can in fact have been acquired as the result of experience. For example: if an obsessional tendency can be hereditary. This would not exclude the possibility that an obsessional *constitution* can also be acquired. Freud suggests the mechanism. Speaking of a later age, he remarks: 'Premature advancement of the ego development ahead of the libido development contributes to the obsessional predisposition.' Hartmann may have had this passage in mind when he says: 'Acceleration of certain integrative processes may become pathological. Premature ego development, for example, may in this sense be considered as one of the factors predisposing to obsessional neurosis.'

The process of cerebral controlling which I describe in early infancy could in its turn be an analage for such a later psychological development. This may be one of the kinds of 'increase of later psychological pressures' which Greenacre has in mind. It is important that we should not assume 'the acquired' to be in all cases 'the therapeutically reversible'. By definition constitution cannot be reversed, but of course its consequences can be better or worse managed, or changed in psychoanalysis. It seems probable, nevertheless, that traits which are in process of being acquired can, during development, be reversed if prophylactically handled at the time. The traits hardest or impossible to reverse would be those of the undifferentiated phase of development which have a biological, physiological, or perhaps ethological impact.

To express this clinically: as psychoanalysts we do not believe that we can retrospectively abolish an 'oral character' such as was developed by the infant I have described. We can and do, however, alter the *consequences* of such constitutional qualities in our clinical practice, recognizing that there is in fact a limit to what is psychoanalytically alterable and a line at which traits have to be accepted as constitutional, even if this line is hard to establish. Bowlby's reminder that there are critical phases in embryology and their application to ethology would represent such dialectical instances in development, and Balint's concept of 'the basic fault', would represent a clinical outcome.

It seems important for prophylaxis that when we are merely uncertain about the origin of a trait we should not, in attributing it to 'constitution', be understood inevitably to mean 'hereditary', but should allow that there may well be an acquired element in the constitution also, whether the patterning becomes symbolic and psychological or remains non-symbolic and psychosomatic or, so to say, ethological. Somewhere in the developmental hierarchy there is, by common consent, a transition from these mainly physical and biological experiences of the undifferentiated phase to psychological ones, the timing of the transition and its role in the personality being a matter of a complementary series. My purpose in this paper has been to show how mothering of very small infants may contribute to this transition during development.

Conclusion

As a clinical sign of the normal transition from the 'virtually biological' to the psychological phase of development I would suggest: onset of a capacity to recognize the mother as different from other women. This ability when present confers a capacity for anticipation which also means the capacity for a more psychologically significant 'disappointment'. This more specific reaction is a development from the less specific tension states which would be the infant's response to frustration of the earliest developed prodromal cues such as recognition of posture or other kinaesthetic, olfactory, more primitive cues.

What I have not seen described elsewhere is the fact that the age at which this wider and more elaborated gestalt of recognition of the mother arrives *depends among other things upon the specificity with which the infant has previously been handled*. Spitz puts this age at six or seven months, but in infants who are handled by one mothering person only and are under unchanging physical and affective conditions specificity arrives earlier. This is shown by the infant's directed smile (which is different from the reflex smile). It can be observed for example that a mother-specific infant at say three months old will for a while smile only at its mothering person and cry if other women approach it. This for a short phase of a week or two; then it will discriminate successfully and can smile again at all suitable people.

The earliest age at which I have seen this specificity of directed smile is at three months and five days in a full-term infant. This infant also at five months had a phase of specificity to its father, when, although it remained friendly to all women, for a few weeks it cried at strange men as though it could not properly discriminate them from its father. I have not elsewhere seen it stressed how the specificity and integration of the infant are influenced by specificity of handling and that this might advance integration in the infant.

To develop sufficient personality integration to recognize the mothering person the infant has to respond to environmental cues which it connects with her. Response to these cues is first acquired by a process best known in Pavlovian conditioning. Then at a certain point the gestalts of individual cues integrate and widen, so that we say the infant can discriminate the mother from other women. Although this achievement may be a useful clinical sign for us, its real importance is metapsychological and lies in its indicating a critical degree of personality integration and reality testing, that is, a relatively elaborated capacity for disappointment. In the case I have described such a capacity for 'disappointment' or delay in some prodromal neural way seemed to be forced onto the infant at only two weeks of age.

By means of the specificity of smiling response we can discriminate the significant difference between two sorts of babies who, I am suggesting, have very different starts in life: the baby with specificity of aims in its first six months of life which speaks of 'good object relations' and the bewildered baby elaborating defensive need systems narcissistically.

The concept of cumulative trauma

M. MASUD R. KHAN

EVERY PHASE OF theory-making in psychoanalysis has influenced the current concept of trauma and its clinical evaluation (Fenichel, 1937). I shall, somewhat arbitrarily, divide the total span of analytic researches into five stages. This is an artificial division to show what new ideas emerge at which stage. One stage does not cancel out the other. They run parallel, reinforcing and partially correcting each other, and each time a new strand is added to the growing complexity of psychoanalytic metapsychology.

In the first phase, 1885 to 1905, while Freud was postulating the basic concepts for the understanding of the unconscious – dream work, primary and secondary processes, the psychic apparatus, symptom formation, and the aetiology of hysteria and obsessional neurosis – the concept of trauma played a very vital and significant role (Freud, 1893b, 1895). Trauma was conceived of essentially as (a) an environmental factor that intrudes upon the ego and which the ego cannot deal with through abreaction or associative elaboration: 'hysterical patients suffer from incompletely abreacted psychical trauma' (Freud, 1893b); and (b) as a stage of strangulated libidinal energy which the ego cannot discharge. The paradigm of this traumatic situation is sexual seduction. We have a vivid account by Freud himself (1950b, Letter 69; also 1914a) and by Jones describing (1953) how frustrated and demoralized

[117]

Freud felt when he discovered that these traumatic events of seduction had never actually happened. During this phase the corresponding theory of anxiety is: 'Neurotic anxiety is transformed sexual libido' (Freud, 1897). The chief defence mechanism discussed is repression.

The second phase, 1905 to 1917, is characterized by systematic attempts at working out infantile sexual development (Freud, 1905b) and psychoanalytic metapsychology (Freud, 1914b, 1915a, 1915b, 1915c, 1917). In terms of infantile sexual development and libido theory the paradigmatic traumatic situations are (a) castration anxiety, (b) separation anxiety, (c) primal scene, and (d) Oedipus complex. Trauma pertains to the strength and urgency of sexual instincts and the ego's fight against them. It is in terms of unconscious fantasy and inner psychic reality that all conflicts and hence traumatic situations are envisaged. During the latter half of this phase Freud worked out his first systematic statement of metapsychology, and we have the concept of ego-libido, primary narcissism, and ego-ideal on the one hand, and a detailed examination of the mechanisms of introjection, identification, and projection on the other. The paper on 'Mourning and Melancholia' (1917) marks the end of this phase, and by opening up the discussion of aggression and guilt starts the next.

The period of 1917 to 1926, the third phase, gives us the 'final phase' of Freud's metapsychological thinking. In *Beyond the Pleasure Principle* (1920a) we have the first statement of the repetition compulsion as a principle of psychic functioning and its relation to the death instinct (principle of inertia in organic life). Here, Freud arrived at his dualistic theory of instincts, and from his earlier distinction between sexual instincts and ego instincts moves on to the duality of life versus death instincts. With the hypothesis of dual instincts and repetition compulsion, and the definition of psychic structures in terms of ego, id, and superego (Freud, 1923a), the concept of trauma took on an exclusively intersystemic and instinctual frame of reference. The vast literature on guilt, masochism, melancholia, depression, and internal anxiety situations documents at great length such traumata and the ego's mode of

[118]

handling them. The extreme and most detailed discussion of such intersystemic and instinctual traumata is perhaps by Melanie Klein (1932) in her description of paranoid and depressive positions. This phase in Freud's own researches achieves its culmination in his revision of the concept of anxiety in *Inhibitions, Symptoms and Anxiety* (1926b).

The fourth phase, 1926 to 1939, is launched by the revision of the concept of anxiety and inaugurates the beginnings of ego-psychology proper. Strachey (1959, pp. 77-86) has given us a masterly summary of the evolution of Freud's concept of anxiety. I shall single out for comment only the fact that in *Inhibitions, Symptoms and Anxiety* Freud clearly distinguished between traumatic situations and situations of danger, corresponding to which are the two types of anxiety: automatic anxiety and anxiety as a signal of the approach of such a trauma. 'The fundamental determinant of automatic anxiety is the occurrence of a traumatic situation; and the essence of this is an experience of helplessness on the part of the ego in the face of an accumulation of excitation . . . the various specific dangers which are liable to precipitate a traumatic situation at different times of life. These are briefly: birth, loss of the mother as an object, loss of the penis, loss of the object's love, loss of the superego's love' (Strachey, 1959, pp. 81-2).

With the revised concept of anxiety and traumatic situations the role of environment (mother) and the need for 'extraneous help' in situations of helplessness comes into the very centre of the concept of trauma. Thus the intrapsychic, intersystemic, and environmental sources of trauma are integrated into a unitary frame of reference. Toward the end of this phase in his two papers 'Analysis Terminable and Interminable' (1937a) and 'Splitting of the Ego in the Process of Defence' (1940b) Freud focused his attention on the ego in terms of the modifications acquired during the defensive conflicts of early childhood, as well as through primary congenital variations and the disturbances of the synthetic function of the ego. This is why I have characterized this phase as inaugurating ego-psychology proper. These new formulations have far-reaching implications for the evaluation of the source and function of trauma.

[119]

The last phase is from 1939 to today. In this the developments of ego-psychology through the researches of Anna Freud
(1936 onwards), Hartmann (1939, 1950b, 1952) and others,
and the whole new emphasis on infant-mother relationship,
have changed our very frame of reference for the discussion of
the nature and role of trauma.

Function of mother as protective shield

In *Beyond the Pleasure Principle* (1920a) Freud set up a conceptual model to discuss the fate of a living organism in an open
environment. 'Let us picture [he said] a living organism in its
most simplified possible form as an undifferentiated vesicle of a
substance that is susceptible to stimulation.' Freud next proceeds to point out that the two sources of stimuli possible are
the external and the internal ones. He continues: 'Then the surface turned towards the external world will from its very situation be differentiated and will serve as an organ for receiving
stimuli' (p. 26). This gradually develops into a 'crust' and eventually into a 'protective shield'. Freud postulated that '*Protection against* stimuli is an almost more important function for
the living organism than *reception* of stimuli. The protective
shield is supplied with its own store of energy and must above
all endeavour to preserve the special modes of transformation
of energy operating in it against the effects threatened by the
enormous energies at work in the external world' (p. 27). Continuing his argument Freud postulated that this sensitive cor-
tex, which later becomes the system Cs., also receives excitations from within. It is, however, less effective against inner
stimuli, and one way the organism protects itself against the
unpleasure from inner stimuli is to project them to the outer
environment and treat them as 'though they were acting, not
from the inside, but from the outside, so that it may be possible
to bring the shield against stimuli into operation as a means of
defence against them'. In this context Freud described as
'traumatic' any

    . . . excitations from outside which are powerful enough to

[120]

break through the protective shield. It seems to me that the concept of trauma necessarily implies a connection of this kind with a breach in an otherwise efficacious barrier against stimuli. Such an event as an external trauma is bound to provoke a disturbance on a large scale in the functioning of the organism's energy and to set in motion every possible defensive measure. At the same time, the pleasure principle is for the moment put out of action. There is no longer any possibility of preventing the mental apparatus from being flooded with large amounts of stimulus, and another problem arises instead – the problem of mastering the amounts of stimulus which have broken in and of binding them, in the psychical sense, so that they can then be disposed of (pp. 29f.). [Developing his argument further, Freud concluded:] what *we* seek to understand are the effects produced on the organ of the mind by the breach in the shield against stimuli and by the problems that follow in its train. And we will attribute importance to the element of fright. It is caused by lack of any preparedness for anxiety, including lack of hypercathexis of the systems that would be the first to receive the stimulus. Owing to their low cathexis those systems are not in a good position for binding the inflowing amounts of excitation and the consequences of the breach in the protective shield follow all the more easily. It will be seen, then, that preparedness for anxiety and the hypercathexis of the receptive systems constitute the last line of defence of the shield against stimuli. In the case of quite a number of traumas, the difference between systems that are unprepared and systems that are well prepared through being hypercathected may be a decisive factor in determining the outcome; though where the strength of a trauma exceeds a certain limit this factor will no doubt cease to carry weight. (pp. 31f.)

The total context of Freud's discussion is the observation of an infant's play with a reel that related to 'disappearance and return' (of the mother) and the traumatic dreams in general. If we replace in Freud's model 'the undifferentiated vesicle of a substance that is susceptible to stimulation' by a live human infant, then we get what Winnicott (1960b) has described as 'an infant in care'. The infant in care has for his protective shield the caretaking mother. This is the uniquely human situation, in so far as this dependency in the infant lasts much longer than in any other species that we know of (Hartmann, 1939); and from this prolonged period of dependency the human infant emerges as a more highly differentiated and independent organism *vis-à-vis* his environment.

My aim here is to discuss the function of the mother in her role as a protective shield. This role as a protective shield constitutes 'the average expectable environment' (Hartmann, 1939) for the anaclitic needs of the infant. My argument is that cumulative trauma is the result of the breaches in the mother's role as a protective shield over the whole course of the child's development, from infancy to adolescence – that is to say, in all those areas of experience where the child continues to need the mother as an auxiliary ego to support his immature and unstable ego-functions. It is important to distinguish this ego-dependency of the child on the mother from his cathexis of her as an object. (Ramzy and Wallerstein, 1958 have discussed this aspect in terms of *environmental reinforcement*.) Cumulative trauma thus derives from the strains and stresses that an infant-child experiences in the context of his ego-dependence on the mother as his protective shield and auxiliary ego (cf. Khan, 1963a,b,c).

I want to stress the point that what I am describing as breaches in the mother's role as protective shield are qualitatively and quantitatively different from those gross intrusions by the mother's acute psychopathology which have been often discussed in our literature in relation to schizophrenic children or overtly hostile and destructive patterns of behaviour in delinquent children (e.g., Beres, 1956; Lidz and Fleck, 1959; Mahler, 1952; Searles, 1959, 1962; Shields, 1962; etc.). The breaches I have in mind are in the nature of maladaptation to the infant's anaclitic needs (Winnicott, 1956a).

The mother's role as a protective shield is a theoretical construct. It should include the mother's personal role *vis-à-vis* the infant as well as her management of the non-human environment (the nursery, the cot, etc.) on which the infant is dependent for his total well-being (cf. Searles, 1960). I should emphasize also that the breaches in this protective-shield role, as I envisage them, are not traumatic singly. To borrow the apt phrase from Kris (1956b), they have the quality of a 'strain', and do not so much distort ego-development or psychosexual evolution as *bias* it. In this context it would be more accurate to say that these breaches over the course of time and through the developmental process cumulate silently and invisibly. Hence the difficulty in detecting them clinically in childhood. They gradually get embedded in the specific traits of a given character structure (cf. Greenacre, 1958). I would like to restrict myself merely to stating that the use of the word trauma in the concept of cumulative trauma should not mislead us into considering such breaches in the mother's role as protective shield as traumatic at the time or in the context in which they happen. They achieve the value of trauma only cumulatively and in retrospect. If the concept of cumulative trauma has value and validity, then it should help us to identify more accurately what sort of ego distortion and disturbance of psychosexual development can be related to what type of failure of environmental provisions, in relation to anaclitic needs in the infant and the child. It should help in replacing such incriminating reconstructions as bad, rejecting, or seducing mothers, as well as such anthropomorphic part-object constructs as 'good' and 'bad' breast. Its place could be taken by a more meaningful examination of the pathogenic interplay of specific variables in the total relationship of an infant-child's psychic and physical equipment and how the environment meets it. This in turn would sponsor the clinical search for effective therapeutic measures rather than merely prescriptive ones. I have given a detailed account elsewhere, from the treatment of a female patient, to show how an early disturbed relation between mother and daughter led to homosexual episodes in her adult life (Khan, 1963a).

In the past two decades, research in ego-psychology and infant-care techniques have gained in complexity and depth. From these researches it is possible to distinguish theoretically between four aspects of a human infant's total experience:

1. The role of the caretaking environment and its contribution toward the release and stabilization of the intrapsychic potentialities and functions (cf. Freud, 1911a, p. 220).

2. The special sensitivity of an infant making demands on the primary environment, which I am designating here as a mother's role of protective shield (cf. Escalona, 1953).

3. The unfolding of the maturational processes, autonomous ego-functions, and libido development.

4. The gradual emergence of the inner world and psychic reality, with all the complexity of instinctual needs and tensions, and their interplay with inner psychic structures and object-relationships.

In our literature, perhaps, one of the most sensitive and elaborate descriptions of the caretaking role of the mother is in Winnicott's writings. According to Winnicott (1956b), what motivates the mother for her role as a protective shield for the infant is her 'primary maternal preoccupation'. The incentive for the mother's role is her libidinal investment in the infant and the infant's dependence on it for survival (cf. Benedek, 1952). From the infant's subjective point of view there is at the beginning little perception of this dependence or of the need for survival.

What the mother's caretaking role achieves in optimal circumstances is:

1. Through making herself available as a protective shield the mother enables the growth of the maturational processes – both of autonomous ego-functions and instinctual processes. The mother's role as a protective shield defends the infant against the mother's subjective and unconscious love and hate, and thus allows her empathy to be maximally receptive to the infant's needs (cf. Spitz, 1959).

2. If her adaptation is good enough, then the infant does not become precociously aware of this dependence on the mother –

hence does not have to exploit whatever mental functions are emergent and available toward self-defence (cf. Freud, 1920a; James, 1960 [*this volume – Ed.*]).

3. The protective shield of the mother enables the infant to project all the unpleasurable inner stimuli on to her, so that she can deal with them and thus sustain the illusion of omnipotence of well-being in the infant. Erikson (1950) has defined this sense of well-being as 'trust', Benedek (1952) as 'confidence', and Kris (1962) as 'comfort' (see also Searles, 1962).

4. Through functioning as a protective shield, and so providing a model, the mother enables the infant's psyche to integrate what J. Sandler (1960) has called a 'qualitative organizing component'. In later ego-development and functioning we can identify this as guiding the synthetic function of the ego on its discriminating role, both in relation to inner instinctual reality and to the demands of the external environment.

5. By providing the right dosage of life experience (Fries, 1946) and need satisfactions through her body care, she enables the infant's inner world to differentiate into id and ego as well as gradually to demarcate inner from outer reality (cf. Hoffer, 1952; Ramzy and Wallerstein, 1958).

6. By lending her own ego-functions as well as her libidinal and aggressive cathexes (through her role as a protective shield) she helps the infant to build up supplies of primary narcissism, neutralized energy, and the beginnings of the capacity and wish for object cathexes (cf. Hoffer, 1952; Kris, 1951). Both what she provides and what emerges through the infant's maturation interact and supplement each other (Erikson, 1946; Freud, 1911a; Hoffer, 1949; Winnicott, 1951).

7. If these tasks are accomplished successfully, then the shift from primary dependence to relative dependence can take place (Winnicott, 1960b). In this stage the function of her role as a protective shield becomes more complex; it takes on an essentially psychological aspect. She has now to help the infant with his first experiences of inner instinctual conflicts on the one hand, and yet sustain for him that flux from primary identification to realization of separateness which is the essence of

disillusionment (Winnicott, 1948b) and a precondition for a true capacity for object cathexes (cf. Freud, A., 1958b; Milner, 1952).

8. If she is successful in these achievements, then the infant gradually becomes aware of the mother as a love object and of his need for her love. This is now an object cathexis which employs instinctual (id) cathexes that have become available in the meantime (Freud, A., 1951).

9. By providing phase-adequate frustrations she sponsors the capacity for toleration of tension and unpleasure, thus promoting structural development (cf. Kris, 1962). Rubinfine (1962), in his valuable discussion of this aspect of maternal care, concludes:

> . . . where need satisfaction is always and immediately available (i.e., deanimated), there should be a relative absence of tension. Without appropriately timed experiences of frustration and delay, there may result retardation in the development of various ego-functions, among them the capacity to distinguish between self and nonself. Such failure of differentiation of self from object, and the consequent failure of defusion of self- and object-representations, leads to interference with the development of the capacity to discharge aggressive drives toward an external object, and results in the turn of aggression against the self.

Winnicott (1952) has stressed the point that a mother should and indeed must fail the id, but never the ego of the infant.

The vehicle of all these transactions between mother and infant is dependency. This dependency is to a large extent not sensed by the infant. Similarly, it is important to keep in mind that the mother's role as a protective shield is a limited function in her total life experience. In the beginning it is an all-engrossing one for her. Still, theoretically it is significant for us to be able to see it as a special instance of her personality and emotional functioning. Spitz's (1962) distinction between the totality of the infant's anaclitic needs and the implementation of the mother's diatrophic attitude in response to these needs is pertinent to remember in this context. Unless we can do this we cannot identify how this role as a protective shield can be and does become invaded by her personal needs and conflicts. It is the intrusion of her personal needs and conflicts that I characterize as her failure in respect of her role as a protective shield. The mother's role as protective shield is not a passive one but an alert, adaptive, and organizing one. The protective-shield role is the result of conflict-free autonomous ego-functions in the mother. If personal conflicts intrude here, the result is a shift from the protective-shield role to that of symbiosis or rejective withdrawal. How an infant will react to these failures depends upon the nature, intensity, duration, and repetitiveness of the trauma.

In our literature three typical instances of this type of failure of the mother as a protective shield have been thoroughly discussed:

1. The most extreme and pathogenic is through the excessive intrusion of the mother's psychopathology. Winnicott (1949a, 1952) has discussed it as failure of the good-enough holding environment leading to psychosis or mental defect. Mahler (1952, 1961) has coined the phrase of symbiotic relationship between mother and child that leads to schizophrenic illnesses. In this context I would like also to mention, among others, the researches of Beres (1956), Geleerd (1956, 1958), Lidz and Fleck (1959) and Searles (1959).

2. The breakdown of mother's role of protective shield has also been discussed in terms of loss of or separation from her. Here again the pioneer researches of Anna Freud and Burlingham (1942, 1944) and Winnicott (1940, 1945b), and the later exhaustive investigations of Bowlby (1960), Spitz (1945, 1951), and Provence and Lipton (1962) stand out as particularly important (also cf. Hellman, 1962).

3. The third instance of breakdown of mother's role as protective shield occurs when either some constitutional sensitivity (Escalona, 1953) or physical handicap (Burlingham, 1961; Sandler, A.M., 1963) impose an impossible task on the mother, or when a severe physical illness in the infant or child creates a special demand which no human adult could possibly meet (cf. Frankl, 1961; Freud, A., 1952b).

[127]

Aetiology of cumulative trauma

I am here tentatively trying to conceptualize a fourth type of partial breakdown of the mother's role as a protective shield, which becomes visible only in retrospect as a disturbance and can be designated as cumulative trauma. I have been specifically guided and helped in arriving at this hypothesis through the researches of Winnicott, Kris, and Greenacre.

Over the past twenty years Winnicott has been persistently drawing our attention to the importance of the mother's caretaking function, the vital role of dependence for the infant's emergence into self-status, etc. James (1962) has recently given us a valuable critique of Winnicott's researches. What is pertinent for my purposes in Winnicott's hypotheses is his elucidation of the role of regression to dependency needs in the therapeutic process (1949b), his researches into the antisocial tendency (1956a), and his careful delineation of the early psychic and affective processes of integration in the child (1945a).

It is Winnicott's basic hypothesis (1952) that all relative failures in infancy of the good-enough holding environment (mother's role as a protective shield) set up a compulsion in the relatively matured child and the grown adult to correct the imbalances and dissociations in ego-integration. This is achieved through regression to dependency needs. In Winnicott's idiom, establishment of 'the false self' is one result of such caretaking environment's failure to adapt through good-enough holding (1949a). What Winnicott calls 'the false self' is a characterological consequence of the disruption and distortion of ego-autonomy. What Winnicott calls 'impingements' are the failure of the mother in infancy to dose and regulate stimuli – both external and internal. Winnicott believes that these impingements are disruptive of true ego-integration, and lead to premature defensive organization and functioning (1948b). What Kris (1962) has described as 'a specific kind of provocative overstimulation which was bound to produce mounting tension in the child without offering appropriate avenues of discharge' and also as 'tantalizing', Winnicott designates as 'impingements'. I am here considering these as some of the most pathogenic genetic elements in cumulative trauma (cf. Erikson, 1950).

Kris in his paper 'The Recovery of Childhood Memories in Psychoanalysis' (1956b) has distinguished between 'shock trauma' and 'the strain trauma'. The latter he has defined as the 'effect of long-lasting situations, which may cause traumatic effects by accumulation of frustrating tensions'. The clinical examples that Kris offers here and in his contemporary paper on 'The Personal Myth' (1956a) leave me in no doubt that 'the strain trauma' and the screen memories or precocious early memories that the patients recount are derivatives of the partial breakdown of the protective-shield function of the mother and an attempt to symbolize its effects (cf. Freud, A., 1958b). Kris's sensitive and consummate account of the predicament of the infant Anne in his paper 'Decline and Recovery in a Three-Year-Old' (1962) is the most apposite material in relation to my concept of cumulative trauma. It is interesting to note in Kris's account that even though the mother and infant were observed from the start, it was only later, i.e., in relative retrospect at 34 weeks, that the fact of disturbed maternal handling constituting a 'tantalizing' situation for the infant Anne could be definitely established.

Greenacre's studies (1954, 1960a, 1960c) have been largely concerned with the vicissitudes of the maturational factor in infancy and its effect on ego and instinctual development. In 1959 she introduced the concept of *focal symbiosis* to identify a specific variant of what Mahler has described as symbiotic relationships. Greenacre defines focal symbiosis as 'an intensely strong interdependence (usually between mother and child, but sometimes, as in my cases, with people other than the mother) which is limited to a special and rather circumscribed relationship rather than a nearly total enveloping one. . . . In limited or focal symbiotic relationships, there is often a peculiar union of the child's special need with the parent's special sensitivity, and . . . the total personality of either parent or child may not be as much involved as in the severe case of symbiotic psychoses described by Mahler' (pp. 244, 245).

Greenacre (1959, 1960a, 1960b) furthermore relates a great deal of the psychopathology of perversions, borderline cases, and body-ego development to focal symbiosis. In her concept of focal symbiosis she has fruitfully extended the range in time and developmental process through which the child and his human environment can involve each other in terms of the archaic dependency relationship.

In the context of these formulations I shall now examine the nature and function of the cumulative trauma. Cumulative trauma has its beginnings in the period of development when the infant needs and uses the mother as his protective shield. The inevitable temporary failures of the mother as protective shield are corrected and recovered from the evolving complexity and rhythm of the maturational processes. Where these failures of the mother in her role as protective shield are significantly frequent and lead to impingement on the infant's psyche-soma, impingements which he has no means of eliminating, they set up a nucleus of pathogenic reaction. These in turn start a process of interplay with the mother which is distinct from her adaptation to the infant's needs. This interplay between mother and infant can have any or all of the effects described below.

1. It leads to premature and selective ego-development. Some of the emergent autonomous functions are accelerated in growth and used in defensive action to deal with the impingements that are unpleasurable (James, 1960 [*this volume — Ed.*]; Winnicott, 1949b).

2. It can begin to organize a special responsiveness to the mother's mood that creates an imbalance in the integration of aggressive drives (cf. Sperling, 1950; Winnicott, 1948a).

3. The involvement of precocious functions with the mother's collusive response militates against developmentally arriving at a differentiated separate 'coherent ego' (Freud, 1920a) and self. This in turn leads to a dissociation through which an archaic dependency bond is exploited on the one hand and a precipitate independence is asserted on the other. A specific result is that what should have been a silent, unregistered dependency state now becomes an engineered exploita-

tion of instinctual and ego-dependence, with a precocious narcissistic cathexis of the mother.

4. As a further consequence the disillusionment that belongs to maturational separating off from mother is side-tracked and a false identificatory oneness is manipulated (cf. Searles, 1962). This way, instead of disillusionment and mourning, an ego-attitude of concern for the mother and excessive craving for concern from the mother becomes established. This concern is quite different from the concern that belongs to sadistic instinctual attack on the mother and the ensuing feelings of guilt (cf. Klein, 1932). This concern is an ego-interest that substitutes for a true object cathexis (cf. Winnicott, 1948a).

5. Through the impingements that derive from failure of mother's role as protective shield, a precocious cathexis of external and internal reality takes place. This organization of inner and outer reality leaves out a very important function of the ego's subjective awareness and experience of itself as a coherent entity. Its synthetic function is also disrupted (cf. James, 1960 [*this volume – Ed.*]).

6. The strain and impingements from the failure of mother's role as protective shield, which I am designating here as cumulative trauma, have their most specific effect on the vicissitudes of body-ego development in the infant and the child. The researches of Coleman, Kris, and Provence (1953), Greenacre (1958, 1960b), Hoffer (1950, 1952), Kris (1951), Milner (1952), Spitz (1951, 1962), and Winnicott (1949a, 1949b, 1951) have stressed the importance of the maternal caretaking procedures (protective-shield role) for the development of the body ego in the context of the earliest stages of the ego-id differentiation and the gradual integration of a sense of self. Here I want to refer, only very briefly, to my inference from clinical material that the breaches in the mother's role as protective shield leave their precipitates most sentiently and effectively in the body-ego development of the child. These residues over the course of maturation and development gather into a specific type of body-ego organization and form the substratum of the psychological personality. Pertinent here are the observational data offered by Coleman, Kris and Provence

(1953), Kris (1951), and Ritvo and Solnit (1958). In the adult patient it is through the clinical observation of the idiosyncrasies of the body-ego behaviour in the transference-neurosis and the total analytic setting that we can hope to reconstruct what are the particular genetic patterns of the cumulative trauma in a given case (Khan, 1963a). The concept of cumulative trauma tentatively offers, in terms of early ego-development and in the context of infant-mother relationship, a complementary hypothesis to the concept of fixation points in libido development. In this sense it tries to map out what were the significant points of stress and strain in the evolving mother-infant (child) relationship that gradually gather into a dynamic substratum in the morphology of a particular character or personality.

Once this interplay between infant and mother starts, it brings into its sphere of action all new developmental experiences and object relations. In many significant aspects this later pathogenic interplay between mother and child aims to correct the earlier distortions through impingements. This is what I think Greenacre (1959) refers to as the drive behind 'the union of the child's special need with the parent's special sensitivity'. That these attempts at recovery only complicate the pathology is an irony of human experience. This is perhaps at the root of many attempts at cure through love and passionate involvement in our adult patients. I have tried to discuss this aspect in my (1962) paper 'The Role of Polymorph-Perverse Body-Experiences and Object-Relations in Ego-Integration' (see also Alpert, 1959; Khan, 1963a; Lichtenstein, 1961).

I have so far stressed only the pathogenic effects on infant development from breaches in the mother's role as protective shield. It would, however, be a gross misrepresentation of the total complexity of the interplay between mother and infant if we fail to state that although the infant ego is weak, vulnerable, and extremely dependent on the mother's role as protective shield, the infant has also a great inherent resilience and potentiality (strength). It not only can and does recover from breaches in the protective shield, but it can use such impingements and strains as 'nutriment' (Rapaport, 1958) toward further growth and structuration (cf. Kris, 1951; Rubinfine, 1962). It is important to remember that though the ego can survive and overcome such strains, exploit them to good purpose, manage to mute the cumulative trauma into abeyance, and arrive at a fairly healthy and effective normal functioning, it nevertheless can in later life break down as a result of acute stress and crisis. When it does so – and this is of great clinical importance – we cannot diagnostically evaluate the genetics and economics of the total processes involved if we do not have a concept like cumulative trauma to guide our attention and expectancy. It has often been remarked in our literature during the past three decades that the character disorders of a schizoid type, which have become the more frequent type of patient in our practice, present a clinical picture whose aetiology needs concepts that include disturbances of infant-mother relationship that were at the time neither gross nor acute (Khan, 1960b; Kris, 1951). I am suggesting that the concept of cumulative trauma can help us a great deal here. The human infant is well endowed to struggle with the vicissitudes of his internal and environmental stresses. What is important for us is to be able to identify in the clinical process what effects this struggle has left and how it has shaped the adult character (cf. Greenacre, 1954, 1960b; Khan, 1963c; Lichtenstein, 1961).

One treacherous aspect of cumulative trauma is that it operates and builds up silently throughout childhood right up to adolescence. It is only in recent years that we have learned to evaluate as pathogenic a certain precocious development in children. Such precocity had previously been celebrated as giftedness or strong ego-emergence or a happy independence in the child. We are also inclined to view with much more caution and reserve, if not suspicion, a mother's boasts of a specially close rapport and understanding between herself and her child.

Clinical experience shows that the phases of maturational development where these impingements from mother's failure in her role as protective shield tend to get organized into an active collusive relationship between mother and child are the late oral, early anal, and phallic phases – the phases where the emergent instinctual process and maturational ego-process test

[133]

the mother with their full need and demand. It is also these stages where the stimulus hunger asks for maximal psychological adaptation, response, and restraint from the mother in her role as protective shield. The chief psychic process involved in such collusive relationships is identification, as Kris (1951) and Ritvo and Solnit (1958) have stressed. This identification remains essentially of an incorporative and projective type, interfering with internalization and assimilation of new object-representations, and thus confuses a proper differentiation and growth of internal psychic structures. This holds true also of the distortion of the libidinal strivings and object relations of the Oedipal phase (cf. Schmale, 1962).

The phase at which the child himself acutely becomes aware of the distorting and disruptive effects of this collusive bond with the mother is at adolescence. Then the reaction is dramatically rejective of the mother and all the past cathexes of her (Khan, 1963b). This, of course, makes the adolescent process of integration at once tortuous and impossible. At this point attempts at integration which wilfully negate past libidinal investments, ego-interests, and object ties are instituted. This leads either to collapse of personality development into inertia and futility, or a short, magical recovery into omnipotent isolation, or a passionate craving for new ideals, new objects, and new ego-interests (Beres and Obers, 1950; Erikson, 1956; Geleerd, 1958; Khan, 1963c; Spiegel, 1951).

Conclusion

The concept of cumulative trauma takes into consideration psycho-physical events that happen at the pre-verbal stage of relationship between mother and infant. It correlates their effects on what later becomes operative as a disturbed relationship between mother and child or as a *bias* in ego and psychosexual development (Khan, 1962, 1963a). Once an infant emerges out of the pre-verbal stage we can never see directly the first impingements and failures in the mother's role as the protective shield. What we see in direct observation or clinically are derivatives of these mental processes and capacities. What I am conceptualizing here as cumulative trauma has been described by Anna Freud (1958b) in another context. She states 'that subtle harm is being inflicted on this child, and that the consequences of it will become manifest at some future date.'

Even though we have now available many sensitive accounts of direct observations of the feeding situations and the total relationship between infant and mother (Robertson, 1962), there is still doubt as to whether we can identify at the point of its actuality the breakdown of the mother's role as protective shield in relation to the infant's anaclitic needs. As Kris's (1962) account of the infant Anne makes abundantly clear, even though an infant was observed by a team of highly skilled professionals, it was only in retrospect that the effects of such breakdown of a good-enough provision of maternal care began to be visible. In the case of Anne we see how the impingements from the mother's handling already began to gather into the structure and function of the cumulative trauma. It is important for us to be able to chart out clearly the earliest nature and role of these failures, because only thus can we organize our clinical expectancy and arrive at true diagnosis. As Anna Freud (1962) expressed it:

. . . if our present direction of interest is no more than a turning of our glance from the effects of dependence on to the contents and processes in the period of dependence, it is still a turning-point of decisive importance. By taking this line we change the direction of our interest from the illnesses themselves – neurotic or psychotic – to their preconditions, to the matrix from which they arise, i.e., to the era where such important matters are decided as the selection of neurosis and the selection of the types of defence.

On basic unity (primary total undifferentiatedness)

MARGARET LITTLE

IN THE ANALYSIS of patients whose transference manifestations are of a psychotic rather than a neurotic kind, I have found two characteristic phenomena which I want to examine. One is a particular position which they attempt to force me to accept; the other is the supreme importance for them of body happenings, as shown in their acting out – i.e., body memory.

These patients are people who cannot in any circumstances take survival for granted. There exist in their unconscious memories experiences of something which we must really regard as annihilation; in many cases there has been in early infancy some actual threat to life – illness of the infant or mother, hostility in the environment, etc.

They have been variously described; objectively, as suffering from, e.g., a 'basic fault' (Balint, M., 1968) or 'psychological catastrophe, or disaster' (Bion, 1958a) and, subjectively, as by themselves – 'I am cut off from my roots', or 'I have a fracture-dislocation.'

Their insistent, prolonged, and exhausting efforts to repair this condition have been described by a number of writers as attempts to establish a 'symbiotic' relationship with the analyst, but I think this use of the word is a misleading one. In my experience it is not a state of symbiosis that the patient seeks to establish but rather one of total identity with the analyst and of undifferentiatedness from him.

[136]

Some clinical illustrations may help us at this point.

1. Miss E. told me that, when I first went to the hospital where she was, in place of the doctor who had been treating her, she had thought to herself 'Here's a new doctor; she wants a patient.'

At first sight this could be seen as a piece of realism, and secondly it can readily be understood as projective identification. It was in this way that I interpreted it to her, and she accepted my interpretation. Only after many years of analysis did I come to recognize that it had meant much more than that, and that although she accepted the interpretation she could not really use it. She had understood my need of a patient and her need of a doctor to mean absolute identity of person between us. Her acceptance of the interpretation also meant identity of person, as did my acceptance of her for treatment, whereby I tacitly confirmed her in her belief, asserted that I too believed it, and was therefore, once more, one with and inseparable from her.

Many years later, when moving towards termination, this patient found it almost impossible to leave me at the end of every session. She would experience agonizing pain in her buttocks and would scream, as she had screamed in childhood when severely beaten. When I recognized the hate aroused in me by her attempting to prolong the sessions in this way and making me feel guilty for not doing so, I could separate myself out from her. Then I could see, and interpret, that she felt *in her body* pain that she believed she was inflicting on mine (as, in her hate, she wished to do). The pain she experienced was remembered in a bodily way and was now psychic, not somatic. Temporarily there was no differentiation anywhere – only massive identity.

This patient's breakdown had followed a threat of separation from her sister with whom she believed herself, in a delusional way, to be identical. Their relationship was a folie à deux. Her recovery has been based on this delusion of total identity with me, which has had to be gradually broken down, as far as factual reality is concerned, while the psychic reality of it has had to be preserved with the greatest care. I will refer to the technical aspects again later.

2. Mrs M. was referred for psychotherapy, as being 'very ill mentally, with various psychosomatic symptoms; if not treated she may develop a serious physical illness and die'.

She was unable to lie on the couch. She found great difficulty in keeping her appointments because she lived a long way off and had a little girl, aged seven. Although the sessions were arranged to fit in with the child's school life, Mrs M. started bringing the child with her and then tried to get her husband to come too.

She painted three portraits of me, all of them with large dark eyes, like her own. She told me that her mother, whom she was said to resemble, had also had them. I drew her attention to the eyes in the pictures and asked if she thought mine were really like that. She looked intently into mine and said 'But that's how your eyes *are*.' (They aren't.) I would contrast this with a neurotic patient who got up off the couch, after spending an hour talking about my white hair, and laughed at his picture of me, finding that it was fair.

Mrs M.'s mother had died when she was born, and her father had laid her beside her mother's dead body 'so that she would have known her, at least for that time'. She drew me a picture of this episode so that I would also have known her.

She gave me enormous bouquets of flowers, usually white ones, circumventing any attempts on my part to understand the unconscious significance of the gifts, and at Christmas she brought me a large card, with a picture of a cat, and the caption 'From one cat to another'.

After a few weeks of treatment she left her husband and child and took a flat where she expected me to live with her. When she found that I did not, she interrupted her treatment altogether and found a lover. He stayed only a few weeks, and shortly after he left her she went into a sanatorium suffering from tuberculosis.

I did not analyse Mrs M., but I came to understand something about her through work with other patients.

I have described as 'delusional transference' (1958) this tenaciously held, absolute belief in the analyst's total identity with the patient himself, and with his parents, both deified and diabolized (i.e., having magical qualities, good and bad). It also extends to everyone with whom either the patient or the analyst has any relation. In effect, it extends to the whole world, both of people and things, of thought, sensation, emotion, and movement. The state of total undifferentiatedness I have called 'basic unity'. It is, actually, a delusion, but a valuable one, and as I shall show later, it is founded in certain factual realities of whose memory it is the psychic representation. It is also a state to which the patients concerned apparently need to regress in order to repair the 'basic fault' or psychic 'fracture-dislocation', i.e., to find their psychic roots.

This unconscious delusion, of course, only exists in certain areas of the patient's psyche, otherwise he would be totally insane; in other areas he is well aware of the reality of the analyst as a different and separate person from himself and from his parents, and non-magical. This awareness of the reality is used as defence against the delusion. Such a use of one reality against another is, in fact, the most difficult of the defences to penetrate, because giving it up exposes the patient to acutely painful states of increasing confusion and depersonalization, which are experienced as chaos or annihilation.

The fear of annihilation, however, is dynamic and all-pervading and therefore governs the patient's reactions and his behaviour, both in relation to the analyst and to his environment. This fear, and the drive to establish identity with the analyst, lead him both to avoid these states of depersonalization and undifferentiatedness and at the same time to seek them, at any cost to himself or to the analyst. By reason of the life-and-death quality of the patient's experiences, his concrete thinking, and inability to make deductions, and the fact that events belonging to earliest infancy are being lived out in a grown-up body, these phases of the analysis contain a large element of actual danger (suicide, death, or attack upon someone, often the analyst), which calls for great care in the management of the case. In fact, the management becomes a vital part of the analysis itself, psychically if not actually, and the body events may become the interpretations. Verbalization then becomes the second stage in a two-stage process, both stages being

[139]

necessary for real insight to be attained, but the second being effective only as a result of the first, i.e., of the body happening.

These states of depersonalization appear temporarily in the course of the analysis of a transference psychosis as states in which, psychically, nothing is differentiated from anything else. There is apparently awareness of one thing only, distress or pain of an overwhelming intensity, such that all else is annihilated, including any sense of being a person, even that of being a person suffering. Discharge, and consequent differentiation, comes through some body event – a movement, a scream, salivation, etc. – by means of which some kind of bodily contact with the analyst occurs. Through repetitions of such events the patient comes gradually to recognize the difference between his body, his sensations, and his emotions, while those of the analyst are discovered as separate from his. The event has concerned two people, and the patient discovers himself as a person who has moved, screamed, etc., in relation to another person, whose separate existence, experience, movements, and responses can also be recognized. The delusion breaks up, recovery begins, and relationship becomes a possibility.

The importance of these body happenings lies in the fact that in those areas where the delusion is operative the patient is to all intents and purposes literally an infant, his ego a body-ego. For him, in these areas, only concrete, actual, and bodily things have meaning and can carry conviction. These areas are separated off from those where deductive thinking, inference, and symbolization operate, but not through splitting mechanisms. The 'basic fault' is a failure of differentiation and integration, splitting being an ego-activity belonging to a later stage of development.

What appears to happen in these patients through their states of frenzy and depersonalization is a process of alternating differentiation and integration in which a kind of first awareness or discovery is experienced, which might be regarded as 'personalization'. The person can then go on to 're-ality testing' later, in connection with verbalization.

This 'first awareness' is often a first awareness of the body, or of some part of it, for these patients behave as if the body were only some kind of appendage to which they happen to be linked, which is more a nuisance than anything and not an essential part of the self. The body is thrown around, in unawareness of sensation, function, or purpose, like that of an infant, and surprise is expressed when these things are found.

The quality of this first awareness has led me to understand the body happenings to which I refer as relating to body memories of prenatal and earliest post-natal life which have not been assimilated. It seems to me that in these patients there is a discontinuity between those earliest body memories and later experience, and that this discontinuity must be repaired before survival can be taken for granted. Only when this has been brought about can certain other processes follow, one of which is the development of the pleasure principle, for pleasure is not a reality and can have no meaning except in survival.

I would like to illustrate what I mean by talking about a lump of plasticine.

A lump of plasticine is homogeneous; it may have shape perceptible from outside, but not from within. Outside it may in fact be related to other objects, but it takes no account of them. Within itself it is nothing other than itself. A piece of it may become protruded, or nipped off, formed into another shape, and stuck on again – i.e., assimilated back to the lump, but differentiated from it, retaining its new shape or character. Here is the beginning of differentiation and integration, and of creation. The basic unity of the plasticine is first broken and then restored; there is coherence and stability, and a fresh place to go on from, but the essential nature of the plasticine (its *physis*, in the original meaning of the Greek word) remains unaltered.

In speaking of the undifferentiated state as it appears in the analysis of adults, I mean such a 'lump of plasticine' state, one to which the patient has needed to regress in order to come forward again by means of new differentiation and the assimilation of new experience, finding and extending his basic unity. (This state of undifferentiatedness may of course be used defensively against the recovery of repressed memories and ideas, but this is not what I am attempting to discuss here.)

The analogy with the lump of plasticine can be strained too

[141]

far, but I am using it to show the difference between a very early state, where psychically, the patient-infant is, so to speak, a lump of plasticine, and a much later one, where ideas of inside and outside, or 'me and not-me', have begun to develop. He may then believe his whole inside to be full of homogeneous plasticine-like stuff, which he can imaginatively put outside himself, filling the whole world with it. In this earlier state nothing exists but himself: it is a monistic state of autoerotism, or more accurately perhaps 'panautism', by which I mean a state in which nothing but the self exists.

Ideas such as projection, introjection, identification, subject, or object can have no meaning in relation to something totally undifferentiated, except from outside it. Differentiation comes about through movement, contact with the outside world (discovery), and assimilation back to the lump, or integration. At this point 'autoerotism' may begin to change into narcissism, narcissism being by definition concerned with the self as both subject and object.

I am thinking here of a passage in Freud's paper 'On Narcissism' (1914b): 'We are bound to suppose that a unity comparable to the ego cannot exist in the individual from the start; the ego has to be developed. The autoerotic instincts, however, are there from the very first, so there must be something added to autoerotism – a new psychical action – in order to bring about narcissism.'

In my view this 'new psychical action' is the beginning of the rhythmic processes of differentiation out from the primordial, undifferentiated state, and integration, or assimilation back, of the differentiates. The tendency toward it is inherent, but when these processes are disturbed, narcissism fails to develop, autoerotism (or 'panautism') remains, and ego-development may be seriously impaired, with grave risk to the psychic life of the individual.

As far as objective reality is concerned, I would repeat, this undifferentiated, 'panautistic' state is a delusional one, and it remains unconscious in transference psychosis until it is uncovered in the analysis; no patient is in fact an infant, or wholly undifferentiated. The delusion, although accepted as true for the patient, is not shared by the analyst (unless, unfortunately, he has something of a countertransference psychosis).

It follows, then, that in the patient's delusion, patient and analyst are one and indivisible, identical and continuous, and without differentiation either within the entity or between the entity and anything in the outer world.

I want now to consider the primordial state of the foetus in intra-uterine life. There is at this time a unity with the mother which is broken up by the birth process. Up to the time of birth, although the foetal circulation is distinct from that of the mother, the mother's respiratory, digestive, and excretory systems are functioning for both, i.e., for the entity.

The foetus is in fact wholly dependent upon the mother, without whom it could not continue to exist. The mother, of course, is not dependent at all upon the foetus. The state of affairs, then, appears more parasitic than symbiotic, but to look upon it in this way is to do so from outside rather than from inside. From inside, as it were from the point of view of the foetus, it is a state of unity, or absolute identity, between foetus and mother.

This intra-uterine state, with its continuity with the mother, provides the infant with the stability which is needed at the outset of life; the total birth experiences, and those which immediately follow, seem to set the pattern which tends to persist. At birth the first major contact with the environment is experienced, and it appears that only if something near enough to the intra-uterine state is re-established and maintained long enough without further disturbance can the experience be assimilated (i.e., linked with prenatal body experience) and become a useful one. Assimilated it can lead on to further differentiation and integration; it can be psychically elaborated and become creative, not disrutive. It becomes in any case a point of reference for every subsequent experience.

That is to say that every subsequent experience tends to become psychically *either* a restoration of the undifferentiated state, out of which differentiation and integration can safely occur, or dissolution, bodily dismemberment, and chaos.

[143]

'Return to the womb' has been thought of as something universally desired, a state of bliss and absence of demand; it sometimes happens that a patient who regresses in analysis is looked down on and thought of as lacking in something positive, that is of value for life. In my experience this view is mistaken. The matter of psychic return to the undifferentiated state (or rather of finding again still existing areas of undifferentiatedness), basic unity, is a matter of life and death; psychic, if not bodily, life or non-life, and new integration between the psyche and the soma depends upon it. The regression is in fact extremely painful and frigthening.

Certain realities of the analytic situation can be used in building up the psychic unity between analyst and analysand. For example, it is a fact that analyst and analysand are parts of one another's lives for the whole duration of the analysis (which concerns both) in an inseparable way. One room and one hour serve both together, as an entity; there are times when one of them thinks, feels, or acts for that entity, rather than for either as a separate being, or even for both as linked together.

The entity is, of course, an imagined one, whose reality for the analyst is limited and different from that of the analysand, who seeks to make it actual. If it be recognized and accepted imaginatively by the analyst, it means that he goes the whole way with the analysand psychically. If not, there is repeated failure to reach the basic unity, repetition of original failure, and repeated hopelessness, out of which nothing comes. The analysis drags on to eventual failure, either in abandonment, or in pseudosuccess, which is only a papering over of the cracks.

In this next part of the paper I am concerned with questions of analytic technique. The underlying principle I have already stated: acceptance by the analyst of the truth *for the analysand* of his delusion of absolute identity between them, his entering into it, and demonstrating both its psychic truth and its objective untruth.

The presence of delusion makes necessary the use of certain extensions of ordinarily accepted technique, and I want here to gather some of them together.

1. Analysis of transference psychosis can only be carried out in regression, and regression to dependence for life (though this does not mean regressive illness in every case). Where ordinary conditions are not enough, some adaptations may be needed to make analysis possible, such as hospitalization, the analyst visiting the patient, altering his room or his timetable, interviewing relatives, etc.

2. Those who look after the patient (in factual reality) become psychically not only extensions of the analyst but identical with him. At times, at least momentarily in the sessions, he takes over (in the delusion) being various aspects of the patient, his ego, his fear, his love, etc., sometimes, even, his body, or part of it.

3. In the areas where the patient cannot use inference, analogy, symbolization, or deductive thinking, realities that are actual, concrete, and bodily are used in order to show the unreality in fact of the delusional ideas. These things are linked secondarily with words, which bring them into relation with those other areas where the delusion does not obtain.

I am speaking here of such things as answering questions, touching or being touched by the patient, or using objects as if they were the things they represent ('symbolic realization', as described by Mme Séchéhaye, 1951), or direct use of the analyst's own emotions. These have been regarded as dangerous, or in some way destructive of the analytic situation itself, but in my experience this is not true. It is true that a much more 'fluid' situation is produced by using them and that this may provoke much more anxiety in the analyst, but that is a different matter.

4. Interpretations are not all verbal. I spoke earlier of a two-stage process of interpretation, in which the first stage is non-verbal, the body happenings or objects becoming the actual interpretations, whose result is discovery, and the second being verbalization, out of which come reality testing and insight. It is as if one were dealing first with a psychotic and then with a neurotic layer, though the transference phenomena remain at a psychotic level until both stages have been passed.

5. In adapting to the needs of the individual patient in this

way, the analyst is limited only by the limits which he finds in himself, or in his patient. There can be no 'absolute' or 'canon' of analysis, or of any particular technique, only the application of the fundamental rule must be allowed to become flexible and extensible.

Limits are in fact found, and there is no occasion for the fear that if once a patient is allowed gratification in a regressed state there will be no end to it. In his regression the patient is psychically an infant, and infants do need gratification and *are* frequently satisfied. It is necessary to remember, and to acknowledge to the patient, that it is not possible to satisfy fully his infant needs in his grown-up body, and that even if it were, it would be at a cost to his mature self, which would be offended. But this very acknowledgement to some extent offsets the lack of satisfaction and is itself a gratification that he can use when combined with the partial bodily satisfaction.

The finding of these limits actually depends upon the unity which does exist between analyst and analysand. It is a difficult thing to describe, but once it has been experienced it becomes understandable.

If the analyst is sufficiently one with his patient psychically, he experiences him at times as himself, or himself at times as the patient. But because of his unity with himself he also experiences what he says or does to be himself. 'What I do is me; what is not me I do not do,' and 'I do this, here, now, with this patient; I do not do it with him at another time, nor ever with that other patient.' It is a part of owning himself, for the patient is his work, and his work and actions are himself.

Conversely there are points at which the patient experiences the analyst as himself, or himself as the analyst and, accepting the analyst's unity unconsciously as his own, will find a limit which the analyst then recognizes as appropriate to himself.

6. These extensions serve the limited and specific purpose of the analysis of delusion, and their use for this purpose is founded in, and inseparable from, classical technique, of which it is a logical development. Without such foundation it would be merely 'wild analysis', or something mystical and truly dangerous.

[146]

For a longer or a shorter time the analyst (or some psychic extension or part of him) is all that stands between the patient and death, and at some moment he has to stand aside and allow the patient to take his life into his own hands, separating himself out from the entity, integrating with himself, and becoming either a living person or a corpse. The analyst can do nothing but be there, a whole and separate individual, with his own unity which he has made available to the patient.

From this moment the delusion breaks up from inside, as it were; the adaptations are gradually discarded, and verbalization increases. I would like to remind you again here of Freud's description of the breakup of a delusion in his commentary on Wilhelm Jensen's story *Gradiva*, entitled 'Delusions and Dreams' (1906).

The outcome of the analysis of a transference psychosis is that the analysand finds and retains a psychic unity with the analyst, while establishing a true separateness from and independence of him. Once this comes about, he becomes capable of forming mature relationships, and of carrying out his analysis within himself.

In my last section I want to say something about the implications and applications of this idea of basic unity, both in the analytic situation, and as we find it in ordinary life, as a normal and as a pathological thing.

It is of course more obvious as a pathological thing. As regards analysis, here is another piece of clinical material. I know that it can be taken in several different ways, but I am asking you to consider with me only the one aspect, that relating to the earliest level of development, the level that is preverbal, existing before object relations are developed, where body experience is all-important. Any kind of differentiation is only just beginning there, so it is also preambivalent and conflict-free.

'I find I haven't told you something, and that it's because I thought you already knew it,' says Rosemary. 'It's so much easier to talk to you when you aren't really there than when you are.'

Rosemary has never sorted herself out from her sister Joyce, who is two years older. All childhood happenings, ideas, or feelings are told of the entity 'we' ('We did this. We hated that'). She and Joyce are indivisible; she 'never feels a person' but is often 'two people', and sometimes 'half a person'. At the beginning of a session she frequently doesn't 'know how to begin'.

Three months after starting analysis, on her way to a session with me, she went into a big store to buy food, to entertain a favourite aunt who was visiting her. She collected some things, as much as she could hold, and then put into a string bag on her arm a bar of chocolate and a box of small cheeses. She paid for everything except these, which she forgot. On leaving the store, she was stopped by the store detective, who accused her of stealing them. Police were called; she was taken to the police station and locked in a cell for some hours, while her identity was checked. Next day she was charged in the magistrate's court, where she appeared without a lawyer, and was remanded for a week.

It never occurred to her to say that she was in treatment, nor, although she asked to be allowed to telephone to say that she had been prevented from keeping her appointment, did it occur to her to let me know what was happening. Several days elapsed before I knew.

Her movement, putting out her hand to take me (in the non-human form of cheese and chocolate) brought her up sharply against the environment, society, and the whole machinery of police, court, etc., and this interfered with the assimilation of the movement. The chain of events that followed effectively disrupted a process that was just beginning in her, and so repeated the happenings of her earliest infancy. They represented all that she most dreads and is constantly expecting.

Rosemary has not yet differentiated her mouth out from the rest of herself, or herself from her devouring surroundings. She suffers from anorexia nervosa, and she describes herself as 'cut off from my roots'.

At the time of her visit to the store Rosemary was function-

ing separately on at least two different levels, and I am understanding the separateness as being due to a failure of fusion,
rather than to a splitting mechanism. There was a person who
could choose and arrange a meal which she would provide for
another person for whom she felt affection. This argues both a
high degree of differentiation and organization and the existence of object relations. At the same time, on the earliest level
she was not yet differentiated out from her environment or
aware of its existence. She was an infant, in whom a movement
happened which should have been creative, leading to differentiation and integration, becoming an assertion or statement of
herself. But the movement was met by the environment in such
a way as to bring about disruption instead.

Although to all outward appearance she was entirely composed and self-possessed, and gave her evidence in court simply
and clearly, it was a matter of years before she could talk about
this episode, and verbal interpretations given at the time
brought no response. When she did finally talk about it it
became clear that the only things that had had any reality for
her were my presence in the court and what I actually said and
did on her behalf. It was important that the magistrate in discharging her said 'I believe your doctor when she tells me that
you are ill', and not 'I believe you when you tell me that you did
not steal'.

Some months later she told me of the only time she had stolen in childhood: Joyce was ill, and Rosemary (age eleven) did
not even know whether she was alive or not; nobody told her,
and she could not ask. The separation was absolute. Rosemary
was sent to stay with this same aunt. In a shop she saw a little
shell purse lined with red silk. She took it and kept it secretly for
years, always feeling guilty, as if she had committed a murder.

Last year I was away from her for some time, and I was very
doubtful whether she would kill herself or get ill and die. I lent
her a book of poems by Walter de la Mare. Some time later she
told me with great difficulty that two years before that she had
found a poem in a magazine in my waiting room; some of the
words 'seemed to belong to her', and she had cut it out and kept

it. When she showed it to me I could see why it had so much meaning for her, as the shell purse had had. I could also understand why she did not tell me at the time about the incident in the store. She believed that I knew it, as she and I were one.

Throughout her analysis she continued to be paralysed with terror, and unable to find any starting point other than something happening in me. She would clutch my hand, and I would speak of it as showing me this terror and relate it to material of the previous day, or to other occasions when she had done the same. Only when I pointed out that the pressure was so great as to be painful to me, or that my fingers had 'gone dead', could she begin to talk. Her silence and immobility would remain total for weeks on end, and only after I showed signs of life in some explicit way (for anything merely implicit was useless) could she begin to tell me what had been going on. It was a matter of amazement to discover that the person to whom she talked when I was not there did not reply, for it was herself, and not me; also that her own part in some of the childhood games was clearly distinguishable from that of Joyce. Her 'we' began to break up.

At last I began to find something of how her analysis could perhaps be done. She began to talk comparatively freely and to feel a person, and the analysis became steadily a more ordinary one. I may add that in the outside world she did not give the impression of being a schizoid or withdrawn personality at all; she was much liked by her fellows and had a good sense of humour and fun.

In the light of this idea of absolute identity between patient and analyst I think we have to reconsider our ideas of such mental mechanisms as projection, introjection, condensation, displacement, and all that Freud included in the term *dream work*.

I spoke earlier of the analyst who experiences the patient as his work, and his work as himself. It is like the poet who speaks of 'my love', meaning both his loved one and his own emotion, which is himself; we can see here how what we have considered to be condensation becomes instead a regression to the primordial, undifferentiated state. Similarly, in the first clinical exam-

[150]

ON BASIC UNITY

ple I quoted, what appeared to be projective identification
turned out to be an assertion of absolute identity with me.

For this same reason, that to them everything is one, patients
who show a transference psychosis bring dreams whose latent
and manifest content are the same.

I have said more about the need to reach the basic unity than
about the fear of it, though I have mentioned this. Fear of the
idea arises from its very nature, for the point of unity is also the
point of annihilation; it is the point of paradox, of chaos, or
absolute ambivalence, where opposites are simultaneously the
same thing and utterly different. It is not only the analysand
who experiences this anxiety; the difficulty is shared by the
analyst, whose task of being simultaneously absolutely one
with, and separate from the analysand, deeply concerned – or
engaged, to borrow Michael Fordham's expression (1960) –
but not involved with him is so difficult already. This fear
results in abhorrence of the word *delusion* and in rigid adherence to verbal technique alone.

I am postulating that a universal idea exists, as normal and
essential as is the Oedipus complex (which cannot develop
without it), an idea of absolute identity with the mother upon
which survival depends. The presence of this idea is the foundation of mental health, development of a whole person, and the
capacity for holistic thinking. It is to be found not only in the
delusions of the mentally sick, where it takes the form of transference psychosis, but also in the sane and healthy.

The most obvious and immediate example is here, right now.
You and I can only understand each other in so far as we possess an area of unity which is a psychic reality, to which temporarily we unconsciously regress. This is how empathy works.
The finding of agreement, or consensus of opinion between
individuals or in any group, depends upon it; in turn agreement
strengthens unconscious belief in survival and so provides the
necessary security for tolerating differences and disagreement
elsewhere.

Professor I. Ramzy, in discussing a paper I presented in
Topeka in 1958, drew attention to the absolute need to preserve our most primitive modes of functioning for the actual

[151]

survival not only of the individual but also of the human race. What I have here called 'basic unity' seems to me to be one of those essential primitive modes.

Contact or communication between the artist and his public depends upon the presence of, and regression to, this unconscious delusion in both. To the artist his creation is his work, is his feeling, is himself; to the hearer or the viewer what is heard or seen is *his* feeling, is his response, is himself. So each psychically *is* the work of art, and *is* the other, in the area where they overlap.

Other manifestations that I would regard as normal can be found in such things as provision of school uniforms, existence of the flag as a national symbol and the behavior of gardeners who give each other plants, until their gardens contain the same things but still remain essentially different and individual.

Where the basic unity has not been established, either in infancy or through analysis, annihilation anxiety persists, and unity will be sought, and avoided, in such things as ideologies, organized religions, secret societies, folies à deux, etc.

I have not the space to go into this in detail here, but it seems to me that in *Group Psychology and the Analysis of the Ego* (1921) Freud has talked about this very thing, especially in his reference to organized groups with a leader.

The relationship between the members of the group is an attempt to deny separateness and difference, while the relationship between the members and the leader simultaneously asserts it. These groups are largely concerned with self-preservation, i.e., with survival, but the price of that survival is loss of individuality. Juvenile gangs of various kinds are largely composed of members who feel not only that their existence is precarious but that it is not real, and that the only certainty is annihilation.

Organized religion offers a defence of a kind against the death that is the certain fate of the isolated. Those who use such a defence but cannot submerge their individuality enough seek in such things as mysticism or pantheism to lose their identity in 'mystical union' with the 'Wholly Other', and to find survival in a life that is merged with that of the cosmos.

[152]

Freud quotes Robertson Smith (Smith, W.R., 1885): 'Identifications which lie at the root of clan feeling rest upon the recognition of a common substance, and may even therefore be brought about by a meal eaten in common.' Here again we have the substance, the concrete thing, and bodily experience. The Christian idea of Communion rests upon the concrete symbols of bread and wine, which are believed to provide a means of resurrection after death, i.e., survival of the body.

I know that this could be understood in terms of relationship of an oral kind, but I want to remind you of the two points from which I started: (1) the attempts made by patients to establish union or identity with the analyst and (2) the importance for them of body happenings.

To sum up:

Within an individual both survival and the ability to find objects with which relationships can be formed depend upon the existence of a unity which comes from the entity mother-infant (or analyst-analysand). From it a rhythm of differentiation and reassimilation or integration comes. It provides the 'stillness at the centre' which allows of movement and perception; it is the *sine qua non* for living continuously in one's body, for having an identity, and for being identical with, and able to make assertion or statement of, oneself.

Ego in current thinking

JOHN PADEL

IN THEIR BOOK *The Language of Psycho-Analysis* (1967) Laplanche and Pontalis have a valuable and lucid article s.v. 'Ego'. In its first five sections they trace the stages in the development and the diversification of the concept in Freud's writings. In the sixth they consider Freud's ideas on the ego from two perspectives: first, the perspective of the ego as an organ which is gradually differentiated from the id, perception in the ego playing 'the part which in the id falls to instinct' – i.e., being both the stimulus to action and also the main source of the process of differentiation; second, the perspective of the ego as 'an internal formation originating from certain privileged perceptions' – perceptions which 'derive not from the external world in general but specifically from the interhuman world'.

Having expounded the first perspective and stated its difficulties, in efforts to resolve which ego-psychology had altered classical theory, Laplanche and Pontalis conclude:

> Not that there is any question of setting out some 'true' Freudian theory of the ego to counter these tendencies of ego-psychology: indeed it is remarkably difficult to integrate all the psychoanalytic contributions to the concept of the ego into a unified line of thought.

It is the second perspective which they consider the one with

[154]

possibilities; it is that of the ego as a formation arising from early perceptions of subject-object ('interhuman') relationships. They have rejected as untrue 'the simple interpretation' according to which Freud used the term ego ('Ich') sometimes in a nonspecific way to designate the personality as a whole and at other times in a precise and specific way, so creating a 'terminological ambiguity'. They firmly reject that way out and also Hartmann's conceptual distinction between the ego as agency and the self as love-object. Such false solutions, they maintain, both destroy Freud's need for, and creative use of, ambiguity and evade the real problems.

At the Rome Congress of 1971 the president-elect of the International Association, Leo Rangell, pleaded that the simple verbs 'I choose', 'I decide', 'I act' be brought back into psychoanalytic theory. He was followed by Max Schur, who said he *thought* he could understand what Rangell had meant: of course the reality of the ego was that it was a mechanism, operated dynamically by the interaction of forces; but the simple verbs that Rangell had mentioned could probably be accommodated in the theory on the understanding that they were metaphors. The obvious answer followed – that Schur had got it the wrong way round: it was the mechanical theory of the ego that was the metaphor. The response of the audience showed that it was a relief to hear that.

Rangell again refers to that repeated plea of his in an article published in the *Journal of the American Psychoanalytical Association* (1982, pp. 868-9) but does nothing to develop psychoanalytic theory in such a way as to accommodate in it the concepts of choice and will. That issue of *J. Am. Psychoanal. Ass.* has seven articles and a summary discussing various aspects of the Self in psychoanalytic theory, mainly as the concept is used in the various theories of Kernberg (himself one of the contributors), Kohut, and Gedo. Most of the writers are critical of the greater importance given to the concept of Self than to the term Ego, but nearly all appreciate the reasons why Kernberg, Kohut, and Gedo originally proposed their different changes and modifications of theory.

While the criticism of Self-theorists, that they do not

[155]

humanize theory in the way that they set out to do, is well made in that issue of *J. Am. Psychoanal. Ass.*, it is probably fair to say that the contributors nowhere mention arguments like that of Paul Ricoeur (1970, pp. 473-4, 483) that the economic and dynamic theories of classical psychoanalysis are themselves solipsistic. Ricoeur points out that the concept of *identification* is quite extraneous to those theories. Taking human relations into consideration, Freud had to give two separate accounts of the genesis and development of the ego – the solipsistic one (Michael Balint and Rickman called it a 'one-person psychology'), by which the pleasure principle has to be modified by the reality principle, so that the ego somehow achieves the inexplicable feat of using the pleasure principle to overcome or override the pleasure principle (anyhow, a learning theory), and an interpersonal account, by which object cathexes are internalized and contribute to the ego's growth.

Despite his verdict that Self-theorists have nowhere improved upon classical structural theory and in the main diminish it, Rangell (p. 881) closes his critical accounts by admitting that 'corrective theoretical formulations . . . are long overdue'. 'Such an advance', he says, 'might not only clarify the long-perplexing area of narcissism and the self but result in . . . a great unification of theory and practice throughout the analytic world.' He then adds a welcome final section in which he considers the vital contributions that group psychology could make towards these long-overdue formulations. (Rangell himself had carefully observed and described the Watergate episode in American politics, but also proposes that group behaviour in psychoanalytic societies urgently needs similar attention!) It must be a mere oversight that Rangell nowhere refers to Freud's *Group Psychology and the Analysis of the Ego* (1921), for he uses in a striking way the notion of the charismatic leader, a figure who, Freud had pointed out, was missing from Trotter's book and yet was required to explain the cohesion of groups, especially the cohesion of primitive and poorly-structured groups.

It is in fact remarkable that, whereas that book of Freud's gives the fullest account of the ego and is half entitled 'the

[156]

analysis of the ego', hardly anybody who discusses ego theory seems to have got from it more than a passing quotation. Yet I believe it was one of the most penetrating pieces of thinking that Freud did and that *The Ego and the Id* (1923a) was a retreat from it – a far less successful attempt to analyse the ego. In the later work Freud combines only some of his insights into the way we live and grow by identifying in relationships, with some of his speculations about the two basic instincts that he postulated to be fighting their unending war in every human psyche.

There are two reasons why the earlier work appears so important. One is that in it Freud makes a sustained effort to relate the external relationships of the individual to the internal relationships of his psyche, to show how the internal derive from the external and affect the external ones subsequently, and to show this particularly (but not only) over a person's attitude to authority, both external and internal. The second reason for the importance of the earlier work is that Freud there attempted to explicate the process of identification more fully than he had done before or was to do afterwards. He even gave a diagram to illustrate one type of change, not merely from an external to an internal object-relationship (for the external object is not lost), but a change which does take place internally in the members of a group with a leader. He uses the concept of identification in earlier and in later papers but never again wrestles with it as he does in *Group Psychology* – so persistently indeed that he almost transcends the limitations of the 'one-person psychology' (Balint, M., 1949, quoting J. Rickman) which his metapsychology has elaborated.

Different theorists have treated identification as a technical term, some by regarding it as just one mode of defence (which of course it sometimes is), others by regularly prefixing to it certain technical adjectives, which crowd out its common meaning. Yet that common meaning is well understood by the uninitiated.

A radio news-report one morning said that a chief of police had made a speech complaining that social workers identified too often with the criminal instead of with the authorities. His

[157]

complaint was essentially an appeal to reverse the identification, to refuse to identify with the felon and to identify with the police instead. Of course a social worker may not have to identify with either, but that chief of police did assume that we would all know what he meant. He knew both that we can and do identify with one member of an opposed pair and also that we are capable of changing over and identifying with the other of that pair – with the police against the criminal. We do this all the time, but most flexibly when we are lookers-on at a relationship and do not have to take sides with one against the other. Consider the effect of a tragic drama upon the spectators present at it. Aristotle said that it stirred up in them pity and terror. In feeling terror they are, of course, identified with the hero in his peril; in feeling pity they are not so identified – it is happening to the hero and not to them, though they have been identified with him at other moments and so are sorry for him now. Aristotle seemed to feel the social and psychological function of drama so important that he termed Man a *mimetikón zōon*. *Mimetikón* includes, but is wider than, the notions 'imitative' and 'representing'; one way to translate his phrase would be by the words 'an animal that identifies with others'.

If identification is the actual way in which our ego is created and grows, we need to know how this habit of identifying with someone else begins, whether restrictedly over short spans of time or largely over long periods. We need also to know how it develops and how extensive it is: is it one aspect of all experience, transient or lasting, from watching a drama to growing up and taking a place in society, or living in and through a marriage?

It is clear that in the act of identifying with someone or something, someone else or something else is excluded. The field is thereby divided. If identifying is a prime ego-function, then dividing the field is closely and necessarily associated with it. In other words, splitting must occur along with or precede the act of choosing; but before either can be done, the field must appear as complex – it must consist of at least two elements in some relation to one another. So holding awareness of a com-

plex field and dividing such a field are also prime ego-functions.

In his paper 'On Narcissism' (1914b, p. 88) Freud describes
the relationship between a male homosexual and his young
partner as one in which the homosexual is identified with his
mother and his partner with himself at a younger age. Freud
then distinguishes the choice of object modelled on mother
from the choice of object modelled on oneself, but insists that
both kinds of object-choice are open to each individual, though
he may prefer one or the other. He goes on: 'We say that a
human being has originally two sexual objects – himself and
the woman that nurses him – and in doing so we are postulating a primary narcissism in everyone, which may in some cases
manifest itself in a dominating fashion in his object-choice.'
This means that such a person finds both kinds of object-choice
less open than do most other people; his preference for one
kind is too strong.

Here Freud portrays the outcome of the suckler–suckling
relationship as the formation of a deep-rooted memory of it
which is the basis of all subsequent relationships but affords
the possibility of choice, flexibility, and change. At one
extreme the individual may identify with mother and so enter
on relationships in which he is more giver than taker; at the
other extreme he may identify with infant-self and be receiver
or taker rather than giver. (Of course neither extreme means
maturity.) But the very fact of being able to choose to identify
with the one *or* with the other means that he also adopted a
third position, from which he could observe self-and-mother as
a couple and be for a while identified with neither. That
detached and observing self forms a third term and has created
a three-term relationship out of a two-term one. The new,
observing and reflective self can identify now more with one
end of the composite unity of self-and-mother, now more with
the other; and re-establishes a two-term relationship by making either identification. Pathology would start from an inability, or from a lessened ability, to take up any one of the three
positions; the normal ego is able to move between them.

[159]

Exchange in that first relationship is of far more than milk and bodily contacts: there is acknowledgement of feelings and of mutuality in feeling, and there is reciprocal observation. In the infant's internalization of the relationship a special place is taken by the mother's eyes; if we suppose that the composite unity of lips-and-nipple, of mouth-and-breast forms the oral nucleus of the ego, the observing eyes, in so far as they are separate, form the nucleus of the later superego. This can be deduced from the observations and recordings made by Donald Gough, who was interested in the time-relations of mutual looking of mothers and sucklings during feeding (1962). For the infant the field of observation is divided; his attention is shown to fluctuate between the oral and the visual, the second of which can both inhibit and facilitate the feeding process. In other words, that exchange of looking can develop both into a discovery of authority, 'a differentiating grade in the ego' (Freud, 1921, pp. 129-33), and, as a desire-desire relationship (Ricoeur, 1970, p. 178), into an exchange of consciousness with consciousness which results in 'a reduplication of consciousness' (ibid., p. 483) and which has operated through an identification in an object-relationship.

So far I have left on one side the actual third person – the father of the future Oedipal stage, whose presence may inhibit or may facilitate the mother-child relationship. Freud is surely right in postulating that the child deals with the third person by identifying with him until (s)he finds him a rival and an obstacle. By the time (s)he makes father's acquaintance, (s)he is well used to alternating between the three-term position and the two-term one and is not for some time forced to choose between *being* and *having*. In *The Ego and the Id* (1923a) Freud supposed that it was the discovery of not being able either to be or to have (unless disaster were to follow) that ended the Oedipal phase, that the child chose instead to *be like* – like the rival in other ways than having the desired object – and *then* first identified with her/his parents by internalizing them in their relationship. Ten years later (*S.E.* 22, p. 64) Freud changed this view without calling attention to the change. He says that on giving up the intense Oedipal cathexes the child develops 'an intensification of the identifications with his parents *which have probably long been present in his ego*' (my italics).

This change of view is highly significant because it means Freud's acknowledgement that loss of object is not the motive or the occasion for identification, though it is certainly both a reason and an occasion for the intensification of it. So we may suppose that all through the Oedipal period (and even well before it) the child has been used to treating the parents' relationship in the same way as (s)he treated the relationship between self and mother – sometimes seeing the pair as separate from self (benign or persecutory to self), at other times identifying with one parent to engage in an object-relationship with the other (hostile or friendly). This means a natural combination of the positive and negative Oedipal positions, with 'the two identifications in some way united with each other' (*S.E.* 19, p. 34).

There is another theme in *Group Psychology and the Analysis of the Ego* which is greatly changed in *The Ego and the Id*. In the latter work Freud repeatedly implies that it is only explicitly erotic cathexes which are converted into identifications. In the earlier one he points out that group situations themselves greatly amplify the emotional significance of the relationships in them and lead to identifications (*S.E.* 18, pp. 103-4 *et al.*). Indeed at the end of chapter 8 he defines a primary group (i.e., a fairly unstructured group) as 'a number of individuals who have put one and the same object in the place of their ego-ideal and have consequently identified themselves with one another in their ego.' And he gives a diagram (p. 116) of three individuals, all relating to an external object, each one of whom puts his own image of the external object in the place of his ego-ideal, so identifying with the others in his ego.

In that diagram Freud represents the internal world of each individual simply as a line with the ego as its mid-point; at the left-hand end is a point standing for the ego-ideal and at the right-hand end a tiny circle stands for the object (the shared external object is further to the right of the line); there is for each line a curve with arrows showing how the object passes to the ego-ideal. We can say that this simple type of internalization is illustrated by a rotation of the right-hand half of the line around the ego, which remains apparently unchanged except in its resulting identification. The type of internalization which has been described in chapter 7 for a male homosexual, for Dora with her cough, for a child who has lost her kitten, and for the melancholic, is different: if we use the diagram, we can say that the right-hand half of the line slides to the left, so that the object occupies the place of the ego, and the ego that of the ego-ideal. In other words, the earlier relationship of ego object is continued in the relationship ego-ideal ego.

'The essence of the matter,' Freud says, 'is whether the object is put in place of the ego or the ego-ideal' (p. 114). It would simplify the whole matter if we thought not about the internalization of an object but always about the internalization of a relationship, direct or reversed, which leads to an identification with some element or aspect of that relationship. If, in Freud's second way of internalizing, the ego-object relationship continues unchanged in the superego-ego relationship, there will be no recovery from the consequent melancholia, mourning, or self-doubt; only when there is exchange between the two agencies, or when a new object is found to take over some share of that previous relationship, can the shadow of the object be lifted from the ego.

From *Group Psychology and the Analysis of the Ego* I draw the conclusion that identification occurs in all human relationships and that it is profound and lasting according as the relationship is or has been important. In that work Freud discusses groups of very different sizes and degrees of organization. Having touched on the many groups that each of us belongs to, he begins with Le Bon's 'crowd' – a fairly large, almost unstructured group, described in words strongly reminiscent of Kipling's 'Bandar Log' (Monkey People). Then he reproduces McDougall's account of a well-structured group, enumerating his five 'principal conditions' for raising mental life to a higher level. These conditions are:

1. The group's continuity – of membership and structure;
2. The formation in each member's mind of an idea of the

group's nature and working, so that he develops an emotional attitude to it;

3. The group's interaction (e.g., rivalry) with other comparable groups;

4. The possession of traditions and customs to fix the group's internal relationships;

5. The group's being definitely structures in a way that expresses its members' specialization and differentiation of work.

Having given three pages to McDougall's psychology of groups, Freud sees that the word 'individual' (ego) could be substituted for 'group' in these five conditions. (He is wrong, of course, about number 5 – unless for 'members' he had adopted Plato's device and substituted 'parts of the self' – or 'identifications'.) Freud covers up the flaw in his argument by moving number 3 to the end of the list: 'the individual, outside the primitive group, possessed his own continuity, his self-consciousness, his traditions and customs, his own particular functions and position, and he kept apart from his rivals.' But Freud uses this insight only to dismiss McDougall, as if the individual were prior to the group instead of having gained his very qualities and attributes in and through membership of various groups, some of which Freud discusses in the rest of the paper. This seems the paper's most serious defect: at the very point where he could have used the social and the individual psychology to illuminate each other he turns away from the social and has to bring it in again in his own way via the artificial groups of the Army and the Church, and via identifications formed in the family, in school, in unstructured groups, and in groups of two – hypnosis and being in love.

This argument is not of minor importance: our answers to it will decide whether or not we think of separate egos and objects managing to achieve relationships, or of relationships which are already there and are mutually explored, internalized, broken, mended, and transformed (or renounced). If the first, if we believe in separateness of the ego from birth (or earlier), then we are liable to think in terms of a one-person

[163]

psychology, to talk about the introjection and projection of objects, and to believe that the internalization of a relationship is secondary to the introjection of an object. If the second, if togetherness is there from birth, then we shall believe that the internalization of relationships (or situations) is primary and may sometimes be accompanied by the phantasy of incorporating an object, that the reduplication of consciousness (Ricoeur, 1970) ensures that we are aware of the mutuality of experience, and that it is therefore our business to work out two- and three-person psychologies – i.e., psychologies of intimacy and of social life – and to show how we manage to live by both, using the mode of each to refresh the other.

We have already a good beginning of each of these psychologies, worked out piecemeal in clinical and theoretical papers by clinicians who began treating patients in the 1920s; I mean Fairbairn and Winnicott. It is not surprising that the three-person psychology began earlier, since, as Michael Balint (1949) pointed out, words are far less relevant in the intimacy of the two-person relationship and, as we all know in psychoanalytic work, are anyway liable to switch the two-person mode into the three-person mode. Moreover, it takes somebody who is completely at home in a therapeutic relationship with a child and who can operate without words, on the child's own level, to be able to discover in subsequent reflection the basic features of an encounter and so, if he can clear his mind of cant, to describe the contributions of each to the two-person interaction in which he has just been taking part. It is no accident that the first approach of a two-person psychology was made by a paediatrician.

Like Winnicott, Fairbairn believed in the importance of the real, as well as the phantasied, relationship. He was very perceptive both of defence and of the exclusion of aspects of the personality which it entails. Because he felt so keenly the need for closeness – certainly in his patients and, I presume, in his own life – he related all pathology to failures to maintain essential closeness at various stages of development, and saw the outcome of failures to do so as necessitating the individual's sustained attempts to divest his object of its most disturbing features, viz. its over-exciting quality and its forbidding authority. This defensive splitting of the object was of course undertaken after internalization and entailed an involuntary splitting of the ego, because of the profound attachment to the exciting object and no less because of the profound reliance upon the overseeing and control which the forbidding authority ensured. (I would also add 'because of the original field divided between mouth/nipple and eyes'.)

So it was not just two aspects of the object that were split off but two aspects of the ego-object relationship. Fairbairn was right to speak of repressed parts of the ego, because they could and did become reunited partially and intermittently with the central ego. Roy Schafer (1976, p. 218) admits the rightness when he says that Fairbairn 'populated the mind with his personified types of ego only'; but his 'populated' seems gratuitously misleading.

One of Fairbairn's most important contributions to our ideas about the functioning of the ego is that what is repressed is always a relationship (though it may be symbolized or represented as an object). On the two-person level the relation is one between self and other; on the three-person level it is one between self-and-other bound in mutual control and self-and-other bound in mutual desire. The idea that what is repressed is always a relationship, simple or complex, is consonant with the idea that I have stated earlier, that what is internalized is always a relationship (or that complex of relationships which is a total situation), although it may be symbolized or represented by an object.

In the last paragraph but one of Freud's published paper on the Rat Man (1909, pp. 248-9) we read his patient's three ways of operating – impulsively, naturally and freely, and compulsively and ascetically. Freud is so taken with this triadic description of the personality that he adds a final vignette of a female patient who can be described in the same way. It is easy, of course, to see here an anticipation of Freud's later structural theory of the personality, but the clinical accounts fit Fairbairn's thinking just as well, since what we have been hearing about are the relationships that the patients try to avoid repeating.

Even in 1931 (1952, pp. 197-277) Fairbairn could give an account of a three-and-a-half-year analysis in which the repressed relationships of his patient keep surfacing as pairs in which we can distinguish early ego-figures and object-figures. He was certainly aware how readily a repressed relationship could be represented by one figure standing both for the ego and for the person with whom the ego had identified.

In two papers (1954, 1958) Fairbairn illustrated the tripartite ego in clinical accounts and suggested in the second paper that transference itself was the consequence of the ego's endeavour to maintain the personality as a closed circuit, and, since the analyst's presence and behaviour made that difficult, to press him too into the closed circuit in order not to allow him to break it.

Fairbairn's papers are often written in one-person-psychology terms, yet the three-person relationships (not only the Oedipal) are always present, with the two-person relationship either just past, threatening to return, or seen as a goal ahead. Moreover, he operated easily with the concept of identification (1952, *passim*, but especially pp. 257-8).

We could ask (with Schafer) why Fairbairn needed the ego-concept at all. I think the answer is that, since he worked with identifications and with split-off aspects of the personality, he naturally never thought of not conceptualizing that central aspect of the personality from which the others had been split, the 'I myself' as attender, judge, and agent. There is much to be said, especially clinically, for Schafer's 'action-language', but even he, in writing of 'Identification and Character-Analysis' (1983, pp. 148-52), decides that he has to speak of 'identifications' (often represented by figures made out of aspects of self and aspects of parents, etc.) instead of 'unconsciously maintained identificatory actions in the realms of overt behaving and private fantasizing.' Schafer may be right and the term ego be on the way out (especially '*the* ego'), but I do not think that his action-language yet allows enough space for passive or for observing experience, though his description of self-imprisoned human beings (ibid., pp. 257 *seqq.*) shows that he understands them very well.

Winnicott, in all his clinical and theoretical writings, seems to keep the intersubjective, two-person experience in mind the whole time. He does not accept the notion of ego present from birth (though he may have allowed the 'psyche-soma' from birth on); this was because he instinctively stressed the potentiality of the infant ('There is no such thing as a baby'): until needs were met there was no ego, no unified experience. Ego formed thanks to the holding and handling during the times in which needs were met – and between these times too, for here the protective shield which the mother provided against impingement (see especially Khan, 1964) was destined to become a vital ingredient of the ego-boundary.

Winnicott wrote making easy transitions from the infant's point of view to the mother's and back again. He never forgets that the mother has two aspects for her child: she is environment and she is object, and she accepts being both at once. She operates with what Rycroft (1968, p. 78) and Sterba (1934) called a creative use of an ego-split. Besides, she gives the child time to choose (Winnicott, 1945a, p. 152; 1952, p. 223) and should not impose on her/him a premature awareness that she is the source of supply. 'We all know that the baby creates the breast' was his statement of the mother's acceptance: 'illusion' was his conceptualization of the baby's one-person/two-person option.

The concepts of the 'transitional object' and the 'transitional phenomenon' (1951, 1971) are perhaps Winnicott's best-known additions to our ideas of ego-functioning. He wrote the first version of his paper on these concepts about fifteen years before he finally made up his mind what symbolism was involved. Transitional objects and phenomena represent that absolute togetherness of mother and child which has been and is no more, which is not even remembered but is used and relied upon as if remembered. The transitional object can stand for mother or an aspect of her, especially when the child is falling asleep: it can stand for the child's own self (to be returned to

[167]

and perhaps punished or comforted) during the time in which the child has been (or has been doing) what mother required. In this way the transitional object facilitates switches in identification; it tells a great deal about ego-functioning, because it represents a flexible past relationship which is now a possession and a component of present relationships.

It would be wrong to leave this cursory account of ego-function as Winnicott wrote of it without mentioning three other ideas. The first is that of the false self, when a premature ego-identification made under stress has supplanted the spontaneous life of the child's ego. The second is that of the use of the mother and other family-members as mirror to the child's ego, in an important stage of transition when observation is developing the overtones of self-observation. The third idea is that *playing* is the best description of healthy ego-function, but that it requires at some early stages the presence of mother – no longer herself to share in playing but simply to be there if needed.

When we are thinking psycho-physiologically, we probably all acknowledge the ego-functions of anticipation, perception, and memory at the input end of the original reflex arc, those of controlled action (including thought and speech) and refraining from action at the output end of the arc, with judgement between, corresponding to what neurophysiologists term 'central delay'. Besides there are the various modes of defence. All these can be spoken of in a one-person psychology. But identification, engaged in not defensively but by way of relating and interacting and leading to a duplication of consciousness, is a concept that still offers scope for new thoughts about the ego.

For example, Stanley Palombo (1976, 1984) has been developing fresh ideas about the use of dreaming. His theories and those of others working on similar lines are not incompatible with those of Freud or Jung but supplement them to fill an important lacuna. At the very end of his paper 'On Dreams' (1901) as well as in his later paper 'Remarks on the Theory and Practice of Dream-Interpretation' (1923b) Freud raised the question, 'Whence the dream-thoughts?' and he acknowledged

[168]

it to be a question that it was not within the scope of psychoanalysis to answer. Palombo's answer is that in transferring items from the day's residue from short-term to long-term memory overnight, in one phase of that transfer we visually recall selected events of the day, and alongside the recall engage in a search of the early-established categories (filed therefore under childhood memories) for matching and then for the establishing of association-points for rapid reference. Palombo raises the question why it should be necessary to visualize the events.

A possible answer is that matching and, even more, internalizing require the processes of identification and of seeing a situation from the points of view of other people present at it. One of my analytic patients would commonly describe a dream-scene and add, 'I was on the left (or the right)', and she explained that she saw herself clearly from another vantage-point. It was then sometimes possible to work out with whom she was identified in seeing the dream-scene as she had first described it. She played a musical instrument, often standing up when performing. Near the end of her analysis she had to play at a concert and was worried by developing a slight, nearly rhythmical spasm of her back muscles. I interpreted her identification with an erect phallus and its pulse to give herself potency in playing. She came back at me sharply: 'That would be a most *un*helpful thought to think on the platform!' But she had had the thought and dismissed it before then. The spasms did not continue and she was free of them at the concert.*

In pulling together some of the threads of this paper I go back

---

* On this topic I was glad to see that Rangell (1982, p. 880) states: 'A clinical finding that links Self-psychology with all that has preceded it in psychoanalytic theory is the equation phallus = self, a common finding in normalcy and pathology for any clinician working at unconscious depths.' The symbolic equation (in Freud's sense of the phrase) of self with parental genital is one of the regular identifications made in childhood. Perhaps the difficulty of making such an identification should be a strong reason against the bringing up of a child by a lesbian couple.

to the late Max Schur's mention of metaphor. We do need metaphor for fresh thought; we also need to be able to discard metaphors when they are dead, but without losing the memory of the values they conveyed when they were living. Even if we stop using the mechanical metaphors of metapsychological theory, there will be no risk, thanks to Freud's own texts and to the new ways of reading them to which such writers as Ricoeur and Patrick Mahony (1982) educate us, that we shall lose touch with their original power. But we do need fresh metaphor in which to rethink the personality, its growth, and its relations with others. There is a very beautiful metaphor for the ego to which Rycroft pointed in the last chapter and post-script of his book *The Innocence of Dreams* (1979, pp. 153-69), using G.M. Hopkins's poem 'The Windhover'. He suggests that ego is related to the imagination that supports it as the kestrel to the air it rides. There is more that I find in that metaphor – one positive idea and one negative. The first is that the kestrel hovers to scan, and in scanning we suppose that it divides the field as a preliminary to action; having selected, it stoops. The second is that we do not postulate for the kestrel that double awareness of features in the field which we do for the feeding infant; still less the awareness of two beings in a close relation to one another. We do not need the notion of identification when we imagine a kestrel, though we know well that it was a large part of the poet's imagining it. He used it as a mirror for his own capacity to home in on his target.

The play of visual attention in which scanning consists has been emphasized by Marion Milner (1969, p. 410 and fn.), who quotes the work of Victor Ehrenzweig. In her book *The Hands of the Living God* she reveals her own capacity to hover and to scan, to help her patient gradually to do likewise, to notice how her patient divides the field and to find meaning in that division, and sometimes to redivide the field herself before stooping to interpret.

Division of a field, whether according to Freud's paired opposites or in any other way, is a basic mode of thought. It makes an unfamiliar field, situation, or aggregate of material intelligible, particularly if more than one pair of opposites can be used. It may also lead to discovering the middles excluded by division into opposites. This indeed is the main point of imposing double binds on other people (e.g., by transference interpretations): it forces them to rethink what they have been taking for granted, even their own identifications. It consists in a switch from a three-person to a two-person mode, and it is most fruitful if it implies some redivision of the field that both persons have been scanning just prior to the moment of the switch.

Christopher Bollas recently called attention to another way of working to the same end (1984). Allowing a mood to develop without interpretation or comment, until it becomes possible to talk about the mood, may lead to a discovery of the situation in which, and the identifications from which, the mood originally derived. A situation between self and important others has been internalized long ago and a recurrent mood may be the essential indicator that search is required, which may bring new awareness of the past situation and of the identifications that are still being imposed upon the present. Here the analyst's presence and scanning without early division of the field can help the patient to attend to his own mood and to what underlies it.

So far I have said nothing about Melanie Klein's ideas about the ego. This is not because I have not gained from reading her papers, for it is impossible to study them without rethinking again and again the relation between ego and object. Partly it is because I have not found in her writings any attention to that doubling of consciousness which is the basis for a two-person psychology. But one paragraph of her paper 'The Origins of Transference' (1952a, p. 55) is absolutely compatible with Fairbairn's notion of the internalizing of situations and re-finding of them in dream or in relation to the analyst. Here she stresses the fundamental importance of the transference *situation* (her italics) and says, 'It is essential to think in terms of *total situations* transferred from the past to the present. . .' I believe that if that were always held in mind, there would be far less disagreement about the introjection and projection of self and/or objects.

[171]

With that proviso it is easier to assent to something she says in her short paper 'The Mutual Influence in the Development of Ego and Id' (1952b, p. 59): 'The internalized objects also form the core of the superego.' But I am especially grateful for the footnote there, which acknowledges her uncertainty about how far and under what conditions the internalized object forms part of the ego, and how far of the superego. It seems to anticipate her thought in the paper 'On the Development of Mental Functioning' (1958), where she says that 'The superego is normally established in close relation with the ego and shares different aspects of the same good object' (p 241). I find this illuminated by Donald Gough's paper and entirely compatible with the idea of the infant's internalization of the total situation of sucking while watched over by mother.

In this paper I have called attention to these ego-functions:

1. Scanning of the field in which one is acting;

2. Division of the field with alternation of attention between at least two features of it and exploration of each from the vantage-point of the other;

3. Reuniting of the field (especially that featuring the two persons – self and other) and viewing of the field from a third position;

4. Re-finding of each object by identification with the other one.

Archimedes is said to have exclaimed, after describing the lever, 'Give me a place to stand and I'll move the earth.' He understood the importance of the third term and the third position! I believe that identification with one person can make it possible to relate more fully to another. Each one of us has sat on mother's knee to smile at father and been held over father's shoulder to make eyes at mother. In that early three-person situation identification and object relation occur together and facilitate one another. Identification is not the consequence of internalizing but accompanies or precedes it. By identifying we internalize a field, a situation, or a relationship.

[172]

Fear of breakdown

D. W. WINNICOTT

MY CLINICAL EXPERIENCES have brought me recently to a new understanding, as I believe, of the meaning of a fear of breakdown.

It is my purpose here to state as simply as possible this understanding, which is new for me and which perhaps is new for others who work in psychotherapy. Naturally, if what I say has truth in it, this will already have been dealt with by the world's poets, but the flashes of insight that come in poetry cannot absolve us from our painful task of getting step by step away from ignorance towards our goal. It is my opinion that a study of this limited area leads to a restatement of several other problems that puzzle us as we fail to do as well clinically as we would wish to do, and I shall indicate at the end what extensions of the theory I propose for discussion.

Individual variations

Fear of breakdown is a feature of significance in some of our patients, but not in others. From this observation, if it be a correct one, the conclusion can be drawn that fear of breakdown is related to the individual's past experience, and to environmental vagaries. At the same time there must be expected a common denominator of the same fear, indicating the existence of universal phenomena; these indeed make it possible for

[173]

everyone to know empathetically what it feels like when one of our patients shows this fear in a big way. (The same can be said, indeed, of every detail of the insane person's insanity. We all know about it, although this particular detail may not be bothering us.)

Emergence of the symptom

Not all our patients who have this fear complain of it at the out-set of a treatment. Some do; but others have their defences so well organized that it is only after a treatment has made consid-erable progress that the fear of breakdown comes to the fore as a dominating factor.

For instance, a patient may have various phobias and a com-plex organization for dealing with these phobias, so that dependence does not come quickly into the transference. At length, dependence becomes a main feature, and then the analyst's mistakes and failures become direct causes of localized phobias and so of the outbreak of fear of breakdown.

Meaning of 'breakdown'

I have purposely used the term 'breakdown' because it is rather vague and because it could mean various things. On the whole, the word can be taken in this context to mean a failure of a defence organization. But immediately we ask: a defence against what? And this leads us to the deeper meaning of the term, since we need to use the word 'breakdown' to describe the unthinkable state of affairs that underlies the defence organization.

It will be noted that whereas there is value in thinking that in the area of psychoneurosis it is castration anxiety that lies behind the defences, in the more psychotic phenomena that we are examining it is a breakdown of the establishment of the unit self that is indicated. The ego organizes defences against break-down of the ego organization, and it is the ego organization that is threatened. But the ego cannot organize against environ-mental failure in so far as dependence is a living fact.

[174]

In other words, we are examining a reversal of the individual's maturational process. This makes it necessary for me briefly to reformulate the early stages of emotional growth.

Emotional growth, early stages

The individual inherits a maturational process. This carries the individual along in so far as there exists a facilitating environment, and only in so far as this exists. The facilitating environment is itself a complex phenomenon and needs special study in its own right; the essential feature is that it has a kind of growth of its own, being adapted to the changing needs of the growing individual.

The individual proceeds from absolute dependence to relative independence and towards independence. In health the development takes place at a pace that does not outstrip the development of complexity in the mental mechanisms, this being linked to neurophysiological development.

The facilitating environment can be described as *holding*, developing into *handling*, to which is added *object-presenting*.

In such a facilitating environment the individual undergoes development which can be classified as *integrating*, to which is added *indwelling* (or *psychosomatic collusion*) and then *object-relating*.

This is a gross oversimplification but it must suffice in this context.

It will be observed that in such a description forward movement in development corresponds closely with the threat of retrograde movement (and defences against this threat) in schizophrenic illness.

Absolute dependence

At the time of absolute dependence, with the mother supplying an auxiliary ego-function, it has to be remembered that the infant has not yet separated out the 'not-me' from the 'me' – this cannot happen apart from the establishment of 'me'.

Primitive Agonies

From this chart it is possible to make a list of primitive agonies (anxiety is not a strong enough word here).

Here are a few:

1. A return to an unintegrated state. (Defence: disintegration.)

2. Falling for ever. (Defence: self-holding.)

3. Loss of psychosomatic collusion, failure of indwelling. (Defence: depersonalization.)

4. Loss of sense of real. (Defence: exploitation of primary narcissism, etc.)

5. Loss of capacity to relate to objects. (Defence: autistic states, relating only to self-phenomena.)

And so on.

Psychotic illness as a defence

It is my intention to show here that what we see clinically is always a defence organization, even in the autism of childhood schizophrenia. The underlying agony is unthinkable.

It is wrong to think of psychotic illness as a breakdown, it is a defence organization relative to a primitive agony, and it is usually successful (except when the facilitating environment has been not deficient but tantalizing, perhaps the worst thing that can happen to a human baby).

Statement of main theme

I can now state my main contention, and it turns out to be very simple. I contend that clinical fear of breakdown is *the fear of a breakdown that has already been experienced*. It is a fear of the original agony which caused the defence organization which the patient displays as an illness syndrome.

This idea may or may not prove immediately useful to the clinician. We cannot hurry up our patients. Nevertheless, we can hold up their progress because of genuinely not knowing;

any little piece of our understanding may help us to keep up with a patient's needs.

There are moments, according to my experience, when a patient needs to be told that the breakdown, a fear of which destroys his or her life, *has already been*. It is a fact that is carried round hidden away in the unconscious. The unconscious here is not exactly the repressed unconscious of psychoneurosis, nor is it the unconscious of Freud's formulation of the part of the psyche that is very close to neurophysiological functioning. Nor is it the unconscious of Jung's which I would call: all those things that go on in underground caves, or (in other words) the world's mythology, in which there is collusion between the individual and the maternal inner psychic realities. In this special context the unconscious means that the ego integration is not able to encompass something. The ego is too immature to gather all the phenomena into the area of personal omnipotence.

It must be asked here: why does the patient go on being worried by this that belongs to the past? The answer must be that the original experience of primitive agony cannot get into the past tense unless the ego can first gather it into its own present time experience and into omnipotent control now (assuming the auxiliary ego-supporting function of the mother (analyst)).

In other words, the patient must go on looking for the past detail which is *not yet experienced*. This search takes the form of a looking for this detail in the future.

Unless the therapist can work successfully on the basis that this detail is already a fact, the patient must go on fearing to find what is being compulsively looked for in the future.

On the other hand, if the patient is ready for some kind of acceptance of this queer kind of truth, that what is not yet experienced did nevertheless happen in the past, then the way is open for the agony to be experienced in the transference, in reaction to the analyst's failures and mistakes. These latter can be dealt with by the patient in doses that are not excessive, and the patient can account for each technical failure of the analyst as countertransference. In other words, gradually the patient

[177]

gathers the original failure of the facilitating environment into the area of his or her omnipotence and the experience of omnipotence which belongs to the state of dependence (transference fact).

All this is very difficult, time-consuming and painful, but it at any rate is not futile. What is futile is the alternative, and it is this that must now be examined.

Futility in analysis

I must take for granted an understanding and acceptance of the analysis of psychoneurosis. On the basis of this assumption, I say that in the cases I am discussing the analysis starts off well, the analysis goes with a swing; what is happening, however, is that the analyst and the patient are having a good time colluding in a psychoneurotic analysis, when in fact the illness is psychotic.

Over and over again the analysing couple are pleased with what they have done together. It was valid, it was clever, it was cosy because of the collusion. But each so-called advance ends in destruction. The patient breaks it up and says: So what? In fact, the advance was not an advance; it was a new example of the analyst's playing the patient's game of postponing the main issue. And who can blame either the patient or the analyst (unless of course there can be an analyst who plays the psychotic fish on a very long psychoneurotic line, and hopes thereby to avoid the final catch by some trick of fate, such as the death of one or other of the couple, or a failure of financial backing).

We must assume that both patient and analyst really do wish to end the analysis, but alas, there is no end unless the bottom of the trough has been reached, unless *the thing feared has been experienced*. And indeed one way out is for the patient to have a breakdown (physical or mental) and this can work very well. However, the solution is not good enough if it does not include analytic understanding and insight on the part of the patient, and indeed, many of the patients I am referring to are valuable people who cannot afford to break down in the sense of going to a mental hospital.

[178]

The purpose of this paper is to draw attention to the possibility that the breakdown has already happened, near the beginning of the individual's life. The patient needs to 'remember' this but it is not possible to remember something that has not yet happened, and this thing of the past has not happened yet because the patient was not there for it to happen to. The only way to 'remember' in this case is for the patient to experience this past thing for the first time in the present, that is to say, in the transference. This past and future thing then becomes a matter of the here and now, and becomes experienced by the patient for the first time. This is the equivalent of remembering, and this outcome is the equivalent of the lifting of repression that occurs in the analysis of the psychoneurotic patient (classical Freudian analysis).

Further applications of this theory

Fear of death

Little alteration is needed to transfer the general thesis of fear of breakdown to a specific fear of death. This is perhaps a more common fear, and one that is absorbed in the religious teachings about an afterlife, as if to deny the fact of death.

When fear of death is a significant symptom the promise of an afterlife fails to give relief, and the reason is that the patient has a compulsion to look for death. Again, it is the death that happened but was not experienced that is sought.

When Keats was 'half in love with easeful death' he was, according to the idea that I am putting forward here, longing for the ease that would come if he could 'remember' having died; but to remember he must experience death now.

Most of my ideas are inspired by patients, to whom I acknowledge my debt. It is to one of these that I owe the phrase 'phenomenal death'. What happened in the past was death as a phenomenon, but not as the sort of fact that we observe. Many men and women spend their lives wondering whether to find a solution by suicide, that is, sending the body to death which has already happened to the psyche. Suicide is no answer, however, but is a despair gesture. I now understand for the first time what my schizophrenic patient (who did kill herself) meant when she said: 'All I ask you to do is to help me to commit suicide for the right reason instead of for the wrong reason.' I did not succeed and she killed herself in despair of finding the solution. Her aim (as I now see) was to get it stated by me that she died in early infancy. On this basis I think she and I could have enabled her to put off body death till old age took its toll.

Death, looked at in this way as something that happened to the patient but which the patient was not mature enough to experience, has the meaning of annihilation. It is like this, that a pattern developed in which the continuity of being was inter-rupted by the patient's infantile reactions to impingement, these being environmental factors that were allowed to impinge by failures of the facilitating environment. (In the case of this patient troubles started very early, for there was a pre-mature awareness awakened before birth because of a mater-nal panic, and added to this the birth was complicated by undiagnosed placenta praevia.)

Emptiness
Again my patients show me that the concept of emptiness can be looked at through these same spectacles.

In some patients emptiness needs to be experienced, and this emptiness belongs to the past, to the time before the degree of maturity had made it possible for emptiness to be experienced.

To understand this it is necessary to think not of trauma but of nothing happening when something might profitably have happened.

It is easier for a patient to remember trauma than to remember nothing happening when it might have happened. At the time, the patient did not know what might have hap-pened, and so could not experience anything except to note that something might have been.

Example
A phase in a patient's treatment illustrates this. This young woman lay uselessly on the couch, and all she could do was to say: 'Nothing is happening in this analysis!'

[180]

At the stage that I am describing, the patient had supplied material of an indirect kind so that I could know that she was probably feeling something. I was able to say that she had been feeling feelings, and she had been experiencing these gradually fading, according to her pattern, a pattern which made her despair. The feelings were sexual and female. They did not show clinically.

Here in the transference was myself (nearly) being the cause now of her female sexuality fizzling out; when this was properly stated we had an example in the present of what had happened to her innumerable times. In her case (to simplify for the sake of description) there was a father who at first was scarcely ever present, and then when he came to her home when she was a little girl he did not want his daughter's female self, and had nothing to give by way of male stimulus.

Now, emptiness is a prerequisite for eagerness to gather in. Primary emptiness simply means: before starting to fill up. A considerable maturity is needed for this state to be meaningful.

Emptiness occurring in a treatment is a state that the patient is trying to experience, a past state that cannot be remembered except by being experienced for the first time now.

In practice, the difficulty is that the patient fears the awfulness of emptiness, and in defence will organize a controlled emptiness by not eating or not learning, or else will ruthlessly fill up by a greediness which is compulsive and which feels mad. When the patient can reach to emptiness itself and tolerate this state because of dependence on the auxiliary ego of the analyst, then, taking in can start up as a pleasurable function; here can begin eating that is not a function dissociated (or split-off) as part of the personality; also it is in this way that some of our patients who cannot learn can begin to learn pleasurably.

The basis of all learning (as well as of eating) is emptiness. But if emptiness was not experienced as such at the beginning, then it turns up as a state that is feared, yet compulsively sought after.

Non-existence
The search for personal non-existence can be examined in the

same way. It will be found that non-existence here is part of a defence. Personal existence is represented by the projection elements, and the person is making an attempt to project everything that could be personal. This can be a relatively sophisticated defence, and the aim is to avoid responsibility (at the depressive position) or to avoid persecution (at what I would call the stage of self-assertion, i.e., the stage of *I am* with the inherent implication *I repudiate everything that is not me*). It is convenient here to use in illustration the childhood game of 'I'm the King of the Castle – You're the Dirty Rascal'.

In the religions this idea can appear in the concept of oneness with God or with the Universe. It is possible to see this defence being negated in existentialist writings and teachings, in which existing is made into a cult, in an attempt to counter the personal tendency towards a non-existence that is part of an organized defence.

There can be a positive element in all this, that is, an element that is not a defence. It can be said that *only out of non-existence can existence start*. It is surprising how early (even before birth, certainly during the birth process) awareness of a premature ego can be mobilized. But the individual cannot develop from an ego root if this is divorced from psychosomatic experience and from primary narcissism. It is just here that begins the intellectualization of the ego-functions. It can be noted here that all this is a long distance in time prior to the establishment of anything that could usefully be called the self.

The psychoanalytic encounter: transference and countertransference

'Slouching towards Bethlehem. . .'
or thinking the unthinkable
in psychoanalysis

NINA E.C. COLTART

AFTER I HAD AGREED to write this paper, my mind went blank for quite a long time. Then I began to realize that a paper for a symposium whose overall title was 'Beyond Words' appropriately had to be generated in that very area, namely, where blankness seemed to be. After a while, the title for the paper announced itself. I was wary of it, since it seemed both eccentric and religious. But it stuck tenaciously. For those of you who do not know it, it is taken from a short poem by W.B. Yeats called 'The Second Coming'. It occurred to me when I re-read it closely that it is a poem about breakdown and the possibility of healing, or could be seen as such. It is mysterious, but then so is our subject. It goes like this (my italics):

> Turning and turning in the widening gyre
> The falcon cannot hear the falconer;
> Things fall apart; the centre cannot hold;
> Mere anarchy is loosed upon the world,
> The blood-dimmed tide is loosed, and everywhere

---

* This paper was first given as a contribution to the English-Speaking Conference of Psychoanalysts in 1982. The conference was in the form of a symposium, whose overall title was simply 'Beyond Words'. This expanded version of Nina Coltart's paper was given as one of the Freud Memorial Lectures at University College London, February 1985.

The ceremony of innocence is drowned;
The best lack all conviction, while the worst
Are full of passionate intensity.

Surely some revelation is at hand;
Surely the Second Coming is at hand.
The Second Coming! Hardly are those words out
When a vast image out of Spiritus Mundi
Troubles my sight: somewhere in the sands of the desert
A shape with lion body and the head of a man,
A gaze blank and pitiless as the sun,
Is moving its slow thighs, while all about it
Reel shadows of the indignant desert birds.
The darkness drops again; but now I know
That twenty centuries of stony sleep
Were vexed to nightmare by a rocking cradle,
And what rough beast, its hour come round at last,
Slouches towards Bethlehem to be born?

This is not a paper on religion. It does not look to Messianic
dogma, nor to Christian symbol to help us out of the anarchic
depths of the unconscious. What caught my attention was the
idea that there is a distinct metaphor for us in the poem which
speaks to the whole of what analysis is about. We can move the
metaphor of the poem from the religious to the analytical.
Some people have seen this as pessimistic; you will gather that
I have seen it differently.

It is of the essence of our impossible profession that in a very
singular way we do not know what we are doing. Do not be dis-
tracted by random associations to this idea. I am not undermining our deep, exacting training; nor discounting the ways in
which – unlike many people who master a subject and then just
do it, or teach it, – we have to keep *at* ourselves, our literature
and our clinical crosstalk with colleagues. All these daily oper-
ations are the efficient, skilful, and thinkable tools with which
we constantly approach the heart of our work, which is a mystery.

The day that one qualifies as an analyst, the analyst that one
is *going to be* is a mystery. Ten years later, we may just about be

able to look back and discern the shape of the rough beast – ourselves as analysts in embryo – as it slouched along under the months and years until, its hour come round at last, there is some clearer sense of ourselves as analysts. The process of doing analysis has slowly given birth to an identity which we now more or less recognize as an analyst, or at least the identity which we have become, and are still becoming, which for us approximates to the notion of 'being an analyst'. This may be very different from that which we long ago had visualized or hoped for.

It is my belief that something very similar obtains also for our work with our patients. However much we gain confidence, refine our technique, decide more creatively when and how and what to interpret, each hour with each patient is also in its way an act of faith; faith in ourselves, in the process, and faith in the secret, unknown, *unthinkable* things in our patients which, in the space which is the analysis, are slouching towards the time when their hour comes round at last. When that hour comes, by dint of all our long, thoughtful, interpretative attempts to familiarize ourselves with the patient's inner world, we begin to see shaping up things that we may have guessed at; or predicted, or theoretically constructed or relied on; or even, almost like by-products of months of careful, steady work, things that take us by surprise. We have been waiting attentively, in Freud's own words, 'for the pattern to emerge'. Those of us who were fortunate enough to be taught by the late Dr Bion value the stress which he laid on the need to develop the ability to tolerate not knowing, the capacity to sit it out with a patient, often for long periods, without any real precision as to where we are, relying on our regular tools and our faith in the process, to carry us through the obfuscating darkness of resistance, complex defences, and the sheer *unconsciousness* of the unconscious.

In parenthesis, there is a possible solution or definition here of that controversial problem, the difference between psychotherapy and psychoanalysis. Although I am currently stressing our ignorance, *there is* always something going on that we more or less *know* something about; the daily *tabula*

[187]

rasa of the analytic session produces a mass of information; and for a patient who comes once or twice a week, it may well be constructive and ego-supportive to get on to a track indicated by one of these signposts. In analysis we can afford to ignore them, in the slow, attentive working towards a deeper nexus of feeling, fantasy, and wordless experience, that is slouching along in an as yet unthinkable form. Clues we note and store away, but need not, often must not, hear them as distracting sirens' songs to be fallen for and followed.

I want to say something more here about the act of faith. It is to do with Wilfred Bion. I have to confess that at the time that I wrote my short paragraph above about being taught by Bion, it was pretty well a summary of what I knew about him. Of course, I knew that he had invented a Grid and I had never talked to anyone who could make real sense of it. But since writing my original paper, I felt a strong urge to read all the works of Bion, and have done so. I was both delighted and horrified by what I found. Delighted because some of it expressed so clearly some of my own ideas; horrified because it began to look as though I had been plagiarizing. But I do not think I can have been. I have concluded that, apart from perhaps being more influenced by the few seminars that I had with him than I realized, we had simply developed individually along similar lines *in some ways*. I stress this because I do not wish time or imaginative conjecture to be wasted in thinking that I am seriously comparing myself to any extent with him. Wilfred Bion was a widely cultured man and I think probably a mystic and a genius. Certain clues in his writings suggest that, in the most modest and dispassionate way, he thought the same. And I am not. Also he did invent that Grid, and he constantly refers to it, and even now that I have read him word for word, it makes little sense to me, and I cannot use it. This may be because Bion was, amongst other things, mathematically minded, and I am innumerate.

To return to the act of faith. Bion *uses* this phrase and by it intends to signify the most highly desirable stance of the psychoanalyst. He says that the act of faith is peculiar to scientific procedure and must be distinguished from the religious meaning with which it is invested in common usage. The essence of its creation – and Bion sees it, as do I, as a positive, willed act – is refraining from memory and desire, a phrase which many people *do* loosely associate with what they know of Bion. He says in *Attention and Interpretation* (1970, p. 30): 'It may be wondered what state of mind is welcome if desires and memories are not. A term that would express approximately what I need to express is "faith" – faith that there is an ultimate reality and truth – the unknown, unknowable, "formless infinite",' which can become at least partly known through evolution into objects of which the individual personality can become aware. The channel for this evolution and the transformation of the apprehension of the ultimate reality, or a bit of it, is the analyst's direct attention and perception, and his capacity to bring together hitherto meaningless fragments of the patient's mental and verbal elements into a thinking process, and communicate this back to the patient.

Bion says that this form of attention, this act of faith, must be what he calls 'unstained by any elements of memory or desire or sensation'. He means in the analyst, of course. 'The more the psycho-analyst occupies himself with memory and desire the more his facility for harbouring them increases and the nearer he comes to undermining his capacity for F [the act of faith]. For consider: if his mind is preoccupied with what is or is not said, or with what he does or does not hope, it must mean that he cannot allow the experience to obtrude. . . , (1970, p. 41). No-one who learns to denude himself of memory and desire, he goes on to say, and of all those elements of sense impression ordinarily present, can have any doubt of the reality of psychoanalytical experience which remains ineffable. It will be seen that Bion has intuition very high in his hierarchy of the tools at our disposal, and is advocating a constant sternly self-disciplined practice. Indeed, at one point, he actually equates intuition with 'analytic observations'.

It must be emphasized, however, in case it is not clear enough already, that Bion is not advocating random speculative commentary unrooted in a huge reservoir of experience, thought, theoretical knowledge, and the capacity to draw upon and correlate all these in the intervals *between* the dark experiencing of the act of faith, and in the interests of making the *evolution* of the total experience comprehensively available to the patient. The philosopher Immanuel Kant said: 'Intuition without concept is blind: concept without intuition is empty.' It seems to me that Bion, and I in my way in this paper, are striving for the merging of the two.

Before I move on from this section on Bion's thought, I just want to quote from a question-answer seminar recorded when Bion was in São Paulo in 1973. It says with such simplicity so much that elsewhere in his writings Bion goes over repetitively at length and in a complex way; the questioner asks: 'How did you come to realize the advantages of suppressing memory and desire during an analytic session?' and Bion replies: 'I found I could experience a flash of the obvious. One is usually so busy looking for something out of the ordinary that one ignores the obvious as if it were of no importance.' Whereas, again in *Attention and Interpretation*, he says, unhelpfully if challengingly, 'There can be no *rules* about the nature of the emotional experience that will show that it is ripe for interpretation.' Here I would add that faith and self-reliance are indeed needed!

The crucial thing about our technical development is that it hinges on a paradox. There is a delicate balance between our reliance on our theories and on our knowledge of human nature in many of its dimensions – (and experience tells us that human nature continually reveals similar patterns which generates good theory) – the balance, I repeat, is between this *reliance*, and our willingness to be continually open to the emergence of the unexpected. *Plus ça change, plus c'est la même chose* may be a good truism for analysts; but it is only true in a restricted sense; it is the changes that are rung that are the essentials of individual humanity. There is a grim stage when we are *learning to be* analysts when we are endangered by our own templates, our theories, and our teachers. We may detect the faint shuffle of the slouching beast, and be tempted to throw a set of grappling irons into the darkness, seize him, label him, hang him round with words, and haul him prematurely to birth. We may then often be stuck with a deformed monster that we have largely created by our own precipitate verbosity; we may then proceed laboriously onwards with a sort of analytic mistake, while the true creature who is not yet ready for the light of day retreats backwards into the darkness again.

The use of the metaphor of the poem here says what I want to say, but perhaps I should explain it a little, and less poetically. The seductive impulse to use the power of one's thinking and theorizing to take possession of the patient too soon can be great, but will, as suggested, be of little ultimate value to him. Precipitate control of the material may lead to a sense of satisfaction in the analyst, and often to quite conscious layers of the patient, whose resistance to exposing his true unknown reality to the light will have been served by it.

Heisenberg's Uncertainty Principle is a hard taskmaster in the everyday life of the consulting room; it seems to me undesirable that one should communicate certainty about a patient to a patient, or, at least, only very occasionally. The whole of our subject, psychoanalysis, can be, and often is, attacked on the grounds that it is unscientific and cannot be supported by any scientific evidence. The most that can be claimed for it is that it is *probable*, and what we use is not rigorous scientific investigation, but the act of faith, supported by rational and imaginative conjectures, themselves inevitably conditioned by our learning and our experience. The act of faith may feel like a spontaneous regression to complete unknowing, and may well be accompanied by dread; it can be disturbing to the analyst and seem like a serious self-induced attack on his ego, which in a way it is. To quote Bion again, with particular reference to trying to capture the rough beast too soon: 'Such depths of ignorance are difficult to dare to contemplate, though I am bound to feel a wish to believe how Godlike I am, how intelligent, as a change from being appalled by my ignorance.' But it may be at the expense of the *true* pattern emerging that we do this.

I am sure I am not saying anything heretical or unfamiliar to analysts at least, if I confess that I sometimes wish ardently, as I settle down for the opening sessions of what promises to be a long analysis, that the first year were already over. This is part of the paradoxical nature of our work. I would not for the world pass up that first year with all its subtle demands on the technique of getting the patient rooted in the analysis, feeling for the available transferences, learning history, and doing first aid, which is often so necessary when things have fallen apart and anarchy has been loosed upon the world.

But after this preliminary work, there comes a time which is exhilarating, when the pace quickens and the gears change. Paradoxically again, this is often the time when darkness begins to close in, but it is a darkness having that special quality of the unknown which is moving towards being known. Freud was speaking of a time like this, I imagine, when he said that sometimes he had to 'blind himself in order to focus on the light in one dark spot'. There is a textural richness which begins to draw deeper analysis out of one's own darkness, and stretch oneself towards the limit of ingenuity, technique, and a rapid use of identifications and intuition, combined with imaginative intensity. During phases like this in analysis it is true to say that one does not *think* at all during some sessions, at least in the ordinary cognitive use of the word. Indeed, one of the most satisfying elements about entering the stage of doing an analysis when the anxiety of the early years is left behind and senility has not yet come, is this freedom from actually thinking while one is actively engaged in working; i.e., when the act of faith is becoming easier. Of course, to say this is not to detract from the high value attaching to the power of attention and total concern with the patient. In fact there is plenty of evidence, not only in our literature, but in that of philosophy and religion, that the attention is more total when temporarily freed from concurrent cognitive processes. This switch into fifth gear cannot exactly be legislated for, although Bion's advice that we should rigorously practise for it is relevant, and it does not by any means always happen. Then we fall back again on thinking, and theorizing, and trying things out in our heads, or just waiting. But in the fifth gear phases, when the act of faith is most fully deployed, when our listening ear seems to be directly connected with our tongue and speech, interpretative dialogue is not a process which I would regard as being under everyday conscious control. Fascinating data derived from bio-feedback experiments show that the nature of the brainwaves actually changes in the states to which I am referring and predominantly alpha rhythm on the EEG takes over from normal waking mixed beta and theta waves. When I gave this paper to the English-speaking Conference, one of the analysts in the discussion took up what I have just said and asked me rather peevishly what I meant by saying that this was fascinating. I fear I was unable to answer satisfactorily. I had myself participated in bio-feedback experiments and had learned to alter my brainwaves, blood pressure and skin resistance. If the phenomenon I have just described is not self-evidently fascinating, then we are on different wavelengths and I cannot justify the use of such a personalized word.

Certain recurring problems in analytic work give valuable encouragement to our reliance on the process that I have just attempted to describe. These are problems which may be rather specially regarded as falling into the arena entitled Beyond Words. One of them is silence. Any silence of more than about 40 minutes in analysis begins to have its own peculiar interest. But there is a very particular challenge issued by profoundly silent patients, who are often, by the way, not diagnosable as such during a careful assessment interview. I make this point because it indicates that profound silence itself, as well as what it conceals, can be a rough beast which is slouching along in the depths of a communicative, articulate patient and whose time may need to come round and *be endured* in the analysis.

I have treated eleven patients in 25 years who have been deeply silent for long periods during the analysis. One for nearly a year, several for months or weeks.

One of these was a man who was in his mid-50s when he started treatment with the complaint of near-suicidal depression. He was unmarried, sexually virginal, powerful, charismatic, and a successful captain of industry. He was not, I decided in the first year, a False Self personality, nor was he, apparently, homosexual or perverse. He had a huge number of acquaintances, but no really close friends. He was a clubbable man. The very fact of starting analysis, and that he had never really talked deeply to anyone about himself, meant that in his case the first couple of years were full of interchange and improvement. But I was suspicious that something else was gathering its forces in the depths of his inner world. He slowly made an eroticized transference, and was somewhat elated for months. I could not exactly predict what the shape of the beast was going to be, but that there was something completely different that had to emerge in time if the analysis was going to work, I did not doubt. He had come to me with his centre not holding, and with things falling apart; and the initial improvement had not truly touched that. In his third year, he suddenly ground to a halt, and fell violently silent, exuding ever-stronger black waves of hatred and despair. I slowly tried out the various technical manoeuvres that I had learned over the years for approaching and entering silence. To no avail. The change in him from late midlife crisis neurosis to something which breathed psychosis was heavy in the atmosphere. He never failed to attend, but his body movements and even his shape seemed to have altered. Very close attention to these things is of the essence when faced with such a massive Beyond Words challenge. He slouched and humped himself grimly and disjointedly up and down my stairs and in and out of my room. His gaze, when he glanced at me, was shifty, evil, and terrified. He was as if possessed. When I spoke about what I saw and felt, he glowered, grunted and sank further into an ungainly heap. He had never wanted to lie on the couch, so all this was face-to-face. I carried dark and heavy projective identifications, to put it one way, which I tried in vain to decode to him, until I was almost as saturated in despair as he was.

One day, without really thinking it out clearly, I suddenly demonstrated an example of what Neville Symington in a recent paper has called the analyst's act of freedom [*this volume – Ed.*]. I simply and suddenly became furious and bawled him out for his prolonged lethal attack on me and on the analysis. I wasn't going to stand for it a second longer, I shouted, without the remotest idea *at that moment* of what alternative I was proposing! This outburst of mine changed the course of the analysis.

It was only in the subsequent interpretative understanding of that parameter, as my outburst would be called, and of the preceding black months, that we came to see how much, to his own surprise and horror, this man had needed to live out, and have *experienced and endured by another person without retaliation*, his primary hatred of a genuinely powerful mother. He had, so to speak, lost her to his only brother who was born when he was eleven months old, and he had been required by her throughout his life to love and revere her unstintingly. He had solved this first great problem of his life by remaining unswervingly loyal to her and it had nearly cost *him* his life. You will see that the act of freedom arose from the exercise of an act of faith. I had given up trying to 'understand' this patient, given up theorizing and just sat there day after day without memory or desire in a state of suspension, attending only with an empty mind to him and the unknowable truth of himself, which had shaped his life, until such a moment as I was so *at one* with it that I *knew it* for the murderous hatred it was, and had to make a jump for freedom – his as well as mine, though I did not think that out at the time – by shouting. These acts of faith can feel dangerous.

I would like to speak briefly here for a moment of another thing that is often, I have the distinct impression, felt to be dangerous in psychoanalysis, albeit in a different way from the encounter with murderous hatred via the act of faith. This is laughing. You hardly ever hear analysts talk about laughing in sessions, and you do not find papers written about it either. Again I return to Bion for a comment though he nowhere has developed it as much as I could have wished. In one of his São Paulo seminars (Bion, 1980), he is talking about how psychoanalysis has changed and developed; he wonders would Freud even understand what some of us are doing now? Then, apparently at random, he goes straight on to say:

[195]

I wonder if it is within the rules of psychoanalysis to be able to laugh at ourselves? Is it according to the rules of psychoanalysis that we should be amused and find things funny? Is it permissible to enjoy a psychoanalytic meeting? I suggest that, having broken through in this revolutionary matter of being amused in the sacred progress of psychoanalysis, we might as well continue to see where that more joyous state of mind might take us. (pp. 94-5)

Then, rather maddeningly, but very characteristically, he says no more about this explicitly, but I think it is significant that he goes straight into a short passage which ends like this:

... I sometimes think analysts are sunk in gloom; so much so that they are often taken by surprise when they discover that there is such a thing as mental pain. One feels that they have only learned that there is a *theory* that there is mental pain, but that they don't believe it exists, or that psychoanalysis is a method of treating it. So when a patient gets better they are surprised. They do not believe it has any-thing to do with the work they are doing; but if we are to go on growing and developing, I believe that the psychoanalyt-ical procedure does a great deal to help that development to take place. Psychoanalysis helps the spirit or the soul . . . to continue; we can help the soul or the psyche to be *born* even, and help it to continue to develop after it is born.

Now the immediate juxtaposition of those two passages makes me think that implicit in the second passage is the message of the first; to put it very simply, that laughter and enjoyment can be therapeutic factors in psychoanalysis. Certainly I believe that one not only can but should enjoy psychoanalytical sessions.

I once thought about writing a paper on laughing in psychoanalysis and perhaps this is the nearest I shall get. I sup-pose there is a fear that I may be deluding myself, and not notic-ing that what it really means is that my technique has got sloppy, or that I have developed a special sort of defence, or both, or many more horrendous things, but certainly with advancing age laughter in sessions seems to occur more often than it did. Of course, it is important to try to continue to analyse and monitor what is happening. I remember that when I was still training, I started to treat a patient in what had to be called five-times-a-week psychotherapy, because I was not yet an analyst. He was not one of my Clinic training cases. He was a man who could make people laugh. He was quite ill, but he was really extremely amusing. I was so serious about my training and what I thought were the sacred rules of psychoanalysis that I used to use a lot of energy trying not to laugh. Of course I analysed the aggression in his jokes, and there was plenty of it, and what was defensive, distracting and seductive about it all. And so I would now. But I also think now that I would laugh first if I felt like it. I am now of the opinion that I deprived both him and me unnecessarily by being so prim. I think I might have got nearer to some true shape or pattern in him *faster*, by responding with a natural reaction and *then* talking about it. If we are too protective of our self-presentation and of what we consider grimly to be the sacred rules of True Psychoanalysis, then we may suffocate something in the patient, in ourselves, and in the process.

Another category of patients who present one with specific Beyond Words problems are those with psychosomatic symptoms. In this I include, of course, the fairly straightforward, pure, and now relatively rare hysterical conversions. The overlap between these and some psychosomatic symptoms of different aetiology can be extending and confusing. For example, I have had the opportunity to treat five cases of asthma of late onset in adults, two in analysis, and three in focal analytic psychotherapy. They could not exactly be classified as hysterics, because I believe hysterical symptoms are rooted in a pathological disablement of the will, while willing and breathing, which is what goes wrong in asthma, do not connect up properly in a psychological sense, i.e., we do not breathe at will. A paralysed limb where the voluntary muscles cease to work hysterically is a different matter. But they were certainly conveying a message of conflict through their asthma attacks, and this *is* what hysterics do. They were also threatening life itself, and two of them very nearly did die in status asthmaticus. If I were to condense into one sentence what the hidden central dynamic was, I would say it was pre-verbal never-thinkable, never-expressible rage with the mother, rooted in a period before the attainment of the depressive position. In silence, eventually, I had to experience this rage directly myself as raged at, before being able to evolve this shape into suitable words.

The special interest of psychosomatic symptoms, to pick up the main metaphor of this paper, is that the rough beast whose hour is not yet come is holed up in the body. There is a lovely quotation from the poet John Donne which refers to the non-pathological aspect of this:

> The blood spoke in her cheek,
> as if her body thought.

The beast has crossed that mysterious barrier whose location eludes us, and moved over into a stronghold from which it is only on rare occasions easy to deliver him. Mostly, he seems inaccessible, and we perceive that part of the mind has lodged on a psychotic island in the body. This image arises from a paper by Herbert Rosenfeld (1985), which sheds light on the treatment of women who not infrequently select the uterus as their psychotic island. We could say that a psychosomatic symptom represents that which is determined to remain unconscious, or unknowable, but which at the same time has actually made itself conscious in a very heavy disguise; it is speakable about only in a dense and enigmatic code. In terms of the metaphor of my paper, we have to ask what is the unthinkable content slouching along in the darkness of the psychosomatic symptom? How do we build a bridge which *really holds* over the secret area of the body-mind divide? Can the unthinkable become thinkable? Can we possibly devise words which have enough compatibility with the physical track chosen by the mind, so that we can send some sort of message down back along that same track via the body to the mind? By ordinary, careful analysis laced with inspiration one may at length interpret the psychosomatic symptom so irresistibly that it yields. A rush of new affects may appear. The now more verbal material may be enriched by new-old memories. Or the symptom may just quietly fade away. Nevertheless, there is a certain mystery which we do well not to ignore. It would be unwise to conclude that because we have apparently cured a genuine psychosomatic symptom by dynamic interpretation we actually *know* how it was *done*. We may be able to derive further theory from it. We may even be able to repeat the performance with another patient with a similar problem. But we do not quite know how it was done. Where and how did our laboriously evolved words and thoughts meet and capture the resolutely unthinkable beast in the unconscious process?

There is a way of visualizing analysis as a spiral process. The seemingly same ground is ploughed over and over again. And yet there is always something new about it. I refer to this spiral effect here because it has a special relevance to our work with psychosomatic symptoms. We may have undermined such a symptom to the point of its yielding. The patient may be in completely different territory, a long way up the spiral. Suddenly the symptom returns. It requires investigation all over again. The original understanding does not influence it in the same way. The mind is so protean that it can colonize the body in a new spirit and skilfully enlist the symptom under a new banner in the ongoing war of resistance in the transference.

Perhaps I may end here by saying that patients with such symptoms, and silent patients, teach us most vividly and memorably that there is always in our work a dimension that is beyond words. Some people *suffer* more from the unthinkable than others, and for these we have to do all in our power to help towards the therapeutic transformation, to bring thoughts to the unthinkable and words to the inexpressible. Gradually the rough beast may, within the framework of the analytic relationship, slouch towards being born, and the new creature emerging from the birth is the increased happiness and peace of mind of the patient. But in all of us there are some things which will never be within our reach; there is always a mystery at the heart of every person, and therefore in our job as analysts.

Elements of the psychoanalytic relationship and their therapeutic implications

JOHN KLAUBER

CONFIDENCE IN the therapeutic success of the analytic method tempts analysts to overlook some of the strains it imposes on both patient and analyst. The development of transference is always traumatic for the patient, as is the longing for relationship with the analyst as a result of their intimacy. The development of psychoanalytic objectivity and distance, which have to be combined with ready empathy, are similarly an arduous task for the analyst. The period of depression which the analyst must endure before he acquires his skill is described, with its accompanying danger of the prolonged dependence of the psychoanalyst on his own training analyst.

The most neglected feature of the psychoanalytic relationship still seems to me to be that it is a relationship: a very peculiar relationship, but a definite one. Patient and analyst need one another. The patient comes to the analyst because of internal conflicts that prevent him from enjoying life, and he begins to use the analyst not only to resolve them, but increasingly as a receptacle for his pent-up feelings. But the analyst also needs the patient in order to crystallize and communicate his own thoughts, including some of his inmost thoughts on intimate human problems which can only grow organically in the con-

[200]

text of this relationship. They cannot be shared and experienced in the same immediate way with a colleague, or even with a husband or wife. It is also in his relationship with his patients that the analyst refreshes his own analysis. It is from this mutual participation in analytic understanding that the patient derives the substantial part of his cure and the analyst his deepest confidence and satisfaction.

The evolution of the theory of technique might be thought of as a gradual victory, but only a partial victory, for the recognition of the relationship. This clearly had its reasons as it was liable to get out of hand in the early days when wild analysis was a danger, as it still does occasionally today. And the technique of interpreting unconscious impulses aggravated resistance, resulting in the sort of sexual battle that Freud described (1915d) in his 'Observations on Transference-Love'. In his last clinical paper (Freud, 1937a) he was struggling similarly with the problem of the negative transference, protesting that the hostility of a former pupil was nowhere to be seen at the time of his analysis. The path to an approach which is less threatened by the patient's feelings was opened gradually between 1928 and 1950 by Wilhelm Reich (1928, 1945), Anna Freud (1936), Melanie Klein (1948), with her concentration on the interplay of object-relationship and character formation and the subtleties of the transference, by Winnicott (1949) and Paula Heimann (1950) with their utilization of the countertransference, and Hartmann (1950a) who began to map an area of functioning outside the 'seething cauldron' of the impulse life. All this supplemented the libido theory, which was too stiff on its own for an adequate description of the affective life, with a series of articulations which would make it more acceptable to the patient and ease the atmosphere of the consulting room. The way was open for an easier discussion of the actual relationship, exemplified by such contributors as Nacht (1957), with his stress on the analyst's 'presence' and Greenson (1974), who regards the analyst's capacity for loving his patient as essential equipment for his job. However, there remains little description of what actually happens between

[201]

patient and analyst except in transference/countertransference terms or any details of the strains imposed on the analyst by fulfilling his obligations.

The strength of the emotions generated in the psychoanalytical relationship is in fact played down. According to a personal communication by Willi Hoffer there was a time when many analysts wore white coats, no doubt to protect themselves. The ubiquity of acting out, to which Limentani (1966) drew attention, provides evidence that tensions which are temporarily unmasterable are regularly generated in the course of analysis. In 1972 I suggested that there was an element of a tease in psychoanalytic therapy since emotions are constantly aroused which the analyst will never satisfy. The patient has to be content with an interpretation instead, and I thought that the capacity to use analysis might be connected with the capacity to cathect the analyst's interpretations, which all patients libidinize, instead of his person. There seems to be little discussion of the possible long-term vicissitudes of the patient's longings and of the question of how far our techniques of analysis of the terminal transference, so far as we can judge them, actually stand up to the hopes that we place in them. It is strange, too, that there seems to be no discussion of the effects on the analyst of forming relationship after relationship of the deepest and most intimate kind with patient after patient, and the mourning which at some level must be involved for each one of them.

Clinical theory and the physical arrangements in the consulting room are designed to protect analyst and patient from these problems. On the whole they are very successful, but I think that the conduct of analysis could often be improved if certain neglected problems were recognized. I should therefore like to consider the nature of the analytical relationship in more detail.

The psychoanalytic relationship consists partly in the replacement of an object-relationship by a mutual identification, or rather by identification supplemented by an attenuated ('aim-inhibited') object-relationship. The nature of the identification is different, however, on the two sides.

[202]

The actual operation of these processes remains somewhat mysterious, but an attempt may be made to conceptualize them as follows. The patient withdraws his unsublimated instinctual energies from the analyst as a person, but cathects him increasingly with them as a fantasy object. His instinctual desires for the analyst of fantasy are reduced, or even neutralized, by interpretations elucidating the archaic origins of his fantasies. The extent to which the ego's functioning can remain autonomous against the massive stimulation of fantasy in the transference and retain a realistic picture of the analyst, and the means by which it does so, are not well clarified. This was clearly the area with which Freud was struggling in 1915 when he decided that the patient's love for the analyst was 'genuine' and compared the dangers of the analyst's position with a seductive patient to that of the pastor who visited the dying insurance agent: the insurance agent was not converted but the pastor left the house insured. On the other hand, the patient's ego clearly makes an affective relationship with the analyst as a person and forms an identification with the therapeutically orientated aspects of the analyst's ego. This identification lasts him in favourable cases for the rest of his life, while the unsublimated aspects of the transference are analysed away during the treatment. This theory implies that the distortion of the person of the analyst by fantasy has been too unrealistic to last and that the patient's passion for truth, his *amor intellectualis*, has been great enough to result in the formation of a powerful new analytic ego and ego-ideal. The fact that the formation of an ego-ideal normally depends on object loss suggests that this is also an area of theory in need of further clarification. Freud was never tired of repeating, however, that there were patients who were not amenable to this transformation; for them only the logic of soup and the argument of dumplings had any effect. One may legitimately wonder whether a great many patients do not fall into an intermediate class between these two extremes.

The analyst does not cathect the patient as a fantasy object in the same way. Occasionally he makes a transference to the patient, typically as a response to the patient's transference, but

[203]

this is quickly brought under control by his own continuing state of spontaneous self-analysis (Gitelson, 1952). The analyst has to identify with his patient's mental and emotional processes in order to achieve empathy, but the identification involved in empathy is not enough. It is too transient and too uncontrolled. In order to achieve continued and deeper understanding, he must not only empathize with his patients but scrutinize their mental processes critically, continually testing the empathetic identifications which he holds inside him with his intellect and with the affects which finally determine his judgement. That is, he must hold the patient inside himself cathected with just the right degree of ambivalence, absorbing some parts of the image into himself and holding others at a distance. Any object-relationship which he forms with the patient will be on a highly sublimated level, any instinctual expression being subjected to considerable modification through the analyst's absorbing preoccupation with the patient as an inner object. The conditions under which he maintains this preoccupation are not the easiest. Into the isolated, physically immobile life of the analyst come a succession of intelligent, mostly personable younger people who bring with them the breath of many different lives. They share with him their deepest feelings, as well as feeding into him considerable instinctual stimulation by the stories they tell, by their appearance, their voices and their smell. On the whole, analysts manage this situation well, but considerable instinctual inhibition is involved. It is perhaps not surprising that their repressed object-relationship occasionally overflows into massive identification, as when they embrace a patient's point of view (for instance of a marriage) or even – occasionally – introject his symptoms.

In order to attain and maintain this high achievement, however, measures have to be taken the drastic nature of which is overlooked. The usual psychoanalytic arrangement of chair and couch abrogates the characteristic cue for human responses. The infant at the breast fixes his eyes on his mother's eyes as he feeds, and the human adult makes love face to face, and not *more ferarum*, 'in the manner of the animals'. For the most intimate and prolonged exchange of secret thoughts that humans have devised the patient is prevented from seeing the analyst's face, while the analyst sees only the back of the patient's head or perhaps the rear side of his face. Sometimes he sits where he can see the patient's eyelids or sclera, thus (among his other reasons for it) allowing himself a small piece of reassurance of which the patient is deprived unless he turns round. The reciprocity of normal human response is also abrogated in other ways. The patient lies down, normally on his back, while the analyst sits. The analyst addresses the patient, or half addresses him; the patient addresses the analyst via the air. The intimacy of the relationship is being offset – perhaps as a necessary precaution – by a set-up perpetuating the authoritarianism and perhaps the magical aura of the nineteenth century hypnotist. It receives its theoretical justification in the rather Helmholtzian notion that, by turning away from the stimulus of the analyst's appearance, the patient is freed from the pull of reality and can produce the derivatives of his unconscious mental processes in less distorted form. There are practical experiences which correspond to this. The use of the couch does facilitate regression and free association in the most neurotic patients. (I will give a more detailed explanation of the mechanism whereby it does so, later.)

It will be more convenient at this point, however, to draw attention to some possible effects of these arrangements on the analyst, in addition to the privacy of thought which they secure him. If the effect of turning away from the analyst is so momentous for the patient, what is the effect of turning away from the patient on the analyst? How does the analyst accommodate himself to being without the basic cue of human expression for ten hours, 200 hundred days a year? Does it impose a strain on him? If so, what is its nature and what means are available for him to alleviate it? I will return to this later. But first I would like to sketch out some aspects of the analytical relationship in more detail. I hope it will not be thought that I exaggerate the difficulties. If I do, I believe that I err in the right direction because I think that they require more open consideration than they receive.

I should like to start with a description of the position of the newly qualified psychoanalyst. This description may not apply with the same force to those who have practised psychotherapy for many years in a psychoanalytically orientated institution as to those who come fresh to more or less full-time analytic work after being students. The newly qualified analyst is confronted by quite severe object loss. First, he probably loses his analyst, and this at a time when analytical support might be very useful to him. Next, he loses the object relations of his daily working life if he gives up his previous career completely, or at any rate a good many of them – the undervalued but important exchanges which do so much to give us the sense of belonging to a community. Above all, his instinctive desire to form object-relationships with his patients is frustrated, lying at the root, perhaps, of much countertransference difficulty until he can accommodate himself to the psychoanalytic way of life. All this may be obscured to some extent and for a time by the relief of qualifying and the excitement of starting his longed-for career. What will not be obscured is the sense of loss of an ego: the intellectual task of following the evolution of unconscious themes in his patients' words and behaviour, relating them to an effective notation and considering them in such a way as to be able to produce a spontaneous and more or less effortless interpretation, is immensely difficult. When it is achieved, it restores the sense of reality to the analyst's ego. Many analysts admit, however, that it took them many years to feel themselves to be analysts and to be able to accept most patients who were recommended, without experiencing some degree of anxiety and guilt. The analyst's professional role is thus for a long time alienated from his full sense of identity. In this plight he must cathect the inner representations of his teachers, first of his analyst, then of the idealized image of the great man or woman who represents authority to him. This feeling of therapeutic inadequacy might be called the depressive position of the newly qualified analyst. The great figures will have a tendency to operate in him as introjects, he will look for opportunities to apply their formulations rather than his own, and he may even find himself occasionally mouthing bad interpretations from the book twenty years later.

To sum up, it will be seen that I regard the beginning of psychoanalytic practice as involving, in addition to its satisfactions, a depressive experience as a result of object loss and separation between the ego and the ego-ideal, against which the analyst tries to defend himself by introjection. Of course, he also defends himself by seeking new teachers in the external world and discussing cases with his colleagues in seminars. I do not think that he can entirely escape the effects of having to relate to patients as internal objects rather than external objects in this way, however. And while he clearly needs support and further education, there may come a danger point at which the search for his own originality and authority becomes submerged by further introjections. This way also lies the danger of idealization of ambivalently cathected leaders, which may overwhelm individual judgment.

If beginning the practice of analysis holds these strains for the analyst, what strains does beginning analysis hold for the patient? To my mind, though it may be heavily concealed by improvement, beginning analysis must be described as a trauma for the patient.

The essence of a traumatic situation, according to Freud, is 'an experience of helplessness on the part of the ego in the face of accumulation of excitation whether of external or internal origin' (1926b), and also 'a breach in an otherwise efficacious barrier against stimuli' (1920a). The barrier that is breached in analysis is, of course, the barrier against the excitation of unconscious fantasy and unconscious memory. The psychoanalytic arrangements are designed to effect this breach for therapeutic purposes. I should say at once that the arrangements and interpretation are also designed to contain the trauma and reduce it from the start. I believe, however, that our confidence in our therapeutic efficiency and the quickening of object-relationship that characterizes the start of a new analysis induce in us a tendency to underrate the drastic nature of what we do.

The patient is asked to sacrifice the reassurance of his previous contact with the analyst, eye to eye, ego to ego. The reason why patients are often, or perhaps always, afraid to lie on the couch is that they understand one of its essential meanings. This is the loosening of the grip of their ego on reality at the very time when enormous intrapsychic demands are imposed on its synthetic function under the influence of a powerful new object-relationship. The abrogation of response by the analyst is compounded by the withholding of a great many normal comments and answers to questions. The patient is thus, so to speak, dropped by the analyst from the point of view of the role that he exercised at the consultation as a member of the externally real, holding environment. The patient who has been 'dropped' in this way has to clutch at a new object-relationship, in the first instance hypercathecting the analyst's words. He is reassured by the genuine object cathexis which he feels from the analyst, but a split has occurred in his ego. The experience of being dropped from the analyst's holding environment to being held by the Word alone results in the analyst's being jet-propelled in the patient's mind into magical status. The patient's new, intensified object-relationship with the analyst becomes steadily more invested with fantasy. Transference phenomena begin to occur. The realistic ego which operates with energies further removed than the fantasies from their instinctual sources, and which makes a realistic relationship with the analyst, is rendered less potent. It is confronted by strange, involuntary thoughts which it tends to repudiate. The patient has begun to enter the world of waking dreams. These dreams take over, or partially take over, in the consulting room, and sometimes outside it, for several years. What the development of the transference has shown is the power of analysis, aided by the couch/chair arrangement, to remobilize the past traumatic introjections which the patient can now no longer contain. He has to rely on a stranger to help him with his problems and, sensing their complexity, he may rightly apprehend that the stranger, whatever his capacity to respond, will fail to understand him adequately in some important areas with which he will have to struggle on his own after the analysis is over. His confidence in his power to continue his own analysis may have been diminished by an assault on the ego, of whose dangers Ernst Kris (1956b) was well aware: the sudden release of repressed memories, to which might be added the effect of wonderful interpretations and sometimes of interpretations which speak too quickly of the patient's aggression rather than of the anxieties behind it. All this aggravates the trauma, and it seems justified to conclude from the recognized phenomenon of the honeymoon period, that the patient instinctively copes with it by employing manic defences.

Of course, the therapeutic action of psychoanalysis starts immediately. In spite of his anxieties, the patient will usually feel enormously reassured by the analyst's ability to demonstrate his capacity to accept and understand his feelings in a way which is a totally new experience for him.

The problem is: to what extent can interpretation resolve the developing wishes directed at the amalgam of the analyst as a real and fantasy object? According to the classical theory only pregenital impulses could be sublimated, though this is now generally doubted. The nature of the capacity for sublimation is clearly relevant, however, to the question of what elements of the transference can reasonably be expected to be resolved. Freud recognized that there was a problem in this area when he referred to the fact that in some respects the patient's love was 'genuine', that is, presumably that it included an element which could not simply be analysed away. The question of how far analysis in fact leaves the patient to struggle with these residual feelings, in spite of our efforts to resolve them, is clearly important for the patient's development in the lifetime that should await him undisturbed after he has left the analyst's room for the last time. If he is left with unreciprocated love and unresolved hostility then this is a difficulty of the psychoanalytic procedure which must be examined.

The residual bond (to which the analyst always responds in some way) is most clearly seen in training analysis. Freud, still rather naïve about transference matters, regarded the bond that springs up between the candidate and his analyst as 'not least' of the gains of analysis. Perhaps we are now entitled to be more suspicious that a prolonged dependency of thought may also sometimes arise. Although a similar bond is less easy to observe in former patients who are not analysts, we may suspect that it remains strong in some of them – those patients, for instance, who, in spite of the gains of analysis, still lead unsatisfying lives; in some depressed patients; and patients whose lives have been dramatically changed by analysis. It has remained strong in those patients who, in spite of their ambivalence, return to the same analyst in an attempt to put things right between them, and in those patients who move over a period of twenty years from one analyst to another. Two other phenomena, or possible phenomena, may also give rise to thought. One is that it seems to be not uncommon for patients to harbour resentment against their former analysts. There must, of course, be many explanations for this, but the tease inherent in stimulating and frustrating emotions could be one of them. The second phenomenon, if it exists, is of a comparable kind on the part of the analyst. There sometimes seems to be almost a tendency among psychoanalysts, or at any rate a temptation, to sabotage their relationship with their patient after termination. If this impression has any truth in it, then it implies that the strain of countertransference feelings is also not easily dealt with. After all, how can we be expected to allow patients to impose so much instinctual restraint on us and not to resent them for it?

Whether it is true or not, it raises questions of the long-term effect of analytic work on the analyst which deserve consideration. The mourning of an analyst for his patients would not be directly comparable in kind to the residual mourning of his patients. Nonetheless, if it is true that the inhibition of object-relationship with the patient imposes a strain, then it is likely to result in some form or degree of introjection to compensate for the gratifying object that has been lost. This may operate in manifold ways, but it could, for instance, be in part by the introjection of the uncivilized parts of particular patients with whom the analyst has to deal, resulting in an excessive tolerance of aggression in certain areas, with strong reaction formations against it in others. My own opinion is that such a process probably does affect many analysts early in their career, but they work through it with maturity. If this is true, it is very important to consider how the atmosphere of psychoanalytic

[210]

training and the organization of a psychoanalytical society could foster it or diminish it.

The therapeutic implications of the views of the psychoanalytical relationship which I have presented centre, as far as the patient is concerned, on the resolution of two problems: the trauma that he has undergone and the mourning that he may be left with. The two problems are related.

Whom does the patient mourn? Is it the analyst with whom his ego makes a relationship, or is it the analyst of fantasy who has attracted to himself previously unconscious impulses and longings? As in normal love and hate, it must always in some degree be both, since the analyst of reality could not mean so much to him unless he also represented the archaic figures with which we need to maintain a relationship throughout our lives. This is the crux of the matter. In the psychoanalyst the patient finds again the amalgam of fantasy and reality that he met in his first analyst of childhood – the mother who understood the thoughts he could not verbalize.

If the patient is to overcome his attachment to the analyst, more is required than simply interpretation of the transference fantasies because, put more accurately, it can only be a question of the interpretation of such transference fantasies as the patient is able, consciously or unconsciously, to make available to the analyst, and the analyst able to recognize and understand. The patient must therefore also reach a less intense relationship with the person of the analyst which has been bathed and interpenetrated by the transference fantasies by a route which allows his ego opportunity to assess the analyst's real attributes.

This underlines that the first requirements of analytic technique must therefore be to facilitate the patient's capacity to communicate his feelings and thoughts as fully as possible. In order to do this, it is of the greatest importance that the analyst should not reinforce the trauma the patient has experienced by behaving in an unnecessarily traumatic way himself. In order to reduce the split between the analyst of fantasy and the analyst apprehended in detail by the ego, a constant aim

[211]

must be to facilitate the integration of the two images by the interpretation of the patient's warded-off perceptions of reality and, sometimes, in my opinion, by the acknowledgment of their accuracy by the analyst.

Much of this may be considered to be the common ground of all analysts, but I believe that in fact pinpointing the problems of trauma and mourning leads to a subtly different attitude and technique. For instance, analysts will be less inclined toward the traumatic use of silence, which drives the patient into silence or into concealing his feelings of rejection and his depression. The use of prolonged silence has already been criticized on these grounds by the Kleinian school. But although we know too little of what our colleagues really do, it seems to me that analysts are often oversensitive in their fear of disturbing the transference. If they become more aware of the traumatic factors involved, they may examine their techniques and be surprised to discover unnecessary areas of traumatization or failure to detraumatize. Do we sometimes pay too high a price for the sophistication of our techniques, for instance, if we reply only with an interpretation? To take another example: some analysts do not reply to Christmas cards. They analyse the patient's motives for sending one when he returns. Is it really sound to imagine that more is to be gained by rebuffing the patient in this way than by reciprocating as a member of society with a common culture and still analysing the motives when they come up? Is it really sound to act as though the patient had no knowledge of one's private life and family, or even of the severe blows that fate may deal one? It seems to me important that the patient should be relieved so far as possible (it is a delicate area) of the oppressive feeling, which he does not necessarily express, that the analyst has adopted a Jehovah-like stance, able to control completely the irruption into the consulting room of human joy or sorrow. Of course there are dangers in this procedure in comparison with the classical idea of the analyst's prime function as remaining, so far as possible, simply a mirror; but these disadvantages have to be weighed against the disadvantages of the patient's suppressing responses through negative attitudes to the analyst's rejection, which may then become difficult to elicit.

The gradual acknowledgement of reality increases the sense of reciprocity with his patient for the analyst too. He feels more real: the split between his professional personality and his real personality is reduced. I am not here suggesting – and I hope I will not be misunderstood – that he should step out of his role or have any object-relationship with his patient which is not confined, and remains confined, within the framework of analysis and termination. The sort of relationship I am describing does not interfere with the development of a hostile transference, though this would clearly be its danger if abused. But it does, I believe, help to prevent the suppression of a secret hostile relationship and transference, and of defensive idealization.

The maintenance of a relationship between patient and analyst that is a hint, and only a hint more reciprocal than is envisaged in the usual model, also protects the analyst against the dangers of introjecting a fantasied ideal of psychoanalysis which may impose on him an illusory standard of normality. This may affect his treatment of patients deleteriously and even disturb his emotional balance for many years. Man does not live by reality alone, even less by psychic reality. It is good for analyst and patient to have to admit some of the analyst's weaknesses as they are revealed in the interchange in the consulting room. The admission of deficiencies may help patient and analyst to let go of one another more easily when they have had enough. In other words, the somewhat freer admission of realities – but not too free – facilitates the process of mourning which enables an analysis to end satisfactorily. The end of analysis is in this way prepared from the beginning.

Affects and the
psychoanalytic situation

ADAM LIMENTANI

IN ANNOUNCING the main topic for the 30th International Psycho-Analytical Congress in Jerusalem in 1977, the Programme Committee noted that the problem concerning affects seemed appropriate as a focus for the discussions, since no two theories agree on it. The truth of this statement is affirmed by the most casual reappraisal of the literature as stated in a number of outstanding contributions such as those of Brierley (1951), Rapaport (1953), Rangell (1967) and Green (1973). Green's *Le Discours vivant*, a very comprehensive work on the subject, has not attracted sufficient attention because it has appeared only in French and in Spanish (1975). Papers written in more recent years have continued to highlight the discrepancy of approach to the problem in various parts of the world, due not entirely to parochialism on the part of some writers, but rather because of the disparities between theory, technique and clinical practice. The major areas of theoretical research are: (1) the drive discharge theory, (2) the debate on the existence of unconscious affects, (3) the relationship to their mental representations and fantasies, (4) the issue concerning the possibility of affects dissociated from the object, (5) the ego as the only seat of anxiety, (6) the problem of narcissistic and schizoid personality disturbances, and (7) the widespread calls for adjustments and modifications of the classical method in the treatment of borderline and narcissistic states,

[214]

which has generated further complications in the matching of theory with practice. Although the task of reviewing the literature has been undertaken by André Green (1977) the subject of the affects in the analytic situation remains vast. In this paper I shall not concentrate on any one aspect of the theory of the affects or of a specific clinical phenomenon, nor will I attempt to supply any answers. I shall, however, underline certain diagnostic features which are fundamental to an understanding of the state of *malaise* existing in the relationship between theory and our clinical daily work.

In the course of a recent address to the British Society, Bion (1976) remarked that 'feelings are the few things which analysts have the luxury of being able to regard as facts.' He added that when analysts embark on theory, they lose their sense of direction 'as they have an inexhaustible fund of ignorance they can draw upon.' As few would dispute so simple yet profound a statement, it is, however, difficult to see how we have reached a situation which was so well summed up by Rangell (1967) when he wrote: 'affects, the original centre, in giving way to subsequent developments have become, wrongly, "the forgotten man". In spite of their ubiquity clinically, [the affects] have in a sense been bypassed, or at least minimized out of proportion, and receive a good deal less of systematic attention than they deserve in our total theoretical metapsychological system.' Rangell was clearly referring to Freud's (1933a) shift of emphasis from representations to the instinctual impulses and to the description of the id as the reservoir of the life and death instincts, later responsible for the developments expressed in the work of Ferenczi and Melanie Klein. The immediate result of this thinking was to link affects with the unconscious fantasies or to regard them as the expression of instincts. The work and experiences described in Balint's and Winnicott's writings have also made us all the more aware of the patient's predicament occasioned by the closeness of bodily feelings to the psychic apparatus. It is prolonged contact with borderline patients that has opened our eyes to the continuous attempts to impinge on the analyst as the object. The understanding of object relations and their implications from the point of view of the countertransference has gained momentum during the last quarter of a century. I am referring to these developments here because it is possible that Rangell's statement may not be easily understood unless it is stressed that his remarks apply to the lack of systematic attention in trying to incorporate the affects in a total metapsychological system.

In our actual clinical work we could hardly overlook the affects as they are often the immediate reason why patients seek treatment, and during analysis the patients continue to note the qualitative and quantitative changes in their affects when assessing their own progress or lack of it.

The success and failure of an analysis could in fact be said to rest on the degree of affective change which takes place during its course. An analysis is most often remembered through the recall of a particular affect which had probably been dominant. Statements such as 'an altogether overwhelming emotional experience'; 'it was very distressing'; 'I could not go through it again'; 'I was depressed all the time'; are not infrequently heard from analysands. Analysts will speak of an analysis as having been a 'stimulating' or 'interesting' one, or, when nothing seemed to be happening for months at a time: 'boring'. Neither analysts nor patients are prepared to admit that a treatment was entirely 'intellectual' whereas it may clearly appear to be so to the observer. Some analyses, on the other hand, are stormy from start to finish, and it is surprising how two people are able to keep their interest going in the face of the strain and stress generated over the years; a factor which must have been aggravated by the very considerable length of most contemporary treatments. Considering the large number of patients seen by a psychoanalyst in the course of a day, it is to be expected that he will have to do something in order somewhat to insulate himself. Some therapists are more successful than others in handling the impact on themselves of their patients' emotional response to the psychoanalytic process, and are therefore able to avoid losing touch with the analysands even when their direct emotional involvement in the relationship is at a low point. The less successful will not infrequently himself become the victim of psychosomatic disorders, and it should be noted here that the defence of intellectualization affords no protection to the analyst against such an eventuality (Sandler, 1972).

I make no apology for focusing on the emotional position of the analyst in the psychoanalytic situation, so vividly described in Gitelson's courageous paper published in 1952. The literature on affects has in fact shown a curious neglect of this aspect of the therapeutic relationship and one has to turn to papers mainly devoted to the countertransference to see it adequately discussed. It was Paula Heimann (1950) who introduced the then revolutionary notion that the countertransference did not simply mean the transference of the analyst towards his patient but that, rather, it was an instrument of research into the patient's unconscious. She also regarded it as being not only 'part and parcel' of the analytic relationship but also a *creation* of the patient and therefore part of the latter's personality. She did warn, however, against its usage as a screen for the analyst's shortcomings and also deprecated the practice of the analyst's disclosing his feelings to the patient, views which the present writer wishes to endorse very strongly. An example of the consequence of such behaviour in the analytic relationship was observed by me in the course of supervisory work. A student-analyst had explained a recent lapse of his attentiveness to his patient as being due to a feeling state which had affected him. The patient's reaction was to become overanxious and deeply concerned about her therapist's mental health. The opportunity was missed for understanding the impact of the analyst's 'unusual' state on the patient in terms of early life experience of a mother who made heavy demands on her child. Further, the patient was not ready to deal with reality. Such unburdening is much more in keeping with Gitelson's view of the therapist's transference which, he believes, should be brought right out into the open. If this is the case, we can assume that the analyst expects something in return for his admission (confession) and such expectation will be coloured by unresolved infantile wishes and needs on his part.

In theory, by turning to the countertransference, the analyst has the tools (his psychoanalytical concepts and his feelings) to control the affective state of the analytic situation at any given moment. The first few years of my life as a psychoanalyst were profoundly affected by a remark from my supervisor, Dr Sylvia Payne, when she was advising me on the timing of a genetic interpretation. Having made a good case for early intervention, she added as an afterthought, 'In the last resort it really depends on how quickly you wish to decrease the level of anxiety in the patient and how much of it you can take.'

It is fashionable nowadays for analysts to believe they can do just that by giving what they consider is a transference interpretation, which allegedly also includes an examination of the countertransference, by imparting it in terms such as 'You want to make me angry.' This 'you and me' interpretation must fail to elicit an appropriate affective response in so far as it leaves out any clarification of the patient's role at the time. It does not say whether he is in the role of a baby or a child who is experimenting or, say, an adolescent who is deliberately provoking an adult; and it is of course quite meaningless in terms of object relations theory, as it gives no indication who the analyst is at that precise moment. Some analysts, no doubt, would argue that so challenging a remark could lead up to an explanation of the use of the analyst as a particular object. But there is little reason for withholding such knowledge if the analyst has it at his disposal. The vicissitudes of affects in the analytic situation can be, and in my contention are, controlled by the analyst; a point which I shall take up again. His personal attitudes, training and theoretical position will all influence him in his interventions, creating a unique atmosphere. The dissociation of his faculties of thinking and feeling will have far-reaching effects on the course of an analysis. A patient will often respond with increasing persecutory anxiety to an excessively *feeling* approach because it can be experienced as seduction, teasing and, finally, frustrating. A collusive approach at the intellectual level can hide the failure to respond to the patient's attempt to escape from his emotions. This situation could be gleaned from the statement of a drug addict: 'My analyst and I agreed to stop after two years because there was no transference.' In my view that was indicative of a two-way transference block and needed careful elucidation *in* analysis rather than termination of the encounter.

In our work we are constantly exposed to both external and internal experiences. Some, but very limited, protection is afforded by placing oneself out of sight. Our narcissism, however, whether healthy or unhealthy, will always be threatened. The situation is further complicated by the ambiguity in the analytic situation which plays a part not always fully appreciated. For instance, at the outset, we invite the patient to enter into a relationship which offers a mixture of satisfaction and frustrations, and with a demand for utter trust which he can hardly experience towards a total stranger. We stipulate that words shall be the method of communication, knowing full well that most affects cannot be adequately described in words. We assure the analysand that both of us will be able to work better if we are not to stare at each other, yet we know how difficult it is for an infant in the first months of life to take his eyes off his mother. We, further, impose restriction on his movements, thus removing one important element from the triad of cognition, affect and motion, which are intensely and intricately interrelated throughout the individual's development. The time limit imposed on the sessions and their periodicity are 'natural expressions of love, and symbolical of good food and care', as Winnicott noted as far back as 1945 (Winnicott, 1945a). It should cause little surprise if certain patients may wish from time to time to use every means at their disposal to express their feelings and to create unforeseen situations which can exercise the analyst's emotional responses as well as his technical skills. This is most likely to occur in borderline states and narcissistic character and personality disorders, when the impact on the analyst from the patient's affects, projections and projective identifications will be at its greatest. Problems of management overlap with the difficulty of understanding the patient.

Allowing the fulfilment of wishes for a physical contact with the therapist and the introduction of non-verbal ways of dealing with outbursts of violence are explained as a genuine and honest desire to maintain contact with the analysand. Yet it is difficult to see how it could be claimed that the psychoanalytic process is not thereby affected or prejudiced.

Psychoanalysts tend to rationalize, hence to justify, taking steps which are outside ordinary practice, but they seldom acknowledge that such steps may be gratifying or defensive. There are also those who, as a result of rigidity in their personality, cannot tolerate the behaviour of a patient when it is clearly disruptive and often incompatible with the classical technique. This is often associated with a blunting of the analyst's capacity for effective response, leading to stagnation or the discontinuation of treatment. The use of reassurance, humouring and an avoidance of transference interpretation is less difficult to understand in this context but, in my opinion, is more likely to produce further complications and an interference, possibly total, with the psychoanalytic process.

Before proceeding to the next section, I should explain that my understanding of the term 'affect' is in accordance with that suggested by Laplanche and Pontalis (1967): 'any affective state, whether painful or pleasant, whether vague or well defined and whether it is manifested in the form of a massive discharge or in the form of a general mood, therefore linking it with states of tension.' Affects are linked with ideas or mental representations. A feeling, as an affective presentation, is an internal rather than an overt activity, yet it is seldom out of touch with the external situation. Muscular, glandular and physiological activities can be associated with feelings.

The concept of 'feeling state' as suggested by Joffe and Sandler (1968) is also valuable in differentiating conditions where somatic changes are not in immediate direct evidence.

The disruption of the classical method is most likely to occur in the treatment of persons, men or women, who are inarticulate and unable to remember many details of their childhood. They may be highly intelligent and often possess outstanding intellect and exceptional talent. The obvious difficulty in verbalization is almost invariably linked with an incapacity to express valid and genuine feelings and emotions. Love and hate are unavailable to them, love even more than hate. They may complain of depression without displaying it, but we do not believe them to be capable of it. On the other hand, should there be anxiety, this will be of a pervasive, inhibiting, paralysing and primitive quality.

The case material which I wish to present is fairly typical of a situation met in contemporary psychoanalytic work when a patient's affective disturbance has a profound effect on the psychoanalytic process. Negative therapeutic reactions expose the analyst to massive countertransference responses. In this clinical outline, I shall deal only with those aspects relevant to our topic. There were two particular features: a major one being that for months on end the patient would be unable to use the couch; and a minor, but no less irritating, one in her attempt to control omnipotently everything in the external and internal world to such a degree that the analyst was unable to elicit any emotional response from her without feeling tempted to abandon the analytic and therapeutic role.

Clinical material

Mrs A. began her analysis at the age of 27, on account of severe, intractable anxiety associated with poorly described feelings of depression and suicidal thoughts. She also complained, from true incapacity, about being inarticulate. She had given up a lucrative occupation which she had pursued without appropriate training, and which had caused her to feel a fraud. She had been married for some years, but there seemed to be little left in the marriage besides devotion on the husband's part and admiration on hers, coupled with a fear that he might leave her. There was little physical contact, neither partner being greatly concerned about it.

Mrs A. had been brought up under unusual circumstances. Her family at first lived in a small village in southern England, in total isolation. An older sister and brother excluded her in every way, forcing her to become totally immersed in an ambivalent relationship with her parents. Her father, from all accounts a very disturbed man, had taken over her toilet training from the start and insisted, with her connivance, on 'cleaning her' until she was nearly eleven years old. The mother, a teacher, preoccupied with supplementing the family income and looking after her own mother, seemed to be almost unaware, or at least unconcerned, about the father's intrusions into the daughter's life. Mother's father had died the day after Mrs A.'s birth. After three months of breast feeding, mother had to go away for some weeks, leaving the child in the care of the maternal grandmother. This shattering episode in Mrs A.'s life was brought into the analysis at the time of the first separation three months after work had begun, when she plunged into a state of total inactivity, blankness, and a whole stream of death fantasies. This incident also marked the disappearance of the early, explosive, erotized transference. On my return I found a patient who had only thoughts and no feelings, and she was soon to discover that she had no more control over her thoughts than her feelings.

After the next separation Mrs A. returned, having lost not only her feelings but her thoughts as well. Her blankness, however, had an excruciating as well as exquisitely painful quality to it which, having communicated itself to me, I could then tell her about. When she complained that she was now suffering again, I recalled reading in a story by Chekhov of a doctor telling his patient: 'You must feel the pain, otherwise you are dead.' However, what was causing such intense psychic pain to my patient was still out of our reach; but it was also clear, to both of us, that the anxiety was there to fend off the experience of other affects of a dangerously intense nature. When I tried to put her in touch with her aggression, or rage, easily available in the transference and in her relationships to a number of clearly bad external objects, she would gesture with her hands as if hoping to touch something, saying: 'Where is it, I cannot feel it.' It was at this time that I would become conscious of the rift created by deep splitting and my patient's capacity for dissociation. The occurrence of negative therapeutic reactions would also make heavy demands on my patience and resilience. One serious relapse occurred after an Easter vacation, when she reported having been present at a Jewish Passover celebration.

[222]

(She, a Protestant, had always been attracted to the Jewish religion as a further escape from her untenable identity.) She had been impressed by a part of the service and had written down her recollection of it on a piece of paper which she handed to me. It read: 'Mouths but they speak not; eyes but they see not; noses but they smell not; hands but they touch not; feet but they walk not; throats but they make no sounds.' This time she had no thoughts, no mind and no body. However, she reported a dream she had had during the vacation in which *she was standing in a street, waiting for a taxi; there were hundreds of them but they were all full. A doctor standing behind her was urging her to get away.* She appreciated the irony in that she had identified me both in the taxis full of people and also in the doctor behind her. She had remembered I existed, but that was no good if there were so many people able to hire me. As she got in touch with the idea of having longed for me during the holidays, she became panicky and no more was possible for that session. The next day she reported having read a book for the first time in years (Mrs A. did not read either books or newspapers). To my surprise it was a book which popularized the understanding of somatic illnesses. She was shocked at reading that repressed anger could cause arthritis and that a baby feels so much when left. This had reminded her of the taxi dream. Mrs A.'s stare during this exchange had become unbearable to me. I was at a loss what to say, having tried in the past every possible approach to get her to use the couch again; I reminded her that in the dream the doctor had been standing behind her, which was how it should be. She then pointed out that the reason why the dream had been so painful was that she could not see me. She was now distinctly irritated and mentioned my persistence in suggesting the use of the couch. She went on to remind me of a 'knocking game' she used to play with her mother when a small infant, in which she would knock with her hand on the side of the cot and her mother would reply with gentle knocks, standing behind her, out of her sight (this was a new detail). She had known about this game all her life but she now had a conviction of remembering the feeling of it. With feeling hitherto unknown to either of us, she asked if I understood that she did not want me to act in the same way as her mother, at least not when I was available to her.

As analysts we often forget that patients do not always attempt to repeat past affective experiences in their analyses; they also try to avoid them. However, persistence in interpreting an obvious resistance had paid well, as it had brought back an early infantile memory of a feeling, linking it with the transference and promoting insight. The feeling had led us to the idea of the disappearance and unavailability of the mother-analyst. This of course does not mean that Mrs A. at other times had not used the eye to eye opportunity she herself had provided, for indulging in her cannibalistic impulses; or as a substitute for instinctual wishes involving the skin; or for hiding defences and for preventing memories from getting through. Writing down and handing over to me on paper her thoughts and fantasies was a symptomatic action used by Mrs A. when under stress. I regarded this as a 'transitional space' valuable in preventing acting out (Khan, 1972b). On the other hand, it is possible that I was not sufficiently discouraging because I welcomed such an action from a patient who had been so inarticulate.

This brief account would be incomplete without the mention of Mrs A.'s love affair with death, which had started when she was four years old. She then played a 'game' in which she would throw herself on the ground and would lie there thinking she was dead until she was disturbed or resuscitated by magical internal means. Her assurances that she would not kill herself had little effect on me until the recovery of this early memory. Afterwards and in the light of all available material, I came to the conclusion that Mrs A., rather than being under the influence of the death instinct, was quite simply anti-life, as she seemed to seek a way of surviving without being or feeling alive. She longed for death, but real death filled her with horror. There must be many meanings attached to the patient's dealings with death and her feeling of deadness which was frequently traced to her mother's similar feeling dating back to the loss of her own father. On the other hand, acting the part of being dead was the ultimate defence against the eruption, into the Conscious system, of unconscious affects linked to destructive instinctual drives and impulses (Laplanche, 1975). A clue to such a possibility was the references to be gathered from an affective response dream which I had during a difficult phase in the treatment. In the dream *the shadowy figure of a woman shows me a life-size rag-doll which I pick up and throw across several rooms, until it lands out of sight in a corner. With the female figure I follow the flight of the doll. As we reach it, it suddenly comes to life. I feel anxious, darkness descends. In the next scene I am in my car with a figure again next to me. An electrical wire is on fire and the engine is about to be set alight. A woman appears and offers to repair the car for a fee which seems excessive.* I wake up with a feeling of curiosity and refreshed. I immediately associated the woman who had offered to repair the car to Mrs A., whose conflicts about the lack of reparative drive had dominated the analysis recently. The doll was similar to a puppet which I had had as a child, and which was safely out of the way in the attic. The reason for having such a dream did not emerge fully until the Monday session when Mrs A. reported having had a dream about loving. As she was reflecting that on Friday she had been upset as she thought I was pushing her too hard, I suddenly recalled that I had been preoccupied with external matters and that I had been somewhat irritable and less than attentive to the patient's relapse into a state of severe anxiety. In the silence that followed, I recalled a third part of the dream in which *balloons containing a bugging device* (day residue) *were floating about my analytic room. As I tried to shoot them down I was aware I should not destroy them.* It may be self-evident that over the weekend I had become conscious of my lapsing from free-floating attention, but what is more relevant is that the dream made me aware that an excess of therapeutic zeal was getting through to the patient, increasing her anxiety and fear of recovery, quite apart from causing me to feel irritable and impatient. I do not propose to go into the personal aspects of the dream material, but I note that having got in touch with my aggressiveness and frustration, a direct response to the negative therapeutic reaction displayed by Mrs A. at the time, I was able to recover my analytic curiosity, hence the feeling of well-being on waking.

Comment

My understanding of this woman's predicament was that a fragmentation of the ego (or a regression to unintegrated state; Winnicott, 1945a) had taken place in the first few months of her life, causing the kind of disintegration which deals with anxiety that cannot be contained by other means such as projection, denial, negation, projective and introjective identification (Segal, 1964). The slightest attempt at integration is followed by a fresh outburst of massive anxiety which screens off every emerging feeling state. Unconscious affects in such cases may never see the light of day. My further attempts to understand her illness have led me to a re-examination of Khan's concept of cumulative trauma which I believe is applicable to this case. Khan (1963 [*this volume – Ed.*]) has underlined the effects of a type of maternal stress in which the mother's protective shield is lost and in the analysis such task falls on the therapist, who should not attempt to be a 'mother'. Also, Khan's idea, formulated in his writings included in *The Privacy of the Self* (1974) concerning affects and threat of annihilation staying hidden and dissociated rather than repressed, appears valid as does his suggestion that when someone has taken himself as an internal object, the fear of annihilation is indeed paralysing. Outstanding in Mrs A.'s was the fact that anxiety linked with psychic pain was equal to anxiety about emptiness and blankness. Concepts such as that of signal anxiety or 'feeling safe' (Sandler, 1972) or splitting processes being responsible for the lack of availability of emotions (Klein, 1946) are not only essential to the comprehension of the material but indispensable.

I shall now discuss, briefly, some problems linked with 'anxiety' and the role of words and reconstructions in relation to the affects.

'Anxiety' in the psychoanalytic situation

Clinically, we recognize the existence of signal, primary, castration, separation, paranoid, depressive, neurotic and psychotic anxiety. Each type carries a specific meaning, function and origin. The list is a formidable one and not encouraging to our hope of finding a single basic theory of the affects. Green (1973, p. 104) has commented on the absence of such a theory in the writings of Melanie Klein, who has influenced many authors who have dealt with this subject. My understanding of this apparent omission is that the stress placed on the analysis of paranoid and depressive anxieties must be taken in conjunction with the concepts of primitive fantasies, early development and object relations. A theory of affects, as such, may be irrelevant to the Kleinian psychology, which could hardly be said to neglect them. However, some amongst our Kleinian colleagues create the impression that all one has to do in order to clarify the most obscure clinical situation is to locate the paranoid or depressive anxiety. It is not always easy to relate this attitude to clinical experience. There are, for instance, individuals (of whom Mrs A. is a clinical example) in whom anxiety dominates their lives to the point of freezing or pushing everything else out of the picture. When they come into analysis, we soon realize that we are not dealing with straightforward signal anxiety. It is more the case of anxiety being used as a screen to conceal other affects, rather than a particular idea or mental representation (see also Jones, 1929; Lewin, 1965). This is a massive effort on the part of the ego to block the affective path to the exploration and study of the thought processes which have gone into the formation of symptoms. To launch into an investigation of a precise genetic and developmental source of the anxiety could be misleading and confusing to the patient.

An interesting hypothesis recently advanced by Calef (1976; working in conjunction with Weinshel), if proved valid, might have interesting repercussions on our clinical work. From the starting point that some instinctual conflicts may terminate in unrepressed satisfactory resolutions (as part of character formation), this author argues that the signal affects determined by such conflicts would be conceived as reliable and trustworthy. In so far as neurotic conflict clouds perceptual consciousness and those functions which demand the development of affect signals, affective signals will be distorted. This in turn will lead to distortions of the more complex secondary affects. (In this context see also Kohut, 1973.) Should this hypothesis be correct, it follows that certain internal structures or functions, as they are functions of functions, may not be direct products of conflict and need not be relegated to the unconscious. According to Calef, we are dealing here with a form of internalization, not necessarily introjection. Some signal affects may therefore be considered as only indirect and not direct products of conflict.

Words, affects and the psychoanalytic situation

> . . . . Words strain,
> Crack and sometimes break, under the burden
> under the tension, slip, slide, perish,
> decay with imprecision, will not stay in place,
> will not stay still.

T.S. Eliot, Four Quartets

Those who have experience in treating cases of sexual perversions and delinquency are quite familiar with the observation of the direct discharge of an impulse in a seemingly total absence of anxiety or guilt. Pre-verbal areas of disturbance, common in these conditions, are linked with feelings being resisted in an entirely autonomous way; the impulsive behaviour being designed to short-circuit affect development. Brierley (1951) has pointed out that affective language is older than words. She regards affects as part of a primitive system of the ego. Uncovering them, tracing their origin and interpreting their relation to the associated impulses and thoughts permits the integration of the primitive ego into the principal ego. The difficulty here is that words will constantly fail us, particularly when they are most needed. The good analytic hour and the rapport with the psychotic or borderline patient will be disrupted by failure to find the correct words for describing a feeling state. Patient and analyst share the frustration. In general we tend to ascribe such difficulties to the material being derivative of some pre-verbal experience. Less attention has been paid to the possibility of the analyst's having unconsciously recognized the patient's feeling in so far as it reminds him of a similar, personal and early pre-verbal experience. Help is impeded as even a long personal analysis may not succeed in supplying us with the exact and precise word which is needed at a given moment. In my supervisions I have noted that some very gifted but disturbed students have a capacity for dealing with such situations, perhaps because they have had very similar experiences in their own analysis. On the other hand, the less gifted but intellectually bound student may be inclined to use cliché or jargon expressions which may be quite difficult to eradicate. Bion (1976) has commented on our having to use words which are debased by common usage, and also on the fact that the analyst needs a discipline beyond that which can be provided by any training. He believes that forging words, which the analyst must keep in working order, will give him a language which he can use and value. It is perhaps in this use of technical language that the most serious collusion occurs between analyst and patient, as if each needed to create a barrier between feelings, impulses and thoughts.

Words are also at the centre of the controversy to which I have already made brief reference, concerning explosive affective situations, actual or threatened violence and a variety of acting in, which occur in the course of treating the more disturbed patients, espesially those with borderline conditions. I believe that the absolutely correct interpretation which could quell the storm exists only in theory. In practice, a theoretically correct interpretation may be quite inadequate for the situation and should not be repeated in exactly the same form. Those who believe that a failure of an intervention to produce a change in a tense situation is always due to incorrect understanding, must either believe in magic or subscribe to a theoretical position which they dare not challenge. Because words are or are assumed to be ineffective, the analyst feels inclined to abandon the analytical stance and he may do so at the slightest sign of approaching trouble.

A parallel situation to that obtaining in psychoanalytic work occurs in the physical treatment of similar states. The neuroleptic drug fluoethixol decanoate, notable for its anti-psychotic action and anxiolytic effect in certain overactive and excitable patients, can have a biphasic effect on mood, low doses tending to be activating and high doses sedating. The following example shows the predicament we face when searching for the correct dosage in our interpretative work.

A girl in her early 20s, Miss B., had a history of sudden outbursts of violent behaviour requiring periods of isolation in her room or in hospital. She warned me about this in the first interview when she told me that her therapist had her ejected from his office by the police. She now wanted 'to get this man out of her system'. Within days she developed a state of mind towards the analyst which was a mixture of animosity and sexualization of the relationship. An interpretation of her increasing ambivalent dependence on the analyst-mother, aimed at decreasing the erotization of the transference, was followed by a session in which she screamed incessantly, keeping up a barrage of insult against him. Her behaviour was then linked with the interpretation given on the previous day, but I only succeeded in increasing what now seemed to be an expression of intolerable tension and narcissistic rage. Preparing for the next intervention, it occurred to me that people outside the room might be afraid. This led to my becoming aware that I was frightened, and I then began to consider the possibility of this feeling being due to projective identification. The situation became clear when she shouted that I had made her feel ugly and unattractive. I rejected the *idea* that this referred to physical ugliness and told her that my interpretation had aggravated her feelings of greed and dependence, and as she anticipated frustration she felt angry and aggressive and in consequence ugly and unattractive inside herself. I felt considerable anxiety in making this type of intervention because I was not sure that the patient could tolerate my abrupt entry into her inner world,

[230]

and I was also aware that I was dealing with a nearly, but not quite, conscious affect.

In dealing with Miss B. and patients with such narcissistic problems, more than repression is involved in the analysis of their affects, which strike us forcibly as being related to tension phenomena. The most thorough exploration of the ambivalence, basic as it is, is not sufficient in relieving tension unless it is accompanied by the analysis of the inner world fantasies and of those 'primitive agonies (anxiety being not a strong enough word)' which Winnicott (1974 [*this volume* – *Ed.*]) has described as lying behind 'the fear of a breakdown that has already been experienced'. In the case in point, a deeper interpretation had the required sedating effect, preferable to reassurance or calling the police. The patient left in a calm state with the feeling of having been understood. As the session was followed by sustained improvement, it is right to speculate on the possible change in the mental representation from that of a persecuting analyst-mother to one able to contain the aggression and greed.

A very different situation from the one just described arises when wordless communications, in the form of acting out and symptomatic actions, occur suddenly in an attempt by the patient to show that all is not lost in the course of analyses which appear satisfactory, both partners doing their duties. The only other clue that the affects are not brought into the analysis as a part of knowing and experiencing (Khan, 1969a) is that the countertransference is seldom in question.

Space does not allow me to enter into a discussion of the connection between the lack of expression of the primary affects and psychosomatic states, and the clinically observed phenomenon of the closeness between explosive acting out and implosion leading to somatic manifestations, a Hobson's choice for so many unhappy individuals (Limentani, 1966; McDougall, 1974).

Some important questions remain. How do the words we use relate to an infant's or child's original experience? The language we use reflects the sophistication of the adult mind, and we know how we value the capacity in the analysand to abstract. What have we achieved when a patient responds to a correct interpretation of his repetitive compulsion, which is aimed at undoing an unpleasant weaning experience, saying, 'You are telling me that I am banging my head against a brick wall.' Is that what a baby feels at the time? Does it feel more than an adult? Are we not expecting an internal change to take place irrespective of verbal inadequacies? Are words the music of thoughts, as a woman said in acknowledgement of the analytic work done? On the other hand, are words, often such shallow and poor mediators of the affective states, all that important to the psychoanalytic process?

Years ago, I had a patient who seldom spoke during the second phase of a very long analysis. He broke his silence once, after some months, to say in answer to a further attempt at interpretation on my part, that I suffered from the delusion that words were necessary in psychoanalysis. We parted when he decided he was well enough to continue his analysis on his own. I never discovered whether he agreed or disagreed with my construction that in making me silent he was undoing the experience of having had a psychotic mother who had talked incessantly and irrelevantly all her life before being removed to a mental hospital. During the long silences I learned to understand his tensions, moods, depressions and a host of non-verbal communications. I have never been able to pass on that emotional experience to my students or my colleagues.

The role of affects in reconstruction
In a timely reappraisal of reconstruction in psychoanalysis, Greenacre (1975) clearly defines the obligatory contributions of the analysand and those of the analyst, which she finds more difficult to define. This is so because the analyst's thinking and cognitive processes are constantly under 'the ebb and flow of his personal and mental and emotional reactions. He may sometimes be clearly aware of this, at other times they are almost or completely subliminal. This part of the analytic work cannot be faked, computerized or even taped. . .' and, I would add, seldom, if ever, accurately reported. But more relevant to

our topic is Greenacre's remark that it is 'the language of the specific reconstruction of actual emotional experiences that furnishes a reliving with a new perspective'. Having further noted that verbal communications must be the most important channel to be used towards the achievement of real knowing, she reminds us of the large number of non-verbal and pre-verbal communications available to the partners in the analytical relationship and asks 'not whether and how these physical eruptions may be analysed but rather how they operate in the basic transference relationship'. I have quoted extensively from this important paper because it touches on the core of the problem we face in the analysis of adults. Although it seems impossible to improve on Greenacre's final statement that the reconstruction brings the child and adult together, in the present writer's view this will not occur in every analysis. In a large number of cases it seems to happen more readily in the course of a second analysis, which almost invariably includes a reconstruction of the previous one. Many patients I have met had a past which they had never lived. A first analysis can restore the past to them, but the affects are swamped by an avalanche of recollections and intellectual constructions (often mainly contributed by the analyst) and reconstructions. The real working through of old and discarded feeling states can in these patients take place only in the course of a second analysis.

Adherence to theoretical beliefs plays a part in the work of reconstruction of traumatic experiences, which have occurred in early life, in association with appropriate affective states. An example of this arose in the course of a discussion in the British Society, when it was agreed that fear of strangers was central to the understanding of the psychopathology of an adult patient. However, one speaker dated the traumatic experience to the eighth month of life whilst another felt that such fear *had* to be related to the paranoid position and therefore it would have to be put back a few months. It seems inevitable that this time difference in the theoretical arguments would itself reflect on the analytic situation and any feeling state which might then be recaptured. Five months is a large slice of an infant's life.

[233]

Afterthoughts

When we speak of the psychoanalytic situation, it is obvious that we are referring to the relationship of a special type which is born out of the specific, and in some way peculiar, nature of the encounter; the affects generated in it will, to some extent, reproduce those which occur or have occurred outside it. The mere fact that reciprocal actual sexual gratification is missing underlines the difference. The opportunity of thinking about the topic discussed in this paper has confirmed the view, which I have held throughout my psychoanalytic career, that any affect or feeling state exhibited by the analysand will have the analyst as the object, in fantasy or in person. It can therefore be best understood in terms of object relations theory. I am less convinced of the possibility of an affect being unrelated to an object, although in theory such an event could be observed outside the analytic relationship. I believe this could happen in the case of a *feeling dream* for example, in the absence of any particular imagery, but again it could well be that such a dream is derived from a pre-objectal state. With Brierley (1951) I would also say that it is the objects which are invested with affects rather than ideas being affectively charged.

Looking at the problem from the point of view of the therapist, it is my belief that although he will follow every lead offered by the patient, he will remain in control of the climate and temperature of the psychoanalytic situation. This requires the development of a special sensibility, a kind of internal pacemaker, which improves in its function with experience. This sensibility is of course part of the countertransference, but it has the special quality of operating mostly at a subliminal level and is therefore not in the immediate field of awareness of the therapist, as is the case with many other countertransference elements. A sudden and excessive demand, stimulated by the patient, will increase the affective load. The analyst's training will prevent immediate discharge and if all is well this internal information will maintain an appropriate level of fruitful emotional exchange. The average level of anxiety will be similarly regulated. Calef (1976) has gone even further in suggest-

[234]

ing that a therapist uses 'the individual influencing machine' and that 'theoretical bias frequently functions more for the purpose of rationalizing the influencing machine than for the therapeutic work itself'. Although the term used by Calef is rather sinister, it deserves serious examination because of the indirect effect on the analysis of the affects generated at certain times in the psychoanalytic situation by the work of reconstruction. Although we are well aware that the affects are only one of many phenomena observed and developed in psychoanalysis, the different ways of handling them by those who practise contribute to the particular quality of the patient's total experience. A number of psychoanalysts (Ferenczi was the first amongst them) will provide a totally emotive analysis by utilizing all the available intellectual abilities in themselves and their patients. At the other end of the psychoanalytic spectrum are those who will rely on a clearly formulated theoretical and technical approach, reaching the basic emotions through the use of their brains. Both extreme groups have their detractors and poor imitators, whose psychoanalytic identity was perhaps never adequately established. Where a satisfactory identification is lacking, imitation may provide a substitute (Gaddini, 1969).

Psychoanalysis is an art but, unlike art itself, it cannot be isolated from meaning. Psychoanalysts, in common with artists, are dissatisfied with their capacity to interpret and externalize the total innermost experiences in themselves and their analysands. Unlike artists, however, they must constantly struggle with the imperative of distinguishing imagination from reality. It is almost a cliché to observe that even in the most talented, artistic expression confers no guarantee of freedom from emotional turbulence, neurosis or psychosis. Writers may long to give musical effect to the words they employ. Musicians, who claim the privilege of an ability to express feelings without being too troubled by precise meaning, will, if pressed, confess to the superiority of language as the true mediator in object relations. Have not painters expressed their frustration by writing on their canvases? It is possible that in the case of the artist we are dealing with an exclusive, albeit highly satisfactory, process of reparation in relation to the internal object, leading to affective tension only being discharged. Psychoanalysis, contrary to commonly held fears, can be helpful to the artist in providing a further outlet in the psychoanalytic situation for the appropriate release of the affects. Greater integration derived from intellectual *and* emotional working through reduces acting out and symptomatic actions quite apart from mobilizing new areas in the personality. As many analysts know, this would enhance rather than impede artistic expression.

It cannot be of little value to remind ourselves that we are not alone in seeking appropriate affective discharges. As psychoanalysts, we are only too aware that our profession is not only impossible (Greenson, 1966), but also extremely difficult.

An enquiry into the function of words in the psycho-analytical situation

CHARLES RYCROFT

IN THIS PAPER I shall attempt to formulate certain ideas about the function of words in the psychoanalytical situation. In doing so I shall continue a line of thought that I began in a paper on symbolism (1956a), in which, following Milner (1952) and Kubie (1953), I took the view that it is misleading to restrict the analytical concept of symbolism to the use of symbols by the primary process, and suggested that words should be included within the general category of symbols even though they can be differentiated from other symbols on the grounds: (a) that their immediate symbolic connections remain conscious, (b) that the displacement of cathexis from the thing-representation is only partial, the word remaining linked to and yet distinguishable from its referent, and (c) that they are conventionalized. These differentiating characteristics enable words to be used by the secondary process for purposes of communication even though they also continue to carry cathexes derived from instinctual sources. In the last paragraph of my paper on symbolism I suggested that it is this dual function of words that makes psychoanalytical treatment possible.

Before coming to the main argument of this present paper I must mention that my contribution to the 'Freud Centenary Symposium on the Theory of Technique' (1956b) was based on an earlier draft of this paper and that several paragraphs and sentences are common to both. However, my contribution to the symposium was designed for a specific purpose and occasion and was limited to a period of twenty minutes. As a result it was a highly condensed and in some ways an unsatisfactory statement of various ideas which I wish to elaborate in greater detail here. I have called this paper an Enquiry to draw attention to the tentative, almost groping nature of much of the thought that lies behind it.

This paper, like its predecessors, is written from a standpoint which conceives of man as a social animal who, in addition to his drive to self-preservation and self-awareness, is also continuously concerned to maintain himself in a reciprocal, adaptive interrelationship with his objects and which sees psychodynamics as the study of the development of the capacity for interpersonal relations, and psychopathology as the study of the ways in which this capacity may break down. I shall start my argument with two very familiar quotations from Freud's *The Ego and the Id* (1923a). The first is Freud's definition of the ego as 'that part of the id which has been modified by the direct influence of the external world . The second is his suggestion that the essential difference between an unconscious idea and a preconscious one is that the latter has been 'brought into connection with verbal images'. Now since words are all learned *from* objects in the external world and their primary function is to communicate *with* objects, these statements imply (a) that the essential quality of preconscious, and therefore conscious, ideas is that they have acquired the quality of communicability and (b) that the ego is that part of the id which is concerned with communication with external objects. The importance of communication and, therefore, of speech, as one though not the only mode of communication, arises from the fact that the capacity for interpersonal relations is not simply a matter of being able to use objects to satisfy libidinal wishes but is the ability to maintain a reciprocal relation between self and object before, during, and after the consummatory acts appropriate to the particular relationship. It also involves the ability to maintain a living internal psychical relationship with the object during its physical absence. In other words it is the capacity to keep in contact or communication with objects that are realistically perceived and are recognized as being separate from the self.

Although words are not, of course, the only tools of interpersonal communication – there are indeed numerous occasions on which the use or abuse of words betrays a breakdown in communication on a more simple, emotional level – it is self-evident that they play an important part in all interpersonal relations. Their use implies at least some recognition of the object as separate from the self and, unlike certain other tools of communication such as gestures and emotional expressions (some of which, at least, are innate) they are very obviously learned within the framework of object-relationships. The capacity for speech is certainly a mental function which shows that the id 'has been modified by the direct influence of the external world'. Furthermore, the important part played by words in all psychotherapeutic procedures shows that they can be a major vehicle in relationships which can alter the participants profoundly. Psychoanalytical therapy in particular shows that they can be used for the expression and resolution of infantile conflicts, including those dating from before the patient's acquisition of speech. The way in which this last can happen has been beautifully described by Ella Sharpe in her paper on metaphor (1940).

One special function of words is their permissive function, which bears a relation to their communicative function analogous to that of the superego to the ego. The acquisition of speech within the framework of object relations leads, as a result of the introjection of objects, to the formation of inner sanctions permitting the formulation and expression of certain ideas and inner prohibitions preventing the formulation and expression of other ideas, which become repressed. Formulation and communication of a previously unconscious idea involves, therefore, the overcoming of an internal resistance deriving from the superego – or, to state the same thing in terms of fantasy, defiance of an internal object. This is why the expression by the analysand of a previously unadmitted idea is preceded by anxiety, or an increase of defences against anxiety, which is followed by a sense of release when the idea is finally communi-

[239]

cated. This is also why the formulation of original ideas, even those of a scientific and impersonal nature, requires moral courage. The analysand and the original thinker or artist both have to face the fear of being neither understood nor approved. They face the fear of isolation from objects, both internal and external. To put the matter the other way round, comprehension and toleration of an idea by the analyst gives the analysand permission to entertain it. I speak here of the analysand acquiring permission to *entertain* previously repressed ideas rather than to *hold* them, since it can obviously happen that the patient has to entertain an idea consciously before he can discover that it is not true, or entertain a wish to do something before he can discover that he does not really want to do it.

In this paper, however, I do not intend to consider the part played by words in the analysand's internal economy, and shall not discuss in any detail the role they play in intrapsychic communication, integration, and the growth of self-awareness. Instead, I shall restrict myself to certain aspects of the inter-communication between analyst and analysand, with special reference to the verbal communications made by the former to the latter.

The purpose of psychoanalytical treatment is to increase the patient's capacity for object-relationships, and the analyst's various technical procedures are designed to establish a special form of relationship between himself and the patient, in which the analyst, while remaining an external object, can also become the temporary representative and personification of the various internal figures dating from his past to whom he is attached at the expense of his capacity for conscious relationships with present-day external objects.

The analyst's first contribution to the formation of a relationship between himself and the patient is the provision of a setting within which this relationship can develop. This setting includes, among other things, a quiet room with a couch in it, a closed door, regular and frequent appointments – and the analyst himself. This setting is itself a communication to the patient, since its details are all signs that the analyst is preparing to take up a certain attitude towards him, that he intends to listen to him, to concern himself with him without requiring him to be concerned with the analyst, and to protect the contact between them from external distraction. This communication is non-verbal and is a silent indication that he intends to provide one component part of an object-relationship, a person who will maintain a steady and sustained interest in *his* object, the patient. He does this, then, in the first instance by means of signs – I am here using the word 'sign' as a technical, semantic term – which indicates the existence of a particular psychological situation. The position of the analyst's chair in relation to the patient's couch signifies the analyst's preparedness to listen to the patient, his arrangements about times of sessions, his willingness to continue to do so, etc. These details are all signs of the analyst's contribution to the establishment of a relationship between himself and the patient, this notwithstanding the fact that the patient may also use any particular detail as a symbol with which to represent specific unconscious ideas within his own mind.

I have here made use of the distinction drawn by logicians between signs and symbols. Signs indicate the existence or presence of some process, object, or condition, while symbols refer to or represent conceptions of processes, objects, or conditions. Psychological signs are also signals, since their function is to communicate to a responding object. A baby's cry is not only a sign that there is a baby in distress: it is also a signal of distress, which tends to evoke an appropriate response in its mother. Similarly signs of sexual interest are signals which tend to evoke either a response or alternatively defences against making a response. Signs play an especially important part in communication of affects, since many forms of emotional expression are probably innate and are immediately comprehensible without recourse to symbolic interpretation. Dreams and symptoms on the other hand are symbolic modes of expression, since they refer to, and are only comprehensible in relation to, conceptions existing in the patient's mind. The words used in analysis are also symbols, since they refer to ideas in the analyst's and patient's mind, but the inflections and tones of speech are signs since they indicate directly the speaker's affective state.

In describing the provision of a setting as the analyst's first therapeutic activity I am, of course, following Winnicott (1958) and Michael Balint (1965), who in different ways and from somewhat differing standpoints have both stressed the importance of the setting and atmosphere within which the analytical process takes place. This setting provides the framework within which explicit, symbolic communication develops. The analyst invites the patient to talk to him, listens, and from time to time talks himself. When he talks, he talks neither to himself nor about himself *qua* himself, but to the patient about the patient. His purpose in doing so is to enlarge the patient's self-awareness by drawing his attention to certain ideas and feelings, which the patient has not explicitly communicated, but which are nonetheless part of and relevant to his present psychological state. These ideas, which the analyst is able to observe and formulate because they are implicit in what the patient has said or in the way in which he has said it, have either been unconscious, or, if they have been conscious, it has been without any awareness of their present and immediate relevance. In other words the analyst seeks to widen the patient's endopsychic perceptual field by informing him of details and relations within the total configuration of his present mental activity which for defensive reasons he is unable to perceive or communicate himself.

The analyst is able to do this, largely though not entirely, because he assumes that although the patient may consciously only be talking to and about himself he is unconsciously also trying to satisfy his need for an object-relationship by making contact with the analyst. As a result his communications tend to be concerned, consciously or unconsciously, with the analyst, just as those of the analyst tend to be concerned with the patient. The difference between the two is that the patient's conception of the analyst is profoundly influenced by projection on to him of the various internal imagos, dating from his past, to which he is attached at the expense of external objects, whereas the analyst's conception of the patient is relatively

[242]

undisturbed by projection. The analyst's communications to the patient tend, therefore, to be concerned precisely with his feelings and ideas about the analyst and the way in which they reflect his experiences and fantasies of infantile and childhood objects. They progressively help the patient to discriminate between his fantastic and infantile preconceptions of the analyst and other figures in his present life and the reality of his adult relationship with them, and therefore make it progressively easier for him to become aware of his thoughts and communicate them to the analyst. His drive to do this is his wish, which has previously been frustrated in so far as he has been ill and therefore isolated, to have a relationship within which he can share experience. The analytical situation enables the patient to communicate, share, and bring into relation with an object, feelings, memories, and thoughts which have previously been either repressed and unconscious or split-off and only experienced in states of dissociation. Since these communications are predominantly verbal, the analytical process brings previously unconscious and unformulated ideas 'into connection with verbal images'. The fact that the analyst is more tolerant and realistic than the infantile imagos which comprise his superego permits ideas, which have previously been repressed, to be verbalized and communicated. In addition the analyst's understanding of the language of dreams, symptoms, fantasies, and defences enables him to translate into words unconscious attempts to communicate which had previously been inaccessible and incomprehensible, while his knowledge of infantile sexuality and the nature of infantile object relations enables him to facilitate the symbolization of pregenital drives which had been intolerable to the patient's ego in their original unsublimated form.

The patient's increasing capacity to be aware of, communicate, and share his mental life cannot, however, be attributed solely to the intellectual content of the analyst's verbal communications. It is also the result of the fact that every correct interpretation, even when it is, as it should be, entirely free of reassurance or suggestion, contains within it a whole number of additional implicit communications about the analyst and

[243]

his attitude towards the patient. In addition to enlightening the patient about, say, his fantasies or defences, it also indicates that the analyst is still present and awake, that he has been listening and has understood what the patient has been talking about, that he remembers what the patient has said during the present and previous sessions – and that he has been sufficiently interested to listen and remember and understand. Furthermore, the fact that it is an interpretation and not a reassurance or admonition indicates that his feelings are neither unique nor incomprehensible and that the analyst is neither shocked nor trying to get him to conform to any preconceptions of his own as to how he should feel or behave. In other words it tells the patient (a) that the analyst is interested in him as another human being and is capable of understanding him, and, (b) that it is possible to have a relationship with another person without violation or distortion of his own subjective experience and intrinsic capacity for growth. I should perhaps stress that I am here referring to interpretations which are correct not only in respect of content but also in respect of timing and affect.

These implicit statements are signs of the analyst's interest in the patient, of his capacity to maintain an object-relationship, at least within the confines of his consulting room. They tell the patient the one thing that he needs to know about the analyst and are the analyst's major contribution to making the contact between himself and the patient a real and not an illusory relationship. They constitute an affective communication, and, as is characteristic of affective communications, it is made by signs and not by symbols. Although it could be communicated explicitly in words, it would be both irrelevant and useless to do so, since it would be an attempt to convey something that the patient can only credit in so far as he has already acquired the capacity for object-relationships. In the transference neuroses, belief in external objects is sufficiently developed to prevent the patient ever seriously doubting the analyst's concern and interest, while in the narcissistic neuroses distrust of external objects constitutes a major therapeutic problem. In the former, therefore, explicit statement of the analyst's interest is useless because it is unnecessary: in the latter it is use-less because it would not be believed. Indeed, many such patients would feel that any expression of positive feeling by the analyst was forced and contrived, even if they believed it. The various psychotherapies which use explicit statements of positive feeling by the therapist probably only work by exploit-ing the patient's capacity to overcome distrust by idealization. In the long run it can only be overcome by signs of real and sus-tained interest and understanding and not by verbal expression of positive feeling.

In addition, therefore, to their symbolic function of com-municating ideas which increase the patient's insight and self-awareness, interpretations also have the sign-function of con-veying to the patient the analyst's affective attitude towards him. They combine with the material setting provided by the analyst to form the analyst's affective contribution to the estab-lishment of a trial relationship in which distrust can be over-come and the patient can increase his ability to make contact and communication with external objects.

In the previous section I have touched on three problems, which if pursued at any length would lead us far from the restricted theme of this present paper. These are (a) the distinc-tion between signs and symbols, and the part played by sign-communication in human relationships in general and the analytical situation in particular, (b) the part played by the analyst's emotional attitude in overcoming the patient's dis-trust of objects, and (c) the nature and psychological status of the analyst's therapeutic attitude. Before returning to the sub-ject of words in the psychoanalytical situation I should, how-ever, like to comment briefly on these three topics.

The clearcut distinction I have drawn between signs and symbols would not, I believe, prove tenable in the precise form I have made it, if more detailed semantic and clinical analysis of the two concepts were attempted. The reason for this is that the concept 'sign' embraces two notions which are not necessarily inseparable. These are (a) the idea that a sign indicates the actual presence of something, in contrast to a symbol, which only refers to or represents it, and (b) the idea that a sign can be understood directly without symbolic interpretation. On every occasion that I have used the term 'sign', I have done so to refer to something which indicates the presence of what it signifies, but the various 'signs' I have mentioned differ in respect of the way in which they are perceived and apprehended. A baby's cry is, most probably, understood and responded to directly and instinctively, and so, probably, are the tones and inflections of speech, but the signs of the analytical setting certainly require some development of the capacity for symbolic thinking before they can be understood. Further analysis of this problem would involve us both in further verbal definitions and distinctions and in clinical examination of *how* affects are expressed, communicated, and perceived. For the purposes of this present paper we need only recognize that they are.

The idea that the analyst's affective attitude helps to dispel the tendency to distrust in narcissistic patients is based on the assumption that distrust cannot be understood in terms of projection of hostility alone, but that it is also a manifestation of the hypersensitivity of the narcissistic ego. Objects and circumstances that are felt to threaten the integrity of the ego always tend to evoke hatred and suspicion, and this defensive reaction is easily aroused in patients who fear that positive contact with an object involves submission to the object's conception of psychical reality and violation or distortion of the subject's own experience of self. In so far as this fear is present the psychoanalytical situation itself may seem peculiarly dangerous, since the analyst's interpretations may be felt as an attempt to impose a certain view of psychical reality and his possession of a psychological theory as evidence that he has a *Weltanschauung* to which he wishes to convert his patients. Furthermore, the very fact that language is derived from external objects and contains within it precipitates of past psychological experience and theories may lead to hatred and suspicion of words themselves. The only patient I have had who openly hated words did so on the ground that their very existence showed the impossibility of any real understanding between human beings. Only when she wrote poetry did she feel that words were her own.

Various attempts have been made to define the nature of the analyst's therapeutic attitude, but they usually fail, I believe, in implying a greater degree of either detachment or involvement than is usually either present or desirable. They range from the idea that the analyst remains a completely detached observer who operates in a state of pure intellect entirely undisturbed by feeling to the opposite idea that it is in the last resort the analyst's love that cures the patient. On the other hand some of the most apt descriptions of the analyst's attitude fail to define it psychologically at all. For instance the phrase 'benevolent neutrality', which grammatically is an oxymoron, a combination of two contradictory terms, implies both that it is an affective attitude and that it is not. My assumption in this paper is that it is a sentiment, in McDougall's (1931) and Shand's sense of the term, that is, an organized, enduring disposition of emotional tendencies, which is maintained more or less consistently, even though it may suffer passing disturbances due to fatigue, preoccupation, etc. This sentiment can be thought of as a specific development of that component part of the capacity for interpersonal relations which makes interest, concern and empathy for the object a natural and spontaneous activity.

The analyst's ability to maintain this sentiment is the result of a number of factors, including (a) the various drives and identifications which have led him to choose psychoanalysis as a profession and enable him to get satisfaction from it; (b) the analytical setting, which is adapted to his needs as well as to the patient's. For instance, it protects him from external distraction just as much as it does the patient. It also restricts to known and tolerable limits the contact he has with the patient; (c) the fact that he has several patients, thereby diminishing the intensity of his involvement with any one of them; and (d) his ability to operate a split in his ego, analogous to that required of the patient (Sterba, 1934), which makes his relationship to his patients an *imaginative* participation in their inner and outer life rather than a direct involvement with them. I have selected these four factors for mention since, taken together, they draw attention to the part played in the psychoanalytical situation by the analyst's capacities and needs.

Although the interest and understanding felt by the analyst is, either consciously or unconsciously, perceived by the patient, it is just as likely to be distorted or denied by him as is any other aspect of the analytical setting. Perception by the patient that he is being understood may, for instance, be used as the basis for a fantasy of complete union with the analyst, as a patient of mine did when she reacted to interpretations which struck her as particularly understanding by going into blissful, hypomanic states of what she called 'transcendental harmony'. In contrast, she treated interpretations which she was not prepared to accept as deliberate sadistic attacks. Less dramatically, other patients may overvalue the feeling of being psychologically understood as a defence against recognizing bodily needs and feelings of physical deprivation. On the other hand, patients who equate being understood with being devoured or penetrated may deny that they are being understood or attempt to make it impossible for the analyst to understand them. Alternatively they may try to prove that the understanding is either insincere and hypocritical or is motivated only by intellectual or financial considerations. They may also try to make the analyst feel that he is failing to understand them in the hope of undermining his self-esteem by making him feel that he lacks a quality of mind essential to being a good analyst. In this they are behaving like revengeful children who try to make their parents feel that they lack parental feelings. Such patients incidentally provide another reason against the analyst expressing his interest in the patient.

To return to the main theme of this paper, I should like to discuss briefly three other factors which influence the total meaning attached by the patient to the analyst's interpretations.

The first is that the patient will, at times, use speech as a symbolic substitute for infantile sexual activities. At such times he will not only use his own speech to discharge oral, anal, or phallic drives, or to gain exhibitionist or narcissistic pleasure, but will also endow the analyst's speech with identical or complementary meanings. In other words he will react to the analyst's speech as though it too had these pregenital meanings or alternatively will endow listening to it with oral, masochistic, or voyeuristic significance.

The second arises from the fact that, logically speaking, every statement implies two other classes of statements, the assumptions that have to be made before the original statement can be formulated and the corollary statements that can be deduced from it. It follows from this that every interpretation the analyst makes implies a whole number of assumptions about mental functioning in general and the patient's individual psychology in particular and also a number of deductions that can be made from it. Patients seem to vary considerably in their capacity to apprehend the full implications of single interpretations. This variation is not only a function of intelligence but also depends on the various factors which influence the rate at which 'working through' takes place. The fact that every interpretation logically implies a number of other interpretations is important in considering the process of interpretation during the course of an analysis, since each interpretation can then be seen as a member of an interpretative series, which tends to assume those that have preceded it and to foreshadow those that will follow it. In other words each interpretation can be thought of as a detail of a total interpretative pattern which emerges during the course of the analysis. I am not, of course, suggesting that this total pattern will necessarily ever become explicit either in the form of a 'complete' interpretation by the analyst or of a total insight of the patient's. To suppose so would be to forget that clinical facts are never as orderly as the theories we abstract from them.

The third factor influencing the meaning attached to interpretations is that all words tend to evoke associated images additional to those necessary to comprehend intellectually the idea which the word is being used to convey. These associated images are responsible for the poetry of words and for the fact that all words, even the most abstract, have shades and overtones of meaning and tend to evoke concrete images.

[249]

Even language which is designed to avoid imaginative reverb-
erations fail to do so since it evokes a feeling of dryness. The
fact that the analyst and patient have a language in common
means, of course, that they tend to share the same associations
to words, but disparity of imaginative associations and reso-
nances can, on occasion, be a source of misunderstanding or
distraction. It can, for instance, obviously happen that the
analyst unwittingly uses some word or phrase which the
patient associates with a particular affective situation quite
other than the one to which the analyst was referring. Alternatively a patient may fail to appreciate the full psychological
meaning of a word used by the analyst and take it in a more
restricted, literal sense than the analyst intends. Thus, a patient
failed to realize that the word 'castrated', which his analyst
often used, had any connection with feelings of being emascu-
lated or unmanned psychologically. He assumed that his
analyst meant anatomical castration and nothing else. As a
result many interpretations he received, though accepted intellectually, lacked psychological reality. In such a case apparent
verbal understanding masks a failure in communication. On
the other hand, when the analyst succeeds in formulating
interpretations in a way that takes cognizance of the patient's
imaginative processes and are meaningful at different levels of
experience, this does much to establish and maintain contact
with the patient as a whole person.

The tendency of words to evoke concrete imagery creates
quite peculiar difficulties in patients who have lost the ability to
distinguish between words and what they signify, since they
tend to react to interpretations as though they were the process
that the interpretation refers to and are liable to confuse literal
and metaphorical meanings. The only neologistic patient I
have ever had developed her highly abstract and tortuous mode
of speech to prevent herself being overwhelmed by the concrete
imagery and physical sensations which normal, everyday
metaphorical speech evoked in her. It is, of course, in schizophrenic and schizoid patients that problems of communication
become most apparent, since their tendency to withdrawal,
introversion, and distrust is due to ambivalence about the wish

to communicate and preoccupation with the hazards that are felt to attach to doing so.

Throughout this paper I have concentrated on the verbal communications made by the analyst and have said little about the verbal behaviour of the patient. As a result I have not discussed the way in which information about the patient's infantile anxiety situations and psychopathology can be deduced from his linguistic habits – a possibility which was first envisaged by Ella Sharpe in her paper 'Psycho-Physical Problems Revealed in Language: an Examination of Metaphor' (1940), and which has since been confirmed statistically in a series of papers by Lorenz and Cobb (1953). Lorenz (1953) suggests that many of our so-called intuitive judgements of others are in fact based on our unconscious perception and evaluation of their linguistic and syntactical habits, and cites examples of the way in which disturbances in object relations, self-awareness, affectivity, etc., are reflected in habits of speech. If this is true it follows, on the principle that what is sauce for the goose must also be sauce for the gander, that the patient must also have material available on which to make intuitive evaluations of his analyst.

My reason for giving greater consideration to what the analyst says to the patient than to what the patient says to the analyst has been my conviction that we are more likely to increase our understanding of the dynamics of the analytical process by viewing it as a relationship, albeit of a unique kind, between two persons, than as a situation in which one person observes another. It must be admitted, however, that this view of the analytical process presents certain difficulties, which can easily be avoided if we limit ourselves to the fiction that we simply observe our patients. These difficulties are both of a practical and theoretical nature.

The practical ones arise from the fact that recognition of the analytical situation as a relation between two persons compels us to take the analyst's psychology into account. I have, for instance, mentioned that the analyst's capacity to get satisfaction from his work contributes to his ability to maintain an appropriate emotional attitude to his patients, and that certain details of the analytical setting conform to his needs as much as they do to the patient's. Further analysis of what I have called the analyst's sentiment would, however, require more detailed information about the analyst's subjective experience and the origin of his need to be an analyst than is at present available.

The theoretical difficulties arise from the fact that the problem of communication in the analytical situation is largely a problem of affects, and, as Rapaport (1953) has pointed out, the clinical and theoretical problems involved are of a complexity which 'makes a definitive formulation of an up-to-date theory of affects certainly ill-advised, if not impossible'. Furthermore, Rapaport's review of past and present theories of affects shows that more interest has been shown in affects as tension and discharge phenomena and as endopsychic signals used by the ego in its work of mastering impulses than in their communicative function. In particular, there is only passing reference, via the connection between affects and empathy, to the assumption made throughout this paper that affects are not only observable but also tend to evoke a response in their observer, and that it is the interaction of affects which is responsible for the sense of contact which is so essential in the analytical situation. I am not, however, claiming that there is anything new in this idea. It is implicit in the clinical concept of 'rapport' and in much of the literature on countertransference. In this paper I have been concerned with the part played by words in maintaining not only intellectual but also affective contact in the analytical situation.

The analyst's act of freedom as agent of therapeutic change

NEVILLE SYMINGTON

IN THIS PAPER I intend to explore a phenomenon with which all analysts are familiar. I will first describe it and then examine what its implications are for theory. I shall refer to it as the 'x-phenomenon'. I shall start with some clinical examples.

I was charging Miss M. a little more than half what my other patients were paying. She had been a clinic patient and I used to sigh to myself and say inwardly, 'Poor Miss M., £X is the most that I can charge her.'

I did not in fact articulate it so clearly as that. In my mind it was like an acknowledged fact that everyone knows, like the unreliability of the English weather. It was part of the furniture of my mind and I had resigned myself to it in the same way as I reluctantly resign myself to the English weather. So the analysis went on and on with that assumption as its unquestioned concomitant until one day a startling thought occurred to me: 'Why can't Miss M. pay the same as all my other patients?'

Then I remembered the resentment she frequently expressed towards her boss who always called her *'Little Mary'*. A certainty began to grow in me that I was the prisoner of an illusion about the patient's capacities. I had been lassoed into the patient's self-perception and I was just beginning to extricate myself from it. I then brought up the question of her fee and in the course of a discussion she said, 'If I *had* to pay more then I know I would.'

She had now clearly told me that she had the capacity in her to pay more and that this could be mobilized if I changed my inner attitude towards her. A few sessions later I said to her, 'I have been thinking over our discussion about the fee. I charge most of my other patients £X and in our discussion I have not heard anything that makes me think that I should not charge you the same.'

For two sessions she cried rather pitifully but then became resolved that she would meet the challenge. Soon she found a job that paid her one third more than her previous salary. In moving job she extricated herself from the patronizing tutelage of the boss who called her 'Little Mary'. She had been able to do this because she had first been freed from the patronizing attitude of her analyst. Shortly after this she finally gave the push to a parasitic boyfriend. Again I think she had been able to do this because she had been able to give the push to a parasitic analyst. These two events were soon followed by other favourable developments. I think the source of these beneficial changes was in that moment of inner freedom when I had the unexpected thought: 'Why can't Miss M. pay the same as my other patients?' I am calling this act of inner freedom the 'x-phenomenon'.

Now I want to take another example. This patient was an obsessional man who used to hesitate sometimes in the middle of telling me something, usually as he was about to tell me some thought he had had since the previous session. As he had often expressed his apprehension that I would think him pathetic I would say to him something like, 'I think you are afraid that if you tell me about the incident in your mind I shall think you are pathetic.'

Of course I was thereby clearly inferring that I would not think him pathetic. With this assurance he would then obligingly tell me the thought in his mind. Then one day I was reading the following passage from *Four Discussions with W. R. Bion*:

Q. . . . She wouldn't be put off by what you suggest; she would get irritated with your reply and insist that you call her by her first name.

B. Why not the second one? Why not whore? Or prostitute? If she isn't one, then what's the trouble? Is she wanting to be called a prostitute or a whore? If not, what is the point of the story? What convinced her that her father was right?

Q. She wants sex with other men besides her husband, therefore in her view, she must be a whore. She's afraid that if she got a divorce from her husband she would run around and have sex with all sorts of men – behave like a free whore.

B. In view of what you are saying I think I would try to draw her attention to the way in which she wishes to limit my freedom about what I call her. It is just as much a limitation if the patient wants you to give the correct interpretation. Why shouldn't I be free to form my own opinion that she's a whore or that she is something quite different? Why be angry with me because in fact I am free to come to my own conclusions?

Q. Her fear is that your own conclusion will be that she is a whore.

B. But why shouldn't I be allowed to come to that conclusion?

Q. So you conclude she is a whore – now where are you?

B. But I haven't said that I do. The point I want to show is that there is a wish to limit my freedom of thought. . . (Bion, 1978, pp. 15-16).

As I read this I had a moment of illumination about my obsessional patient. I had been a prisoner of this patient's controlling impulses and at the moment of reading this passage from Bion I had a new understanding in which I felt freed inwardly (though this had outward concomitants). The next time he expressed his apprehension that I would think him pathetic I said to him quietly, 'But I am quite free to think that.'

He was much taken aback. It was possible then to see how much he operated by controlling my thoughts and the thoughts of others. A great fear was that if he allowed me to think my own thoughts then I might have the thought: 'How nice it would be to get away from Mr X.'

Then on to his feeling that no one ever *wanted* to be with him. This was linked to childhood experiences where his parents never wanted to be with him but farmed him out with child minders while they pursued their business interests in various parts of the world. We were able to look at his need to wind himself around me like a boa-constrictor and try to substitute my thinking and feeling for his, to make me into his ego, as it were. It was then possible to link his failure to be able to think and feel with the absence of a mother or analyst who wanted to be with him. The foundation of the thinking capacity seems to lie in the internalization of this maternal desire. Again the source of all this interpretative work and insight started from the moment of my own inner act of freedom. So this was another case of the 'x-phenomenon'. The remaining examples I want to take are from a patient about whom I shall need to give more background.

This patient was referred after an episode of hallucinatory psychosis. I took her on largely because of her strong motivation to get better. She regularly hallucinated in the sessions and communicated with what I shall call 'telegraphic bits'. It may have been a regression to holophrastic speech. After a long silence she would just say 'crocodile' and then some minutes later she would look at some point in the room and say 'blue circle'. I found myself reading *Alice in Wonderland* to help me into the right gear. I abandoned myself to crazy fantasy through which I linked these discrete elements. This phase of treatment progressed satisfactorily and eventually the hallucinations disappeared and she was able to address me if not as a person, at least as a distinct entity. I learned later that until that point she had not been able to distinguish between me and her boyfriend and in fact thought that I was him. From the moment that she saw me as distinct the honeymoon period of treatment was over for me.

In the initial interview she had told me the content of the hallucinations which had led her to seek treatment. In these hallucinations she was merged with her mother and savagely

[256]

attacking her boyfriend. It became clear, only slowly, that one of the principal reasons why she wanted treatment was to overcome her sadistic fantasies and actions towards any object of her love. The honeymoon period was over when I became the target of her sadism. Her sadistic attacks were subtle, unrelenting and certainly threw me off balance. She honed in on those areas of my own vulnerability with a devastating precision and she was unrelenting. For instance for a long period she said she felt I was not the right person for her and she began to investigate other possible therapists. She twice sought the advice of a female colleague. In all this she reiterated frequently that in my attitudes, tones of voice, gestures and in my manner of dressing I conveyed male chauvinist attitudes and that I was unsympathetic to the needs and predicaments of women. This was not articulated neatly like that. It was hinted at on occasions, raged about at others and only slowly was it possible to decipher what she was saying. At other times she would scream exasperatedly at me, and so intensively that I was unable to think. She would reproach me with fury for not attending to the matters which she had insistently brought to my attention. I was usually quite in the dark and realized that she probably thought she had asked me something or told me about some thought or event but had not in fact done so or had told me so elliptically that either the phenomenon itself or its import had escaped me.

Now, in her persistent accusation that I was dominating towards her because she was a woman and I was a man, I was aware of two things. In the first place I knew that she was sadistically attacking me and secondly, that, operating at a psychotic level of perception, she was more sensitive to my own unconscious attitudes than a patient in a classical transference neurosis. My problem therefore was on the one hand not to allow myself masochistically to become a victim of her sadism and yet not to dismiss out of hand the content of what she was saying. Yet, of course, in that hesitant and divided state of mind, I was the perfect victim. The treatment went through a particularly bad patch that lasted for about a year. I thought to myself that perhaps I was not the right person for her, perhaps she did need a woman, perhaps my male chauvinist attitudes were getting in the way of clear interpretation and so on. And the more I wavered inwardly the more furious and attacking she became. During this time she also complained regularly about rigidity, that I needed to be more flexible, I needed to consider other approaches or needed more analysis myself. For a long time I wavered inwardly as if I were standing on marshy ground.

Then about three years into treatment she adopted a new manner of behaving in the sessions. Instead of sitting in her normal chair (she did not use the couch) she walked past me and sat in a chair behind me. I resolutely remained in my chair. Sometimes she pulled her chair right up behind mine and on one occasion she poked my arm with her finger. Then, instead of sitting behind me, she took to standing behind me and I continued to keep to my chair determinedly interpreting and continued to do this for some eight sessions. Then one day I became uncomfortable with this procedure. I did not feel at ease and I was not able to respond spontaneously. Although I was interpreting, it was not out of an inner freedom but defensive in character. I decided that next time she walked past me and stationed herself behind my chair I would move across to the other side of the room. I could not say quite why I decided to do this but I knew that I could not interpret freely when I felt this discomfort. So the next time she took up her standing routine I got up calmly and moved to a settee on the other side of the room. As she saw me do this she turned and said in tormented fury, 'Why did you move?' (it had a tone which denoted that I had no right to move as I had just done) and at the same time she moved back to her own chair and I moved back to mine. 'What thoughts do you have about why I moved?' I asked. 'Just sheer male dominance', she said in defiant rage. Now, at this point I had an inner conviction that it was no such thing. I felt an inner certainty which I had not possessed before. I felt quietly confident that I had not acted out of any such motive and that I was not reacting to her sadistically.

'Can you think of no other possible interpretation of my action?' I asked her. 'No,' she said, 'it's just sheer male dominance'. Whereupon I said that it seemed that we had reached a deadlock and then there was a tense silence and there was an atmosphere that was pregnant with fury. Then at the end of about twenty minutes the atmosphere began to ease and I felt that we both had come through a crisis like two swimmers who had just managed to cross a turbulent river and reached terra firma. Some ten minutes after that she said, 'I don't know about you but I am feeling better', smiling slightly. That composite moment when I acted and then when in response to her I experienced an inner certainty that I had not had before is another instance of the 'x-phenomenon'. She was more able to listen from then on and in certain ways communication became easier and there was greater clarity, although a great deal remained obscure and communication was still badly impaired.

With the same patient there was another instance that is less easy to describe but I shall attempt to do so. I had a very clear notion that my role as analyst was to interpret to the patient my understanding of the unconscious import of what lay behind her manifest communications but a stage was reached with her when she could not bear any interpretations. She screamed that she could not sort anything out unless I accepted the surface meaning of what she said and also unless I accepted responsibility for what belonged to me in the process. She could not sort out what was her, could get no insight into herself, until she was clear who she was and who I was. In other words she needed to separate out the two elements that made up herself and me from the agglutinous mass that they were for her at the time. At this stage the only way in which it was possible for her to do this was, at various junctures, for me to express what my feelings were. It was important to her to know that they were really mine; several times she asked me if these were my feelings or those of all analysts; I told her that they were mine. Sometimes she would ask whether these were feelings shared by all analysts and I told her truthfully that I did not know.

After a period of this type of communication it became possible for her to express some separateness and then it was possible to interpret in the normal way again. (I say 'in the normal way' because I think the communications about my feelings

[259]

were interpretations. They were interpretations about the way she was merged with me through the superego structure of her personality. I will come back to this later in the paper.) There was a transitional stage when I would couch interpretations in this sort of way, 'I want to express to you the thought that is in my mind. . .' and then I would go on with the substance of the interpretation.

Finally I was able to interpret what I thought was in her mind. I understood this as being a transition from being a fused object in the transference to a separate one and that the interpretations had to be in a mode that was acceptable to the different psychological states that accompanied those phases. Again when I acted from personal freedom rather than follow some specific technical regulation that is supposed to be followed in an analysis then therapeutic shifts occurred and, I might add, a great deal of insights and learning in the analyst. (I hope it will not be inferred that I am scorning analytic technique; this would be the very opposite of what I am intending to say. After all the soul of analytic technique is to free analyst and patient from the normal social constraints and so favour development of the inner world. The problem is when 'classical technique' becomes the agent of a new social constraint.) I hope that these illustrations of the 'x-phenomenon' are sufficient to convey my meaning.

My contention is that the inner act of freedom in the analyst causes a therapeutic shift in the patient and new insight, learning and development in the analyst. The interpretation is essential in that it gives *expression* to the shift that has already occurred and makes it available to consciousness. The point though is that the essential agent of change is the *inner* act of the analyst and that this inner act is perceived by the patient and causes change. Even the most inner mental act has some manifest correlate that is perceptible, though this perceptibility may be unconscious and probably is. The psychotic is particularly sensitized to these minute changes. I will give two examples of this from the last patient that I took my clinical material from. In the first example it was an instance of an inner emotional state and in the second a specific inner mental act. Shortly before seeing my patient one day I received news that another patient of mine had committed suicide and I was upset, to put it mildly. There was a silence for the first twenty minutes of the session, then she looked at my desk and I made an interpretation that I cannot now remember but I shall not forget her response, 'I am not taking stick for your bad experience.' She was in tune with my emotional state in relation to which my interpretation bore little importance and she sensed this. She perceived it in the atmosphere. I am quite sure that she had no external knowledge of what had occurred.

The other occasion was when I was trying to decide on which day to finish prior to Christmas and I was thinking about this during a silence. The moment I said to myself inwardly that I would make Tuesday the last session she said at that precise moment, 'You have interrupted my thoughts, you have just stolen something from me.' I had of course. Instead of being in reverie with her I had stolen a chunk of shared thinking in favour of an administrative decision. As far as she was concerned I might just as well have spoken my thoughts out loud because she felt my inner act so that even an inner judgement has some perceptible external correlate. I do not think that the mental, emotional and sensational spheres ever exist in isolation. The most inward mental act reverberates through the sensational and perceptual spheres. The psychotic patient is tuned in to these inner spheres in a way that is not so of neurotics or normal people. The psychotic is not cut off from reality but rather one minute aspect of reality is enlarged so that the rest of the mental or emotional field is crowded out. It is like the zoom lens on a television camera that swoops down on one object of interest and that one object then takes up the whole television screen. I am insisting therefore that the inner act of the analyst affects the patient, especially is this so in the psychotic and borderline patient. The focus of this paper though is that the analyst's inner act of freedom causes a therapeutic shift in the patient. To account for this further contention it seems that some theoretical ramparts are needed to support it.

I think at one level the analyst and patient together make a single system. Together they form an entity which we might call a corporate personality. From the moment that patient and analyst engage in what we call an analysis the two are together part of an illusory system. Both are caught into it. Recent literature stresses that the analyst is not just a mirror but this is a gross understatement. The analyst is lassoed into the patient's illusory world. He is more involved in it, more victim to it than the average social contact. As the analytical work proceeds the analyst slowly disengages himself from it. In this way transference and countertransference are two parts of a single system; together they form a unity. They are the shared illusions which the work of analysis slowly undoes. Psychoanalysis is a process which catalyses the ego to ego contact: that area of the personality that is non-corporate, personal and individual. In this way psychoanalysis is working in the opposite way to religion, whose central social function is to bind people together into corporate entities. We need to look at this corporateness as belonging to a part of the personality where fusing takes place and how we can assimilate this to psychoanalytic theory.

In all the instances of x-phenomenon that I have given, the analyst's personal feelings have been shrouded by illusory feelings, emanating from the patient's unconscious superego. This could be formulated by saying that the feelings belonging to the superego have cloaked the feelings belonging to the ego. However the term superego needs to be amplified in the way that the sociologist Talcott Parsons (1952) has done:

> the place of the superego as part of the structure of the personality must be understood in terms of the relation between personality and the total common culture, by virtue of which a stable system of social interaction on the human levels becomes possible. Freud's insight was profoundly correct when he focused on the element of moral standards. This is, indeed, central and crucial, but it does seem that Freud's view was too narrow. The inescapable conclusion is that not only moral standards, but *all the components of the common culture* are internalized as part of the personality

[262]

structure. Moral standards, indeed, cannot in this respect be dissociated from the *content* of the orientation patterns which they regulate. (p. 23)

These illusory feelings in the patient are partly the internalized values of the family of origin, of his class and national allegiances together with the impulses, especially the destructive ones, from within. The impulses from within are strengthened and supported by the cultural values. At the beginning of the analysis (and often for a long time) the patient and analyst are held in thrall by the power of this personal-cultural illusion. This is possible because the patient and analyst become part of a system through which communication takes place. In his passive role where he does not assert his own view of the world the analyst allows himself to be swept into the personal-cultural contents of the patient's superego and interprets within that framework. Analyst and patient are part of a system and are joined through the superego parts of their personalities. It is through the superegos that corporate personality is effected. When the patient first comes to the analyst's consulting room it is probable that a fusing takes place of the analyst and patient via the superegos of each. Transference and countertransference are emotional expressions of this fusion.

If this model is accepted, then it follows that within the corporate personality there is a process of resistance and transference occurring in the whole entity, in other words in the patient and analyst. There is, however, also a process of analysis occurring in both persons, in the total entity. The process of analysis is the guarantee that there can be movement out of a locked situation. A female patient once asked me, 'What guarantee have I that something in your unconscious will not block my progress? You may unconsciously envy my desire to have a baby and my capacity to have one and therefore block me subtly.' I observed that it seemed she assumed that all the analytic power lay within me. She immediately retorted that it did not lie within her. I pointed out that she seemed to feel that if it was not in her and not in me then it did not exist at all. This was linked to her view that I had possession of the process. When she began to realize that this was not so she felt grief and realized that neither she nor I had control over the speed of development. She often said that she could not move until I moved first.

For a very long time I did not understand this. Only after about three years of treatment I suddenly realized that she meant that she could only move when an inner act of freedom had occurred within me. I had not realized at this stage that she was able to 'know' when these occurred. She was reliant on x-phenomenon but for a long time she had the fantasy that it was within my power to summon it at will. She became sad as it began to dawn on her that I had to wait, just as she did. So in the corporate entity there is a shared illusion or delusion (transference/countertransference) and shared resistance and there is also a process which we call psychoanalysis which fights a slow but persistent battle in both against the shared resistance and illusion. The analytic process catalyses the individual to individual existent reality. The x-phenomenon is a product of the analytic process. The latter works at a deep level, at a pre-verbal, primary process level. It finds its verbal expression in interpretation. Interpretation expresses this deep change and effects the final consummation of it at the conscious and manifest level. The sudden access of personal feeling in the analyst that breaks another bond of the illusory stranglehold in which both patient and analyst are held in thrall is immediately experienced by the patient and exists prior to insight. It implies a form of communication between analyst and patient that supersedes man's methods of perceiving the nonhuman world. The analytic procedure capitalizes on this special form of human communication.

It could be argued that what I am describing is a particular instance of projective identification but I do not think this does justice to those psychological events which, for want of a better term, I have called the x-phenomenon. Projective identification means that feelings which belong to the patient are projected into the analyst and lodge there like a foreign body. What I am describing is a joint process in which the real feelings of analyst and patient are aroused by the resistant process. The analyst's

[264]

feelings are *his* feelings even though they may have been stirred up by the patient. Patient and analyst are responsible for the feelings that are generated in the situation. Often the patient is 'blamed' for feelings experienced by the analyst and this is called projective identification. This type of description implies that there are only two blameable objects in the room: patient and analyst. There is a third term: the process in which both are involved.

What I have said so far may seem to contradict Freud's view that our only knowledge of the external world is through perception, mediated consciously by the ego. In nearly all Freud's writings he followed the scientific view of his day which was that man's knowledge of his fellow man is via his senses and does not differ essentially from his knowledge of the nonhuman world. Before Freud formulated the structural model he ascribed this type of knowledge to consciousness and thought that the unconscious did not have *direct* access to the external world. When he came to formulate the structural model he thought that the agency whose role is to mediate the external world to the organism is the ego and that the superego and id do not have direct contact with it. Now he does not specifically say whether he considers that this mediating role of the ego is just the conscious part of the ego but there are two passages which contradict all his other assertions on this matter:

> I have had good reason for asserting that everyone possesses in his own unconscious an instrument with which he can interpret the utterances of the unconscious in other people. (1913, p. 320)

> It is a very remarkable thing that the *Ucs.* of one human being can react upon that of another, without passing through the *Cs.* This deserves closer investigation, especially with a view to finding out whether preconscious activity can be excluded as playing a part in it; but, descriptively speaking, the fact is incontestable. (1915c, p. 194)

He is here talking about a special type of knowledge that exists between human beings that does not pass through the normal

[265]

sense organs or through that conscious part of the personality inhabited by word-presentations. This particular type of knowledge therefore antedates any interpretation that the analyst may give.

That there is a special type of knowledge by which human beings know each other that is quite different in kind from the way in which men know the physical universe was, I think, first articulated by Giambattista Vico. Until Vico all knowledge had been divided into three different kinds: metaphysical or theological, deductive and perceptual. Under this last category were included empirical observation and experiment. To these three types of knowledge Vico added another: knowledge that we have of ourselves and other human beings. In the case of human beings we are not just passive observers, he said, because we have a special knowledge 'from the inside' and we have a right to ask why it is that human beings act in the way they do. This type of knowledge is active and not passive because we can only know something from the inside if human beings have created it. God is therefore, according to Vico, the one who has perfect knowledge as he is the creator of all, but in the case of the special knowledge that human beings can have of each other it is a similar type of knowledge: it is knowledge *per caussas*. But Vico has not had a great following among thinkers within the human sciences. What he has asserted has been taken for granted by all great writers of prose or poetry but has not been studied seriously within the social sciences. Probably Max Weber, the sociologist, is the best-known follower of Vico's viewpoint. He distinguished between the ordinary knowledge by which we know the physical universe which he called *Wissen* and that special type of knowledge proper only to the knowledge of human beings by human beings and this he called *Verstehen*. Although this special type of knowledge has been central to clinical work in psychoanalytic practice there does not seem to be a metapsychology to account for it. The idea that a scientist might take this type of knowledge seriously is also scorned by almost all schools of thinking within academic psychology.

Vico said that it was possible to enter into the world of past cultures 'from the inside' by studying the poetry and myths that belonged to them. To gain this special type of knowledge man needs to be equipped with *fantasia*. Vico considered that this type of knowledge was superior to the knowledge that we have of the non-human world; this is because human culture has been created and can therefore be known from the inside. Now this idea that culture is a human creation and can therefore be known from the inside can, I think, be applied to the sort of knowledge that we have of a patient in the psychoanalytic situation. Once we accept clearly that there is the 'constitutional factor', or the biological given with its associated drives, then the rest of what we are concerned with is the product of human creation. What we analyse is a product of the inner fantasy life in interaction with first the mother, then the mother and father, siblings and finally the whole social environment. Theoretically it would be possible for all these elements to be analysed and understood. This understanding is of a special kind and arises through an act of insight which has been generated and made possible by the analytical process. We need to get some clue as to how this act of insight occurs.

Let us say I take hold of Kant's *Critique of Pure Reason* and read this statement: 'If we have a proposition which contains the idea of necessity in its very conception, it is a judgement *a priori* (1781, p. 26), I may understand it straight away but, on the other hand, I may not. If I do not it is because I have a false idea and this blinds the intellect. I will be able to understand when I can banish the false idea and allow the idea that Kant is proposing to be grasped by my intellect. I may be quite resistant to doing so because it may mean I have to give up many fond ideas which are comfortable to my way of life or habit of mind. To understand Kant I need to adopt a passive attitude so that I can become receptive to his ideas but I must actively be prepared to banish mine. At the moment of understanding I become Kant, as it were, through an action of the ego, whereby I dispel my superego contents and because of this I remain separated and become slightly more of an individual. At the moment of understanding activity and passivity come together and form a single psychological event.

[267]

Now, in the psychoanalytical situation, something very similar occurs. The patient's communications and the analyst's feelings and thoughts become the raw material out of which understanding arises. The analyst does not only have his own false ideas to clear away but needs to be passive to the analytical process and combating the resistance that he and the patient are locked into. The attempt to understand is being continually sabotaged by a parallel process that stimulates and fosters false ideas. Received theoretical positions may be used by the resistant process, as they also may be used by the benign psychoanalytical process. The patient and analyst as a corporate entity are involved in these two processes. Belief in the psychoanalytical process seems to be the essential ingredient for both parties. However, it seems that it may be the special role of the analyst to carry this belief for the patient as well as for himself, especially early on in treatment.

The act of understanding is rooted in what is most personal, in the ego, but the false ideas are located in the superego. At the moment of insight, expressed in interpretation, the illusions or false ideas are banished both in analyst and in patient. A personal, ego to ego, contact is established and replaced by an illusion or false belief that held the two together until that time. This belief that held both together is that social glue in microcosm that binds together the numerous communities and groupings of society. This type of togetherness is quite different from the ego to ego contact that occurs at particular moments in analysis. This type of contact is a revolution because new reality, new growth begins. In fact it is the only true revolution that does occur within human affairs. Because subsequent to this personal act of understanding new concepts have to be imported into the superego in order that the latter agency can now reflect the new changes that have taken place in the ego.

In order to separate, the patient needs to get access to the analyst's core feelings. His interpretations need to flow from here to as great an extent as possible if the patient is to be able to separate. This is most especially true for the psychotic patient whose fusion at the superego level is greatest and whose need for ego to ego contact is also greatest. It greatly concerned

[268]

one patient whether what I said to him was what *I* thought or felt or was just a received dictum of the psychoanalytical tradition and therefore just a superego content. Each time a resistance was overcome it was then possible to reach further into what I truly thought or felt and then he was able to separate himself a bit more from that mother glue. He became more able to separate himself from the analyst and from his maternal object intrapsychically. My greatest problem in his analysis was to reach those feelings which were most truly mine. In the case of that patient the problem was particularly acute but on reflection I think this may be a central problem in every analysis.

The psychoanalytical setting is concerned to foster a particular type of communication which is demonstrated most clearly in those moments which I have called the 'x-phenomenon'. This level of communication occurs from the very first moment when the patient enters the consulting room and with it a certain patterning of unconscious knowledge. The goal of the interpretative work is to make this conscious. At the same time there is another process at work, in both the analyst and the patient, whose goal is to sabotage the analysis. This process is located in the superego and makes use of illusions and cultural myths as its instrument. We call this process resistance but I have wanted to emphasize that this is a system in which both analyst and patient are involved, not something that is just located in the patient. The 'x-phenomenon' implies that there is a knowledge that is pre-verbal and that it is anterior to speech and therefore to interpretation. At this level of knowledge the patient knows unconsciously the analyst's internal attitudes. If, for example, the analyst is unconsciously envious of the patient in some particular way then the patient perceives it and only a change in the analyst's inner attitude will enable the patient to move forward psychically. The moment the analyst becomes aware of his or her attitude and is freed from it then the patient perceives it. That is to say he or she perceives a change within the self and may make declarations to that effect without knowing the cause. The interpretations that follow the x-phenomenon become conscious articulations of a change that

[269]

has already occurred unconsciously at the ego to ego level. The interpretations help them to re-establish the superego so that its myths and values change and become tuned in to the changes that have occurred within the ego.

With the exception of Winnicott I think that most analysts operate on the assumption that people are separate entities. I think that the x-phenomenon and the particular form of knowledge that it must imply means that people are individuals and yet part of a corporate entity. Because we are parts of a corporate entity then as soon as analyst and patient come together in the same room there is an immediate adaptation and fusing. The corporate entity instantly establishes itself. Socially this occurs when two people meet but in this case ego to ego contact is kept to a minimum, so also the joint illusion is kept to a minimum. In psychoanalysis the latter is enhanced but only, so to speak, so as to hypercathect it and work through it and give place to the personal.

Regression and the psychoanalytic situation

The unobtrusive analyst

MICHAEL BALINT

THE MORE the analyst's technique and behaviour are suggestive of omniscience and omnipotence, the greater is the danger of a malignant form of regression. On the other hand, the more the analyst can reduce the inequality between his patient and himself, and the more unobtrusive and ordinary he can remain in his patient's eyes, the better are the chances of a benign form of regression.

Thus we have arrived at one of the most important problems of modern analytic technique, which is how much of the two therapeutic agents – interpretation and object-relationship – should be used in any one case; when, in what proportion, and in what succession should they be used? This problem is important in every case, but is especially acute in the treatment of a regressed patient when the work has reached the area of the basic fault. Since, as we have found, words have only a limited and uncertain usefulness in these areas, it seems to follow that object-relationship is the more important and more reliable therapeutic factor during these periods, while in the states after the patient has emerged from his regression, interpretations will regain their importance.

The question now arises as to what sort of technique the analyst can use to create the object-relationship which, in his opinion, is the most suitable for that particular patient; or, in other words, will probably have the best therapeutic effect. The

[273]

first analyst who experimented with these effects fairly systematically was Ferenczi. Viewed from this angle his 'active
technique' and his 'principle of relaxation' were deliberate
attempts at creating object-relationships which, in his opinion,
were better suited to the needs of some patients than the atmosphere of an analytic setting created according to Freud's classical recommendations. Ferenczi recognized fairly soon that,
whatever he tried to do, the result was that his patients became
more dependent on him, that is, he became more and more
important for them; on the other hand he could not recognize
the reasons why this had to happen. Today we may add that his
technique, instead of reducing, increased the inequality between the patients and himself, whom they felt to be really
omniscient and all-important.

It was fairly early in my career that I realized that keeping to
the parameters of classical technique meant accepting strict
selection of patients. In my beginner's enthusiasm this was
unacceptable, and under Ferenczi's influence I experimented
with non-verbal communications; starting with 1932 I
reported on my experiments and results in several papers; most
of them reprinted in *Primary Love and Psycho-Analytic
Technique* (Balint, M., 1965). Of course, my techniques and
my ways of thinking have undergone considerable change during the years, and though I am fully aware that my present ideas
are anything but final, they have again reached a stage at which
I can 'organize' them, that is, express them in sufficiently concrete form so that they can be discussed and, above all,
criticized.

In my endeavour to overcome the difficulties just mentioned,
for some years now I have experimented with a technique that
allows the patient to experience a two-person relationship
which cannot, need not, and perhaps even must not, be expressed in words, but at times merely by what is customarily called
'acting out' in the analytic situation. I hasten to add that all
these non-verbal communications, the acting out, will of
course be worked through after the patient has emerged from
this level and reached the Oedipal level again – but not till then.

May I recapitulate here the several trains of thought that led me to these experiments. On many occasions I have found to my annoyance and despair that words cease to be reliable means of communication when the analytic work reaches the areas beyond the Oedipal level. The analyst may try, as hard as he can, to make his interpretations clear and unequivocal; the patient, somehow, always manages to experience them as something utterly different from that which the analyst intended them to be. At this level explanations, arguments, improved or amended versions, if tried, prove of no avail; the analyst cannot but accept the bitter fact that his words in these areas, instead of clarifying the situation, are often misunderstood, misinterpreted, and tend to increase the confusion of tongues between his patient and himself. Words become, in fact, unreliable and unpredictable.

This clinical observation is so important to my train of thought that I will show it from yet another angle. Words – at these periods – cease to be vehicles for free association; they have become lifeless, repetitious, and stereotyped; they strike one as an old worn-out gramophone record, with the needle running endlessly in the same groove. By the way, this is often equally true about the analyst's interpretations; during these periods they, too, seem to be running endlessly in the same groove. The analyst then discovers to his despair and dismay that, in these periods, there is no point whatever in going on interpreting the patient's verbal communications. At the Oedipal – and even at some of the so-called 'pre-Oedipal' – levels a proper interpretation, which makes a repressed conflict conscious and thereby resolves a resistance or undoes a split, gets the patient's free associations going again; at the level of the basic fault this does not necessarily happen. The interpretation is either experienced as interference, cruelty, unwarranted demand or unfair impingement, as a hostile act, or a sign of affection, or is felt so lifeless, in fact dead, that it has no effect at all.

Another train of thought started with the discovery of the ocnophilic bias of our technique (Balint, M., 1959, 1968). Nowadays analysts are enjoined to interpret everything that happens in the analytic situation also, or even foremost, in terms of transference, i.e., of object-relationship. This otherwise sensible and efficient technique means that we offer ourselves to our patients incessantly as objects to cling to, and interpret anything contrary to clinging as resistance, aggressiveness, narcissism, touchiness, paranoid anxiety, castration fear, and so on. A highly ambivalent and strained atmosphere is created in this way, the patient struggling, prompted by his desire for independence, but finding his way barred at every point by ocnophilic 'transference' interpretations.

The third train of thought originated from my study of 'the silent patient'. Silence, as is more and more recognized, may have many meanings, each of them requiring different technical handling. Silence may be an arid and frightening emptiness, inimical to life and growth, in which case the patient ought to be got out of it as soon as possible; it may be a friendly exciting expanse, inviting the patient to undertake adventurous journeys into the uncharted lands of his fantasy life, in which case any ocnophilic transference interpretation may be utterly out of place, in fact disturbing; silence may also mean an attempt at re-establishing the harmonious mix-up of primary love that existed between the individual and his environment before the emergence of objects, in which case any interference either by interpretation or in any other way is strictly contraindicated as it may destroy the harmony by making demands on the patient.

The last train of thought is connected with my ideas about the area of creation, an area of the mind in which there is no external organized object, and any intrusion of such an object by attention-seeking interpretations inevitably destroys for the patient the possibility of creating something out of himself.

Objects in this area are as yet unorganized, and the process of creation leading to their organization needs, above all, time. This time may be short or very long; but whatever its length, it cannot be influenced from outside. Almost certainly the same will be true about our patients' creations out of their unconscious. This may be one of the reasons why the analyst's usual interpretations are felt by patients regressed to this area as inadmissible; interpretations are indeed whole, 'organized', thoughts or objects whose interactions with the hazy, dream-like, as yet 'unorganized' contents of the area of creation might cause either havoc or an unnatural, premature, organization.

The outward appearance of all these, widely different, states is a silent patient, seemingly withdrawn from normal analytic work, 'acting out' instead of associating, or possibly even repeating something instead of recollecting it; and, last but not least, he may also be described as regressing towards some primitive behaviour instead of progressing towards complying with our fundamental rule. All these descriptions – withdrawal, acting out, repetition instead of remembering, regression – are correct but incomplete and thus may lead to mistaken technical measures.

Thus the technique that I found usually profitable with patients who regressed to the level of the basic fault or of creation, was to bear with their regression for the time being, without any forceful attempt at intervening with an interpretation. This time may amount only to some minutes, but equally to a more or less long stretch of sessions. As I have mentioned several times, words at these periods have anyhow ceased to be reliable means of communication; the patient's words are no longer vehicles for free associations, they have become lifeless, repetitive, and stereotyped, they do not mean what they seem to say. The standard technical advice is correct in this case too; the analyst's task is to understand what lies behind the patient's words; the problem is only how to communicate this understanding to a regressed patient. My answer is in accepting unreservedly the fact that words have become unreliable and by sincerely giving up, for the time being, any attempt at forcing the patient back to the verbal level. This means abandoning any attempt at 'organizing' the material produced by the patient – it is not the 'right' material anyway – and tolerating it so that it may remain incoherent, nonsensical, unorganized, till the patient – after returning to the Oedipal level of conventional language – will be able to give the analyst the key to understand it.

In other words, the analyst must accept the regression. This means that he must create an environment, a climate, in which he and his patient can tolerate the regression in a mutual experience. This is essential because in these states any outside pressure reinforces the anyhow strong tendency in the patient to develop relationships of inequality between himself and his objects, perpetuating thereby his proneness to regression.

I wish to illustrate what I have just said by referring to an episode from an analysis which, at that time, had been going on for about two years. The patient remained silent right from the start of the session for more than 30 minutes; the analyst accepted this and, realizing what possibly was happening, waited without any attempt whatever at interference; in fact, he did not even feel uncomfortable or under pressure to do something. I should add that in this treatment silences had occurred previously on several occasions, and patient and analyst had thus had some training in tolerating them. The silence was eventually broken by the patient starting to sob, relieved, and soon after he was able to speak. He told his analyst that at long last he was able to reach himself; ever since childhood he had never been left alone, there had always been someone telling him what to do. Some sessions later he reported that during the silence he had all sorts of associations, but rejected each of them as irrelevant, as nothing but an annoying superficial nuisance.

Of course, the silence could easily have been interpreted as resistance, withdrawal, a sign of persecutory fear, inability to cope with depressive anxieties, a symptom of a repetition compulsion, etc.; moreover since the analyst knew his patient fairly well, he could even have interpreted or guessed one or the other topic emerging in the associations and also some of the reasons why the patient felt that particular idea irrelevant and was rejecting it. All these might have been correct interpretations in every respect – except in one: they would have destroyed the silence and the patient would not have been able to 'reach himself', at any rate, not on that occasion. There is one more unintended side-effect of any, however correct, interpretation: it would inevitably reinforce the patient's strong repetition-compulsion, there would again be someone there, telling him what to feel, to think, in fact what to do.

Furthermore, all this happened in an exclusively two-person

relationship; the dynamic problem to be dealt with did not have the structure of a conflict for which a 'solution' had to be found. The situation demanded somewhat more skill from the analyst than, say, the understanding of verbal association; by finding a correct answer to the silence, the analyst was running the risk of raising expectations in his patient that this would possibly happen time and again and trigger in this way the development of addiction-like states; another risk was to impress the patient that he has got an analyst so wise and so powerful that he can read his patient's unspoken thoughts and respond to them correctly, the risk of becoming 'omnipotent'; and lastly, words would have been unreliable in this situation, more likely than not they would have forced the patient prematurely into the Oedipal area and created further obstacles to the therapeutic work instead of removing some. Of course, all these are characteristic signs that the analytic work has reached the area of the basic fault.

The right technique, as long as the patient is regressed to this level, is to accept 'acting out' in the analytic situation as valid means of communication without any attempt at speedily 'organizing' it by interpretations. Emphatically, this does not mean that in these periods the analyst's role becomes negligible or is restricted to sympathetic passivity; on the contrary, his presence is most important, not only in that he must be felt to be present but must be all the time at the right distance – neither so far that the patient might feel lost or abandoned, nor so close that the patient might feel encumbered and unfree – in fact, at a distance that corresponds to the patient's actual need; in general the analyst must know what are his patient's needs, why they are as they are, and why they fluctuate and change.

From another angle, the technical problem is how to offer 'something' to the patient which might function as a primary object, or at any rate as a suitable substitute for it, or in still other words, on to which he can project his primary love.

Should this 'something' be (a) the analyst himself (the analyst who undertakes to treat a regression), or (b) the therapeutic situation? The question is which of these two is the more likely to achieve sufficient harmony with the patient so

[279]

that there may be only minimal clash of interest between the patient and one available object in the present. On the whole, it is safer if the patient can use the therapeutic situation as a substitute, if for no other reason than because it diminishes the risk of the analyst becoming a most important, omniscient, and omnipotent object.

This offering to the patient a 'primary object', of course, is not tantamount to giving primary love; in any case mothers do not *give* it either. What they do is to behave truly as primary objects, that is, to offer themselves as primary objects to be cathected by primary love. This difference between 'giving primary love' and 'offering oneself to be cathected by primary love'.may be of fundamental importance for our technique not only with regressed patients, but also with a number of difficult treatment situations.

To describe the same role from a different angle, i.e., using different 'words': the analyst must function during these periods as a provider of time and of milieu. This does not mean that he is under obligation to compensate for the patient's early privations and give more care, love, affection than the patient's parents have given originally (and even if he tried, he would almost certainly fail). What the analyst must provide – and, if at all possible, during the regular sessions only – is sufficient time free from extrinsic temptations, stimuli, and demands, including those originating from himself (the analyst). The aim is that the patient should be able to find himself, to accept himself, and to get on with himself, knowing all the time that there is a scar in himself, his basic fault, which cannot be 'analysed' out of existence; moreover, he must be allowed to discover *his* way to the world of objects – and not be shown the 'right' way by some profound or correct interpretation. If this can be done, the patient will not feel that the objects impinge on, and oppress, him. It is only to this extent that the analyst should provide a better, more 'understanding' environment, but in no other way, in particular not in the form of more care, love, attention, gratification, or protection. Perhaps it ought to be stressed that considerations of this kind may serve as criteria for deciding whether a certain 'craving' or 'need' should be satisfied, or recognized but left unsatisfied.

The guiding principle during these periods is to avoid any interference not absolutely necessary; interpretations particularly should be scrutinized most meticulously, since they are felt more often than not as unwarranted demand, attack, criticism, seduction, or stimulation; they should be given only if the analyst is certain that the patient *needs* them, for at such times *not giving* them would be felt as unwarranted demand or stimulation. From this angle, what I have called the dangers of ocnophilic interpretations may be understood better; though the patient is in need of an environment, of a world of objects, such objects – foremost among them the analyst – must not be felt as in any way demanding, interfering, intruding, as this would reinforce the old oppressive inequality between subject and object.

I hope this clinical description will help the reader to understand why so many analysts have quite so many different terms to describe it. All of them had the following features in common: there was the suggestion that no oppressive or demanding object should be present; that the environment should be quiet, peaceful, safe, and unobtrusive; that it should be there and that it should be favourable to the subject, but that the subject should be in no way obliged to take notice, to acknowledge, or to be concerned about it. Once again, these common features are the exact characteristics of what I called primary objects or primary substance.

To provide this sort of object or environment is certainly an important part of the therapeutic task. Clearly, it is only a part, not the whole of the task. Apart from being a 'need-recognizing' and perhaps even a 'need-satisfying' object, the analyst must be also a 'need-understanding' object who, in addition, must be able to communicate his understanding to his patient.

Some pressures on the analyst for physical contact during the reliving of an early trauma

PATRICK J. CASEMENT

IS PHYSICAL CONTACT with the patient, even of a token kind, always to be precluded without question under the classical rule of abstinence? Or are there some occasions when this might be appropriate, even necessary, as Margaret Little has suggested in relation to episodes of delusional transference (1957, 1958), or as Balint and Winnicott have illustrated in relation to periods of deep regression? (Balint, M. 1952, 1968; Winnicott, 1954a, 1963a).

I shall present a clinical sequence during which the possibility of physical contact was approached as an open issue. There seemed to be a case for allowing a patient the possibility of holding my hand. The decision to reconsider this was arrived at from listening to the patient and from following closely the available cues from the countertransference. The clinical material clearly illustrates some of the issues involved in this decision.

The patient, whom I shall call Mrs B., is in her 30s. She had been in analysis about two and a half years. A son had been born during the second year of the analysis.

When she was eleven months old Mrs B. had been severely scalded, having pulled boiling water onto herself while her mother was out of the room. She could have died from the burns. When she was seventeen months old she had to be operated on to release growing skin from the dead scar tissue. The operation was done under a local anaesthetic. During this the mother had fainted. (It is relevant to the childhood history that the father was largely absent during the first five years.)

Soon after the summer holiday Mrs B. presented the following dream. *She had been trying to feed a despairing child. The child was standing and was about ten months old. It wasn't clear whether the child was a boy or a girl.* Mrs B. wondered about the age of the child. Her son was soon to be ten months old. He was now able to stand. She too would have been standing at ten months. (That would have been before the accident.) 'Why is the child in my dream so despairing?' she asked. Her son was a lively child and she assumed that she too had been a normal happy child until the accident. This prompted me to recall how Mrs B. had clung to an idealized view of her pre-accident childhood. I thought she was now daring to question this. I therefore commented that maybe she was beginning to wonder about the time before the accident. Perhaps not everything had been quite so happy as she had always needed to assume. She immediately held up her hand to signal me to stop.

During the following silence I wondered why there was this present anxiety. Was it the patient's need still not to look at anything from before the accident unless it was seen as perfect? Was the accident itself being used as a screen memory? I thought this probable. After a while I said she seemed to be afraid of finding any element of bad experience during the time before the accident, as if she still felt that the good that had been there before must be kept entirely separate from the bad that had followed. She listened in silence, making no perceptible response during the rest of the session.

The next day Mrs B. came to her session with a look of terror on her face. For this session, and the five sessions following, she could not lie on the couch. She explained that when I had gone on talking, after she had signalled me to stop, the couch had 'become' the operating table with me as the surgeon, who had gone on operating regardless, after her mother had fainted. She now couldn't lie down 'because the experience will go on'. Nothing could stop it then, she felt sure.

In one of these sitting-up sessions Mrs B. showed me a

photograph of her holiday house, built into the side of a mountain with high retaining walls. She stressed how essential these walls are to hold the house from falling. She was afraid of falling for ever.[1] She felt this had happened to her after her mother had fainted.

(Here I should mention that Mrs B. had previously recalled thinking that her mother had died, when she had fallen out of her sight during the operation, and how she had felt that she was left alone with no one to protect her from the surgeon who seemed to be about to kill her with his knife.) Now, in this session, Mrs B. told me a detail of that experience which she had never mentioned before. At the start of the operation her mother had been holding her hands in hers, and Mrs B. remembered her terror upon finding her mother's hands slipping out of hers as she fainted and disappeared. She now thought she had been trying to re-find her mother's hands ever since, and she began to stress the importance of physical contact for her. She said she couldn't lie down on the couch again unless she knew she could, if necessary, hold my hand in order to get through the reliving of the operation experience. Would I allow this or would I refuse? If I refused she wasn't sure that she could continue with her analysis.

My initial response was to acknowledge to her that she needed me to be 'in touch' with the intensity of her anxiety. However, she insisted she had to know whether or not I would actually allow her to hold my hand. I felt under increased pressure due to this being near the end of a Friday session, and I was beginning to fear that the patient might indeed leave the analysis. My next comment was defensively equivocal. I said some analysts would not contemplate allowing this, but I realized that she might need to have the possibility of holding my hand if it seemed to be the only way for her to get through

---

[1] 'Falling for ever' is referred to by Winnicott as one of the 'unthinkable anxieties' along with 'going to pieces', 'having no relationship to the body' and 'having no orientation' (1962, p. 58).

this experience. She showed some relief upon my saying this.[2]

Over the weekend I reviewed the implications of this possibility of the patient holding my hand. While reflecting upon my countertransference around this issue I came to recognize the following key points:

1. I was in effect offering to be the 'better mother' who would remain holding her hand, in contrast to the actual mother who had not been able to bear what was happening.

2. My offer had been partly motivated by my fear of losing this patient, which was especially threatening to me just then as I was about to present a paper on this patient to our Society.

3. If I were to hold this patient's hand it would almost certainly not, as she assumed, help her to get through a re-experiencing of the original trauma. (A central factor of this had been the *absence* of her mother's hands.) It would instead amount to a bypassing of this aspect of the trauma, and could reinforce the patient's perception of this as something too terrible ever fully to be remembered or to be experienced.

I therefore decided that I must review with the patient the implications of this offer as soon as I had an opportunity to do so.

On the Sunday I received a hand-delivered letter in which the patient said she had had another dream of the despairing child, but this time there were signs of hope. *The child was crawling towards a motionless figure with the excited expectation of reaching this figure.*

On the Monday, although she was somewhat reassured by her dream, Mrs B. remained sitting on the couch. She saw the central figure as me representing her missing mother. She also stressed that she hadn't wanted me to have to wait to know about the dream. I interpreted her fear that I might not have been able to wait to be reassured, and she agreed. She had been afraid I might have collapsed over the weekend, under the

---

[2] At the time I was thinking that this offer of the possibility of holding my hand might, in Eissler's (1953) terms, be a permissible 'parameter'.

weight of the Friday session, if I had been left until Monday without knowing that she was beginning to feel more hopeful.

As this session continued, what emerged was a clear impression that Mrs B. was seeing the possibility of holding my hand as a 'short-cut' to feeling safer. She wanted me to be the motionless figure, controlled by her and not allowed to move, towards whom she could crawl with the excited expectation that she would eventually be allowed to touch me. Mrs B. then reported an image, which was a continuation in the session of the written dream. She saw the dream-child reaching the central figure, but as she touched this it had crumbled and collapsed. With this cue as my lead I told her I had thought very carefully about this, and I had come to the conclusion that this tentative offer of my hand might have appeared to provide a way of getting through the experience she was so terrified of, but I now realized it would instead become a side-stepping of that experience as it had been rather than a living through it. I knew that if I seemed to be inviting an avoidance of this central aspect of the original experience I would be failing her as her analyst. I therefore did not think that I should leave the possibility of holding my hand still open to her. Mrs B. looked stunned. She asked me if I realized what I had just done. I had taken my hand away from her just as her mother had, and she immediately assumed that this must be because I too couldn't bear to remain in touch with what she was going through. Nothing I said could alter her assumption that I was afraid to let her touch me.

The following day the patient's response to what I had said was devastating. Still sitting on the couch she told me her left arm (the one nearest to me) was 'steaming'. I had burned her. She couldn't accept any interpretation from me. Only a real physical response from me could do anything about it. She wanted to stop her analysis to get away from what was happening to her in her sessions. She could never trust me again. I tried to interpret that her trust in her mother, which had in a fragile way been restored after the accident, seemed to have been finally broken after her mother had fainted. It was this ultimate breach of that trust which had got in the way of her subsequent relationship to her. I felt it was this that she was now in the process of re-enacting with me in order to find that this unresolved breach of trust could be repaired. She listened to this, and was nodding understanding, but she repeated that it was impossible to repair.

The following day Mrs B. raged at me still for what she saw as my withdrawing from her. The possibility of holding my hand had been the same to her as actual holding. She felt sure she would not have abused the offer. It had been vitally important to her that I had been prepared to allow this, but my change of mind had become to her a real dropping away of the hand she needed to hold on to. To her I was now her mother who had become afraid. Her arm seemed to be on fire. To her I was afraid of being burned too.

Mrs B. told me that the previous day, immediately after her session with me, she had become 'fully suicidal'. She had only got out of this by asking a friend if she could go round to see her, at any time, if she felt that she couldn't carry on. She had ultimately needed to see her friend. It had been her friend's availability which had prevented her from killing herself. She then rebuked me with the fact that her friend could get it right. Why couldn't I? I told her she did not need from me what she could get from others. She needed something different from me. She needed me not to buy off her anger by offering to be the 'better mother'. It was important I should not be afraid of her anger, or of her despair, in order that I stay with her throughout the relived experience of no longer having her mother's hands to hold on to. She needed me to remain analyst rather than have me as a 'pretend' mother. It was also crucial I do nothing that could suggest I needed to protect myself from what she was experiencing or was feeling towards me. She listened and became calmer. Then, momentarily before leaving the session, she lay down on the couch. She thus resumed the lying position.

I shall now summarize the next two weeks. Mrs B. dreamt of *being lost and unsafe amongst a strange people with whom she could not find a common language.* I interpreted her anxiety as to whether I could find a common language with her. In one

[287]

session she had a visual image of a child crying stone tears, which I interpreted as the tears of a petrified child (herself). She dreamt of *a baby being dropped and left to die*. She dreamt of *being very small and being denied the only food she wanted. It was there but a tall person would not let her have it*. In another dream *she was in terror anticipating some kind of explosion*. Throughout this she persisted in her conviction that she could never trust me again, and she experienced me as afraid of her. Alongside this she told me her husband had become very supporting of her continuing her analysis, even though he was getting a lot of 'kick-back' from it. This was quite new. I interpreted that at some level she was becoming more aware of me as able to take the kick-back from her, in her analysis.

Shortly after this Mrs B. reported the following two dreams in the same session. In the first *she was taking a child every day to meet her mother to get some order into the chaos*, which I interpreted as her bringing her child-self to me in order to work through the chaos of her feelings towards me as the mother she still couldn't trust. She agreed with this but added she didn't bring the child to me by the hand. She had to drag her child-self by the hair. In the second dream *she was falling through the air, convinced that she was going to die despite the fact that she was held by a parachute with a helicopter watching over her*. She could see the contradictions (sure of dying whilst actually being safe) but this did not stop her feeling terrified in the dream, and still terrified of me in the session. She stressed that she didn't know if I realized she was still feeling sure she was dying inside.

On the following Monday Mrs B. told me she had dreamt that *she had come for her last session as she couldn't go on. She had begun falling for ever, the couch and the room falling with her. There was no bottom and no end to it*.

The next day the patient felt she was going insane. She had dreamt *there was a sheet of glass between herself and me so that she couldn't touch me or see me clearly. It was like a car windscreen with no wipers in a storm*. I interpreted her inability to feel that I could get in touch with what she was feeling, because of the barrier between her and me created by the storm of her feelings inside her. This prevented her seeing me clearly, just as it had with her mother. She agreed and collapsed into uncontrolled crying, twisting on the couch, tortured with pain. At the end of this session she became panicked that I wouldn't be able to tolerate having experienced this degree of her distress.

On the Friday she spoke of a new worker in her office. She had asked him how long he had been trained. She then realized she was asking him for his credentials. I interpreted her anxiety about my credentials and whether I had the necessary experience to be able to see her through. I added that maybe she used the word 'credentials' because of the allusion to 'believe'. She replied 'Of course, credo.' She said that she wanted to believe that I could see her through, and to trust me, but she still couldn't.

The next week Mrs B. continued to say she didn't think she could go on. She had had many terrible dreams over the weekend. The following day she again sat up for the session. For much of this session she seemed to be quite deluded. Awareness of reality was fleeting and tenuous. For the greater part of the session she was a child. She began by saying she didn't just talk to her baby, she picks him up and holds him. Then, looking straight at me she said, 'I am a baby and you are the person I need to be my mother. I need you to realize this, because unless you are prepared to hold me I cannot go on. You have got to understand this.' She was putting me under immense pressure. Finally she stared accusingly at me and said 'You *are* my mother and you are *not* holding me.'

Throughout this I was aware of the delusional quality of her perception of me.[3] In this session there was little 'as if' sense left in her experience of me, and at times there seemed to be none. It was meaningless to her when I attempted to interpret this as transference, as a reliving of her childhood experience. Not only was I the mother who was not holding her, in her terror of me I had also become the surgeon with a knife in his hand who

---

[3] I now understand this in terms of the psychic immediacy of the transference experience.

seemed to be about to kill her. At this point there seemed to be no remaining contact with me as analyst.

I reflected upon my dilemma. If I did *not* give in to her demands I might lose the patient, or she might really go psychotic and need to be hospitalized. If I *did* give in to her I would be colluding with her delusional perception of me, and the avoided elements of the trauma could become encapsulated as too terrible ever to confront. I felt placed in an impossible position. However, once I came to recognize the projective identification process operating here I began to surface from this feeling of complete helplessness. This enabled me eventually to interpret from my countertransference feelings. Very slowly, and with pauses to check that the patient was following me, I said to her, 'You are making me experience in myself the sense of despair, and the impossibility of going on, that you are feeling. I am aware of being in what feels to me like a total paradox. In one sense I am feeling it is impossible to reach you just now, and yet in another sense I feel that my telling you this may be the only way I can reach you.' She followed what I was saying very carefully, and slightly nodded her head. I continued, 'Similarly I feel as if it could be impossible to go on, and yet I feel that the only way I can help you through this is by my being prepared to tolerate what you are making me feel, and going on.' After a long silence Mrs B. began to speak to me again as analyst. She said, 'For the first time I can believe you, that you *are* in touch with what I have been feeling, and what is so amazing is that you can bear it.' I was then able to interpret to her that her desperate wish for me to let her touch me had been her way of letting me know she needed me to be really in touch with what she was going through. This time she could agree. She remained in silence for the last ten minutes of this session, and I sensed that it was important that I should do nothing to interrupt this in any way.

The next day Mrs B. told me what had been happening during that silence. She had been able to smell her mother's presence, and she had felt her mother's hands again holding hers. She felt that it was her mother from before the fainting that she had got in touch with, as she had never felt held like that since then. I commented that she had been able to find the internal mother that she had lost touch with, as distinct from the 'pretend' mother she had been wanting me to become. We could now see that if I had agreed to hold her physically it would have been a way of shutting off what she was experiencing, not only for her but also for me, as if I really couldn't bear to remain with her through this. She immediately recognized the implications of what I was saying and replied. 'Yes. You would have become a collapsed analyst. I could not realize it at the time but I can now see you would then have become the same as my mother who fainted. I am so glad you didn't let that happen.'

To conclude I will summarize part of the last session in this week. Mrs B. had woken feeling happy and had later found herself singing extracts from the opera *Der Freischütz*, the plot of which (she explained) includes the triumph of light over darkness. She had also dreamt *she was in a car which had got out of control having taken on a life of its own. The car crashed into a barrier which had prevented her from running into the oncoming traffic. The barrier had saved her because it had remained firm. If it had collapsed she would have been killed.* She showed great relief that I had withstood her angry demands. My remaining firm had been able to stop the process which had taken on a life of its own, during which she had felt completely out of control. The same dream ended with *the patient reaching out to safety through the car windscreen which had opened to her like two glass doors.*

Discussion

This case illustrates the interplay between the various dynamics operating. My initial offer of possible physical contact was, paradoxically, tantamount to the countertransference withdrawal which the patient later attributed to me in my decision not to leave this offer of that easier option open to her. In terms of Bion's (1962) concept of 'a projective-identification-rejecting-object' the countertransference here became *the container's fear of the contained.* A further complicating pressure came from the fact that I was shortly to present a paper on this patient to our Society, and I was genuinely afraid of being exposed there as having failed had my patient left the analysis, or had she needed to be hospitalized, just prior to my presenting that paper concerning her. By offering the possibility of the patient holding my hand I was in effect seeking to lessen these risks to myself, and this is an example of Racker's (1968) concept of *indirect countertransference*, in that my response to the patient here was being influenced by some degree of persecutory superego being projected by me on to my professional colleagues.

The resulting sequence can be understood in the interactional terms of Sandler's (1976) concept of *role-responsiveness* or in terms of Winnicott's description of the patient's need to be able to experience in the present, in relation to a real situation between patient and analyst, the extremes of feeling which belonged to an early traumatic experience but which had been 'frozen' because of being too intense for the primitive ego to encompass *at that time* (Winnicott, 1954b, 1963b. See also Winnicott, 1974 [*this volume – Ed.*]). There had come to be a real issue between this patient and me, in the withdrawal of my earlier offer of the possibility of holding my hand. In using this to represent the central element of the original trauma the patient entered into an intensely real experience of the past as she had perceived it. In so doing she was able, as it were, to 'join up with' her own feelings, now unfrozen and available to her. The repressed past became, in the present, a conscious psychic reality from which (this time) she did not have defensively to be psychically absent. During this I had to continue to be the surviving analyst, and not become a collapsed analyst, in order that she could defuse the earlier fantasy that it had been the intensity of her need for her mother that had caused her mother to faint.

The eventual interpretative resolution within this session grew out of my awareness of the *projective identification process* then operating. I am understanding this here as the product of interactional pressures upon the analyst from the patient, which are unconsciously aiming to evoke in him the unbearable feeling state which the patient could not on her

own yet contain within herself (cf. Ogden, 1979). It is a matter
for speculation whether I would have been so fully subjected to
the necessary impact of this patient's experience had I not first
approached the question of possible physical contact as an
open issue. Had I gone by the book, following the classical rule
of no physical contact under any circumstance, I would certainly have been taking the safer course for me but I would
probably then have been accurately perceived by the patient as
actually afraid even to consider such contact. I am not sure that
the reliving of this early trauma would have been as real as it
was to the patient, or in the end so therapeutically effective, if I
had been preserving myself throughout at that safer distance of
classical 'correctness'. Instead I acted upon my intuition of the
moment, and it is uncanny how precisely and unwittingly this
led me to re-enact with the patient this detail of the original
trauma, which she needed to be able to experience within the
analytic relationship and to be genuinely angry about. It is this
unconscious responsiveness to unconscious cues from the
patient to which Sandler refers in his (1976) paper 'Countertransference and Role-Responsiveness'. Winnicott also speaks
of this when he says: 'In the end the patient uses the analyst's
failures, often quite small ones, perhaps manoeuvred by the
patient . . . and we have to put up with being in a limited context misunderstood. The operative factor is that the patient
now hates the analyst for the failure that originally came as an
environmental factor, outside the infant's area of omnipotent
control, but that is *now* staged in the transference. So in the end
we succeed by failing – failing the patient's way. This is a long
distance from the simple theory of cure by corrective experience' (1963b, p. 258).

With regard to the recovered analytic holding I wish to add
one further point. Because this was arrived at experientially
with the patient, rather than by rule of thumb, it did more than
prove a rightness of the classical position concerning no physical contact. 'En route' this had instead acquired a specificity for
this patient which, in my opinion, allowed a fuller reliving of
this early trauma than might otherwise have been possible.

I shall conclude with a quotation from Bion's (1962) paper

'A Theory of Thinking'. He says, 'If the infant *feels* [my italics] it is dying it can arouse fears that it is dying in the mother. A well-balanced mother can accept these and respond therapeutically: that is to say in a manner that makes the infant feel it is receiving its frightened personality back again but in a form that it can tolerate – the fears are manageable by the infant personality. If the mother cannot tolerate these projections the infant is reduced to continued projective identification carried out with increasing force and frequence' (pp. 114f). Bion continues: 'Normal development follows if the relationship between infant and breast permits the infant to project a feeling, say, that it is dying into the mother and to reintroject it after its sojourn in the breast has made it tolerable to the infant psyche. If the projection is not accepted by the mother the infant feels that its feeling that it is dying is stripped of such meaning as it has. It therefore reintrojects, not a fear of dying made tolerable, but a nameless dread' (p. 116).

I know that Bion is here describing an infant's relationship to the breast. Nevertheless I believe that a similar process, at a later developmental stage, is illustrated in the clinical sequence I have described. I consider that it was my readiness to preserve the restored psychoanalytical holding, in the face of considerable pressures upon me to relinquish it, which eventually enabled my patient to receive her own frightened personality back again in a form that she could tolerate. Had I resorted to the physical holding that she demanded the central trauma would have remained frozen, and could have been regarded as perhaps for ever unmanageable. The patient would then have reintrojected, not a fear of dying made tolerable, but instead a nameless dread.

Attachment and new beginning: some links between the work of Michael Balint and John Bowlby

J. R. PEDDER

IT HAS BEEN SAID that in the years following psychoanalytic training, there is a need for a period of recovery or convalescence. This is perhaps necessary if the training is not to be over-idealized. Every analyst needs to discover his own ideas. During this phase of my own development I was presented with the problem of a patient who was depressed and quickly became severely regressed, and often demanded some form of contact such as to hold my hand. I felt intuitively that this would be unhelpful, which of course also agreed with the view of my internal supervisor-ego that it would be wrong. However, not wanting to accept this merely as dogma, I set out to discover for myself what I thought. I found Michael Balint's writings on benign and malignant regression particularly helpful. I was also interested at the time in John Bowlby's work on attachment theory. The first two volumes on attachment and loss (1969, 1973) had been published, and these suggested a possible new way of viewing such patients' needs in a framework other than that of classical libido theory.

A little while later another patient arrived whose needs, I hoped, would be more in the area of benign regression; fortunately, this proved to be the case and led to a new beginning. This paper gives an account of her case and the theoretical problems I was trying to work out. The technique used has not become a standard part of my therapeutic repertoire, and I have not handled a case in a similar way since. Perhaps I now rely more on the interpretative mode. However, I am certain that stranger things happen in analysis than orthodox accounts sometimes seem to suggest. Most analysts must, at times, have to face such issues but, although they are sometimes discussed informally, they are seldom actually written about. I feel we should always be prepared to be surprised and hopefully not too thrown by the unexpected.

Author's Preface, 1985

Bowlby's definitive three-volume work (1969, 1973 *et seq.*) crowns a lifetime's researches into the early and late effects of childhood separation. He has recently (Bowlby, 1975) summarized this work. In his reconsideration of instinct theory he argues that attachment behaviour should be 'conceived as a class of behaviour that is distinct from feeding behaviour and sexual behaviour and of at least as equal significance in human life'. He considers the 'most likely function of attachment behaviour is protection, mainly from predators' and therefore crucial to the survival of the species.

Bowlby's work has been criticized (e.g., Engel, 1971) for discarding the dynamic and economic points of view and not adequately distinguishing psychological from behavioural frames of reference. However, as Matte Blanco more favourably comments, 'its impact upon ideas regarding the psychobiological foundations of psychoanalysis is bound to be great' (1971). It is suggested here that Bowlby's concept of attachment behaviour could provide the psycho-biological foundation which Michael Balint was looking for.

Balint (Balint, M., 1968) twice speaks of 'attachment behaviour' – once in discussing the 'ocnophilic bias of our modern technique' when he refers to 'object-seeking, clinging, attachment behaviour' (p. 169); and earlier in referring to Bowlby (1958), 'these phenomena have been known for some considerable time; recently under the influence of ethology they are referred to as "attachment behaviour"' (p. 165).

This paper pursues these links and also discusses, in the light

[296]

of Bowlby's view of the importance of attachment behaviour, the question of whether it can ever be appropriate to gratify a patient's wish for physical contact with the analyst, e.g., the wish to hold a hand, during a period of regression in analysis.

Balint (1968) makes a valuable distinction between malignant 'regression aimed at gratification' and more benign 'regression aimed at recognition'. The former might occur in hysterical patients whose problems lie in the area of Oedipal conflict and belongs to three-person psychology. Few would suggest that the regressive wishes of such patients should be gratified. We accept Freud's dictum, 'The treatment must be carried out in abstinence' (1915d, p. 165). Language and interpretation should suffice; though interestingly enough Freud himself soon modified this to *'Analytic treatment should be carried through as far as is possible, under privation – in a state of abstinence'* (1919a, p. 162, Freud's italics).

The more benign regression may occur in those whose problem lies at the level of what Balint has termed the basic fault and belongs to two-person psychology. In the latter type of case the regression may herald a 'new beginning' if the patient's needs are recognized and met.

Khan (1969b) makes the distinction between these two levels very clear in his essay on Balint's researches on the theory of psychoanalytic technique. At the area of the Oedipal level, 'the provision of frustrations' is the key; in the area of the basic fault 'the provision of recognitions' may be essential to a new beginning.

Balint first mentioned such needs in 1937: 'Very often these wishes do not go further than to be able to touch the analyst, to cling to him, or to be touched or stroked by him.' Yet he provided few details of how he actually met such needs. Thus he writes, 'Another patient . . . wanted and had to hold one of my fingers for quite some time during a particular period of her analysis' (1968, p. 133). A little later he refers to 'some sort of physical contact with the analyst, the most frequent form of which is the holding of the analyst's hand, or one of his fingers, or touching his chair, etc.' (1968, p. 145). Yet Balint does not seem quite sure how to understand such needs in terms of

[297]

instinct theory. Of the first example he writes, 'with a little effort one could find – or create – *an instinct to cling* [my italics] for the explanation of the satisfaction observed in her case' (p. 134). Whereas further on he says 'this contact is definitely libidinous, on occasion may even be highly charged' (p. 145).

Now 'an instinct to cling' which Balint had first mentioned in his 1937 paper sounds very like the expression of attachment behaviour; whereas if the 'contact is definitely libidinous' this sounds more like the gratification of an erotic instinct, which so alarms us all because of Freud's original reservations and the consequences of Ferenczi's 'Grand Experiments'. Balint has reviewed the tragic disagreement between Freud and Ferenczi in this area which he feels made it so hard for him (Balint) to get the subject a fair hearing (1968, pp. 149-56).

Although Balint can speak of an 'instinct to cling' it seems hard for him not to think of it as something erotic. When he writes, 'the level of gratification never goes beyond that of mild *fore-pleasure*' (1952, p. 231, my italics), this seems to be subsuming hand-holding under the heading of erotic behaviour, as of course it could well be, whereas if we see hand-holding as at times an expression of attachment behaviour our perspective shifts.

Bowlby (1958), in his review of the psychoanalytic literature on the nature of the child's tie to his mother, expresses the view that the 'Hungarian school' comes closest to his ideas on attachment and particularly in Balint's concept of primary object love. He quotes Balint (1937): 'This form of object-relationship is not linked to any of the erotogenic zones; it is not oral, oral-sucking, anal, genital, etc. love but is something on its own. . .'

Winnicott (1960a) appears to be making a similar distinction between meeting needs and satisfying instincts when he writes, 'It must be emphasized that in referring to the meeting of infant needs I am not referring to the satisfaction of instincts' (p. 141). The case described here is also a good example of how 'when a False Self becomes organized in an individual who has a high intellectual potential there is a very strong tendency for the mind to become the location of the False Self, and in this case there develops a dissociation between intellectual activity and psychosomatic existence' (p. 144), in that her breakdown occurred while pursuing a postgraduate degree which represented the interests of her false self.

In the same paper Winnicott argues that, by contrast, spontaneity is the hallmark of the True Self: 'The spontaneous gesture is the True Self in action.' This reminds one of Balint's patient whose 'new beginning' was heralded by the spontaneous gesture of a somersault during a session (1968, p. 128).

Lastly, my patient well illustrated Winnicott's (1960a) comment:

> In analysis of a False Personality the fact must be recognized that the analyst can only talk to the False Self of the patient about the patient's True Self. It is as if a nurse brings a child, and at first the analyst discusses the child's problem, and the child is not directly contacted. Analysis does not start until the nurse has left the child with the analyst, and the child has become able to remain alone with the analyst and has started to play (p. 151).

Case history

A young teacher in her mid-20s was referred by a general psychiatrist sympathetic to analysis. She had previously been under treatment from psychiatrists of a different school and received heavy doses of mixed antidepressant drugs as an inpatient. She told me she had become depressed at the age of 21 while doing a postgraduate degree abroad. She had returned home, been admitted to hospital for several months and thereafter stood the heavy doses of drugs for some eighteen months. She was longing to talk to someone and 'break down the shell around herself', which the drugs had only increased. She had often said to her previous psychiatrists that there were a lot of things she wanted to talk about but they had replied in the vein: 'Never mind about that, we'll wait till you feel better.'

She was the second of three siblings; she had a brother three years older and a sister two years younger. At first she gave an idealized picture of her childhood; she had enjoyed primary school and all went well until she moved to secondary school.

Father was a lawyer and worked long hours, Mother cared for the family but seemed to have been not really available emotionally to the children. At secondary school my patient was often away with minor physical illnesses, some of which she admitted she faked. After leaving school she did a first degree and then won a scholarship to do a doctorate abroad where her depressive breakdown occurred.

Towards the end of our first meeting she said she wanted 'therapy' rather than 'analysis', by which she meant something 'healing rathᵔr than dissecting', and we agreed to start with twice-weekly sessions.

At our second meeting she hesitated between the chair and the couch and then sat down. She thought I would expect her to use the couch; she needed to respond to others' expectations because she was afraid of revealing her real self. She felt she had lost her spontaneity at university; now she could only find herself secondhand through literature. I suggested that this loss had perhaps happened much earlier in childhood and her early years had not been as ideal as she supposed. Her response to this in the next session was to tell me about her separation from her mother from the age of eighteen months to two years, which had not emerged in the initial semiformal history-taking. Mother had been ill during her next pregnancy and she had been sent to stay with an aunt for six months. She often feels that this aunt was more of a real mother, so the separation from her when she returned home at age two was even more painful. Thereafter as a child she was extremely anxious about further separations and very clinging if taken to a party. When they went on holiday she would always, as a priority, secretly locate the police station in case her parents should go away and leave her. At age ten this anxiety had (consciously) 'switched off like a tap' to be replaced by the minor physical illnesses which often kept her away from secondary school.

With the history of childhood separation I expected her to be anxious about holiday breaks and made prophylactic interpre-

[300]

tations to that effect. However, she insisted at first that she was unaffected and went away at school half-terms in addition to usual holidays. I had begun seeing her in January and typically at Easter she denied she would miss me and arranged to go and look after a girlfriend abroad who was having emotional troubles. This 'compulsive care-taking' of others (Bowlby) was a marked feature; she was at the time taking a special remedial class for backward and difficult children.

The treatment seemed to go well and she gradually weaned herself from all the drugs she had been on. We covered a lot of fairly obvious and classical analytic themes, for example envy of her elder brother and his phallic capacities. She dreamt they went to a fairground shooting-range. He was given a good gun and she got one with a crooked barrel. Conversely she was terrified of others' envy of her. At school she hid her family's acquaintance with a well-known author and (during treatment) nearly hid from me that she had helped make a television programme.

In appearance she was a handsome girl with a fine head of hair which together with her dress was in somewhat unisex style. The referring psychiatrist had mentioned sexual difficulties, but what she referred to as 'lesbian' tendencies seemed so obviously like a search for the mother she had lost. Either she was interested in being cuddled and discovering whether her body was acceptable; or she related to women in a more narcissistic way and looked after them. She had a boyfriend throughout treatment, but someone who had been married, separated, not divorced, and had another girlfriend, so he was essentially unavailable and this allowed her to remain uncommitted to either sex. She was determined not to acknowledge her needs at any level. Her sister she portrayed as the younger pretty one who was prepared to seduce men to give her anything she wanted. 'My sister makes up her mouth like a cunt,' she once cried with indignation. She seemed determined to deny any needs of her own at oral or genital levels. She was specially afraid of revealing her needs to be loved and that if she said 'I need you' to a man it might be mistaken for a sexual invitation.

Towards the summer break she was able to talk more of her

[301]

feelings about the coming separation and how in her mother's presence she had sulked whenever depressed but refused to let mother comfort her. She acknowledged her need for a 'companion' on her journey of discovering herself ('a Sancho Panza', she suggested) but feared I would be overwhelmed by her inner chaos.

Just before the summer break she had a dream (prompted by seeing a girl she was attracted to in a shop) in which a chest of drawers (mother's breast) was snatched from her by her sister. We agreed that it related to the coming break and to childhood. She was afraid that men, or myself, or mother (who was always pressing her to get married) would take her away from women too soon. She did not read analytic works but said spontaneously it was unfair that men do not have women's task of giving up their original sexual object-choice.

After the break she reported a dream in which she did not bother to stop in her car to give mother a lift, thus reversing and revenging both the situation of the break and of the childhood separation.

In retrospect I realize she perhaps had flu or colds and stayed away rather more than average – once obviously when she feared I was exasperated by her demands and she stayed in bed to nurse herself, thus repeating the pattern of adolescence. I think I missed these repetitions at the time because she was always so *reasonable* about ringing up to say she could not come.

In October she had a dream which seemed to herald the beginning of getting in touch with the child part of herself. She dreamt that a little girl was riding a tricycle (she knew she had been on tricyclic antidepressants), went head first into a brick wall and fell unconscious. Someone dialled 999 but when the ambulance arrived it wasn't needed because the little girl was beginning to recover consciousness.

Just before the Christmas break she overslept and missed a session in pre-emptive revenge. The next night she dreamt I was having a party for patients and she was excluded in a corner.

Over Christmas she had a homosexual affair perhaps both in

defiance of me and of mother (who is always pressing her to marry) and at the same time in search of mother.

And so we proceeded gaining insights which interested her and seemed plausible and yet there was still something missing. She had always resented the sexual stereotypes presented by her parents and copied by her older brother and younger sister. She defied both in a no man's land between the two. In June she was rather more depressed when she seemed at last to be giving up her fantasy of a penis and arranged for the first time to see a gynaecologist herself about her dysmenorrhoea as though beginning to accept her female identity. She protested, of course, at my commenting to this effect but seemed to confirm it by producing a dream in which she is given a pen which at first writes with yellow ink but it then turns to blood.

After the second summer break the child part of her appeared more in dreams and she seemed more in touch with the rage of this child when, e.g., in a dream the child was being excluded by adults. And yet there was very little sign of this protesting child during sessions.

I had a growing sense of unease about this reasonableness and realized that I had probably colluded with her reasonable false-self organization because she was so agreeable and cooperative. I eventually made an intervention of unusual length for me in which I told her of this feeling I had developed. I said I spoke with some hesitation because I did not want her to think I felt this cooperative part of her was at all phoney, superficial or insincere; clearly it was a deep part of her character and had positive values which made people depend and rely on her, though this in itself must be a problem for her because it made it even harder to reveal the unreasonable protesting child-part of herself. Again I said it was very agreeable the way she always came on time, marched straight to the couch, plonked herself down and got straight on with her dreams and associations; the way she always rang to let me know if ill and if my wife took the message she would say, 'What a nice girl that sounds', etc.; but that all this, charming and agreeable as it was, must be at considerable personal cost.

Well, that did it. Of course at the time she agreed with me as reasonably as ever, but three days later, after the weekend, she came rather earlier than usual and I found her in the waiting room streaming with tears – certainly not put on just to show me another compliant aspect of herself but dark, silent, painful depression. I arranged to see her daily when possible. She was terrified of her real self emerging and afraid of going mad. She felt 'at the end of a springboard'.

That week of black depression was followed the next Monday by hyperactivity and excitement. She had eaten and slept little over the weekend. She paced up and down the consulting room, smoking furiously. She sat in a hard chair, a soft chair, knelt or lay on the floor or sat cross-legged, facing me on the couch. She talked incessantly, at times incoherently. I nearly lost my nerve and thought of referring her back to the psychiatrist, fearing she might be a fullblown manic depressive after all, but managed to contain her excitement. She was clearly terrified of her 'devouringness' which she was taking out on the cigarettes. She said that in letting herself see round my room she was 'broadening her horizons' and for the first time daring to see the effect of herself on me. She had not considered this before, having had a fantasy of myself as the stage-analyst writing notes behind her.

On Wednesday of that week we could not find a time to meet. She had a dream in two parts. In the first part there was a wounded elephant trapped in the corner of a cage; in the second part a friend (who, like herself, had been a refugee as a child) murdered a man. We agreed that the elephant was the child-part of her who had never forgotten how wounded she had felt over being a refugee, but that she was still terrified of the murderous rage she felt about it and about my not seeing her on Wednesday, which had to be put into the friend.

Her fear of her devouringness was intense. She even arranged to visit the dentist that week and she drank more than usual. Spontaneously she reflected on the nature of remorse and of being 'bitten back' for one's greed.

Despite the distress of this period, she felt it to be a positive crisis and did not want to ease her distress with the drugs which

ATTACHMENT AND NEW BEGINNING

she still had available from before. She went home to her parents for the next weekend and felt able for the first time to get them to recognize her depression without her being in the least vindictive about it.

Her next dream was of leading a sad orangutan up to the back door of a nunnery where they were left outside, peering in through the half-glass door (which is like my consulting room); clearly the depressed primitive part of herself, which she still feared would be unacceptable to me.

A few days later she dreamt she wanted Carol (the girlfriend to whom she was attracted) but Carol goes abroad (a reversal of the situation of her adult breakdown). She (the patient) has head lice in the dream. I said she feared I would reject her (like Carol) because of her lousy head. She turned over, face down, on the couch and buried her head in the pillow, extending her arms out loosely to either side of the pillow. Her hands moved around restlessly, reaching silently in my direction for some ten minutes. Eventually I said I thought she wanted me to take her hand, though she felt unable to say so, and then I did.

This seemed an important new beginning and she was later able to say that she had been terrified of being too demanding in asking me to hold a hand, fearing I might not trust her and might have mistaken her wish to be held as sexual.

About six weeks after the collapse of her false-self reasonableness she had a dream in three parts which seemed to link up her whole life.

1. She was walking alone in a field looking for milk (as one might on holiday).

2. She was a child with her mother and the aunt who had fostered her. They had arrived at a seaside resort (where she had in fact gone at age two, following the separation) looking for a boarding house. They had been promised a fine view of the sea but when shown around the boarding house, the windows were almost entirely bricked up and the sea was only just visible if you stood on the furniture. Mother could not afford anything better; she was too poor.

3. She was an adult and went into a bookshop, but the manager had nothing she wanted. It was like the library where her

breakdown had occurred when she had felt so imprisoned by her books.

We agreed that the three parts linked up her whole life; her fear of being alone without milk/nourishment; her fear that I/mother would be too poor and not have the resources to offer her so that she would have to be boarded out with a poor view of the sea/mother; and thirdly, her breakdown abroad where she had gone in compliance with her family's high academic standards and achievements but had felt imprisoned in the books, as indeed she had also perhaps felt restricted in the earlier part of her treatment by the manager/myself who was not really then giving her what she wanted.

Discussion

Perhaps my experience with this case amounts to no more than a personal rediscovery of what many analysts have written about the two levels of analytic work and the insufficiency of work at a verbal level for some patients.

Thus Little (1960[*this volume-Ed.]*) writes: 'Verbalization then becomes the second stage in a two-stage process, both stages being necessary for real insight to be attained, but the second being only effective as a result of the first, i.e., of the body happening'; or Balint: 'I wish to emphasize that *the satisfaction did not replace interpretation*, it was in addition to it. In some treatments interpretation preceded and in others followed satisfaction, as the situation demanded' (1968, p. 134).

Winnicott (1959) wrote:

Only the True Self can be analysed. Psychoanalysis of the False Self, analysis that is directed at what amounts to no more than an internalized environment, can only lead to disappointment. There may be an apparent early success. It is being recognized in the last few years that in order to communicate with the True Self where a False Self has been given pathological importance it is necessary for the analyst first of all to provide conditions which will allow the patient to hand over to the analyst the burden of the internalized environment, and so to become a highly dependent but a real, immature, infant; then, and then only, the analyst may analyse the True Self. This could be a present-day statement of Freud's *anaclitic dependence* in which the instinctual drive leans on the self-preservative. (p. 133)

And perhaps in place of this rather tortuous idea of one drive leaning on another, we could see anaclitic dependence as an expression of a single drive of attachment or an 'instinct to cling'.

Khan (1972a) summarizes his view of the two levels thus:

It is my belief that in all psychotherapeutic work with patients, psychotherapists and analysts have to provide two distinct types of relating from their side. One type of relating is covered by interpretative work, which helps the patient to gain insight into his internal conflicts and thus resolve them. The other sort of relating, which is harder to define, is more in the nature of providing coverage for the patient's self-experience in the clinical situation. The knack of any psychotherapeutic work is to strike the right balance within these two types of functions in the therapist.

The anxiety about meeting the patient's needs at the deeper level seems to have been exaggerated by the fear of irreversible regression. In 1952 Balint saw no reason to modify what he had already written in 1937:

My clinical experience was briefly this: At times when the analytic work has already progressed a long way, i.e., towards the end of a cure, my patients began – very timidly at first – to desire, to expect, even to demand certain simple gratifications, mainly, though not exclusively, from their analyst. On the surface these wishes appeared unimportant: to give a present to the analyst or – more frequently – to receive one from him; to be allowed to touch or stroke him or to be touched or stroked by him, etc.; and most frequently of all to be able to hold his hand or just one of his fingers. Two highly important characteristics of these wishes are easily seen. First: they can be satisfied only by another

[307]

human being; any autocrotic satisfaction is simply impossible. Second: the level of gratification never goes beyond that of mild fore-pleasure. Correspondingly a really full satisfaction followed by an anticlimax can hardly ever be observed, only a more or less complete saturation. Thus, if satisfaction arrives at the right moment and with the right intensity, it leads to reactions which can be observed and recognized only with difficulty, as the level of pleasure amounts only to a *tranquil quiet sense of well-being.* (1952, p. 231)

My patient demonstrated clearly both the need for 'another human being' and the 'tranquil quiet sense of well-being' after the need was met. She also confirmed that the 'level of gratification never goes beyond that of a mild fore-pleasure' though, as emphasized earlier, I feel that the very word 'fore-pleasure' is here out of place since the need that is being met is not really erotic but the search for basic unity or attachment.

Problems of management in the analysis of a hallucinating hysteric

HAROLD STEWART

IT IS NOT OFTEN that one has the opportunity of analysing a patient who fights with a 'ghost' during the course of treatment, and so I thought the case merited clinical discussion. I shall have little to say about the theoretical aspects of hallucinatory phenomena, but there are grounds for a discussion about various parameters that I used during the analysis which I think were necessary to sustain the analysis and bring it to a fairly successful conclusion.

Elizabeth Zetzel in her paper 'The So-called Good Hysteric' (1968), which mainly concerns women patients, made a useful classification of hysterical patients into four grades according to their psychopathology and prospects of analysability. My patient would, I think, fall somewhere between her third and fourth grades and I shall briefly delineate what these grades represent. To quote:

> Third, there are women with an underlying depressive character structure who frequently manifest hysterical symptomatology to a degree which disguises their deeper pathology. Fourth, there are women whose manifest hysterical symptomatology proves to be pseudo-Oedipal and pseudo-genital. Such patients seldom meet the most important criteria for analysability.

She describes the fourth group as follows:

However, while their symptoms may present a façade which looks genital, they prove in treatment to be incapable of recognizing a genuine triangular situation. For them, as for Oedipus himself, the parent of the same sex has not remained a real object in any meaningful way. Such patients all too readily express intense sexualized transference phantasies. They tend, however, to regard such phantasies as potential areas of realistic gratification. They are genuinely incapable of the meaningful distinction between external and internal reality which is a prerequisite for the establishment of a therapeutic alliance and the emergence of an analysable transference neurosis.

My patient was not quite as ill as this and was, perhaps, also not a typical hysteric since severe depressions were one of her presenting symptoms. A panel discussion on hysteria in Paris (Laplanche, 1974) showed the difficulties in defining the hysterical character, when compared say to the obsessional, and I do not wish to enter into that discussion here. I will, therefore, arbitrarily label her as a hysterical depressive character and proceed to describe her and the relevant aspects of the analysis which has lasted now for seven years.

She was referred to me by a colleague working in a hospital to whom a physician, on realizing that my patient might have some emotional disturbances to account for the recurrent fevers which had been present over a four-year period, had referred her. She was 29 years old, looked rather wild and scruffy, wore torn jeans, and although she complained of depressions which had started with her first sexual experience ten years previously, did not have the typical depressive *facies*. During these depressions, she said she felt split in two, one part of herself wanting to be bad, in fact, turned out to be almost a compulsion. She felt unloved and unwanted by everyone including her family and was unable to involve herself in any real way with anyone. She had obtained a good degree in sociology but was now working in a situation far below her capabilities. She was having an affair with a a married man, was sexually subservient to him, was frigid and felt vaguely guilty about sex.

There was little sense of identity or self-esteem. At the second session, she told me she wanted to be a man, that she felt that she was like a man and was a compulsive clitoral masturbator. This masturbation was experienced as if she was masturbating a penis that felt real, even though she knew that she did not possess one in reality, and she felt herself to be a man attacking a young child.

Her attitude towards her father, a successful professional man, was of scorn and contempt for his feebleness in the family circle, and she was frightened to some extent of her mother, who apparently held the family together, but who, in the patient's childhood, had shown uncontrollable tempers towards her children, doing them physical violence and then complaining to the children that they had hurt her by making her be violent towards them. She had a sister two years older than herself and two brothers, two and eight years younger, none of whom she really got on with. She had a delusional idea that her father was not her actual father but that she had someone called her 'real father', whom she had seen only once when she was five years old. This was by a canal near her home when she was out walking and he was described as a tall, dark man wearing an overcoat which, however, was buttoned-up in the female fashion. Her actual father had been in the Forces since her birth in 1939 and had only occasionally been home until his demobilization in 1946. At about this time she also thought she remembered her father's batman, her father being an officer, exposing himself or doing something to her when he was staying in her parents' home.

The only pleasurable experiences that she remembered from childhood were of her maternal grandmother who stayed with them during the war. She had been a kind, gentle, motherly woman, the only sane adult of the family and her departure at the end of the war, when her father returned, was a great loss to the patient. However, just to complicate matters, this grandmother used to see ghosts that no-one else saw, but as these ghosts were benevolent by nature they were not seen as frightening experiences.

The early stages of analysis were characterized by a careful and suspicious attitude towards me while she talked and expanded on her themes, but interspersed were runs of sessions when she would become mocking, provocative, denigrating towards me and the analysis and anything I might say was twisted in these ways against me. These attacks of her being bad ended by her saying she was sorry about them and hoped she had not hurt me. The attacks were based on her father's attitudes and behaviour towards her since childhood, as he had constantly mocked, undermined or ignored anything constructive that she had tried to do. Her saying she was sorry was more placatory than genuine. Her mother's attacks were rather different and I shall now come to these.

After this initial gentle testing of me, the situation changed and I was faced with a difficult technical problem. For much of the time she wanted to be like a baby, to be with me or inside me, and hated the ends of sessions and weekend breaks. The problem arose from the fact that on occasions she would impulsively rush off the couch during a session and try to overpower me in a physical struggle, principally in order to find out, by feeling with her hand, whether I had an erection or not. At first I could stop her with verbal interpretations but these soon became useless and I had to decide what to do. This uselessness at times of verbal interpretations is a phenomenon well recognized by all psychoanalysts who deal with very disturbed patients. I could have used threats by telling her that if she continued with this behaviour, I would have no alternative but to stop treatment, and possibly this threat might have worked. But I suspected that because of the very unrealistic nature of her desires, her behaviour was more compulsive than impulsive. Furthermore, I knew that she was the sort of person who, if prohibited from doing something, would immediately have to do it in order to see if the prohibitor meant what he said, and this would have meant the end of the analysis. I therefore adopted a different course, which was my first parameter, but which depended on a specific factor. This was that, physically, I was bigger and stronger than she, and hence I could physically prevent her from finding out what she wanted to know. This meant physical struggles with the patient and I was concerned that this might then become a form of instinctual gratification for her with the danger of an addiction to an actual physical surrender to me becoming part of the analysis for her. I also had to examine my own countertransference concerning close physical contact with a female patient, but I decided that this was not the motivation of my decision. I wondered whether, if I were smaller, her acting out would not have occurred, but I doubt it because of the compulsive nature of her actions.

The result of doing this was very satisfactory for the course of the analysis. Over a period of months, instead of her becoming addicted to this behaviour, it slowly decreased in frequency as she discovered that I and not she had control of the situation, that I was being the sane, responsible person in the situation – perhaps like her grandmother – and she was gradually able to introject me as a sane control who did not punish or denigrate her or make her feel terribly guilty about her activities. In the analysis of her acting out activities that is essential if parameters are used, it became clear that I was regarded as a phallic mother or a combined-parent figure and she was attempting to try to differentiate the sexes by the presence of absence of the penis. She herself was also the phallic mother, violent and uncontrollable, and I, the helpless child-victim of her childhood experiences. I was also the narcissistic extension of herself, the phallic mother to do with as she pleased, with my penis being her penis. She was also envying and wishing to damage my penis, particularly its symbolic use as a penetrating analytic organ, since her father always thought of himself as intellectually superior to her. Last, but not least, she also wished to see if, as a woman, she was arousing and conquering me sexually.

Gradually she became intensely dependent but ambivalent towards me, confused, empty and depressed and was now unable to work at her job. She dragged herself to her sessions and for the rest of the day did little but stay in her room. Her parents, who lived in a provincial town, were paying for her analytic fees and she existed on sickness and social security benefits.

She now started writing letters to me to keep in contact over weekends and holidays and these were indicative of her state of mind. I quote from one letter:

> Dear Darling Dr Harold, I love you, I adore you, I worship you, and I cannot bear to be away from you. I hate you for arousing such feelings in me and not giving them any real outlet. . . Take me back to your womb. I want to experience the world from inside you. I cannot exist separated from you. . . Take off all your clothes. Show me that you have a penis. Show me that you can erect. I cannot bear it if you don't want me. . . Go back to the devil you sprang from. Stop torturing me. Take your claws out of my body. Take your pick and shovel from my mind. You are plunging me into chaos. I want my hatred to worry you, to provoke in you the same degree of anxiety that I have to cope with. I hate your placid, self-sufficient manner. I think you are the most undesirable, unattractive, unsexy, uneverything object I have ever seen. I want to rip your clothes off. I want to whip you till the thickness of the lash is doubled by the particles of your flesh and blood tumbles from it like a waterfall.

Other letters were quite incoherent and unreadable. She was afraid of madness and of driving others mad. She was keeping contact with me for the whole week by means of letters as well as sessions and was fearful that this constant contact and dependence would drive us mad. But at least the contact was now verbal and no longer physical and I believe she was now experiencing me not only as the phallic mother but also as her phantasy 'real father'; you will recall the feminine aspect of him in the way the overcoat was buttoned-up.

It was about a month before the Easter break of the third year of analysis that I became very concerned about her. After a Friday session, I developed the strong feeling that she might conceivably attempt to kill herself to escape from her torment and the coming weekend and Easter break, and I decided to act on my countertransference feeling. I telephoned her to suggest that if she felt she could not cope with the weekend she could telephone me if she so wanted to. She thanked me, did not telephone and for the next week was more cheerful, presumably as a result of my display of concern about her. However, the outcome was the introduction into the analysis of a new form of communication that needed to be dealt with.

She came to the session with a packet containing some drawings. She placed the packet on my desk, left it unopened, and showed every sign of severe anxiety. She sat on the couch and told me she had done the drawings over the weekend and that she wanted me to see them. Yet at the same time she was quite terrified of their possible effect on me and did not want me to look at them then. Towards the end of the session she was fairly silent, rather hostile and anxious about me, saying she felt a looming black shape in the room. She was terrified about being in the room with the drawings which I had left still in their packet on my desk. She could not bear the anxiety and, most unusually for her, left fifteen minutes early; usually she did not want to leave. At the next session, however, she felt more confident and was now prepared to look at them and discuss them with me.

The drawings were of three distinct types. The first was of separate discrete drawings done in charcoal, several to a sheet, the drawings varying from simple representations of objects to a more complex design of objects. The second type was a sheet covered completely with a highly organized complex design, particularly of faces, done in black and white with a felt pen. The outlines within the design were quite sharp. The third type was also a complex design covering the sheet but the outlines were less clear, there were no recognizable objects and, most significantly, the outlines were in colour. It was these last drawings that were so very frightening to her, particularly one in black and red which she described as showing her obscenity and violence. It is perhaps to be expected that colour and indeterminate shapes would be the vehicle for the expression of a person's primitive aggressive sexual phantasies, rather than clearcut black and white drawings.

Her initial terror of my response concerned what I might think of her having such phantasies and at the same time she must have felt that she had projected the blackness of the aggression in the form of the looming black shape into my room and so made it unsafe, but the reality of my normal response to her had allowed her to distinguish the reality of me and my room from her projections.

These sort of pictures continued to be brought along to sessions and my problem was of knowing how to deal with them. Because of the similarity of the styles, I had realized from the first that the patient had probably read Marion Milner's (1969) book *The Hands of the Living God* and this she confirmed. This was probably another reason why the coloured pictures were so frightening to her, since they had not been copied from Milner's patient's style. But I also realized that I could never understand or interpret her drawings as Marion Milner did, as I do not possess her sort of artistic creativity, intuition and insight for such use in the analytic situation. So I had to treat them like dreams, asking for her associations to the drawings and attempting to link them with her past and with the transference in the usual manner. But I also did not show an overinterest in them since I thought that if I did, my patient would most probably flood me with drawings. In the event she drew until the Easter break and after that almost dried up pictorially. It is of some interest that she later went to art classes for the first time in her life and has proved to have a good deal of talent, a good example of a removal of an inhibition.

The drawings were concerned with problems of separation together with her sexual and sadistic phantasies on almost every libidinal level or type of object-relationship. Perhaps the most important aspects were her fear of the nature of her vagina, which was shown as having teeth or a beak, and fears of vaginal orgasm, as opposed to clitoral orgasm. The vaginal orgasm was seen as destructive not only to the erect penis of her partner, but also to the penis which she felt was hidden away inside her and only came out when she felt sexually excited and frustrated in her near-delusional phantasy. She had experienced puberty as castrating, as it meant that a real adult male penis had not developed at that time and hence if she now properly experienced her vagina, this would be the final blow to her desires to possess a penis of her own. The main threat to this blow was the analysis and the emergence of her femininity. She now had intercourse with a man, had no orgasm, but for the first time realized the terror of her vagina being the way it was in her drawings.

Her last picture was a complete coloured mess on the paper and it was done just before a holiday break. This came after one of her mocking, denigrating sessions and she described the picture as a smearing of shit all over my walls. This followed reading an account of the treatment of a woman called Mary Barnes. It could be shown to her that her behaviour had represented this shit – smearing over my insides to destroy everything inside me, including the potential babies I might return with after the break, and also to damage me for abandoning her and leaving her to hold her mad baby inside which she saw as empty and worthless. A dream also connected this with feelings of her abandonment by her mother when she, the patient, had been hospitalized for a fortnight when she was three years old, and for being abandoned when she had started going to school.

We have now arrived at the time when her hallucinations began, in the third year of analysis, during the summer break. I received a letter from her during the holiday when she was motoring in Europe – although she was unable to work, she could still drive. I shall quote the relevant passages from it:

This holiday is proving disastrous. I have been attacked by a ghost, abandoned by the bloke I went with, and raped by a madman. I was staying in a youth hostel when I was assaulted in the night by an ancient Spanish roué, dressed in clothes from the Regency period, perhaps. I struggled with him for what seemed ages, finally fighting him off. Then I put my hand straight through him and realized he was a ghost. Up till then I had been convinced he was real. Then I was aware of his decaying body rotting away beside me on the bed, and I sat at the end of the bed frozen with horror for about an hour. After a very long time, it dawned on me that perhaps it wasn't a real ghost but a hallucination. I didn't know what alternative was the worst, but I began semi-automatically to analyse my reasons for producing such a vicious ghost. Anger seemed to be predominant in me. I was angry with the fellow I went with because he's a lazy, insensitive, self-satisfied bastard and there was no real contact between us. But I think I pushed onto him my angry transference feelings, also my sexual feelings, to a lesser extent.

It seems to me that her analysis of the situation is essentially correct in relating the hallucination to her experience of me, although I do not think I am quite as bad as all that, but I think her feelings were of murder and fear of murder, rather than anger, as shown by her horror of the decaying, rotting body. This is one of the points made by Bion (1958b) in his paper 'On Hallucination', where he quotes Freud to the effect that the patient's state of mind and feeling is under the sway of the pleasure principle, and in that phase of development the patient's actions are not directed towards a change in the environment but are intended to unburden the psychic apparatus of accretions of stimuli. My patient seemed to be doing this as well as trying to change the environment in that she did fight with her hallucination.

I expect I could be phantasized as an ancient Spanish roué, and the fight she was having could also reflect her actual experiences of her physical struggles with me, but her mention of the Regency period clothes is very significant. She comes from one of the English towns that are graced by the Regency style and atmosphere and there seems little doubt that this ancient roué also contains the reference to her father and her childhood. This well fits in with Freud's view, mentioned in 'Constructions in Analysis' (1937b), that this is method in madness, and it is the fragments of historical truth which give the compulsive belief in delusions and hallucinations its strength, since it derives from infantile sources. I also think that this mixture of present and past experience that is contained within the hallucination is a good example of a compromise symptom.

Two further incidents occurred on this holiday which confirmed the feelings of anxiety concerning suicide that I had had, by her flirting with death in a near-suicidal way. She went swimming in the sea but so far out in a heavy current that she had to be saved by local fishermen while clinging to some rocks. After this she drove back about a thousand miles across Europe with the rubber on her tyres so worn that the canvas was exposed. These actions represent an extreme challenge to death and also help to confirm my method of dealing with her challenging acting out in the early stages of the analysis.

On her return she had intense desires for intercourse with me and, when thwarted, masturbated continuously. She then saw another ghost in her bedroom, and this was a little man three feet tall with fair hair and blue eyes who carried a rope and a bucket. She had a great fear on seeing it but then said to herself that it was a ghost and it disappeared. Apparently it resembled her younger brother, who was born when she was eight years old. She then had more mocking, denigrating sessions and behaved badly to her parents while at their home. I was able to show her that the attacks on me followed the separations of the holiday and my refusal to have intercourse with her, and also displayed the envy of her mother for having the younger brother. The three-foot-high ghost probably represented the third year of her analysis and was her baby in the form of a hallucination. The attacks on her parents were to destroy their intercourse and happiness and also to destroy her own treatment, since they were paying for it, out of guilt for her attacks and also to show what a useless analyst I was. At the next session she told me she realized the correctness of this and then disclosed her phantasy of having two babies inside her, one a mocking, green, envious baby and the other a pale, almost lifeless baby that she had to keep starved. This one was the sensitive, feminine baby that could easily be hurt. The compulsive, angry, envious penis phantasies came from the first baby and her problem was that the more loving she felt, the more she hated the separations from me and so this second baby had to be kept starved of love although she desperately desired it. This corresponds with Bion's views on hallucinations.

At the session after this she told me that she had seen her 'real father' again for the first time since childhood and he had said something to her but she didn't know what. She realized she had been hallucinating, but following this experience she felt that her mind had altered and somehow come together for the better, and she now started to make herself a dress. This was the first breakthrough of her feminine self. This 'real father' was probably me representing some good split-off infantile aspect of her actual father for whom she had always longed.

At the next session she told me of having had a hallucination of a large penis on herself, then she became her mocking, biting, attacking self, but at the end of the session wanted to kiss me better. She then saw the film *The Devils*, which is about the nuns of Loudon, and later that evening had a persistent vision of her genitals rotting away. On putting her hand there, she felt a large hole where they had rotted away and was terrified. She then realized that this was another hallucination, a negative hallucination this time, and was then able to feel her genitals. She wanted to know if she was going mad and I said that for that moment she had been mad. She broke down and cried, but then linked her hallucination with the hysterical mad nun in the film who had licked the blood of her beloved priest's wounds after his torture, putting her tongue into them. I linked up her torturing treatment of me in the previous sessions with the priest's torture and of her intense desire to remove the source of her sexual desires by hallucinating away her genitals or to give herself the penis instead. She accepted this and told me that I tormented her with desire but did not gratify her, and so she tortured me in return but was then afraid of driving me away. She was also tortured by humiliation at her failure to seduce me, but she then became afraid that she would hallucinate me away completely and that she would not be able to see or hear me and then she would be quite mad. This so bothered her that she gave my telephone number to her sister in case this might occur. She also broke down in tears at her art class. These events were important since, for the first time, she was really acknowledging to herself and to others that she was ill.

She now had a significant dream of my wife being pregnant and her feeling left out. Her associations were to a period of her childhood when her father had recently returned from the Forces; her parents had then quarrelled a lot and temporarily separated into different bedrooms, her father's being next to hers. She had then been shattered when her younger brother had been born when she was eight years old. This dream was soon followed by a pregnancy phantasy where she felt very heavy and wanted to urinate excessively. Apart from the transference aspects, she came out with the idea that her father had wanted to kill her when she was two years old. This was the time when her first brother was born and the conclusion must be that she had wanted to kill her father when the brother had been born. Thus her murderous feelings of jealousy and abandonment by her father at the birth of both brothers, together with desires for their disappearance, came out more fully into the open. By now she was wearing the new dresses that she had made, used cosmetics and perfume and in every way was more feminine. After eighteen months off work, she was not able to return and, of equal importance, she was able to allow herself to regress much further during her sessions since she was developing the confidence that at the end of the session she would reintegrate and not stay in a regressed chaotic state. She was developing a real sense of self.

By this time she had had several types of hallucinating experience and we began to recognize that there were various levels of this experience. The first was in recognizing that she could see things around her, but knew all the time that the experiences were not real and came from her imagination. The second was a state where she was not sure if the experiences were real or not, which made her feel afraid and so she switched her mind off in case they did become real.

The third state was where things came on her very suddenly out of the blue with the conviction of reality and it took some time before she was able to recognize that these experiences were not real. This state was usually preceded by feelings of anxiety, and she could not say why she should feel anxious. In my view the third state contains truly dynamic unconscious experience-phantasies coming from the id and the anxiety preceding their emergence is probably a subliminal awareness of them by the deeper layers of the ego. In a previous paper (Stewart, 1966) I have discussed hallucinations in terms of ego-splitting. Since they represent instinctual and affective states, the anxiety on the ego's part is hardly surprising when the danger of their becoming conscious arises. The first state, when she is aware of their unreality from the start, must represent preconscious ego phantasies, and the second state a borderline area between the first and third states.

So far, the third state had always occurred outside the sessions and I pointed out that she was keeping these experiences in their immediacy away from me. The effect of this statement was to make her feel I was persecuting her by trying to drive her mad in the sessions by asking her to hallucinate. She felt I was not interested in her as a person but only as an object from which I could learn about mental functioning – a statement with some truth in it. She also felt that she could now triumph over me by keeping me frustrated in not producing these phenomena. Yet, at the same time she knew and acknowledged that I was right and that the chances were that she would not be driven mad by them. But I also knew that in showing this interest in her hallucinating states, it was quite on the cards that she would produce them for me in abundance in typical hysterical fashion. In the event, I do not think she did, but before getting on to them, another phenomenon turned up which was in fact rather similar to a proper hallucination.

While talking on the couch, she would suddenly shout out a word or phrase that could have had meaning in the context of the rest of what she was saying, yet by its nature seemed to come from another layer of the mind as an intrusion of a rather explosive nature. It often contained a parapraxis that altered the sense of what she was meaning to say. For example, during the session when she felt I was trying to drive her mad by suggesting she bring her hallucinations into the consulting room, she felt confused with the knowledge that I was also the person who was trying to help her and had enabled her to return to work. She felt she loved me, wanted to put her arms around me, wanted me to put my penis inside her, and then shouted, 'Perhaps the penis is too exciting for you.' She then said that she had been going to say quietly, 'The penis is too exciting for me.' The problem here was to know (a) whether she was talking to herself and admonishing herself as though she were two people, like Lewis Carroll's Alice in Wonderland, or (b) whether she was telling me that I, the analyst, could not cope with the excitement that I might have in my penis and so was perhaps driving her mad by overstimulating her and so creating confusion, or (c) whether both were correct. Since she started the next session by telling me I was analysing myself, having just seen my new copy of Kohut's *Analysis of the Self*, and also telling me that I was writing notes to myself, on seeing a scrap of paper with writing on it on my desk, it seemed that the notion that I could not cope with the excitement in my penis was correct. But when she next said that last night she thought that I was inside her and that she was me, it seemed that the possibility of the penis being too exciting for her might also be correct and that she dealt with the exciting penis by incorporating and identifying with it. So in analysing her, I was also analysing myself. Furthermore, 'you' and 'me' could represent projected and introjected objects from the past. This may illustrate some of the problems involved in interpretation and understanding and the potential overdetermination of these statements.

I was seeing her in the early evenings and it being winter, it was dark outside and she now wanted to have only one light on in the consulting room so that it was rather dim and peaceful. She would go into a reverie-like state, like a child in a nursery with the dim light, and I had to remain very still in my chair, since any undue movement on my part would disturb her reverie and also make her feel, in a near-delusional way, that I was undoing my trousers or masturbating and this frightened her. She had the phantasy of being a small child sitting on my knee and of being bounced up and down on it by me, exciting her until she wet my trousers. She wanted to suck my penis, my breast or her thumb, and had an intense desire to masturbate. She then suddenly jerked round, felt that I was hitting her and shouted that she mustn't do that. This seemed to refer either to her wetting with excitement or to her desires to masturbate. At the next session she felt she was being driven mad by her desires to urinate and to masturbate and wanted to cut off my hands.

[323]

She also had the compulsive phantasy that I had undone my trousers and was playing with my penis. She then jerked round, shouting, 'You shouldn't do things like that.' She then thought that she had meant to say, 'say things like that', instead of 'do things like that', which again contains the problem of who the 'you' is, but she went on quickly. She covered herself with her coat, which had been on the couch, and held her genitals, saying, 'I must masturbate.' She then felt horrified at this action of hers. I moved slightly in my chair and she screamed, 'I don't know what I'm so frightened of.' I did not know whether she was afraid she might have excited me sexually and that I might assault her sexually in some way, since there had been so many references during the analysis to a real or phantasied traumatic sexual assault on her as a child; or whether she was having the phantasy that she was me, or I her, and that she was secretly masturbating in phantasy and controlling me and that my punishment was towards this aspect of her masturbation rather than a straightforward Oedipal punishment. It was even more complicated since I did not know whether the penis was father's or mother's, although I strongly suspect the latter since mother was felt to possess everything.

The next session was devoted to her playing a very complex game with various objects in my room, having them stand for various part-objects or aspects of mother, father, analyst or herself. It was like watching a child playing with its toys. A most important object was my ashtray, which is a container on a tall column, kept by the side of the couch for the use of patients, and this stood for the phantasy penis. It emerged that her possession of this was essential to prevent the confusion in her mind of all the other parts moving around and splitting. She made a slip about her being the 'baby analyst', which I think referred to her feeling of not being the adult analyst, who has the penis with its penetrating and understanding qualities to bring things together, but only a baby amateur analyst; but I also think it referred to her feeling of having had to try to understand the confusing aspects of her family from an early age and to be the father, who was absent and later devalued.

This was followed at the next session by her telling me that the batman, her father's army valet, always used to wash his hands. She then placed her hand on her genitals and told me she could notice a strong smell of soap in the room. I could not smell anything myself, but she then bit her hand which, she screamed, was 'his soapy hand'. Here was the first hallucination, an olfactory one, during the session and it was associated with a fairly obvious identification with this person, concerning the hand and the genitals and linked with a masturbatory action. I must confess that I could not clearly see the transference aspect unless this was an attempt to wash away the guilt she experienced from having tried to possess my analytic penis for herself only and using me as her batman. A great deal of the analysis concerned her desire to be a man, and for her to possess the penis represented a defence against internal chaos, depression and emptiness. On one occasion when I collected her from the waiting room, she hallucinated that my trousers were undone and my penis was showing, but her associations were to the fact that she had seen my trousers in a different colour from the one they were and that this colour corresponded to her mother's trousers. This led her on to realizing that she also experienced me as a mother who was false and phoney, untrustworthy and interested only in money and sex. I had always felt quite sure that one aspect of her emphasis on the penis and its possession was a defence against her vaginal desires and phantasies with the jealous rivalries and envies of her mother's vagina and womb at both Oedipal and pre-Oedipal levels, and as I previously mentioned, in the transference I was usually either a phallic mother or the phantasy 'real father' with his feminine overcoat, making it a bisexual transference figure. Yet at the same time, the hallucinations and verbal interruptions continued to suggest early traumatic assault by a man, not by her violent mother, and of her having witnessed parental intercourse. I had the classical difficulty of not knowing if I was dealing with actual traumatic experience or with unconscious phantasy. In one session she shouted, 'No, don't,' and then had the phantasy of a large man bending over her and her feeling little. She suddenly realized that she had used the same words to the little ghost who had resembled her younger

[325]

brother but there was now a reversal of sizes, and this realization caused more mind-clearing.

There were other hallucinations but, most interestingly, she
revealed a strange practice that she used in her bedroom. She
would construct an artificial penis for herself with a stuffed
rubber glove tied around her, and also make a female doll-like
figure. She would then draw the curtains so that the room was
very dim and would then have intercourse with the doll, she
being a man and the doll a little girl. At times she would reverse
the constructions and make a man and she would be the little
girl and the man-doll would have intercourse with her. This
was an acting out of her masturbation phantasy. Perhaps the
most important aspect of this is the negative one that the two
figures were never equal, i.e., man and woman, and this corresponded with her view that, in spite of everything she said, her
mother was basically seen as having a worse deal out of life
than her father and was always in the inferior position.

She was by now feeling greatly improved, was working hard
at her job, cleaning and painting her flat, painting well at art
classes and also doing some writing, which she had always
wanted to do. She had also found herself a proper boyfriend
and he was an interesting choice. He was a large man who suffered from impotence and she treated him on behavioural
therapy lines sexually and gave him the sexual potency he had
lacked. It was as though she was creating a potent adult penis
for herself and at the same time repairing the damage the penis
had suffered for which she had felt guilty throughout her
analysis. It was just before having intercourse with him on one
occasion that she had what she described as a 'devastating hallucination'. It was not of a penis this time, but of a 'violent
cunt', twisted and distorted like a Francis Bacon painting, and
she now realized how terrified she was and had been of her
mother and of her mother's violence which she had experienced as a child, together with the violence that she felt existing
in herself and her genitals. The penis phantasy had long been a
defence against this 'violent cunt' phantasy and she now in
experience realized that I had been right in this assessment
from the start. She is now capable of vaginal orgasm, is married

to this man and wanting children, knowing she will have her violence towards them under control; and I continue to see her once a week.

I realize that this has been a rather patchy picture of an analysis, but I hope it has illustrated the problems I faced in what many people would describe as an almost unanalysable patient. I believe that without the introduction of the various parameters mentioned, this analysis would not have survived. A word should be said about the sort of parents found in these severe hysterical patients. Brenman, in the Panel on 'Hysteria Today' (see Laplanche, 1974), considered that one of the ingredients specific to the hysterogenic mother is a mother overwhelmed by anxiety and unconsciously conveying to the infant that the infant's anxieties are really catastrophic. My experience has also been that this process has not been unconscious but that the mothers have been both physically violent and unpredictable in reaction to their infants, so that the situation really was catastrophic for the infant. Furthermore, the fathers have usually been absent or disillusioningly disappointing to their infants, leaving both mother and infant to deal with each other without adequate support.

To finish, I would like to quote the nursery rhyme from the beginning of Zetzel's paper. The second and third lines even contain the mechanism of displacement upwards:

There was a little girl,
And she had a little curl,
Right in the middle of her forehead,
And when she was good,
She was very, very, good,
But when she was bad,
She was horrid.

Female sexuality

Technical problems found in the analysis of women by a woman analyst: a contribution to the question 'What does a woman want?'

ENID BALINT

IN A FOOTNOTE to his introductory remarks to Freud's 1925 paper on female sexuality, Strachey quotes Ernest Jones as saying that Freud said: 'The great question has never been answered – what does a woman want?' In both his 1925 and 1931 papers one of Freud's most important additional contributions to the subject of female sexuality concerned the little girl's pre-Oedipal attachment to the mother which, he said, was stronger and of longer duration and richer in content, leaving behind many more opportunities for fixation and character formation than he had previously realized. He stressed also that the girl's sexual aims in regard to the mother are active as well as passive and contain a wish to give her a baby as well as to bear her one and that she fulfils them in indirect ways. In 1925 Freud admitted that we know less about the sexual life of little girls than of boys, and that the sexual life of the adult woman is a 'dark continent for psychology'. In spite of much recent research into this subject this is still largely the case. In this paper I shall concentrate only on the many obscure aspects of a woman's attachment to her mother which are a part of this 'dark continent'. These need to be clarified if we are to understand more about her sexual life and approach the question 'What does a woman want?'

The problem of what brings the powerful attachment to the mother to an end has often been discussed. It involves more than a simple change of object (i.e., from mother to father) and often ends in hate of the mother, which may last throughout life although it is usually carefully overcompensated for in adult life. Lampl-de Groot's important contribution (1928) to the subject gives clinical material to illustrate the immense difficulty a little girl has in giving up her possession of her mother and changing from possessing her to have her solely as a loved object to be identified with. The little girl feels that the possession of her mother can only be maintained if she, the girl, is not castrated, i.e., if she has a penis. It follows therefore that if the little girl cannot give up the possession of the mother, she denies castration and either forms no relationships with men at all and keeps her mother as her most important possession, or, while secretly denying castration, forms relationships with men with whom she is frigid but still remains inwardly attached to her mother. In my experience, however, as I hope to show, such women are not necessarily frigid. They never identify with their mothers or with any mature woman but, in spite of this, can establish satisfactory relations with men in many ways. However, the men are never really at the centre of their life; their real preoccupation remains with women and how to care for and satisfy them; but on the condition that their own bodies are for men: they do not give or get any direct physical bodily satisfaction with women: they wish to care for them but at a distance. Lampl-de Groot speaks of one of her own patients who wished to become an analyst, not so that she could identify with her, the analyst – but so that she could get rid of the analyst's analyst (a man), and thus take his place by herself becoming the analyst's analyst, i.e., care for her in a non-sexual, or sexually-inhibited role.

Helene Deutsch (1946) describes the woman's struggle to get away from her mother while at the same time showing an intensified and anxious urge to remain under her protection. She also sees the attachment to the mother as continuing in adult life, and says that:

> In all the phases of a woman's development and experience the great part played in her psychologic life by her attach-

[332]

ment to her mother can be clearly observed. Many events in her life are manifestations of attempts to detach herself, attempts made in thrusts; and the woman's psychologic equilibrium and eventual fate often depend on the success or failure of these attempts.

Helene Deutsch thinks that if the little girl cannot detach herself from her mother successfully she will continue in adult life to need a considerable amount of tenderness and motherly protection and find life unbearable without it. In the analyses of the women on which I base this paper this wish is shown as having been reversed; namely, these women avoid motherly protection and wish instead to give it to other women and perhaps enjoy it vicariously.

This problem first came to my notice during the analysis of two women patients who, although dissimilar in most ways, seemed to present similar features in the transference; also in their relations to men. In both analyses the work apparently went well; they did not make me feel frustrated or inadequate. In fact, I often felt I was doing well with both of them, particularly during the hour itself. During the work some of their conflicts in relation to men were made conscious and some resolution of them took place. However, one area of work was repetitious and unfruitful; namely that in relation to their mothers. Although they spoke about their mothers, little unconscious material came to light, either in fantasy or in memories, and little change occurred in their feelings about or their attitude to their mothers, or to me. Furthermore although each patient presented very different (almost opposite) transference patterns, in neither analysis did these problems vary from day to day.

My feelings of unjustified satisfaction during the sessions put me on my guard and I gradually came to see this as a major technical problem. It appeared that both patients wished to satisfy and please me but since their wish was acted out it was difficult to analyse: in one it was erotized, in the other not. Both patients felt in different ways that coming to analysis regularly and producing dreams and free associations satisfied me – who was seen as the mother, seldom as the father – and thus their major problem was solved day by day. In addition, as this desire was satisfied in the transference their relationships with men became less tense and artificial, although on the whole their unconscious relation to objects remained the same. I was doubtful whether they would ever be enabled to introject their mothers – or, if they had done so, identify with the introjects in a way which would enable them to give up their peculiar, distant though intimate satisfaction from trying to please, and care for them and come to value men in a wholly satisfactory way.

Both these patients were married women with children; both had lovers; both were referred to me because of 'marital problems'; both liked their husbands and thought that they were nice, good, even interesting men, but both were cool and critical of them while being capable of being warm, intimate and loving with their lovers, with whom they had good relationships – not only sexual. Neither saw her lover as superior to, or even nicer than her husband. There was plenty of evidence to support the hypothesis that they were in the sexual phase dominated by the Oedipal complex, which should present no particular problem to the analyst.

For instance, they denied that their mothers were satisfied by their fathers or had ever had satisfactory sexual relationships with them. In this way they denied their envy of their mothers, or hostility to them. They both also denied feelings of guilt because of their relationships with their fathers, although they admitted to fantasies about being given babies by them, and of being preferred by their fathers. Both valued their vaginas, but there was evidence of a denial of castration and an avoidance of penis envy. Both patients were girlish in their appearance and manner, although one was in her 40s and one was in her 30s, and it seemed as if neither could really show herself to be a fully adult woman who could be satisfied genitally by her own husband, i.e., by her children's father. They could, however, as they had in fantasy with their own fathers, have their husband's babies and be mothers of their children. They denied guilt but could have no pleasure from their husbands. One of them concentrated on pleasing (to begin with erotically, and later in a more caring way which was only sometimes a reaction formation against hostile feelings); the other one on utterly failing to please – their mothers and me.

Their mothers were more important to them than their husbands, although they could give pleasure to and receive pleasure from men if they were not their husbands. They appeared to have less severe superegos than I at first suspected and were thus able to enjoy some relationships in spite of their hostility to their mothers. Both these women had older brothers with whom they had been intimate when they were young, and perhaps they had thus to some degree solved their Oedipal problems by transferring some of their sexual strivings from their fathers to their brothers, thus diminishing the hostility and guilt they felt towards their mothers at the Oedipal level.

During the first few years of the analyses I worked with these ideas, to which both patients agreed in an unconvincing way, with little protest (although one, as I will show, became confused) but the work did not change their attitudes to their mothers or to me. Their analyses remained repetitive, i.e., one patient's attachment to me being based on an aim-inhibited sexual drive and a hope of overcoming my hostility, and the other on a hopeless attempt to be near to me which sometimes involved a search for a penis with which to do so.

I will now give some material about the two patients separately before coming back to theoretical considerations.

Early in her analysis Mrs X. acted out her wish to satisfy and please me – the mother-analyst – in a teasing erotic way, secretly imagining that I was satisfied each time she entered my room. She thus identified with a penis; I was related to as an external object and simultaneously as one who could be identified with (Freud, 1923a). She dreaded touching me but entering my room symbolically represented entering my body and giving me pleasure and so set her free to have pleasure with her lover. She was anxious when she left my room which she did with the greatest care and tact. She never touched me and lay on the couch as if she were not really supported by it. She told me that she hated men when they withdrew after intercourse, and was sad and never happy after intercourse because she would then have to wait until the next time before she was needed by the man again. He would be indifferent to her for the time being and would go to sleep. She wanted to be wanted all the time, to be the need-satisfying object for her lover, which was easy (because she had a vagina); and for women, which was more difficult as her vagina was no good to women.

In spite of this the task was not felt to be hopeless or impossible. Early in her analysis she had many lovers, as she thought that I would be aroused and stimulated and amused by stories of them, as her mother had appeared to be by her childish sexual games. She never for a moment risked my envy as it was always made abundantly clear to me that men did not really matter to her, which was in a way true. However, she herself enjoyed her relations with men in a rather offhand way.

When later in her analysis Mrs X. realized that her sexual aims in relation to women were unrealizable, I was given up as an external sexual object and she began to get in touch with an early, more primitive, repressed introjected object who was felt to be truly feminine and for whom she could feel concern. This object represented her nanny who had looked after her from the age of two and a half years until she grew up and withdrew from her. The patient had been truly dependent on this nanny who had been strict and was thus felt to be caring and dependable. The patient had identified with the caring nanny and was herself able to look after – i.e., care for – her when she in turn was ill. A relationship of mutual concern (Balint, E., 1972) had developed between them. The nanny had responded to the patient's care, unlike her mother who had not. It may be significant that until this nanny's arrival the patient had been looked after by a series of nannies and that her mother had breast-fed her with frequent interruptions for test weighing, i.e., she was given the breast, taken off it, put back and later given a bottle to supplement.

Freud (1923a) discussed the problems which arise when the ego's object identifications are incompatible with one another, and says that this may result in a disruption in the ego. Mrs X. was saved this disruption, perhaps because she did not introject her mother but kept her as an external sexual object. The nanny was therefore the only real feminine introject and her identification with this introject was kept apart and secret. Soon after the identification with and relation to the nanny was remembered, the mother (as well as myself) was given up as a sexual object and the patient then tried to care for, i.e., love, her mother in a non-exciting, non-sexual way. The mother then withdrew from her.

The patient responded by resorting again to attempts to please her mother erotically. She tried to hide her emerging femininity; became very thin and started to dress like a boy. When this too failed, she behaved like a stupid hysterical girl, making scenes in public, once more hiding her maturity and pleasure in and ability to relate to her husband and children. Following this episode Mrs X. went through a period of grief and hopelessness in the analysis, until she accepted her mother's rejection and started liberating herself from her. She then slowly began to change: she dressed like a woman and let me see how much she loved and valued her husband.

During this time she seldom related to me as she had before but started to show her care and love for me which I saw now not as a reaction formation but based on her emerging ability to come to terms with reality. The transference manifestations changed from time to time but on the whole, however, she related to me as she had been related to by her nanny. She also stopped treating her husband as she felt her mother had treated her and her father, i.e., as inferior beings – objects needing continual sexual stimulation.

The second patient, Mrs Y., was aged 43 when she came to analysis. Her mother had died a few years before the beginning of the analysis. The mother had probably been a lifelong depressive. This was revealed by her diaries which, although in the patient's possession, were only read by her after many years of analysis when some resolution of her problems had taken place. The diaries described her mother's struggles to make a close relationship with my patient, her only daughter, and to be able to hold her close when feeding her. This the mother failed to do, and in order to bear the strain of feeding her baby at all she had smoked cigarettes and read continuously during the feeds.

Mrs Y. had few memories of her early relationship with her mother but the analysis soon uncovered memories of early relationships with her brothers and father. When she was very young her older brother, John (which was the name of her lover), cared for her, although later he became the main object in the Oedipal phase. Her relationship to her mother was unreachable. She was represented in dreams as a frozen, icy box or coffin or unreachable bare room. This part of her inner world was not related to her other love-objects – nor was it integrated into her ego – and seemed a foreign body frozen and untouchable inside her.

Mrs Y. had been told that analysis was a painful treatment, and she thus knew that if she was upset and hurt I was a good analyst and was doing my job properly. I would therefore be happy, so she was content. Although I was seen as an ugly hunchback she did not mind; in fact, her hostility and envy of me were thus diminished. I was felt to be near to her when she was upset and she felt adequate so long as this situation continued. According to the patient her brothers and her mother and father were all intelligent and she was the stupid member of the family. However, during the analysis she felt that if she understood me and I was willing to work with her she could not be so stupid after all; otherwise I would be bored with her. To her stupid meant castrated.

However, she could not bear it if I showed her the Oedipal conflicts expressed in her dreams, nor when her dreams and associations led us to her earlier experiences with her mother. Still more difficult was it for her when I likened the conflicts of these early years with the conflicts she was having in her present life with her husband and with her lover. When these interpretations were made she got confused, felt attacked and could not understand me. In spite of this she continued to give me dreams and associations in which her present life was connected with her past and with the frozen, isolated part of her inner world which represented her mother. I tried to help her feel her sorrow and need to warm her mother but this also

[338]

made her feel that I was attacking her – was angry with her and, therefore, I too would become distant. She could not accept or really understand the meaning of my words; they became part of the isolated, frozen past. One day, however, she dreamt about her search for a penis and went to buy one at the chemist's shop. With this she could warm up her mother: she was then able to remember some of her mother's clothes, the contents of her cupboards and the books on her shelves; these representations of her mother gradually became familiar objects, i.e., not part of the frozen mother inside her. When these became loved and grieved over she began to take her memories of her mother out of cold storage.

Mrs Y. always dreamt profusely and usually wept when telling me her dreams: however, one day she came into the room looking happier than usual and told me that she had had a truly marvellous dream – quite different from the usual ones.

It was about a piece of marvellous velvet; the most beautiful material, texture, colour, she had ever seen: but it was not hers. It was Hope's (the name of a friend of hers). Here the patient wept. She, the patient, could not have the velvet – or touch or stroke it unless she were Hope – and she was not. 'But still,' she said, 'it was a marvellous dream. I never imagined such beautiful stuff.' She then spoke about her mother and soon realized that the velvet represented her mothers's body. She went on to speak about her father's attitude to her mother when she (the mother) was 'blue' (her phrase – I did not yet know the colour of the velvet which was first said to be golden – but later became a lovely blue colour like her mother's eyes). Father could do nothing for mother and so when she was depressed he used to go to his shed and mend his boat. The patient then wept again, and spoke about hopelessness. No one could cure or soothe or stroke her mother – only Hope could stroke her. Later in the same session Mrs Y. spoke about her lover, who often stroked her but did not touch his own wife; nor could she let her husband touch her.

The meaning of this dream was, of course, overdetermined: it proved a turning-point in the analysis, which for some time became centred on the theme of hopelessness. This was connected with not being able to help or care for or satisfy mother, or to get near to her. I, the analyst, was no longer seen as the angry hunchback, and gradually the frozen isolated part of the patient, the unloved frozen mother, receded. Mrs Y. later began to form relationships with women and she cared for an old, angry woman whom she tended before she died. Later still she was able to let her husband leave her. This involved being able to release him and let *him* give up the hopeless relationship with her and his hope of pleasing her. She is still in analysis and is discovering what it is like to be a woman and to be able to relate to the world – which involves giving up her relationship with unhelpable people – and of being able to receive help from the analyst.

Theoretically the question is: was Mrs Y.'s inability to accept and give satisfaction to her husband based on the early failure with the depressed mother who fed her? Did she in this way act out and preserve her relationship with her mother, i.e., her husband had to relate to her as she had related to her mother and was not allowed to warm her or leave her? Or were her strivings based on a later structure, the result of her Oedipal wish to have her father and give up her attachment to her mother? Her relationship with her husband enabled her to postpone the acceptance of her failure to revive her mother and her relationship with her analyst enabled her to deny her failure to be nourished by her. She had first to feel the hopelessness and then give up centring her life around it before she could give up her hostility and fear and perhaps reach the depressive position, thus making reparation possible.

Summary and theoretical considerations

I have presented material to illustrate some of the difficulties encountered by a woman analyst when analysing women patients whose mothers were either depressed or withdrawn. These patients' main preoccupation is with the satisfaction of their mothers, without giving up their pleasure in their genitals with which they satisfy men. They enjoy and value their vaginas but not their total femininity. This dual aim (i.e., the satisfaction of their mothers and of men) necessitates: (a) a denial of castration, (b) the undervaluing of husbands, i.e., fathers, (c) a particular form of relationship with the women who, they feel, do not have the sexual pleasure they have. They have a horror of touching these women but want to render them harmless and to warm or stimulate them.

My thesis is that a state of primitive concern is one factor in the structure of human relationship and can be reached during the analysis of some patients once their defences against their hostility, their reaction formations to their aggressive tendencies and a period of hopelessness are overcome. Their early primitive emotional feelings can then be used in mature object-relationships.*

It is open to question whether these patients should be thought of as latent homosexuals. In my opinion they should not because, although they are preoccupied with women, this is more because of their love and fear and pity for their mothers and their wish to keep them alive, than because of their libidinal drives which are directed towards men.

In the analysis these patients have first to accept that they cannot satisfy their mothers sexually: they then internalize them (if they have not already done so) and feel love and concern for their introjects. Lastly, they have to go through a period of hopelessness and grief because their love and concern are useless to their mothers. They do not then turn to another woman to satisfy sexually, but find other women to care for and love. I do not see this as connected mainly with guilt feelings. They can also then form loving and not only sexual erotic

---

* John Klauber, who made a valuable contribution to my paper when I read it to the British Psycho-Analytical Society, has given me permission to refer to his ideas. He restated the underlying problem as being connected with the way the judgements of the ego impose themselves on the drives, and on the important role played by the ego in coming to terms with the realities of the mother's character. This in turn he saw as depending on the basic health in the child which can survive the bad parts of its early experiences and eventually utilize the good parts for mature object-relationships.

[341]

relationships with their husbands. It should once again be noted that these women do not turn to women for sexual or body satisfaction. They relate to women as love-objects – and objects for mutual concern – but not mainly as drive-satisfying objects.

These patients illustrate the technical difficulties inherent in the analysis by a woman analyst of those women patients whose preoccupation it is to satisfy a depressed mother while having sexual lives of their own. I have tried to show how difficult it is to follow the threads of their instinctual life and how these run parallel with the ego's struggle to maintain its object-relationship. The analyst has to understand the conflicts appropriate to the Oedipal and pre-Oedipal phases and see how they relate to the primitive object-relationships in which the origins of mutual concern can be traced. In the patients I describe the instinctual drives do not deviate but their failure to satisfy their mothers is acted out in their relationships with their husbands and lovers, who are kept as necessary but only partially satisfying objects, and with their analysts whom they feel they can satisfy for ever. I have emphasized these patients' needs to care for their mothers, and not what I assume to be the earlier need to be cared for by them.

I want to make an attempt at some generalizations, in order to give a partial answer to the question in my title, 'What does a woman want?' I am (I think rightly) afraid of generalizations because I believe they tend to blur the clinical material on which they are based and inevitably omit many important issues, but perhaps it is appropriate at this stage to try to do so.

I suggest that women want, both in their relationship with men and with women, to use that primitive structure in human relations, namely the capacity for mutual concern (Balint, E., 1972). Owing to its primitive nature it can only be satisfactorily expressed by the body itself, or by feelings in the body based on inner representatives of the body and by body memories. The vagina is that part of a woman's body which is felt to be the most important area with which to express mutual concern with men (this does not exclude the use of the rest of her body). However in her relation to women she is at a loss to know how to express it unless she has herself introjected and identified with a satisfactory satisfying woman's body, which satisfied her and which she felt she satisfied when she was an infant. I assume that if she was satisfied by her mother's body she rightly felt that her own body satisfied her mother. I do not think it is adequate to think in terms of identification with parts of a woman's body or of the environment created by the mother. Furthermore, I suggest that unless a woman can experience mutual concern with women her relationship with men is likely to be impoverished, and men may be undervalued and not experienced as objects for mutual concern.

Woman and her discontents: a reassessment of Freud's views on female sexuality

WILLIAM H. GILLESPIE

THE VAST DIMENSIONS of the subject of female sexuality have obliged me to limit my field rather carefully. I have therefore taken as my starting point Freud's own views on female sexuality. As we all know, Freud was a true scientist and his career was a voyage of discovery, during which new vistas kept presenting themselves; and so, of course, we have to reckon with Freud's changing views, for some of them were altered quite radically in his later years. Some, however, were retained relatively unchanged, and it is these steadfastly held opinions that led to a controversy, which became particularly lively in the 1920s. The opposition was led largely by women analysts, but they had the powerful support of Ernest Jones. This controversy is part of the intellectual environment in which Melanie Klein's lines of thought and clinical activity took shape, and so one begins to appreciate how far-reaching have been its consequences.

I have attempted to discover some of the germs of Freud's views on female sexuality by scrutinizing his early published works and the correspondence with Fliess. The first important statements emerged in 1894-5, in Draft G. of the Fliess papers (Freud, 1950a) and in the paper on anxiety neurosis published on 15 January 1895 (Freud, 1895). Draft G. is remarkable for the so-called sexual diagram; the same ideas are presented purely verbally in the 1895 paper, where Freud makes it quite

clear that his view of the sexual process applies, in the first
instance, to men. I will quote:

> In the sexually mature male organism sexual excitation is
> produced – probably continuously – and periodically
> becomes a stimulus to the psyche . . . This somatic excita-
> tion is manifested as a pressure on the walls of the seminal
> vesicles, which are lined with nerve-endings; thus this vis-
> ceral excitation will develop continuously, but it will have to
> reach a certain height before it is able to overcome the resis-
> tance of the intervening path of conduction to the cerebral
> cortex and express itself as a psychical stimulus. When this
> has happened, however, the group of sexual ideas which is
> present in the psyche becomes supplied with energy and
> there comes into being the psychical state of libidinal tension
> which brings with it an urge to remove that tension. A
> psychical unloading of this kind is only possible by means of
> what I shall call *specific* or *adequate* action. This adequate
> action consists, for the male sexual instinct, in a complicated
> spinal reflex act which brings about the unloading of the
> nerve-endings, and in all the psychical preparations which
> have to be made in order to set off that reflex. Anything
> other than the adequate action would be fruitless, for once
> the somatic sexual excitation has reached threshold value it
> is turned continuously into psychical excitation, and some-
> thing must positively take place which will free the nerve-
> endings from the load of pressure on them – which will,
> accordingly, remove the whole of the existing somatic exci-
> tation and allow the subcortical path of conduction to re-
> establish its resistance. (pp. 108-9).

This view seems to depend on a close analogy with that other
vesicle, the urinary bladder; in principle the difference would
reside in the more complicated specific action required in the
sexual act.

Freud goes on to say:

> . . . in essentials this formula is applicable to women as well,
> in spite of the confusion introduced into the problem by all

the artificial retarding and stunting of the female sexual
instinct . . . Where women are concerned, however, we are
not in a position to say what the process analogous to the
relaxation of the seminal vesicles may be. (p. 109)

Freud's inability to discover a female analogue to the seminal
vesicles is surely damaging to the theory. Another point to
which I would draw attention, however, is his remark about
the 'artificial retarding and stunting of the sexual instinct', for
it shows how much, at this early date, Freud was alive to the
importance of social factors in producing effects that might be
mistakenly attributed to inherent differences between the
sexes. Similar remarks can be found in other parts of his early
writings. For example, in Draft G. he writes:

Women become anaesthetic more easily because their whole
upbringing works in the direction of not awakening somatic
sexual excitation, but of changing all excitations which
might otherwise have that effect into psychical stimuli . . .
This is necessary because, if there were a vigorous somatic
sexual excitation, the psychical sexual group would soon
acquire such strength intermittently that, as in the case of
men, it would bring the sexual object into a favourable position by means of a specific reaction. But women are
required to leave out the arc of the specific reaction; instead,
permanent specific actions are required of them which
entice the male into the specific action. (p. 204) [Note the
word 'required'.]

I think that what Freud says here about the 'permanent specific
actions' required of women which entice the male into the
specific action is particularly interesting in connection with
fairly recent work by one of our British colleagues, Dr Michael,
whose investigations of rhesus monkeys (Michael, 1968) have
shown that the male's sexual activity or lack of it varies not
with his own hormonal state, but with that of his female partner. Considerations like this, which in a way Freud had anticipated by more than a half-century, just as he anticipated the
discovery of sexual hormones themselves – such considera-

[346]

tions should make one suspicious of formulations which ascribe sexual activity to the male and passivity to the female, a trap which Freud continually found himself escaping by a hair's breadth.

Already in 1897 (Freud, 1950a, Letter 75) Freud's exposition of the origins of repression foreshadowed the views about the role of the clitoris which were to play so important a part in his theory. The 'something organic' in repression is a question of the abandonment of former sexual zones, i.e., the regions of the anus and of the mouth and throat, which originally instigate something analogous to the later release of sexuality. Memories of excitations of these abandoned sexual zones, thanks to 'deferred action' (i.e., the intensification due to sexual maturing) – such memories give rise not to libido but to unpleasure, analogous to disgust – 'just as we turn away our sense organ . . . [from a stinking object] in disgust, so do our preconsciousness and our conscious sense turn away from the memory. This is *repression*' (p. 269). If psychically bound this leads to rejection (*Verwerfung*), the affective basis for morality, shame, etc. Disgust appears earlier in little girls than in boys, but the main distinction emerges at puberty, when a further sexual zone is (wholly or in part) extinguished in females which persists in males, that is, the region of the clitoris. 'Hence the flood of shame . . . till the new, vaginal, zone is awakened.'

It was, of course, in the *Three Essays*, published eight years later (Freud, 1905b) that Freud elaborated all this more fully. He writes there:

> If we are to understand how a little girl turns into a woman, we must follow the further vicissitudes of this excitability of the clitoris. Puberty, which brings about so great an accession of libido in boys, is marked in girls by a fresh wave of *repression*, in which it is precisely clitoridal sexuality that is affected. What is thus overtaken by repression is a piece of masculine sexuality . . . When at last the sexual act is permitted and the clitoris itself becomes excited, it still retains a function: the task, namely, of transmitting the excitation to

the adjacent female sexual parts, just as – to use a simile –
pine shavings can be kindled in order to set a log of harder
wood on fire . . . When erotogenic susceptibility to stimulation has een successfully transferred by a woman from the
clitoris to the vaginal orifice, it implies that she has adopted
a new leading zone for the purposes of her later sexual activity . . . The fact that women change their leading erotogenic
zone in this way, together with the wave of repression at
puberty, which, as it were, puts aside their childish masculinity, are the chief determinants of the greater proneness of
women to neurosis and especially to hysteria. These determinants, therefore, are intimately related to the essence of
femininity. (pp. 220-21)

I hope you will forgive me if I now make a jump forward of 70
years. The subject will be the same, but the approach that of
observation and physiological enquiry, which by 1965 had
caught up with the Freud of 1895. I am referring to the clinical
researches of Masters and Johnson (1966). This work has, I
believe, aroused criticism and resistance in many people, sometimes rationalized as disapproval of scientific scopophilia. Sexual matters continue to be in some ways taboo, despite all
appearances to the contrary, and for my part I see Masters and
Johnson's bold and direct approach to the subject of human
sexual activity as something quite analogous to Freud's own
attitude in defying Victorian convention by handling these
matters verbally with patients; and so I experience some of the
hostile criticism of Masters and Johnson as *déjà vu*. What they
have described are facts, unless the contrary is proved by
further research; the theories that may be built on these facts
are, of course, an entirely different matter; they have been used,
for example, by Sherfey (1966) to support an extreme feminist
point of view.

At this point I am not discussing feminism but the significance of clitoris and vagina in female sexuality. With the help
of special apparatus Masters and Johnson were able to make
direct observations on the changes in the female genitalia during sexual activity. These showed that: 'The female's

physiologic responses to effective sexual stimulation ... develop with consistency, regardless of the source of the psychic or physical sexual stimulation.' But note carefully that they are speaking of physiological, not psychological responses. They also observe that actual orgasmic experiences are initiated in both sexes by similar muscle components. As regards the clitoris during intravaginal coitus, it is kept in a state of continuous stimulation through the transmitted effect of alternate penile thrust and withdrawal even though, as Sherfey says, it is not being touched and appears to have vanished, owing to its erection and retraction into the swollen clitoral hood. Sherfey adds:

> Furthermore, it is also obvious why the thrusting move-
> ments of the penis will necessarily create simultaneous
> stimulation of the lower third of the vagina, labia minora,
> and clitoral shaft and glans as an integrated, inseparable
> functioning unit with the glans being the most important
> and, in far the majority of instances, the indispensable
> initiator of the orgasmic reaction.

With this last remark in mind, namely, that the glans of the clitoris is generally the indispensable initiator of orgasm, let us return to the *Three Essays* and note that Freud had expressed just the same thought when he wrote of 'transmitting the excitation to the adjacent female sexual parts, just as ... pine shavings can be kindled in order to set a log of harder wood on fire'. But there is a vital difference, and I suspect that it is betrayed by Freud's phrase 'the adjacent *female* sexual parts' (my italics) – does not this mean, even if unintentionally, that the clitoris is *not* a female sexual part, and that it must therefore be given up? Does not Freud's theory of the pseudo-male clitoris which has to be given up imply an insistence that the female *must* be castrated – it is 'required of her', to use his phrase? After all, this female castration is actually practised in certain cultures. If I may be permitted to misquote Scripture: From her that hath not shall be taken away even that which she hath. And so Freud, having expressed so beautifully, by his simile of kindling, this true insight into the function of the clitoris, at once

[349]

extends his concept in a different direction – mistakenly, I submit. He assumes that the transfer of excitation from the clitoris to the adjacent sexual parts is not merely a matter of topography but one of maturational development. He says:

> before this transference can be effected, a certain interval of time must elapse, during which the young woman is anaesthetic. This anaesthesia may become permanent if the clitoridal zone refuses to abandon its excitability ... [Women may be] anaesthetic at the vaginal orifice but are by no means incapable of excitement originating in the clitoris or even in other zones. (p. 221)

And from this there arises the unrealistic and idealized concept of vaginal orgasm, about which I have written elsewhere (Gillespie, 1969).

With the knowledge at his disposal at the turn of the century, to say nothing of the paternalistic cultural background against which he was working, combined with Victorian prudery, the amazing thing is not Freud's erroneous conclusion but the fact that he was able to achieve so much insight into female sexuality. Often, over the years, he expressed the difficulty he found in exploring this 'dark continent'. It is a corner of precisely this darkness on which Masters and Johnson have been able to throw some light, in a highly literal sense, with their illuminated phallus and colour cinematography.

Freud did not make public any comprehensive revision of his views until the appearance of his very important paper on 'Some Psychical Consequences of the Anatomical Distinction between the Sexes' (Freud, 1925), although already in 'On the Sexual Theories of Children' (Freud, 1908) he is speaking of the castration complex and female penis envy, one of the main themes of the later paper. Now the visual discovery of the penis begins to assume a leading place. 'She has seen it [the penis] and knows that she is without it and wants to have it. Here what has been named the masculinity complex of women branches off' (Freud, 1925, pp. 252-3). And Freud explains how the hope of obtaining a penis may persist indefinitely and account for strange actions; or its absence may be disavowed and so she may behave as though she were a man. Alternatively, she remains aware of the wound to her narcissism and develops a sense of inferiority, which she may extend to womankind in general, in this way showing at least one male characteristic. She becomes in general more prone to jealousy than a man. Her loving relationship with her mother becomes loosened, for she holds her mother responsible for her inferior equipment. She also turns against masturbation for the same narcissistic reason. But through the equation 'penis-child' she is able to give up the wish for a penis of her own; with the wish for a child in view she takes her father as a love object and her mother becomes the object of her jealousy. So she reaches her Oedipus complex in this roundabout way and has 'turned into a little woman' – *faute de mieux*, one feels obliged to add. To quote again: '*Whereas in boys the Oedipus complex is destroyed by the castration complex, in girls it is made possible and led up to by the castration complex*' (p. 256, Freud's italics). Ideally, in the boy, the Oedipus complex exists no longer, the superego has become its heir. So what of the female superego? Freud says:

> I cannot evade the notion (though I hesitate to give it expression) that for women the level of what is ethically normal is different from what it is in men. Their superego is never so inexorable, so impersonal, so independent of its emotional origins as we require it to be in men . . . We must not allow ourselves to be deflected from such conclusions by the denials of the feminists. (pp. 257, 258)

Of course the feminists and their latterday counterparts of the women's liberation movement have done much more than deny Freud's conclusions; they have counterattacked vigorously and denounced Freud as a male chauvinist. But what should concern us is not whether Freud's views give offence – this they have always done in one way or another – but whether they are correct. The essential point concerns the nature of femininity. Is it something natural to the female child, or is it something that she has to learn to accept, after failing to achieve a more desirable condition? And if it is true that many females in our culture are reluctant to accept their role as feminine women, is this because that role is inherently unattractive for anatomical and physiological as well as for psychological reasons; or is it because society, dominated by men as the feminists maintain, has decreed that the feminine role is to be weak, submissive and enslaved? The femininists would say that Freud, with his scientific authority, has supported powerfully the male chauvinistic forces from which liberation must be achieved. Some of his remarks can easily be used to support this view of his attitude to female development and its deviations from *his* idea of the normal or desirable. For example, in his last comments on the subject (Freud, 1940a), he says: 'It does little harm to a woman if she remains in her feminine Oedipus attitude . . . She will choose her husband for his paternal characteristics and be ready to recognize his authority' (p. 194). How very convenient for a paternalistic husband, one can hear the feminists say.

For the present let us postpone any attempt to assess Freud's attitude and alleged anti-female prejudice and let us consider briefly some of the criticisms and attempted rebuttals of Freud's views that have been made by other psychoanalysts, mostly women. Perhaps the most outspoken, and one of the earliest, was Karen Horney (1926, 1932, 1933). For her, the 'undiscovered' vagina is the denied vagina; vaginal erotism is primary and not a derivative of oral erotism (in this she opposes the views of both Helene Deutsch and Melanie Klein). It is only anxiety that prevents the seeking of pleasure in the vagina – anxiety connected with the size of the father's penis, with observations of female vulnerability, and with injury caused by masturbation, either physically or in fantasy. Ernest Jones (1933) repeatedly cites Horney with approval and explicitly endorses her concept of the denied vagina. Of course Jones's paper covers a very much wider field and is greatly influenced by the views of Melanie Klein. It is a masterly piece of work and cannot readily be summarized.

No doubt it is equally impossible to summarize Klein's views; but they have been so influential and are in important respects so much at variance with Freud's earlier views that

[352]

some attempt should be made to compare the two. Klein's conception of female sexual development was clearly formulated already in 1932 and, so far as I know, never fundamentally changed. She agrees with Freud to the extent that the girl wants to have a penis and hates her mother for not giving her one. What she wants, however, is not to be masculine through possessing a penis of her own, but to incorporate her father's penis as an oral object to replace the disappointing mother's breast. So far from being an outcome of her castration complex, this wish is the result of her dominant feminine instinctual components and the most fundamental expression of her Oedipal tendencies, for these are orally rooted. Here Klein differs from Horney, who believed in *primary* early vaginal erotism. Although Helene Deutsch also held that the father's penis as an object derives from the mother's breast, she believed that all this, together with the emergence of the vagina, occurs only at sexual maturity. Klein disagrees with Freud's view that the girl's sexuality is essentially masculine and clitoris-orientated until puberty. She holds that after an initial breast-dominated phase common to both sexes, the boy passes next through a feminine phase with an oral-sucking fixation on the father's penis, just like the girl. So – it is the boy who is feminine, not the girl who is masculine!

According to Klein, the clitoris overshadows the vagina in early sexuality because of the girl's fears concerning the inside of her body, for she unconsciously knows of the vagina. In this area Klein is very much in agreement with Horney. Klein, however, adds that although clitoral masturbation fantasies are at first largely pregenital, the later fantasies centred on the father's penis assume a genital and vaginal character and thus, *to begin with*, take a feminine direction – 'being often accompanied, it would seem, by vaginal sensations'. Here I would remind you of Masters and Johnson and Sherfey, who stress the integral nature of the clitoral-vaginal complex of organs. It was not possible for Freud to know of this, and I believe this led him to a false antithesis between clitoris and vagina.

Klein agrees with Freud that there is a difference between the girl's superego and the boy's, but for her the difference is of

[353]

another kind. The impulsion to introject the paternal imago, represented by the father's penis, is much stronger in the girl because vaginal introjection is added to oral introjection, and so she is more at the mercy of a very potent superego. Later on, in coitus, she attempts to introject a 'good' penis to counteract the introjected 'bad' penis. She is thus more dependent on her objects, and this dependence is increased by her lack of a penis of her own.

In 'Female Sexuality' (1931) Freud criticized some of the views I have been discussing, but strangely failed (as Strachey points out) to take note of the fact that these writers were in part reacting to his own paper (Freud, 1925) on the anatomical distinction. By this time he had discovered the intensity and long duration of the little girl's attachment to her mother, so that the pre-Oedipal phase in females gains a new importance; he freely admits his inability to see his way through any case completely, and likewise the possibility that women analysts may have the advantage over him here. However, he still feels justified in assuming that for many years the vagina is virtually non-existent and may not produce any sensations before puberty – and from this there follows the theory of two phases, first masculine, then feminine. He also notes that the clitoris, with its virile character, continues to function in later life in some obscure way. Some of this obscurity has now, I think, been removed by Masters and Johnson. Essentially, then, Freud holds fast to his theory of a normal masculine phase based on the clitoral zone, and a consequent feeling of being a castrated creature when this phase has to be abandoned, and the superior male organ has to be acknowledged. But the girl rebels against this and may develop a feeling of general revulsion against sexuality, or she may cling assertively to her masculinity, or thirdly, by a circuitous route she may arrive at the normal female attitude, taking her father as her object. Her Oedipus complex, having been created, not destroyed, by the castration fantasy, itself escapes destruction. The pre-Oedipal attachment to the mother is far more important in women than men, and their struggles with their husbands essentially repeat the struggle with the mother rather than with the father. The girl emerges from the phase of mother-attachment with the reproach, not only that the mother did not give her a penis, but also that she did not give her enough milk.

It may perhaps be agreed that in this paper on female sexuality Freud is feeling his own way rather than accepting uncritically what was being urged by his analytic opponents. Nevertheless, a few of these independent conclusions do seem to show Freud moving slightly closer to them – for example, the enormous importance for the girl of the initial relationship with her mother, and the possibly equivalent reproaches that she was not given a penis and was not given enough milk, which surely suggests that behind all the fuss about the penis there lies an earlier concern with the breast. It is interesting to note, in passing, that Freud resisted the temptation to conclude that the girl's strong ambivalence towards her mother is due to her inability to direct her hostility on to her father, as the boy does, for he says that this conclusion would be premature before we have studied the pre-Oedipal stage in boys – something which he does not seem to have accomplished subsequently. This is hard to reconcile with his statements about the great obscurity of female sexual development. In his lecture 'Femininity' (1933a, Lecture 33) Freud expresses himself more confidently in that he simply inculpates the castration complex for the girl's specific and greater hostility to the mother, as well as for her greater proneness to envy and jealousy. In general, this lecture recapitulates earlier formulations, and the same may be said of chapter 7 in 'An Outline of Psycho-Analysis' (Freud, 1940a).

The need for limitation has led me to exclude two very important subjects from my discussion of Freud's views – namely narcissism and masochism. To discuss them adequately would require at least two further papers. I have also been unable to consider properly the very interesting and thought-provoking contributions of our French colleagues (Chasseguet-Smirgel, 1964), for example Grunberger's point that, since the origin of narcissism is to be found in the mother's love for her baby, the fact that, as he alleges, every mother is ambivalent towards her girl baby helps to account for female

[355]

complaints about being a woman, and for women being narcissistic before all else. Chasseguet-Smirgel herself also stresses the narcissistic wound inflicted on the little girl by an omnipotent mother, and her inability to overcome this as the boy does with the help of his penis; so that penis envy really arises out of the need to cope with the omnipotent mother. Turok stresses the anal level of the conflict with the mother, who takes control of the girl's sphincter and demands possession of her stool. I think Turok would probably agree that what this stands for is the girl's internal, female sexual world. Penis envy is a manifestation of repression of the true underlying anal conflict, and the idealized penis represents the value of what she has lost all hope of having in herself, namely female genital maturity.

Before returning to Freud for a final attempt to bring together and review his theories, I want to say a few words on a phylogenetic theme; my attention was drawn to it first by David Attenborough's television programme on courtship and mating among animals. It was a beautiful and remarkable film, and it aroused in me the thought – how is it that we can observe and have rather intimate knowledge of the sexual lives and practices of so many species of land and aquatic animals, in such striking contrast to the little that we really know and have observed in the case of the human animal? And in view of this discrepancy how can one despise and condemn the attempts, however imperfect, of researchers like Master and Johnson? One of the pictures that specially intrigued me was that of a male and a female fish expelling their sexual products into the same piece of water, first one, then immediately the other, in each case with what *could* be interpreted as orgastic wrigglings. Then, whilst I was preparing this paper, I received a reprint from Werner Kemper of Berlin of a paper (Kemper, 1965) with a title that could be translated 'New Contributions from Phylogenetics to Female Biopsychology'. To my delight, he describes there this very phenomenon of fish reproduction, including the 'convulsive movements of manifestly (*offensichtlich*) orgastic nature'. Kemper's thesis is that there are four other important reasons, besides those listed by Freud, why female sexual development is so much more complicated and

WOMAN AND HER DISCONTENTS

leads so much more frequently to dissatisfaction than is the case in the male. These are phylogenetic in nature, and the first of the four is illustrated by the fishes mentioned above, together with the well-authenticated assumption that life – and so our ancestors – began in the sea (and of course Kemper is well acquainted with Ferenczi's 'Thalassa'). The point is that the female fish appears to enjoy an orgasm in no way different from the male's; in each case it is a matter of orgastic pleasure in the act of expulsion of a bodily product (*Ausstossungslust*). The male creature, who now appears as the arch-conservative, has had the good fortune to be able to preserve this way of sexual life right through his development into a land animal, a viviparous mammal, and finally man himself; but not so the female, who has been 'required' (if I may use Freud's word in this connection) by the process of evolution to develop a vagina and uterus out of her cloaca, and to get what sexual pleasure she can from taking the male's sexual product into it in the service of internal impregnation. Hers is the plastic, adaptive sex, but she had been obliged to give up the pleasure that her fish-ancestress had shared with her male partner. Is it too fanciful to suggest that the lack of female orgasm, which is, I believe, the rule in most mammals, can be understood in this sense; and to suggest that the human female, in our day at least, has learned again how to have an orgasm with the aid of just those muscle groups that go into action during male orgasm? And I would add too that the fact that nearly simultaneous orgasm is generally an essential factor in producing ultimate pleasure could readily be seen as a reflection of the fact that, in the case of fishes, near-synchronicity is of the essence, for without this condition fertilization will not occur. The suggestion arising from all these ideas is that woman's dissatisfaction with her role is rooted a great deal more deeply than mere envy of the male's possession of imposing external genitalia. As Decter (1973) has convincingly argued, the extreme exponents of women's liberation are going far beyond the demand for a fair deal from men; they are demanding to be liberated from that unfair share in the reproductive process which evolution has imposed on the female of the viviparous species.

If we return now to Freud's early formulations, we can see that from the beginning he perceived that human society as we know it has imposed various requirements on the female, such as the demand that she leave out the arc of the male specific reaction and develop instead permanent specific enticing actions calculated to induce the specific reaction in the male. He also observed that frigidity often depends on a woman's marrying without love; that is, on social pressure.

A little later, however, he began to stress the overriding importance of the clitoris in childhood sexuality, which he declared to be masculine in both sexes. In this case it is inevitable that the little girl should compare herself unfavourably to the male, with very damaging consequences to her narcissism. Thus, behind the social factors which he had earlier recognized, he felt sure from this point onwards that there is an unavoidable problem for the female based on the slogan that anatomy is destiny, and he held fast to this conviction to the end. Despite Freud's belief in the essentially masculine (i.e., phallic and active) nature of the little girl's sexual strivings, he admitted that she shows characteristics that are clearly feminine. This is a point that has been emphasized by a number of analytic critics of his theory, beginning perhaps with Horney. However, when we take into account the more recent work such as the observations of Stoller (1968) on transsexualism and related problems, it becomes clear that in this area we need to be very cautious in coming to firm conclusions, since gender identity is independent of genetic sex; indeed even the anatomical sex does not necessarily correspond to the genetic constitution, and without the appropriate hormonal influence at a certain stage of embryonic development the genetic male will develop into a female, though the genetic female continues as such with or without the appropriate hormones. Thus we cannot confidently draw any conclusions about the significance of so-called feminine behaviour in little girls, since the type of behaviour that a child exhibits is determined to such an important degree by what is expected of it by parents who assume, or who wish, its sex to be this or that.

A striking change was introduced into Freud's thinking

when, with his recognition of the vital importance of early attachment to the mother and its difference in the two sexes, he abandoned the notion of parallelism between male and female development. Nevertheless, he clung persistently to his conviction of the crucial influence of the girl's traumatic discovery of the penis, just as he continued to stress the boy's traumatic discovery of the no-penis. In both sexes these discoveries belied the initial assumption that everyone is like oneself automatically. Freud seems not to have considered seriously the possibility that the occurrence of such sudden traumatic discoveries might depend on current conventions of child-rearing. Nowadays it can seldom happen that a child is prevented from seeing the bodies of children of the opposite sex – a prohibition that was common in Freud's time and indeed in my own. It would be interesting to hear the comments of child analysts on this point.

At one place (1933a, Lecture 33) Freud admits that some may accuse him of an *idée fixe* in believing in the influence of lack of a penis on the configuration of femininity. You may well ask – am I making this accusation? If you insist that I answer yes or no I should find myself in difficulty. It does seem to me that Freud overemphasized the traumatic effect resulting from the visual impression of the unfamiliar genitals of the other sex, and I cannot help comparing Freud's unshakable belief in this idea with his earlier traumatic theory of neurosis, produced by sexual seduction. It was many years before he recognized this error, and many more years before he admitted it publicly. Is it not possible that this theory of a castration complex resulting from a traumatic visual experience is a kind of residue from the neurosis theory, something that he clung to as if it were a treasure saved from the wreckage?

Why indeed should the little girl be so disturbed and so overcome by inextinguishable envy at the mere sight of an unexpected excrescence on the little boy's body? If it were a matter of witnessing an adult erection, that would be different, but this is not what Freud had in mind. Surely we must agree that the girl's reaction is not the result merely of recognizing that he has something that she does not possess, but much more the result of her fantasies about it, based, on the most obvious and superficial level, on its urinary capacities, which would seem to offer more ego control and narcissistic gratification in the function. I would agree that the problem of where the female is hiding her penis is a big one for the boy, and I would suggest that this teasing conundrum constitutes an important ingredient in the impression of female insincerity and the dark obscurity in which she hides her sexuality; when Freud speaks of these things one senses a certain feeling of frustration and annoyance. When the clitoris is finally discovered as the answer to the problem, its diminutive size and lack of any obvious function lead naturally to the view that it is merely a vestigial penis, and that the girl's valuation of it shows that she is trying, in a pitifully inadequate way, to be a boy. The boy – and in this context I suggest that Freud had retained some of his boyishness, just like the rest of us chauvinist males – the boy in this way has his revenge for the female's insincere concealment – a concealment compounded of anatomy and prudery.

But the essence of the matter is that even if one admits the justice of these criticisms, Freud was in a much deeper sense right, if it be conceded that when he talks of the penis he is no more talking simply of a concrete anatomical organ than is Melanie Klein when she talks of the breast. I know that when one feels tempted to say that the penis stands for many less concrete things, rather than the other way round, one is in danger of going the way of Jung. Neverthe ess, I think one is justified in saying that the anatomical difference between the sexes is important not so much for itself but because it is the outward and visible sign of the vastly more extensive differences in the reproductive roles which evolution has decreed shall be allotted to men and to women. Whatever psychological significance, if any, one may be prepared to attach to the contrast between a female fish and a woman, it cannot be denied that the evolutionary process that has produced the mammals has called for a profound internalization of female sexuality, and that this has had very far-reaching psychological consequences, some of which take the form of resentment and dissatisfaction with the female role. Other consequences, of course, are of an opposite kind and can afford intense satisfactions which men cannot share except by identification and empathy. There is clearly a difference of opinion in analytic circles between those who would agree with Freud that the girl who settles for femininity does so only because she gives up the hopeless struggle to be a man, and others who hold that femininity is a primary thing, but has to be abandoned for a time out of fear of the mother, and that the girl's masculine clitoral sexuality is temporarily substituted for it. But it seems to me that the meaning of the clitoris is still somewhat obscure, for Masters and Johnson have demonstrated that it plays an important part in normal female sexual excitement and orgasm. Does this mean that Freud was mistaken in assuming that the clitoris is necessarily associated with masculine, penetrative strivings? Is it not possible that its excitement leads normally to the wish to be penetrated vaginally, so producing further stimulation of the clitoris as well as of the vagina? This is one of the many questions that I must leave unanswered.

Reflections on Dora:
the case of hysteria

GREGORIO KOHON

FREUD IN 1886, in his 'Report from Paris' (Freud, 1886a)
– the first paper in the English Standard Edition of his complete
works – separates hysteria as a psychic illness from biological
sex. This is what he has learned from Charcot in Paris, he tells
us, and to which he adds the notion of hysteria as caused by a
psychic trauma which occurred at some point in the past history of the subject. In the same way that they were formerly
treated as witches, nowadays – says Freud – female hysterical
patients can easily be identified as 'liars', women who 'deceive
us'. In the discussion that followed the presentation of this
report to the College of Professors of the Faculty of Medicine in
Vienna (Andersson, 1962), it was suggested that Freud should
present the case of a male hysteric, which in fact he does a few
months later (Freud, 1886b). This last lecture becomes his first
published paper on hysteria.

By including men among hysterical patients, Freud joins in
the attempt to give scientific status to the proposition of hysteria as a psychiatric diagnosis.[1] Nevertheless, despite this separation between hysteria and biological sex the cases of hysteria in women form the entire contribution to the *Studies on*

---

[1] For a historical view of the development of the concept of hysteria
and the various attempts to distinguish between the biological sex and
the illness see Ilza Veith's (1975) book.

Hysteria (Breuer and Freud, 1895). Psychoanalysis truly began with women. As will be suggested in the third part of this paper, the connection between women and hysteria makes sense to me, and Freud never seems to have abandoned this idea, which in fact has been present in psychoanalysis ever since (see for example Zetzel, 1968).[2] Freud first mentioned it in 'Heredity and the Aetiology of the Neuroses' (1896); reaffirmed it in the *Three Essays* (1905b); and finally stated it in 'Inhibitions, Symptoms and Anxiety' thus: 'there is no doubt that hysteria has a strong affinity with femininity, just as obsessional neurosis has with masculinity' (1926b, p. 143).

I think that in the development of the Oedipal drama of the women there is a hysterical stage, in which the subject – caught up in her need to change object from mother to father – can get 'fixed', unable to make the necessary choice. If it were true then – as Freud suspected – that a woman will choose a husband according to the image of her father, and establish with him in fantasy the same relationship that she had with her mother (Freud, 1931), I would like to suggest that a woman always at heart remains a hysteric. What I am referring to is not unknown to psychoanalysts in their practice: a female patient will say that she is in love with her male analyst but nevertheless make a maternal transference to him, 'and one that is often fiercely denied and frequently has delusional undertones' (Green, 1972).

It is with Dora that psychoanalysis becomes what we know it to be: the problem of transference is introduced for the first time in her case, and in doing so, Freud opens a different window to a hitherto very obscure world. In the historical continuity of thinking about hysteria there is, at this point, a rupture, a necessary conversion from the study of hysteria as carried out up to the time of Charcot, to that done by Freud (Pontalis, 1977). It is an irrevocable change of direction which will eventually make possible, in its ultimate consequences, the invention of the analytic situation. It is to hysterical patients

---

[2] It has also been present, in a different way, in everyday language, retaining in this case the derogatory meanings attached to the word.

that we must be grateful, and it is to Freud's genius that we owe
the discovery that what happens in dreams also happens in hysteria: in both cases, by disguising itself, desire can then find its
satisfaction. Hysteria, after Freud, can no longer be considered
as a syndrome from which both men and women could suffer,
but rather as a reflection of an internal conflict: it exists independently of the symptoms presented by hysterical patients.
Freud's attempt took him even further than he intended at the
beginning: hysteria is not just a psychiatric diagnosis which
would include conversion hysteria, anxiety hysteria, etc., but is
a human problematic, specifically female, present in all of us.
In 'Dora', for example, Freud's position is already clear: what
is important is that she reacts to a sexual encounter reflecting a
certain conflict in a particular way; what is relevant in her sexual life resides in her unconscious fantasy (Namnum, quoted in
Laplanche, 1974).

The number of papers written on the case of Dora is
astonishing, and there seems to be no end to our wish to know
more about her. Those concerned with sociology, history and
political science, literary critics and novelists, all seem
interested – for one reason or another – in her case. In 1979, a
film was made about her (McCall et al., 1979); and three years
before, the Company of Renaud-Barrault put on a play in the
Théâtre d'Orsay dedicated to her (Cixous, 1976). Why such a
fuss? And what is the connection – if any – between our wish to
know, our curiosity, and hysteria?

Of the five so-called 'clinical cases' of Freud[3] the 'Fragment
of an Analysis . . . ' (1905a) is the only one that refers to a
women. The history of Dora is extraordinary. It is a 'literary
masterpiece', which according to Marcus initiates a new genre,
and thanks to which he associates – with a certain irony –
Freud with Nabokov, Proust, Mann, Joyce, Ibsen and Borges
(Marcus, 1974).[4] What is admired is its literary value and the

---

[3] For some – no doubt, interesting – reason, the case of female
homosexuality is never included in this group (Freud, 1920b).

[4] Today we find works of fiction attempting to imitate Freud's style
and presentation. See, for example, the first part of *The White Hotel*,
D. M. Thomas, Penguin Books, 1981.

[364]

Ibsenian way in which Freud holds his readers in suspense (Ellenberger, 1970; Meltzer, 1978). The story unfolds before our eyes, suggesting more and more complexities in the relationships created between the various characters. Dora might well arrive at Freud's door with 'her script written in advance' (Mannoni, 1969), but Freud takes possession of the script and transforms it. What could have been a 'classic Victorian domestic drama' is now a family novel of mysterious complexity: time passes in it, but the repressed comes back once and again in the form of stories within other stories, in the various betrayals of the characters who were themselves betrayed (Marcus, 1974).

Freud seems exalted – and perhaps also excited? – by the way in which he discovers the connection between Dora's sucking of her finger and her knowledge of fellatio; how he interprets the sensation of pressure on her thorax and associates it with Herr K.'s erect penis; how he comes to the association between her playing with the reticule and masturbation. His exaltation is no longer that of a young doctor on an ambitious quest for a name and fame; there is now a persistent search for the truth – although we do not know whether it is Dora's truth or Freud's. The intolerant therapist of the *Studies* has now been transformed into a psychoanalyst (Meltzer, 1978).

Freud knows that he has a powerful instrument which will permit him – by following a method which he considers precise, namely the analysis of dreams – to uncover the secret of the symptoms of his patients. The conversion in this is total: he not only is convinced that he can do it, but, according to him, anybody can. Apparently Dora satisfies Freud's desires and his special interest in sexual matters by offering him her 'pathogenic material' without major obstacles, but she arouses his curiosity when, for example, 'she plays at having secrets', quickly hiding that unimportant letter in the waiting room. Dora speaks about the little jewel box in her first dream, and there is a box to be opened in the second, while Freud, in a letter to Fliess, talks about his collection of picklocks with which he is gently unlocking the case of an eighteen-year-old girl (Freud,

1950b). And in analysing that first dream, Freud (1905a) states: 'A regularly formed dream stands, as it were, upon two legs.' The development of a mutual seduction in the relationship between Dora and Freud seems fairly evident.[5] Many of his interpretations, and the way they were made, could not be understood by Dora except as an attempt at a parental, incestuous seduction (Blos, 1972).

According to Dora's account, Herr K. had found a way of being alone with her in his shop, from which they could see a religious procession in the main square. After closing the outer door and the shutters, Herr K. 'suddenly clasped the girl to him and pressed a kiss upon her lips. This was surely just the situation to call up a distinct feeling of sexual excitement in a girl of fourteen who had never before been approached. But Dora had at that moment a violent feeling of disgust . . . ' (Freud, 1905a, p. 28). This is where Freud makes the connection between one of her symptoms and the possibility that Dora had felt the pressure of the erect penis of her father's friend. But Freud goes further, defining Dora's conduct in the same scene and her reaction as 'already entirely and completely hysterical'. Freud shows here his prejudice, his intolerance and frustration: there is a parallel, a repetition of the same scene in the analysis, in which a new friend of her father's, this time Freud, not only tries to impose his will and what could be seen as his penetrating interpretations, but also his 'not too impractical' solution – the possibility of marrying Herr K.

Freud is going to feel as rejected as Herr K. Dora, instead of responding in a supposedly 'healthy' way on both occasions, disappoints not only Herr K. but also Freud. Freud's frustration is evident in various ways. When he insists upon the necessity of speaking plainly on sexual matters and of being frank and open with our patients, Freud says: 'It is possible for a man to talk to girls and women upon sexual matters of every kind

---

[5] With reference to the erotic link between Dora and Freud, see the interpretation that Anzieu (1959) makes of Freud's dream of the round table. Cf. also the comments that Decker (1982) makes about Freud's libidinal involvement in the choice of Dora's name.

without . . . bringing suspicion upon himself . . . The best way of speaking about such things is to be dry and direct . . . I call bodily organs and processes by their technical names, and I tell these to the patient if they – the names, I mean – happen to be unknown to her' (p. 48). It is at this precise moment that Freud resorts to French: '*J'appelle un chat un chat*'; and a few lines later: 'The right attitude is: "*pour faire une omelette il faut casser des oeufs*".' We could think, with Marcus (1974), that Freud would have been the first to smile at the observation that in this splendid declaration about direct and frank language, its author disappears, not once but twice, into quotations in French.

The criticisms of Freud, leaving aside here those that come from feminist authors, have been multiple and varied. Freud's mistake was in failing to interpret the transference enough (Muslin and Gill, 1978); in not maintaining a neutral attitude in the treatment (Langs, 1976); in having ignored the pathology of the milieu (Rieff, 1971); in not having recognized that what Dora wanted was the total, exclusive and absolute love of her mother (Lewin, 1973); in not having understood Dora's problems in terms of her genetic, adolescent development (Erikson, 1961); in failing to recognize the defence mechanisms typical of the adolescent period, or his own countertransference reactions to them (Glenn, 1980); in not having paid enough attention to the real disappointment with her father and other men during Dora's years of development (Scharfman, 1980).

Some of these criticisms – and here I can only consider them globally without necessarily doing them justice – are undoubtedly valid. Whether they are based on what would have been Freud's 'technical' errors, or on 'theoretical' deficiencies, they are all concerned to find a more exact alternative 'model'. Almost a century later, it is relatively easy to see what Freud might have done 'wrong'. It happens in our daily work: with hindsight we can always make the 'right' interpretation. However, for me there is still a different question: since we have the opportunity to know a bit more about Freud's intervention, what can we learn about Dora?

than twenty years after her treatment with Freud, s referred by her own doctor for a consultation with ιcιιx Deutsch (Deutsch, F., 1957). Her symptoms are hysterical ones: *tinnitus*, loss of hearing in one ear, dizziness. Very rapidly Dora starts making a list of her complaints: the indifference of her husband, how her son has abandoned her, her unhappy life, her frigidity, her disgust and dislike of sexual relations, her rejection of a second pregnancy because of her fear of labour pains, her sleeplessness (she waits insomniac every night until her son comes home and she attributes his lateness to his interest in girls), her conviction that her husband is unfaithful to her with other women, and how she considers that all men are mean and selfish. What a change is produced in Dora, the unbeloved, when she realizes that Deutsch, being an analyst, also knows Freud's work: how could she miss such an opportunity? Dora is transformed: she becomes flirtatious, seductive and with great pride reveals her identity to Deutsch.

Her symptoms disappear at the time of her second visit in which she now describes her chronic premenstrual pain, her vaginal discharges, her unhappy childhood, her mother's compulsions and obsessions, her lack of love, her constipation (her mother's only real preoccupation and from which she now also suffers). Miraculous and rapid cure! A few days later, Dora's brother calls Deutsch to thank him.[6] He tells Deutsch how difficult it is to get along well with Dora, how suspicious she is of everybody, that she always and chronically tries to put people against each other. Dora was jealous and possessive of her son who, contrary to his mother's hopes, developed a successful career as a musician. She clung to him in the same way that she had clung to her husband who died of a heart attack, tortured by his own inhibitions and by the paranoid and suffocating behaviour of Dora. Dora's palpitations, her anxiety attacks, her chronic fear of death, kept everybody in a constant state of alarm all through her life and, finally, her death from cancer of the colon was an acknowledged blessing for all those who sur-

---

[6] We know that Dora was in reality Ida Bauer, Otto Bauer's sister. He was one of the main socialist leaders in Austria (Rogow, 1979).

rounded her. From all points of view, Dora seems to have been 'one of the most repulsive hysterics' (Deutsch, 1957).

From reading his 'Fragment', it is clear that Freud did not like Dora. It is also clear that Freud did perhaps feel attracted and seduced by Dora; perhaps there are reasons for thinking that they had both embarked on a game of mutual seduction, but this need not necessarily imply that he liked her. To think, as some authors suggest, that if only Freud had taken her on again as a patient when she returned to him fifteen months later, Dora would have developed differently, is the result of groundless optimism. Dora's insincerity is quite evident: when she asks for more, what she wants is more revenge, and this is, in effect, the content of the communication that she makes to Freud. Freud appears to our eyes as seduced and abandoned; he obviously felt hurt and offended by Dora's behaviour but, nevertheless, this could not come as a surprise since, in the first dream she told him, Freud had understood that Dora had decided to abandon the treatment. His struggle was irremediably lost from the start.

We know that Freud found his reasons to explain his failure: Dora forced new questions, principally related to the problem of the transference and the question of homosexuality. The problems that were presented forced new theoretical positions and we find ourselves, through the years, with his need to revise his previous conceptions. We have then a Freud of the footnotes, different from that of the original text, still stuck to a notion of genital heterosexuality, Oedipal and simple (Mitchell, 1982). We see him, confronted with the homosexuality of his patient, struggling with himself and with that simplistic, initial Oedipal theory. Lacan points out the true prejudice which leads Freud astray in his intervention: from his belief in an ideal, natural Oedipus complex arises 'his need to insist upon Dora's love for Herr K. as a displacement of her love for her father' (Lacan, 1951). The vacillations and the confusion about the history of the publication of his work do not now seem so mysterious: Freud had placed himself 'rather excessively in the place of Herr K.' (Lacan, 1951).

Dora had managed to provide Freud with the illusion of

power only to take it away. She convinced him that he could 'be the analyst', an infernal game in which all Freud seemed to have done was to follow the designs of Dora's neurosis. The comparison of a hysteric with a bullfight is very appropriate here: at all times the bullfighter, like the hysteric, does nothing which is not designed *to make the bull do something* (Racamier, 1952). *Dora continues waving her cape in front of us, as she did in front of Freud. And Freud's text, in its turn, continues provoking in us this wish to know more, and we never seem to be satisfied. In this sense, Freud's text – and perhaps any text on hysteria – is 'hysterical' too: it tantalizes us, waving a cape that hides nothing behind it. But it is that illusion of power, that very blindness which, ironically, will allow Freud to move forward. At the end, Freud confesses: 'I do not know what kind of help she wanted from me.' It is in this confession that psychoanalysis has found its object.*

'transforming your hysterical misery into common
unhappiness . . . ' Sigmund Freud

Today we face the question of the existence or non-existence of hysteria. The word has disappeared from certain psychiatric manuals, and at one of the last International Congresses of Psychoanalysis there was a panel dedicated to this subject (Laplanche, 1974). Is hysteria really a thing of the past? The liberation of sexual morality, the loss of a certain 'innocence' in women, the change in the 'feminine ideal', the social acceptance of sexuality, would all have been contributory factors in the disappearance of hysteria as such. There is a certain theoretical simplicity behind all of this which considers the presence of a neurotic conflict as a conflict about present sexual impulses. The liberation of sexual morality has, of course, had innumerable consequences for the individual and society, but only with difficulty could it affect the Oedipal unconscious fantasy, the unconscious psychic scenario, the incestuous fantasies. A certain contemporary sexualism has slowly pervaded psychoanalysis, turning sexuality (as understood by Freud) into genitality. This has been the misunderstanding of the

[370]

sexologists who believe that what is repressed is the 'knowledge' about sex. For them the sexual process would be a more or less physiological 'need', equivalent to other physiological needs: all that is required is 'information' about it. The liberation of desire – which is different from the liberation of sexual morality – would originate in the informed knowledge about the 'sexual facts', which nowadays includes knowledge about the Oedipus complex. Therefore the resolution of conflicts would result from a 'healthy sexual practice'. The Oedipal drama has been transformed into a totally banal sequence of 'events' and 'anecdotes': everybody can talk – and even joke – about it. But the joke is on us: *what makes sexuality in human beings specifically human is repression*, that is to say, sexuality owes its existence to our unconscious incestuous fantasies. Desire, in human sexuality, is always transgression; and being something that is never completely fulfilled, its object cannot ever offer full satisfaction.

Theoretical simplistic 'naturalism' has gone hand in hand with the desexualization of the theory, a question that has been a fundamental, controversial issue in the history of psychoanalysis.[7] What I am referring to, for example, is present in the discussion reported by Laplanche, in which psychoanalysts of different persuasions discuss *hysteria*. Many of our colleagues would hold – as was suggested in that Panel – that hysteria is only a defensive technique to maintain at a distance and under control anxieties which are defined as primitive, psychotic and not sexual (Laplanche, 1974). This way of defining hysteria as a defence is best illustrated in the work of

---

[7] This issue was, of course, at the centre of the disagreements between Freud and some of his followers, and formed the basis for many of the splits in the psychoanalytic movement. More recently, Lacan and the French authors whom Lacan he influenced so strongly have developed a criticism of what is seen as the desexualization of the theory, and its 'naturalistic' assumptions. It would not fall within the scope of this paper to expand on this point. I would like to refer the reader to Mitchell's and Rose's 'Introductions' to the writings of Lacan on *Feminine Sexuality* (Mitchell & Rose, 1982).

authors like Fairbairn. It is the result of the elimination from the theory of the role of sexuality in the aetiology of the neuroses, which is the central pillar of Freudian thought. In Fairbairn's theories, drives are not pleasure-seeking but object-seeking; hysteria always reveals the presence of oral conflicts, which in his view are the ones that really count; he believes that the Oedipal conflict has been 'overestimated' – 'it involves a certain misconception', he claims – being for him a sociological phenomenon more than a psychological one; guilt is not connected to incestuous wishes in a triangular situation but to fantasies of theft of love that was not freely given; the father as an object is a rather 'poor second' (Fairbairn, 1941).

Hysteria is then torn away from the Oedipal constellation, and the Oedipus complex is relegated to a secondary place: it is no longer that through which the relationship between baby and mother is transcended; it no longer serves as the principal agent of the psychic structuring of the child. Not only is the Oedipus complex made to appear earlier in life but it is transformed into something radically different: it ceases to be the model of sexuality and meaning for the subject.

In changing the concept of the Oedipus complex, the idea of the existence of a prohibition of incest and the castration complex is, consequently, also changed. By eliminating the castration complex as the mark that distinguishes the difference between the sexes; and by attempting, at the same time, a supposed revaluation of the concept of femininity and of women, we meet up again with a belief in a process of biological identification based on a differentiation of the sexes which is supposedly 'natural' and 'given'; we return to the notion that women and men are 'created in nature' (Mitchell, 1974).

However, it is not possible for us as psychoanalysts to appeal to biology to explain the difference between the sexes. We must not confuse the universal uncertainty of the unconscious with the apparent biological reality. What there is in the unconscious is *a danger and a threat* for the man, and *a desire and an envy* for the woman, and not – as is assumed – an overvalued penis and an undervalued vagina. A penis, just as much as a vagina, does not secure or guarantee anything for the subject about becoming a sexual human being (Masotta, 1976). What the idea of bisexuality denotes is precisely the uncertainty of that process and the struggle through which all human beings *become* either a woman or a man.[8]

There are also those authors who stress the processes of identification with either parent as the cause and explanation for the differentiation of the sexes. In this case, the 'naturalism' resides in believing that the sexual difference is imposed on the already 'created' man or woman, by the culturally determined roles. This position also accounts for many of the separations and divisions in the psychoanalytic movement. Freud opposed both the biological as much as the sociological determinism in the theories that tried to explain the differentiation of the sexes from those points of view. As Mitchell points out: all these explanations look similar to Freud's 'but the place accorded to the castration complex pushes them poles apart' (Mitchell and Rose, 1982). Lacan had insisted on this very same point in his comments on Jones' theories, asking himself how Jones managed to be so much in agreement with Freud when his ideas were so radically different (Lacan, 1955-6).

In the development of psychoanalytic theory it has been justly recognized that — independently of the sex of the child —

---

[8] This is not to argue that there might be anatomical, physiological and endocrinological evidence that points to the existence of a potential bisexuality in both sexes. There seems to be some evidence too that this bisexuality develops in different forms for men and women (Nagera, 1975). At every stage in the process of development in the human embryo the female precedes the male, males are developmentally retarded in comparison with females, *except for their sexual differentiation:* this is the only aspect in which the male precedes the female. The male differentiation is completed at sixteen weeks, while the female is at twenty weeks (Hutt, 1972). This could suggest that bisexuality is more relevant for women, which also seems to be indicated by the presence of two fully developed leading sexual organs, the clitoris and the vagina. It was this presence that made Freud think of women as having two phases in their sexual life, and the controversial notion of the change from clitoral pleasure to vaginal pleasure (Freud, 1925, 1931).

[373]

what counts is the threat of the loss of the mother. This has produced a remarkable progress in both our theoretical and clinical practices but what has been left still unresolved is the mystery of the presence of the father (Le Guen, 1974). The father has disappeared from the theory. For Freud, the mere existence of the father brought about the castration complex and the Oedipus complex. In trying to vindicate the mother, the theory has transformed the father into a kind of appendage of the mother.[9]

The relevance of these important changes in psychoanalytic theory for the consideration of hysteria can be seen more clearly at this point. We can understand why, for example, psychoanalysts claim not to find hysterics any more in their consulting rooms:[10] patients may be hysterics but since the theory looks for something else, it also finds something else. One could take this even further: we can turn around, look at the cases of hysteria treated by Freud, and maintain that they were in fact more disturbed, borderline patients. As a result of the change in the theory, we would be in the position of concluding that hysteria does not exist now, nor did it exist then.

> 'Lacking an edifice, we need at least an outline. This is
> what I propose – a pencil mark on tracing paper, a
> blueprint.' Serge Leclaire

Psychoanalysis is like a nomadic tribe, never settling in any one

---

[9] The *natural* figure of the father will be confused again and again with the *normative* figure throughout Freud's work, thus causing an ambiguous reading of many of his ideas. This confusion is central in the text of 'Dora', and we can understand why it has aroused so much interest among feminists: the question of the father relates to the status of the transference; the problem of the transference takes us to consider the place of the father in the aetiology of the neuroses (see Cixous and Clément, 1975; Gearhart, 1979; Moi, 1981; Rose, 1978).
[10] French analysts seem to have less difficulty in finding hysterical patients than their English colleagues. This is the result of their different theoretical outlooks.

place (Pontalis, 1977). There is no map or boundary other than those that psychoanalysis has created for itself. Hysteria has not only motivated the emergence of psychoanalysis but it also perpetuates its existence. In this context, it makes sense to talk about the double vision that the analyst needs to have: analysis has to invent the patient, not only investigate him (Malcolm, 1980). Psychoanalysis created, in the first instance, the possibility of its existence by inventing a new illness: the transference neurosis. Identified as a nomadic people, sometimes we may not see the frontiers, the innumerable paths which lead us to narcissism, to the different psychoses, to the obsessional phenomena. But hysteria is always there, defining the Freudian psychoanalytic field, and 'not as a witness to dogmatic orthodoxy, but as a central element of a psychopathology which offers its meaning to our thinking' (Green, 1964). This is where hysteria and obsessional neurosis come together, as transference neurosis, giving a central place to the castration complex within the Oedipal drama: the inevitable presence of the proto-fantasies of the primal scene; paternal or maternal seduction; the disguises by displacement and condensation; the possibility of a coexistence between regression and the reality principle; and the ever-present prohibition of the taboos (Green, 1964).

If we bring hysteria back to the constellation of the Oedipus complex, we could then see that together with the parallelism of the development of men and women we have to stress the differences and the asymmetry that exist. In so far as the Oedipal developments are asymmetrical there is, for example, an important difference between female and male homosexuality, and in the general structure of perversions in women and men.

In the case of women, the question is not the change from clitoral pleasure to vaginal pleasure but the need to change the object from mother (and the acceptance of her castration) to father (and the possibility of having his babies). In connection with the acceptance of the castration of the mother, it should be stressed that the notion of penis envy only makes sense in reference to, and in connection with, the notion of a phallic mother: it originates in the universal belief of children that the mother has a phallus, *not in the existence of a real penis in the father.* The misunderstanding about penis envy (the assumption that this concept undervalues women) has created a concept of compensation: envy of the womb. Of course men are envious of women but the issue here is a different one: instead of trying to explain the difference of the sexes, this concept would do away with the differences!

The change of object from mother to father is what is problematic for the woman — as relevant and problematic as not having to change objects is for the man. In this sense, bisexuality might be more relevant for women than for men, and it is in this connection that hysteria — with what I propose as the divalence of the hysterical stage — 'has more affinity with femininity' than with masculinity. While the question that the obsessional neurotic asks is: *Am I dead or alive?*, the question that the hysteric poses is: *Am I a man or a woman?* (Leclaire, 1971). Many hysterics would try to resolve this dilemma by forcing themselves to be a woman by making a child (see the case described by Lemoine-Luccioni, 1976). In other cases, they would remain dissatisfied heterosexuals, only being able to reach orgasm through fantasizing either that they are making love to another woman, or that they are active participants in their partner's sexual encounters with other women. A frequent case nowadays is that of a more or less active bisexual woman, struggling to decide — in her supposed 'process of sexual liberation' — whether to be homosexual or heterosexual.

It is said that the hysteric is made for psychoanalysis and, in effect, hysteria is what encouraged its development, forced its birth. Nonetheless, I would like to suggest that *that which defines psychoanalysis also limits it.* Hysteria is considered the neurosis closest to normality, the prototype of the neurotic individual. It is all apparently there, nothing could be clearer: the question of the third one, the Oedipal conflict, the enigma of sexuality through somatizations. It is, however, present only in appearance for when we look at it, there is nothing really there. Dora characterizes the issue of female desire only in that hysteria is a caricature of 'normality'. The hysteric disguises herself: she will pretend to be a woman, she will put on the fancy dress of what she thinks will constitute her 'feminine self'. What must remain hidden under the disguise is her castration, which she rejects and which paradoxically is what defines her as a woman. The 'feminine' will appear only in her symptoms. The hysteric takes her own masked body and dresses up with it, uses it as if it were a brand-new dress, just bought, resplendent, full of sequins, but not very satisfying. Joan Rivière, in fact, extended this to all women: 'Womanliness . . . could be assumed and worn as a mask . . . much as a thief will turn out his pockets and ask to be searched to prove that he has not the stolen goods' (Rivière, 1929). Could this be a rebellion against the law of the father in this patriarchal society? Perhaps, but then the hysteric is the result of the failure of that rebellion. Men support her in this failure, nourish her and respond to her seductions,[11] which they enjoy. They are united with her in the reassuring and comforting fantasy which seems to tell us that femininity lies after all in the guise of what the hysteric wants us to believe is a 'real woman'. Being a true caricature of the feminine, it is also a caricature of everything else: heterosexuality, homosexuality, perversions, the couple, desire . . . and psychoanalysis – *attempting to change the truth of what the analyst is, and is doing, and of what the patient is, and is doing* (Brenman, quoted in Laplanche, 1974).

Whilst at the root of the Oedipal conflict lies ambivalence, that 'simultaneous existence of contradictory tendencies, attitudes or feelings in relation to a single object, especially the coexistence of love and hate' (Laplanche and Pontalis, 1967), I would like to suggest that what characterizes hysteria is divalence. This concept was created by Pichon-Rivière, but he used it in a different way and in a different context. For him, divalence was what characterized – in his version of Melanie Klein – the paranoid-schizoid position, and it refers to the double aspect of good and bad within each partial object. Divalence would be for him 'primary', since ambivalence can only take place after the constitution of a total object (Bleger, 1967;

---

[11] See Temperley's (1975) paper on the complicity of the husbands of hysterics with their wives.

Pichon-Rivière, 1970, 1971). However, I would like to use the notion of divalence to suggest that it develops together with the constitution of whole objects, father and mother, and it defines a specific moment in the development of the individual, in which the subject is confronted with the choice between these two objects. It is a *hysterical stage*, present in every woman, probably throughout her life. It characterizes, within the context of the Oedipal drama, something specifically female.

Nagera has delineated two sub-stages of the Oedipus complex in the girl. In the first one, which he calls the phallic-oedipal, the mother is still the primary libidinal object; the girl is in an active position in relation to the mother. In the second, which would be the Oedipal phase proper, the father has become the primary object of the girl's libidinal interest, and her position is receptive in relation to him (Nagera, 1975). The hysterical stage I am describing would come in between these two phases, it would take place at that precise moment in which the subject, after the full recognition of sexual differences, has to make the change from mother to father. However, I am referring to it as a *stage*, not in a developmental sense, but more as a place where something happens, on which a performance takes place, a drama is developed, and at the same time, as a distance between two stopping places.

This change of objects – a movement between two places, between two positions – is a very problematic one: we know about it through the failures in achieving it. To my mind, the patient described so richly by Stewart (1977 [*this volume* – Ed.]) is an example of what could happen with some hysterics who fail – for whatever reasons – to overcome this stage. Through the patient's confusion, and through her divalence, the analyst becomes a 'bisexual transference figure'.

While the obsessional subject must decide if he loves or hates his object, how the scales of his ambivalence will tip, and is paralysed by this conflict between love and hate which seems impossible to resolve, the hysteric wanders between one object and the other, paralysed between the two, unable to choose between them, frozen in a gesture of apparent resolution. Thus the conflict of ambivalence is superimposed, and is 'secondary' to that of divalence in hysteria, so that the subject can feel ambivalent towards either one of her objects at a given moment, without being able to choose one or the other. Although playing the role of a seductress, trying to win her idealized father on to her side, she is also in strong phallic competition with him for the mother. Freud speaks of Dora's love for her father as a 'reactive symptom', as a defence against her love for Herr K. It makes more sense though to think that what 'still exercised power in the unconscious' in Dora, what was suppressed, was her phallic attachment to her mother. There is plenty of evidence to suggest an unconscious identification of Dora with her father, and Krohn and Krohn (1972) suggested that this identification could be seen as 'a defence against her hostility and rivalry with him or as an expression of an unconscious wish to love woman as a man' (see also Lacan, 1951; and Mitchell, 1982).

In fact, 'stuck' in her divalent stage, the hysteric seems to map one triangular situation on top of the other in her unconscious: in one triangular set, she occupies the place of her mother – whom she displaces through her rivalry with her, and tries to seduce father. In another set, she is in an aggressive rivalry with father for the conquest of mother. The two situations combine but never quite mix, nor are they resolved: at the end, the hysteric will always feel betrayed by both mother and father, and will never find satisfaction. The 'extreme ambivalence' that we find described in the literature, and that would mark the relationship of the hysteric with men, stems from her divalent position. The hysteric cannot define herself as a man or as a woman because she cannot finally choose between her father or her mother. The hysteric will always remain in the middle, moving constantly between one and the other, without getting close to either one: petrified half-way, she postulates the impossible. She is half participating, half excluded: 'Thanks to the support of a possible double identification, she will remain in an unsatisfied desire, with a more or less intense verbosity and relative happiness, sheltered from a frigidity which is her safeguard and the guarantee of her ambiguous disinterest' (Perrier, 1974).

[379]

The beautiful butcher's wife will continue to desire caviare, of precisely which she will deprive herself (Lacan, 1958); or like that other one who, liking good meat, when invited to a restaurant where excellent meat is served, ends up ordering fish (Israel, 1972). Thus we can understand why an author like Masud Khan (1975a) casts doubt on the treatability of hysterics, recommending his students not to interpret to hysterical patients the erotic transference (Khan, 1975b). Extraordinary teaching, ironic comment, which would turn psychoanalysis upside-down and which, nevertheless, makes sense: *to speak of sexual désire to an hysteric is to try to impose a notion which is inaccessible to the subject.* In spite of the apparent transparency of her discourse, the hysteric 'cannot determine the object of her desire' (Masotta, 1976). Because of her divalence, she will be condemned to be a 'go-between' (Slipp, 1977). She will reject whoever loves her, and will die in desperate passion for an inaccessible other, always believing that all she dreams of is 'a desire that would be born of love' (Safouan, 1974), when in fact her problem is how to bear love when sex is present (Green, 1982). For Dora it is Herr K. but it is not Herr K., in the same way that it is Frau K. but it is not Frau K. either. What Dora does is to get interested in the relationship between two people, never as two separate people. The identification with one of them only makes sense to her if seen from the perspective of the other one. That creates the game of multiple identifications, which ultimately leaves the hysteric empty and desperate: the labyrinths of her desire lead nowhere, except to the preservation of that very desire.

In that blind alley the hysteric cannot answer the fundamental problem that is posed to her: since there is a difference between the sexes, *who is she, a woman or a man?* Anna O., in 1922, transformed now into a social reformer and a campaigner for universal love, shows her confusion when she says: 'If there were any justice in the world, women would make laws and men would have babies' (quoted in Ellenberger, 1970).

The question of femininity
and the theory
of psychoanalysis

JULIET MITCHELL

THIS PAPER IS not about psychoanalytic concepts of femininity; it is about the connection between the question of femininity and the construction of psychoanalytic theory. I suggest that for Freud, 'femininity' sets the limits – the starting – and the endpoint – of his theory, just as its repudiation marked the limits of the possibility of psychotherapeutic cure:

> We often have the impression that with the wish for a penis and the masculine protest we have penetrated through all the psychological strata and have reached bedrock, and that thus our activities are at an end. This is probably true . . . The repudiation of femininity can be nothing else than a biological fact . . . (1937a, p. 252)

This intimate relationship between the problem of femininity and the creation of theory has not characterized other psychoanalytic work. This is largely to do with the shifting orientation: from neuroses to their underlying psychoses; from Oedipal to pre-Oedipal. In part it is to do with a difference to the nature of the theoretical constructions. After Freud the theoretical concepts belonging to psychoanalysis were there to be added to, repudiated, confirmed. By and large, alterations and alternatives emanate directly from the clinical work. But Freud had a different task: it was to make *other* concepts psychoanalytical.

[381]

For Freud the notion of the unconscious is there, an idea waiting in the circumambient literature; it is transformed into a theory by his application of it to the material he observed. Freud's patients correct, repudiate or confirm his concepts which remain always larger, wider in application than their particularity in the clinical setting. But if we take Melanie Klein as an example we can see a different intellectual process. When she starts her work the theory and practice of psychoanalysis is already established. Immersed in her practice she comes to question specific aspects of the existent psychoanalytic theory. Her patients do not lead her back into an overarching theory but forward to a new description which relates only to what is observed and experienced. There is no preoccupation with the nature of theory as such, or with the nature of science, or with making psychoanalysis scientific. This is assumed. Not so for Freud.

What did Freud consider to be the nature of theory? I am going to give two quotations which will mark the framework. First, from the *New Introductory Lectures*:

> We cannot do justice to the characteristics of the mind by linear outlines like those in a drawing or in a primitive painting, but rather by areas of colour melting into one another as they are represented by modern artists. After making the separation we must allow what we have separated to merge together once more. (1933a, p. 79)

and in 'Why War?', his address to Einstein:

> It may perhaps seem to you as though our theories are a kind of mythology and, in the present case, not even an agreeable one. But does not every science come in the end to be a kind of mythology like this? Cannot the same be said today of your own Physics? (1933b, p. 211)

Lines drawn to communicate what we know is only a blurred merging. Myths – symbolical stories set up to explain other stories.

When he first used hypnosis with patients, Freud (like

[382]

others) was aware that the treatment echoed an important hyp-
noid state within the hysterical attack itself. At least within
Freud's psychoanalytic theory, there remains, I believe, always
this homologous structure: a characteristic element of the illness is taken up and repeated in the treatment and then, in its
turn, finds a place at the centre of the theoretical construction.
The famous reflection at the end of the Schreber case is an indication:

> Since I neither fear the criticism of others nor shrink from
> criticizing myself, I have no motive for avoiding the mention
> of a similarity which may possibly damage our libido theory
> in the estimation of many of my readers. Schreber's 'rays of
> God' which are made up of a condensation of the sun's rays,
> of nerve fibres, and of spermatozoa, are in reality nothing
> else than a concrete representation and projection outwards
> of libidinal cathexes, and they thus lend his delusions a strik-
> ing conformity with our theory . . . It remains for the future
> to decide whether there is more delusion in my theory than I
> should like to admit, or whether there is more truth in
> Schreber's delusion than other people are as yet prepared to
> believe. (1911b, pp. 78-9)

And later:

> I have not been able to resist the seduction of an analogy.
> The delusions of patients appear to me to be the equivalent
> of the constructions which we built up in the course of
> analytic treatment – attempts at explanations and cure . . .
> (1937b, p. 268)

If for Freud a scientific theory was a myth (there is nothing
pejorative in this), then we should remember both how his case
histories read like *romans-à-clef* and how, if uneasily, he was
well aware of this:

> I have not always been a psychotherapist. Like other
> neuropathologists, I was trained to employ local diagnosis
> and electro-prognosis, and it still strikes me myself as
> strange that the case histories I write should read like short

stories and that, as one might say, they lack the serious stamp of science. (1893a, p. 160)

If the theory is a myth, the case history a short story, then of course the essence of the illness is in some way a story too. As one commentator has put it: 'Charcot sees, Freud will hear. Perhaps the whole of psychoanalysis is in that shift' (Heath, p. 38). I don't believe tht this particular transition is the whole of psychoanalysis; but I do feel that it is important. Rather than stress language, the talking cure, I would emphasize here the listening treatment. Hysterics are creative artists, they suffer from reminiscences, they have heard something that has made them ill:

> The point that escaped me in the solution of hysteria lies in the discovery of a new source from which a new element of unconscious production arises. What I have in mind are hysterical phantasies, which regularly, as it seems to me, *go back to things heard* by children at an early age and only understood later. The age at which they take in information of this kind is very remarkable – from the age of six to seven months onwards. (1950a, Letter 59)

In these early papers – before *The Interpretation of Dreams* and an interest once more in the visual and in perception – the stress is on the aural and its connection with the formation of unconscious phantasies. Charcot saw and classified and dismissed what he heard:

> You see how hysterics shout. Much ado about nothing . . .
> [She is said to talk] of someone with a beard, man or woman
> . . . Whether man or woman is not without importance, but let us slide over that mystery. (quoted in Heath, p. 38)

But Freud decided that these tales of sound and fury did signify something. The move from seeing to hearing, from Charcot to Freud, is the move away from observation and the attendant blindness of the seeing eye.

Stories had two dimensions: what they are about and who tells them. Freud first believed that the stories were true and then that they were true as stories. Hysterics tell tales and fabricate stories – particularly for doctors who will listen. At first Freud was over-credulous. He thought they were about what they said they were about on a realistic plane, he then realized his patients were telling stories. The stories were about psychic reality: the object of psychoanalysis. What they are about, then, is first seduction and then phantasy; who tells them – this is the beginning of psychoanalysis as a theory and therapy of subjectivity.

Social historians of western Europe and America consider that hysteria reached epidemic proportions during the nineteenth century. It was primarily a disease of women. Alice James, sister of the novelist Henry and philosopher William James, will do to illustrate my theme here. Like Dora, Alice's conversion symptoms seem mainly to have been constructed from an identification with her father: a hysterical paralysis of the leg for his amputation. No one doubted that Alice was as able as her brothers; but she made her illness into her career, writing her diaries to parallel the communications of her body. She described her own feelings:

> As I used to sit immovable reading in the library with waves of violent inclination suddenly invading my muscles taking some one of their myriad forms such as throwing myself out of the window, or knocking off the head of the benignant pater as he sat with silver locks, writing at his table, it used to seem to me that the only difference between me and the insane was that I had all the horrors and suffering of insanity but the duties of doctors, nurse and strait-jacket imposed upon me, too. Conceive of never being without the sense that if you let yourself go for a moment you must abandon all, let the dykes break and the flood sweep in, acknowledging yourself abjectly impotent before immutable laws. (quoted in Strouse, p. 118)

She also commented:

> When I am gone pray don't think of me simply as a creature who might have been something else, had neurotic science been born. (ibid., p. ix)

[385]

Many nineteenth-century doctors got furious with their hysterical patients, finding themselves locked in a power struggle in which their opponent's best weapon was the refusal to be cured. Freud and subsequent analysts are familiar with the problem. Freud's understanding of this – in characteristic fashion – moved from the notion of a social gain in illness (removal of middle-class women from intolerable situations) to a psychological one where it bifurcated. It became on the one hand, the theories of resistance, the negative therapeutic reaction, and, particularly, after the case of Dora, of transference and countertransference. On the other hand, after a difficult trajectory which I am going to try to trace here, it led to the concept of a fundamental human repudiation of femininity – a repudiation which, for Freud, was the bedrock of psychoanalysis both as theory and therapy.

I think – and I want to be tentative here – that psychoanalysis had to start from an understanding of hysteria. It could not have developed – or certainly not in the same way – from one of the other neuroses or psychoses. Hysteria led Freud to what is universal in psychic construction and it led him there in a particular way – by the route of a prolonged and central preoccupation with the difference between the sexes. The sexual aetiology of hysteria spoke to Freud from the symptoms, stories and associations of his patients and the otherwise unattended to, accidental comments of his colleagues. But the question of sexual difference – femininity and masculinity – was built into the very structure of the illness.

There are two aspects to Freud's interest in Charcot's work that I think should be stressed. They are separate, but I suggest Freud brought them together. Charcot emphasized the existence of male hysteria. He also organized the disease. When Freud returned from Paris to Vienna the first paper he presented was on male hysteria. In his report, he commented of Charcot's work:

> Hysteria was lifted out of the chaos of the neuroses, was differentiated from other conditions with a similar appearance, and was provided with a symptomatology which, though

sufficiently multifarious, nevertheless makes it impossible any longer to doubt the rule of law and order. (1886a, p. 12)

At the same time, when Freud's friendship with Fliess was at its height, he wrote to him congratulating him on his work on menstruation with these words: '[Fliess had] stemmed the power of the female sex so that it bears its share of obedience to the law' (quoted in Heath, p. 46). The search for laws, lines to sort out and the blurred picture; laws that in the end are anyway only myths.

The laws about the human psyche will be one and the same thing as the laws about sexual difference. Hysteria was the woman's disease: a man could have it. In Freud's hands hysteria ceases to be a category pertaining to any given sector of the population, it becomes a general human possibility. And a possibility not only in the sense that anyone can have it, but in that it provides the clues to the human psyche itself.

We can see Freud stumbling from the specificity of hysteria to the construction of subjectivity in the general human condition in these early writings from the 1880s and 1890s. Always it is via the dilemma of sexual difference.

Conditions related *functionally* to sexual life play a great part in the aetiology of hysteria ... and they do so on account of the high psychical significance of this function especially in the female sex. (1888, p. 51)

Hysteria necessarily presupposes a primary experience of unpleasure – that is, of a passive nature. The natural sexual passivity of women explains their being more inclined to hysteria. Where I have found hysteria in men, I have been able to prove the presence of abundant sexual passivity in their anamnesis. (1950a, Draft K.)

Her hysteria can therefore be described as an acquired one, and it presupposed nothing more than the possession of what is probably a very widespread proclivity – the proclivity to acquire hysteria. (Breuer and Freud, 1895, p. 122)

Freud tried all sorts of explanations as to why an illness so

[387]

clearly found predominantly in women, should also occur in men. But it was a cry of Eureka! when he wrote enthusiastically to Fliess: 'Bisexuality! I'm sure you are right!' Bisexuality was a postulate of something universal in the human psyche. But while bisexuality explained why men and women could be hysterics it did not account for why it was their femininity that was called into play.

At the level of the story, the tale Freud heard was of paternal seduction. After holding on to this information with conviction he writes to Fliess that something is hindering his work. The obstacle has something to do with Freud's relationship to Fliess – the relationship of a man to a man which, by 1937, was to be the other expression of the bedrock of psychoanalytic theory and therapy, once more, a repudiation – this time, on the man's side – of femininity, of passivity in relation to a man.

Many commentators, including Freud himself, have observed that it was Freud's femininity that predominated in this relationship with Fliess; it is possible that it was his femininity that rendered that friendship eventually untenable. Freud referred on several occasions to his own neurosis as 'my mild hysteria'. He did so frequently at the time when he was blocked in his work on hysteria. He has a breakthrough: 'I no longer believe in my neurotica.' Hysterics are not suffering the trauma of paternal seduction, they are expressing the phantasy of infantile desire. Is this true of hysterics or of everyone? Freud's clinical listening and his self-analysis come together:

> One single thought of general value has been revealed to me. I have found, in my own case too, falling in love with the mother and jealousy of the father, and I regard it as a universal event of early childhood, even if not so early as in children who have been made hysterical . . . If that is so, we can understand the riveting power of *Oedipus Rex* . . . (1950a, Letter 71)

Hysteria, the Oedipal illness; source of the concept of the Oedipus complex, discovered through the hysteria of Freud, a male analyst. Universal bisexuality; universal Oedipus complex; hysteria the most Oedipal neurosis, the one that most utilizes bisexuality. Women more Oedipal, more bisexual, more hysterical. These connections were to remain for many years in search of a theory that explained them. What was universal, what specific to hysteria, what to femininity?

Something else that came to be connected was going on with Freud's investigations. These early texts are preoccupied with two aspects of hysteria: the absences or gaps in consciousness and the splitting of consciousness. Anna O.'s illness reveals the absences, Miss Lucy R.'s the splitting.

> [The] idea is not annihilated by a repudiation of this kind, but merely repressed into the unconscious. When this process occurs for the first time there comes into being a nucleus group divorced from the ego – a group around which everything which would imply an acceptance of the incompatible idea subsequently collects. The splitting of consciousness in these cases of acquired hysteria is accordingly a deliberate and intentional one. At least it is often *introduced* by an act of volition; for the actual outcome is something different from what the subject intended. What he wanted was to do away with an idea, as though it had never appeared, but all he succeeds in doing is to isolate it psychically. (Breuer and Freud, 1895, p. 123)

The splitting of consciousness, the disappearance of meaning, the unconscious – these cease to be confined as characteristics of hysteria and again become universalized. Freud finally distinguishes his theory of hysteria from Pierre Janet's on the grounds that Janet argues that hysteria's defining feature was splitting and Freud that it was conversion. For Freud, splitting was a general condition. Freud came back to the question at the end of his life. In the fragmentary paper on 'Splitting of the Ego in the Process of Defence' (1940b) he is uncertain whether, in 1938, he is on to something new or merely saying again what he has said before. It is a return to the preoccupation with splitting that had marked his work on hysteria 50 to 60 years before. I shall argue that what he says at the end is both old and new. What is new is that by the end of the 1930s he has brought it into line with the problem of sexual difference. In the early

[389]

days, it went only side by side with that question – he had not yet established the point of their connection.

Not yet connected with splitting, then, in the early work on hysteria there remained the problem of the division into masculinity and femininity. In the 1890s Freud came very close to sexualizing repression. Fliess offered one version of this argument, the other was to be Adler's mistake. In a draft entitled 'The Architecture of Hysteria', Freud wrote: 'It is to be expected that the essentially repressed element is always what is feminine. What men essentially repress is the paederastic element (1950a, Draft M.). How close to and yet how different is this from the repudiation of femininity as the bedrock of psychoanalysis in 'Analysis Terminable and Interminable' in 1937. But sexualizing repression was not an idea that Freud held on to for long. Six months later, in the letter to Fliess in which he tells of the hold-up in his self-analysis, he comments: 'I have also given up the idea of explaining libido as the masculine factor and repression as the feminine one . . . ' (1950a, Letter 75). And yet – with all the difference in the world – in Freud's theory libido remains 'masculine' and it is not that repression is feminine, but that femininity is repudiated.

The concept that brought together Freud's observation of splitting and the dilemma of sexual difference as it was posed in hysteria, was the castration complex. I don't want to go into details of the concept here – merely to note whence it arose, what it explained and how forcefully it was (and maybe still is), rejected by other analysts. It came from Freud's pursuit of the internal logic of what he needed to describe. He used both Fliess's biological and Adler's sociological accounts as buffers from which his theory needed to bump away. In a fascinating two pages at the end of the paper on 'A Child is being Beaten' (1919b), he explains why these accounts fail. The concept of castration arose, too, from a listening ear tuned to the problem in the case histories, in particular, in that of Little Hans. What it explained was briefly this: how the formation of the human psyche was inextricably linked with the construction of a psychological notion of sexual difference.

For Freud, the child's first question is hypothesized as

'Where do babies come from?' The second (or maybe chronologically the other way round for girls) is: 'What is the difference between the sexes?' The theoretician in Freud reformulated his own hypothesis – the child's imagined questions – as the myth (or theory) of the castration complex: lines around blurred fields of colour.

The splitting that set up the unconscious is repeated in a split that sets up the division between the sexes. For this reason, the 1938 paper on the splitting of the ego uses as its exemplary instance the conscious acceptance of the castration complex and the simultaneous unconscious repudiation of the possibility of its implications (femininity) as expressed in the setting up of a fetish object.

For Freud the final formation of the human psyche is coincident with the psychological acquisition of the meaning of sexual difference. In Freud's theory this is not there from the beginning, it has to be acquired:

> If we could divest ourselves of our corporal existence, and could view the things of this earth with a fresh eye as purely thinking beings, from another planet for instance, nothing perhaps would strike our attention more forcibly than the fact of the existence of two sexes among human beings, who, though so much alike in other respects, yet mark the difference between them with such obvious external signs. But it does not seem that children choose this fundamental fact in the same way as the starting point of their researches into sexual problems . . . A child's desire for knowledge on this point does not in fact awaken spontaneously, prompted perhaps by some inborn need for established causes. (1908, pp. 211-12)

The story told is about the acquisition and repudiation of this knowledge.

Sexual difference – but why should it be femininity that is repudiated? Before Freud, many doctors and commentators thought that hysterics were women trying to escape or protest their female role; Freud toyed with the possibility that all that was feminine was repressed, the repressed feminine would thus

[391]

have been the content of the unconscious itself. We are all familiar with how often women are thought to be more in touch with the unconscious, more intuitive, nearer the roots of nature – in Ezra Pound's words:

. . . . the female
Is an element, the female
Is a chaos
An octopus
A biological process

Freud's answer was: no, 'we must keep psychoanalysis separate from biology'; repression must not be sexualized. But femininity *does* come to represent this point where meaning and consciousness vanish. Because this point is chaos, that which has been made to stand in for it – made to indicate the gap – is unbearable and will be repudiated. In the loss of balance, something to fill the gap will be hallucinated, a breast; produced as fetish, envied – a penis. The clinical experience of splitting and of castration is horror – penis envy, hallucination, fetishism are quick relief.

It is commonly held that castration rests on deprivation – what is taken away from one, as, for instance, in weaning. I would suggest, however, that what it rests on and organizes into its sexual meanings is, on the contrary, splitting. It only then 'subsequently' uses deprivation. One cannot experience absence, a gap – mankind, like nature, abhors a vacuum – one can only experience this unexperienceable as something taken away. One *uses* deprivation to describe the indescribable – the indescribable are splitting and the castration complex.

Freud talks of splitting where Klein perceives 'split-off parts' which can be communicated to the analyst by projection. The similarity of vocabulary conceals essential differences. I am not sure that the splitting of which Freud talks could be experienced in the transference. It can be witnessed in fetishism, but on the other side of the fetish object there is nothing there: no object, therefore, no subject. In my limited experience all the analyst can do is bear witness; all the patient can do is experience the most intense horror, a horror that is about absence but which can become filled with phantasmagoria. The emptiness of chaos made carnate, a plethora of unorganized feelings and objects.

In splitting, the subjectivity of the subject disappears. The horror is about the loss of oneself into one's own unconscious – into the gap. But because human subjectivity cannot ultimately exist outside a division into one of two sexes, then it is castration that finally comes to symbolize this split. The feminine comes to stand over the point of disappearance, the loss. In popular imagery, castration is usually thought of as something cut off, missing, absent, a wound, a scar. Analytically, I believe it is experienced not only in these pallid indicators of absence but as something appallingly out of place: something there which should not be there. The trauma captured in splitting is that one isn't there; the same trauma that castration comes to symbolize is that one is incomplete; the trauma that can be lived over and over again in the endless byways of life's failures and imperfections. The loss can only be filled up:

> If one of the ordinary symbols for a penis occurs in a dream doubled or multiplied, it is to be regarded as a warding off of castration. (1900, p. 357)

Because human subjectivity cannot ultimately exist outside a division between the sexes – one cannot be no sex – then castration organizes the loss of subjecthood into its sexual meanings. Something with which the subject has identified, felt to be his or herself (something that satisfies the mother, the phallic phase – *being* the phallus for the mother – completing her), disappears, is missing. Castration is 'discovered' in the mother who is no longer perceived as whole, complete – something is missing, the baby has left her. The baby goes absent – vanishes from the mirror. Bisexuality is a movement across a line, it is *not* androgyny. For Freud there is no sexual distinction symbolized before the castration complex has done its organizing of the desires expressed within the Oedipal situation. There are male and female, active and passive, multifarious *behavioural* distinctions between boy and girl infants, but no notion in the psyche that one is not complete; that something can be missing.

[393]

The castration complex is not about women, nor men, but a danger, a horror to both – a gap that has to be filled in differently by each. In the fictional ideal type this will be for the boy by the illusion that a future regaining of phallic potency will replace his totality; for a girl this will be achieved by something psychically the same: a baby. Phallic potency and maternity – for men and women – come to stand for wholeness.

Hysteria was, and is – whatever the age or generational status of the man or woman who expresses it – the daughter's disease: a child's phantasy about her parents: the 'daughter' in the man or woman has not found a solution in homosexuality, maternity, or a career. To 'her' femininity really seems to equal the gap indicated by castration or, in Joan Rivière's words, it is enacted as 'a masquerade' to cover it. She is good at this but it cannot satisfy.

In the 1920s some important developments took place culminating on the one hand in ego-psychology and on the other in object relations theory, both Kleinian and non-Kleinian. There was a series of important and unresolved disagreements about the nature of female sexuality, but my point here is that despite an insistence on the problem, the question of femininity ceases to be what motivates the theoretical constructions. I propose to single out a few trends within Melanie Klein's work to indicate the implications of this.

In deciphering phantasy, Freud heard the child in his adult patients. Klein worked with children and found the infant in their phantasies. But there is a difference: the child and infant merge in Klein's way of thinking – their phantasies cope with the inner and outer realities in the present. For Freud, too, through his notion of the repetition compulsion, the child is alive in the adult's present. But for Freud the present always contains a construction of the past: the subject from birth to death is first and foremost, indeed, entirely, a historical subject, nothing other than what he makes of him or herself. This sense of history is not there in Klein's theory nor in her practice. Right until the end of his life, Freud's theory emphasized the analytic task of reconstruction of a history; Klein's highlighted interpretation and the analysis of the transference experience in which the task is to understand (largely through projection and introjection) what is being communicated between two people within the analytical session. Experience of psychic mechanism elicits the story which is no longer a tale told, but something revealed, discovered in process.

Where phantasy to Freud was the story – conscious or unconscious – that the subject tells about himself, for Klein it is the mental representation of the instinct and, simultaneously, a capacity to deal with inner and outer worlds. It joins instinct to object: primitively the oral drive phantasizes an object; a breast or some substitute that can be sucked, for instance, a penis. And in turn, the object alters the inner ego; what is taken in from outside transforms the inside:

> The analysis of early projective and introjective object relationships revealed phantasies of objects introjected into the ego from earliest infancy, starting with the ideal of the persecutory breast. To begin with part-objects were introducted, like the breast and, later, the penis; then whole objects like the mother, the father, the parental couples. (Segal, 1964, p. 8)

The boy and the girl have both the same and different drives: where their biology is different, their urges must differ. For Klein, the instinct is biological; for Freud it is 'our main mythology'. The boy and girl have the same objects. In Klein's theory, the object they first take in is predominantly part of the mother, then the whole mother; this gives them both in Klein's theory a 'primary femininity'. There is a shift of emphasis which, I believe, is crucial. For Klein, what you have got you transform by your phantasies and then take it in and it becomes you. For Freud, it is the attachment to what you have had to abandon that you take in. Freud's subject is constituted by filling the interstices where something is missing: one hallucinates, has delusions, tells stories. Klein's person becomes him- or herself by taking in what is present. Psychically the mother in Freud's scheme is important when she goes away (the *fort/da*

[395]

game), the penis when it is not there (penis envy). Klein's concept of envy (interestingly enough also the bedrock of her theory and therapy) is for a mother who has everything.

For Klein the theory sets up a situation in which the ego phantasizes directly out of its instincts and body feelings onto an object. Whereas Freud's 'body-ego' is always a homunculus standing on its head, for Klein, the objects (despite the accreted confusing phantasies) are, in essence, taken for what they are biologically and socially. The mother is a woman, feminine. The penis, even when inside the mother, is a masculine attribute. So, for instance, when the object of the oral phase moves from breast to penis, for the girl this becomes the heterosexual moment. The projecting penis is masculine where the breast is not. The gendered object gives meaning.

> For the little girl, this first oral turning to the penis is a heterosexual move paving the way to the genital situation and the wish to incorporate the penis in her vagina. But at the same time it contributes to her homosexual trends in that . . . the oral desire is linked with incorporation and identification, and the wish to be fed by the penis is accompanied by a wish to possess a penis of her own. (Segal, 1964, p. 97)

Freud listens to a story, constructs a myth. The unconscious shows they are only stories, myths. It is the gap, the point where the story vanishes, the subject disappears. (Ego-psychologists believe the story is the whole truth and nothing but the truth – the story is all.) But, what we are witnessing in Klein's description is not the unconscious as another scene, that gap which has its own laws, but an unconscious that is filled, replete with a chaos of phantasmagoria, an unconscious as full as the external world seems to be. Her theory is about such an unconscious.

Perhaps I can give another analogy, tentative; a thought-in-flight. Freud's theory is a myth, a story of a story – the subject's narrative structuring of him- or herself. It stops, it fails, it needs re-telling another way. Though a novelist writes of characters of different sexes, he or she never writes of anyone of no sex or in the middle of the dividing line – Virginia Woolf's *Orlando*,

whose hero/heroine must change sides, highlights this. In Freudian theory, masculinity and femininity are only their difference from each other. Difference is articulated by something imagined to be missing. From the position of something missing, each sex can be imagined as having what the other has not. In essence this is what a novelist's story is all about.
· But there is another literary analogy that could act as a possibility for theory. Not a myth, but a symbolist poem. This is what Klein's theory suggests. The wish to bite indicates the oral drive; the oral drive, aggression; aggression is Klein's (not Freud's) death drive. Physical impulse becomes a conception, the conception a theory. In a symbolist poem, the symbol shapes the product. The task is not to produce hypothetical lines around blurred fields of colour but to let the image produce its own shape. The poem, however, does not speak to sexual differentiation. As Adrienne Rich writes:

> If they ask me my identity
> what can I say but
> I am the androgyne
> I am the living mind
> you fail to describe
> In your dead language,
> the lost noun, the verb surviving
> only in the infinitive.

As far as femininity is concerned, we have moved from the hysteric whose femininity, being about nothing, had nothing she wanted, to the feminine boy and girl who, in imaginatively taking in their mother, have everything. But I believe there is a confusion in the conceptualization here. This mother who has everything is not 'feminine'; she is complete. The poem is not, as many people – including Klein in her theory of primary femininity – argue, feminine, even if it partakes of the mother. Of course, the mother is where femininity in its positive filling in of a gap has landed and the association must retrospectively be made. But this poem and this mother are about notions of plenitude, fullness, completeness. Nothing is missing. The verb is in the infinitive. There is no 'I' nor 'other'. In the story sexual

[397]

THE BRITISH SCHOOL OF PYSCHOANALYSIS

difference is symbolized around absence – the abandoned
object cathexis, the envy of what is missing that once, imaginatively, was there. Here in the poem, the envy is for what is there
and it is everything – milk, breast, faeces, babies, penises. What
Klein is describing here is the raw material, the plenitude of
objects and feelings which the story relies on when it comes to
construct itself, to fill in its gaps. It is perhaps poetic justice that
the hysteric who must repudiate her femininity which is about
nothing comes to rest on a mother who has all. But we must
allow the story to tell us something about the poem as well. In
describing what he calls the deployment of sexuality in the
nineteenth century Michel Foucault (1976) argues that there
took place:

> A hysterization of women's bodies: a threefold process
> whereby the feminine body was analysed – qualified and
> disqualified – as being thoroughly saturated with sexuality;
> whereby it was integrated into the sphere of medical prac-
> tices, by reason of a pathology intrinsic to it; whereby,
> finally, it was placed in organic communication with the
> social body (whose regulated fecundity it was supposed to
> ensure), the family space (of which it had to be a substantial
> and functional element), and the life of children (which it
> produced and had to guarantee, by virtue of a biologico-
> moral responsibility lasting through the entire period of the
> children's education): *the Mother, with her negative image
> of 'nervous woman', constituted the most visible form of
> this hysterization.* (my italics)

Motherhood purports to fill in the absence which femininity
covers over and which hysteria tries not to acknowledge. From
their positions along a continuum, motherhood and hysteria,
to have or to have not, to be or not to be, constantly question
each other.

Addenda

BIBLIOGRAPHY

Alexander, F., Eisenstein, S., and Grotjahn, M. (eds) (1966) *Psychoanalytic Pioneers*, New York: Basic Books.

Alpert, A. (1959) 'Reversibility of pathological fixations associated with maternal deprivation in infancy', *Psychoanal. Study Child* 14: 169-185.

Andersson, O. (1962) *Studies in the Prehistory of Psychoanalysis*, Stockholm: Scandinavian Univ. Books.

Anzieu, D. (1959) *El Autoanálisis de Freud y el Descubrimiento del Psicoanálisis*, Vol. 2 México: Siglo XXI, 1979.

Balint, A., and M. (1939) 'On transference and counter-transference', in Balint (1965).

Balint, E. (1963) 'On being empty of oneself', *Int. J. Psycho-Anal.* 44: 470-480.

—— (1968) 'Remarks on Freud's metaphors about the "mirror" and the "receiver"', *Comprehensive Psychiatry* 9: 344-348

—— (1972) 'Fair shares and mutual concern', *Int. J. Psycho-Anal.* 53: 61-65.

Balint, M. (1933) 'On transference of emotions, in Balint (1965).

—— (1937) 'Early developmental states of the ego. Primary object-love', in Balint (1965).

—— (1949) 'Changing therapeutic aims and techniques in psychoanalysis', in Balint (1965).

—— (1952) 'New beginning and the paranoid and depressive syndromes', in Balint (1965).

—— (1959) *Thrills and Regressions*, London: The Hogarth Press.

[401]

—— (1965) *Primary Love and Psycho-Analytic Technique*, London: Tavistock Publications.

—— (1968) *The Basic Fault*, London: Tavistock Publications.

Benedek, T. (1952) 'The psychosomatic implications of the primary unit: mother-child', in *Psychosomatic Functions in Woman*, New York: Ronald Press.

Beres, D. (1956) 'Ego deviation and the concept of schizophrenia', *Psychoanal. Study Child* 11: 164-235.

Beres, D., and Obers, S.J. (1950) 'The effects of extreme deprivation in infancy on psychic structure in adolescence', *Psychoanal. Study Child* 5: 212-235.

Bergman, P., and Escalona, S.K. (1949) 'Unusual sensitivities in very young children', *Psychoanal. Study Child* 3-4: 333-352.

Bianchedi, E.T. de, Antar, R., Podetti, M.R.F.B. de, Piccolo, E.G. de., Miravent, I., Cortiñas, L.P. de., Boschan, L.T.S. de, and Waserman, M. (1984) 'Beyond Freudian metapsychology – the metapsychological points of view of the Kleinian School', *Int. J. Psycho-Anal.* 65: 389-398.

Bion, W.R. (1958a) 'On arrogance', *Int. J. Psycho-Anal.* 39: 144-146.

—— (1958b) 'On hallucination', *Int. J. Psycho-Anal.* 39: 341-349.

—— (1962) 'A theory of thinking', in Bion (1967).

—— (1967) *Second Thoughts*, New York: Jason Aronson, 1977.

—— (1970) *Attention and Interpretation*, London: Tavistock Publications.

—— (1973) *Brazilian Lectures 1*, Rio de Janeiro: Imago Editora, 1974.

—— (1976) 'Evidence' *The Scientific Bulletin of the British Psycho-Analytical Society*, No.10 (1981)

—— (1978) *Four Discussions with W.R. Bion*, Perthshire: Clunie Press.

—— (1980) *Bion in New York and São Paulo*, Perthshire: Clunie Press.

Bleger, J. (1967) 'Enrique Pichon Rivière, su aporte a la psiquiatría, y al psicoanálisis', *Acta Psiquiát. Psicológ. America Latina* 13: 346-350.

Blos, P. (1972) 'The epigenesis of the adult neurosis', *Psychoanal. Study Child* 27: 106-135.

Bollas, C. (1976) 'Le langage secret de la mère at de l'enfant', *Nouv. Rev. Psychanal.* 14: 241-246.

—— (1978) 'The aesthetic moment and the search for transformation', *Ann. Psychoanal.* 6, New York: Int. Univ. Press.

—— (1982) 'On the relation to the self as an object', *Int. J. Psycho-Anal.* 63: 347-359.

—— (1983) 'Expressive uses of the countertransference – notes to the patient from oneself', *Contemporary Psychoanal.* 19: 1-34.

—— (1984) 'Moods and the conservative process', *Int. J. Psycho-Anal.* 65: 203-212.

Bowlby, J. (1958) 'The nature of the child's tie to his mother', in Appendix to Bowlby (1969).

—— (1969) *Attachment and Loss*, Vol. 1, *Attachment*, London: The Hogarth Press.

—— (1973) *Attachment and Loss*, Vol. 2, *Separation: Anxiety and Anger*, London: The Hogarth Press.

—— (1975) 'Attachment theory, separation anxiety and mourning', in D.A. Hamburg and H.K. Brodie (eds) *The American Handbook of Psychiatry*, Vol. 6, New York: Basic Books. (1960) 'Seperation anxiety', *Int. J. Psycho-Anal.* 41: 89-113.

Brenman, E. (1978) 'The narcissism of the analyst: its effect in clinical practice', *The Scientific Bulletin of the British Psycho-Analytical Society*, No. 3.

Brenman Pick, I. (1985) 'Working through in the countertransference', *Int. J. Psycho-Anal.* 66: 157-166.

Breuer, J., and Freud, S. (1893) 'Preliminary Communication', *S.E.* 2.

—— (1895) *Studies on Hysteria*, *S.E.* 2.

Brierley, M. (1951) 'Affects in theory and practice', in *Trends in Psychoanalysis*, London: The Hogarth Press.

Brome, V. (1982) *Ernest Jones – Freud's Alter Ego*, London: Caliban Books.

Brown, D.G. (1977) 'Drowsiness in the counter-transference', *Int. Rev. Psycho-Anal.* 4: 481-492.

Burlingham, D. (1961) 'Some notes on the development of the blind', *Psychoanal. Study Child* 16: 121-145.

Calef, V. (1976) 'The psychoanalytic process', Panel discussion, Ass. for Child Psychoanalysis, Kansas City. Unpublished paper.

Chasseguet-Smirgel, J. (ed.) (1964) *Female Sexuality: New Psychoanalytic Views*, Ann Arbor: Michigan Univ. Press, 1970.

—— (1975) *The Ego Ideal. Psychoanalytic Essay on the Malady of the Ideal*, London: Free Association Books, 1985.

Cixous, H. (1976) *Portrait of Dora*, London: John Calder, 1979.

Cixous, H., and Clément, C. (1975) *La jeune née*, Paris.

Coleman, R.W., Kris, E., and Provence, S. (1953) 'The study of variations of early parental attitudes', *Psychoanal. Study Child*, 8: 20-47.

Decker, J.S. (1982) 'The choice of a name: Dora and Freud's relationship with Breuer', *J. Amer. Psychoanal. Assn*. 30: 113-135.

Decter, M. (1973) *The New Chastity*, London: Wildwood House.

Deutsch, F. (1957) 'A footnote to Freud's "Fragment of an analysis of a case of hysteria"', in F. Deutsch (ed.) *On the Mysterious Leap from the Mind to the Body*, New York: Int. Univ. Press, 1959.

Deutsch, H. (1946) *The Psychology of Women*, Vol.1, London: Research Books.

Edkins, A. (1979) 'Why I like Ess', London: *Bananas*.

Eissler, K.R. (1953) 'The effect of the structure of the ego on psychoanalytic technique', *J. Amer. Psychoanal. Assn*. 1: 104-143.

—— (1965) *Medical Orthodoxy and the Future of Psycho-Analysis*, New York: Int. Univ. Press.

Ellenberger, R.H.F. (1970) *The Discovery of the Unconscious*, London: Allen Lane.

Engel, G.L. (1971) 'Attachment behaviour, object relations and the dynamic-economic points of view', *Int. J. Psycho-Anal*. 52: 183-196.

Erikson, E.H. (1946) 'Ego development and historical change', *Psychoanal. Study Child* 2: 359-396.

—— (1950) 'Growth and crises of the healthy personality', in Erikson (1959).

—— (1956) 'The problem of ego identity', *J. Amer. Psychoanal*. Assn. 4: 16-21.

—— (1959) *Identity and the Life Cycle*, New York: Int. Univ. Press.

—— (1961) 'Reality and actuality', *J. Amer. Psychoanal. Assn*. 10: 451-474, 1962.

Escalona, S. (1953) 'Emotional development in the first year of life', in M.J.E. Senn (ed.) *Problems of Infancy and Childhood*, New York: Josiah Macy Jr. Foundation.

Fairbairn, W.R.D. (1941) 'A revised psychopathology of the psychoses and psychoneuroses', in Fairbairn (1952).

—— (1952) *Psycho-Analytic Studies of the Personality*, London: Routledge and Kegan Paul.

—— (1954) 'Observations on the nature of hysterical states', *Brit. J. Med. Psych*. 29: 112-127.

—— (1958) 'On the nature and aims of psycho-analytic treatment', *Int. J. Psycho-Anal*. 39: 374-385.

BIBLIOGRAPHY

Fenichel, O. (1937) 'The concept of trauma in contemporary psychoanalytic theory', in Fenichel (1954).

—— (1954) *Collected Papers of Otto Fenichel*, 2nd series, New York: Norton.

Fliess, (1953)'Countertransference and counteridentification', *J. Amer. Psychoanal. Assn.* 1: 268-284.

Fordham, M. (1960) 'Countertransference', *Brit. J. Med. Psych.* 33: 1-8.

Foucault, M. (1976) *The History of Sexuality*, Vol.1, Harmondsworth: Penguin Books, 1981.

Frankl, L. (1961) 'Some observations on the development and disturbances in childhood', *Psychoanal. Study Child* 16: 146-163.

Freud, A. (1929) *Introduction to the Technique of Child Analysis*, New York and Washington: Nervous and Mental Disease Publ. Co.

—— (1936) *The Ego and the Mechanisms of Defence*, Revised ed. 1966. London: The Hogarth Press, New York: Int. Univ. Press.

—— (1951) 'Observations on child development', in A. Freud (1968).

—— (1952a) 'A connection between the states of negativism and on emotional surrender', in A. Freud (1968).

—— (1952b) 'The role of bodily illness in the mental life of children', in A. Freud (1968).

—— (1953) 'Some remarks on infant observation', in A. Freud (1968.

—— (1954) 'The widening scope of indications for psycho-analysis', in A. Freud (1968).

—— (1958a) 'Adolescence', in A. Freud (1970).

—— (1958b) 'Child observation and prediction of development', in A. Freud (1970).

—— (1962) 'The theory of the parent-infant relationship', in A. Freud (1970).

—— (1968) *Indications for Child Analysis and Other Papers*, New York: Int. Univ. Press, London: The Hogarth Press, 1969.

—— (1970) *Research at the Hampstead Child-Therapy Clinic and Other Papers*, New York: Int. Univ. Press, London: The Hogarth Press.

—— (1979) 'Personal memories of Ernest Jones', *Int. J. Psycho-Anal.* 60: 285-287.

Freud, A., and Burlingham, D. (1942) *War and Children*, New York: Int. Univ. Press, 1943.

—— (1944) *Infants without Families*, Revised ed. 1973. New York: Int. Univ. Press, London: The Hogarth Press.

Freud, E., Freud, L., and Grubrich-Simitis, I. (eds) (1978) *Sigmund Freud: His Life in Pictures and Words*, New York and London: Harcourt Brace Jovanovich.
Freud, S. (1886a) 'Report on my studies in Paris and Berlin', *S.E. 1*.
—— (1886b) 'Observation of a severe case of Hemi-Anaesthesia in a hysterical male,' *S.E. 1*.
—— (1888) 'Hysteria', *S.E. 1*.
—— (1893a) 'Some points for a comparative study of organic and hysterical motor paralyses', *S.E. 1*.
—— (1893b) 'On the psychical mechanism of hysterical phenomena: a lecture', *S.E. 3*.
—— (1895) 'On the grounds for detaching a particular syndrome from Neurasthenia under the description "Anxiety Neurosis"', *S.E. 3*.
—— (1896) 'Heredity and the aetiology of the Neuroses', S.E. 3.
—— (1897) 'Abstracts of the scientific writings of Dr. Sigm. Freud (1877-1897)', *S.E. 3*.
—— (1900) *The Interpretation of Dreams, S.E. 5*.
—— (1901) 'On dreams', *S.E. 5*.
—— (1905a) 'Fragment of an analysis of a case of hysteria', *S.E. 7*.
—— (1905b) *Three Essays on the Theory of Sexuality, S.E. 7*.
—— (1906) 'Delusions and dreams in Jensen's *Gradiva*', *S.E. 9*.
—— (1908) 'On the sexual theories of children', *S.E. 9*.
—— (1909) 'Notes upon a case of obsessional neurosis', *S.E. 10*.
—— (1910) 'The future prospects of psycho-analytic therapy', *S.E. 11*.
—— (1911a) 'Formulations on the two principles of mental functioning', *S.E. 12*.
—— (1911b) 'Psycho-analytic notes on an autobiographical account of a case of paranoia (Dementia Paranoides)', *S.E. 12*.
—— (1912a) 'The dynamics of transference', *S.E. 12*.
—— (1912b) 'Recommendations to physicians practising psychoanalysis', *S.E. 12*.
—— (1913) 'The disposition to obsession neurosis', *S.E. 12*.
—— (1914a) 'On the history of the psycho-analytic movement', *S.E. 14*.
—— (1914b) 'On narcissism: an introduction', *S.E. 14*.
—— (1915a) 'Instincts and their vicissitudes', *S.E. 14*.
—— (1915b) 'Repression', *S.E. 14*.
—— (1915c) 'The unconscious', *S.E. 14*.

BIBLIOGRAPHY

—— (1915d) 'Observations on transference-love (Further recommendations on the technique of psycho-analysis III)', *S.E.* 12.

—— (1917) 'Mourning and melancholia', *S.E.* 14.

—— (1919a) 'Lines of advance in psycho-analytic therapy', *S.E.* 17.

—— (1919b) 'A child is being Beaten', *S.E.* 17.

—— (1920a) *Beyond the Pleasure Principle, S.E.* 18.

—— (1920b) 'The psychogenesis of a case of homosexuality in a woman', *S.E.* 18.

—— (1921) *Group Psychology and the Analysis of the Ego, S.E.* 18.

—— (1923a) *The Ego and the Id, S.E.* 19.

—— (1923b) 'Remarks on the theory and practice of dream interpretation', *S.E.* 19.

—— (1925) 'Some psychical consequences of the anatomical distinction between the sexes', *S.E.* 19.

—— (1926a) *The Question of Lay Analysis, S.E.* 19.

—— (1926b) *Inhibitions, Symptoms and Anxiety, S.E.* 20.

—— (1927) 'Postscript to *The Question of Lay Analysis*', *S.E.* 20.

—— (1931) 'Female sexuality', *S.E.* 21.

—— (1933a) *New Introductory Lectures on Psycho-Analysis, S.E.* 22.

—— (1933b) 'Why War?', *S.E.* 22.

—— (1937a) 'Analysis terminable and interminable', *S.E.* 23.

—— (1937b) 'Constructions in analysis', *S.E.* 23.

—— (1940a) *An Outline of Psycho-Analysis, S.E.* 23.

—— (1940b) 'Splitting of the ego in the process of defence', *S.E.* 23.

—— 'Extracts from the Fliess papers', *S.E.* 1.

—— *The Origins of Psychoanalysis: Letters to Wilhelm Fliess*, New York: Basic Books, 1954.

Fries, M.E. (1946) 'The child's ego development and the training of adults in his environment', *Psychoanal. Study Child* 2: 85-112.

Gaddini, E. (1969) 'On imitation', *Int. J. Psycho-Anal.* 50: 475-484.

García, G.L. (1980) *Psicoanálisis–Una Política del Síntoma*, Zaragoza: Alcrudo Editor.

Gearhart, S. (1979) 'The scene of psycho-analysis: the unanswered questions of Dora', *Diacritics*, March: 114-126.

Geleerd, E.R. (1956) 'Clinical contribution to the problem of the early mother-child relationship', *Psychoanal. Study Child* 11: 336-351.

—— (1958) 'Borderline states in childhood and adolescence', *Psychoanal. Study Child* 13: 279-295.

Gillespie, W.H. (1963) 'Jubilee oration. The British Psycho-Analytical Society: retrospect and prospect, fiftieth anniversary', London: The British Psycho-Analytical Society.
—— (1969) 'Concepts of vaginal orgasm', Int. J. Psycho-Anal. 50: 495-497.
—— (1979) 'Ernest Jones: the bonny fighter', Int. J. Psycho-Anal. 60: 273-279.
Gitelson, M. (1952) 'The emotional position of the analyst in the psychoanalytic situation', Int. J. Psycho-Anal. 33: 1-10.
Glenn, J. (1980) 'Freud's adolescent patients: Katharina, Dora and the "homosexual woman"', in M. Kanzer and J. Glenn (eds) Freud and His Patients, New York: Jason Aronson.
Glover, E. (1949) 'The position of psycho-analysis in Britain', in Selected Papers on Psycho-Analysis, Vol.1, On the Early Development of Mind, London: Imago Publishing Co. Ltd, 1956.
—— (1966) 'Psycho-analysis in England', in Alexander et al. (1966).
Goldstein, K. (1959) 'Abnormal mental conditions in infancy', J. Nerv. Ment. Dis. 128: 538-557.
Gough, D. (1962) 'The visual behaviour of the human infant in the first few weeks of life', Procs. Royal Soc. Medicine 55: 308-310.
Green, A. (1964) 'Neurosis obsesiva e histeria. Sus relaciones en Freud y desde entonces', in J. Sauri (ed) Las Histerias, Buenos Aires: Ediciones Nueva Visón, 1975.
—— (1972) 'Aggression, femininity, paranoia and reality', Int. J. Psycho-Anal. 53: 205-211.
—— (1973) Le Discours vivant. La Conception psychanalytique de l'affect, Paris: Presses Universitaires de France. (Spanish edition: México: Siglo Veintiuno Editores, 1975).
—— (1977) 'Conceptions of affect', Int. J. Psycho-Anal. 58: 129-156.
—— (1982) 'Freud and Winnicott', Public lecture, The Squiggle Foundation, London.
Greenacre, P. (1953) Trauma, Growth and Personality, London: The Hogarth Press.
—— (1954) 'Problems of infantile neurosis', Psychoanal. Study Child 9: 18-24, 37-40.
—— (1958) 'Towards the understanding of the physical nucleus of some defence reactions', Int. J. Psycho-Anal. 39: 69-76.
—— (1959) 'On focal symbiosis', in L. Jessner and E. Pavenstedt (eds) Dynamic Psychopathology in Childhood, New York: Grune and Stratton.

—— (1960a) 'Regression and fixation', *J. Amer. Psychoanal. Assn.* 8: 703-723.

—— (1960b) 'Further notes on fetishism', *Psychoanal. Study Child* 15: 191-207.

—— (1960c) 'Considerations regarding the parent-infant relationship', *Int. J. Psycho-Anal.* 41: 571-584.

—— (1975) 'On reconstruction', *J. Amer. Psychoanal. Assn.* 23: 693-712.

Greenberg, J.R., and Mitchell, S.A. (1983) *Object Relations in Psycho-Analytic Theory*, Cambridge and London: Harvard Univ. Press.

Greenson, R. (1966) 'That "impossible" profession', *J. Amer. Psychoanal. Assn.* 14: 9-27.

—— (1974) 'Loving, hating and indifference towards the patient', *Int. Rev. Psycho-Anal.* 1: 259-266.

Hart, B. (1911) 'Freud's conception of hysteria', *Brain* 33 (131): 338-366.

Hartmann, H. (1939) *Ego Psychology and the Problem of Adaptation*, London: The Hogarth Press, New York: Int. Univ. Press. Eng. trans. 1958.

—— (1950a) 'Comments on the psychoanalytic theory of the ego', in Hartmann (1964).

—— (1950b) 'Psychoanalysis and developmental psychology', in Hartmann (1964).

—— (1951) 'Technical implications of ego psychology', in Hartmann (1964).

—— (1952) 'The mutual influences in the development of the ego and the id', in Hartmann (1964).

—— (1964) *Essays on Ego Psychology*, London: The Hogarth Press, New York: Int. Univ. Press.

Heath, S. (1982) *The Sexual Fix*, London: Macmillan.

Heimann, P. (1950) 'On countertransference', *Int. J. Psycho-Anal.* 31: 81-84.

—— (1956) 'Dynamics of transference interpretations', *Int. J. Psycho-Anal.* 37: 303-310.

Hellmann, I. (1962) 'Hampstead Nursery follow-up studies: 1. Sudden separation and its effect over twenty years', *Psychoanal. Study Child* 17: 159-176.

Hoffer, W. (1949) 'Mouth, hand and ego integration', *Psychoanal. Study Child* 3-4: 49-56.

Parsons, T. (1952) 'Superego and theory of social systems', in *Social Structure and Personality*, New York: Free Press of Glencoe.

Perrier, F. (1974) 'Estructura histérica y diálogo analítico', in J.D. Nasio (ed.) *Acto Psicoanalítico, Teoría y Clínica*, Buenos Aires: Ediciones Nueva Visión.

Pichon-Rivière, E. (1970) *Del Psicoanálisis a la Psicología Social*, Tomo 1, Buenos Aires: Editorial Galerna.

—— (1971) *Del Psicoanálisis a la Psicología Social*, Tomo, 2, Buenos Aires: Editorial Galerna.

Pontalis, J.B. (1977) *Entre el Sueño y el Dolor*, Buenos Aires: Editorial Sudamericana, 1978.

—— (1978) 'Ida y Vuelta', in Winnicott *et al.* (1978).

Provence, S., and Lipton, R.C. (1962) *Infants in Institutions*, New York: Int. Univ. Press.

Racamier, P.C. (1952) 'Histeria y teatro', in J. Sauri (ed.) *Las Histerias*, Buenos Aires: Ediciones Nueva Visión, 1975.

Racker, H. (1968) *Transference and Countertransference*, London: The Hogarth Press.

Ramzy, I., and Wallerstein, R.S. (1958) 'Pain, fear and anxiety', *Psychoanal. Study Child* 13: 147-189.

Rangell, L. (1967) 'Psychoanalysis, affects, and the human core', *Psychoanal. Q.* 36: 172-202.

—— (1982) 'The self in psychoanalytic theory', *J. Amer. Psychoanal. Assn.* 30: 863-891.

Rapaport, D. (1953) 'On the psychoanalytic theory of the affects', *Int. J. Psycho-Anal.* 34: 177-198.

—— (1958) 'The theory of ego autonomy', *Bull. Menninger Clin.* 22: 13-35.

R ch, A. (1951) 'On countertransference', *Int. J. Psycho-Anal.* 32: 25-31.

Reich, W. (1928) 'On character analysis', in R. Fliess (ed) *The Psychoanalytic Reader*, London: The Hogarth Press, 1950.

—— (1945) *Character Analysis*, 2nd ed. New York: Orgone Institute Press.

Rickman, J. (1951)' Reflections on the function and organization of a psychoanalytic society', *Int. J. Psycho-Anal.*, 32: 218-237.

Ricoeur, P. (1970) *Freud and Philosophy*, London: Yale Univ. Press.

Rieff, P. (1971) *Introduction – Freud: Dora – An Analysis of a Case of Hysteria*, New York: Collier Books.

Riesenberg Malcolm, R. (1985) 'Interpretation: the past in the present', *The British Psycho-Analytical Bulletin*, No. 5.

BIBLIOGRAPHY

Ritvo, S., and Solnit, A.J. (1958) 'Influences of early mother-child interaction on identification processes', *Psychoanal. Study Child* 13: 64-85.

Rivière, J. (1929) 'Womanliness as a masquerade', *Int. J. Psycho-anal.* 10: 303-313.

Rivière, J. (ed) (1952) *Developments in Psycho-Analysis*, London: The Hogarth Press.

Robertson, J. (1962) 'Mothering as an influence on early development', *Psychoanal. Study Child* 17: 245-264.

Rogow, A.A. (1979) 'Dora's brother', *Int. Rev. Psycho-Anal.* 6: 239-259.

Rose, J. (1978) '"Dora" – fragment of an analysis', *m/f*, No. 2: 5-21.

—— (1982) 'Introduction II', in Mitchell and Rose (1982).

Rosenfeld, H. (1985) 'The relationship between psychosomatic symptoms and psychotic states', in *Yearbook of Psychoanalytic Psychotherapy*, Vol. 1, Emerson, N.J.: New Concept Press.

Rosolato, G. (1962) 'La histeria – Estructuras psicoanalíticas', in J. Sauri (ed) *Las Histerias*, Buenos Aires: Ediciones Nueva Visión, 1975.

Rubinfine, D.L. (1962) 'Maternal stimulation, psychic structure, and early object relations', *Psychoanal. Study Child* 17: 265-282.

Rycroft, C.F. (1956a) 'Symbolism and its relationship to the primary and secondary processes', in Rycroft (1968).

—— (1956b) 'The nature and function of the analyst's communication to the patient, in Rycroft (1968).

—— (1968) *Imagination and Reality*, New York: Int. Univ. Press.

—— (1979) *The Innocence of Dreams*, London: The Hogarth Press.

Safouan, M. (1974) 'In praise of hysteria', in Schneiderman (1980).

Sandler, A.M. (1963) 'Aspects of passivity and ego development in the blind child', *Psychoanal. Study Child* 18: 343-360.

Sandler, J. (1960) 'The background of safety', *Int. J. Psycho-Anal.* 41: 352-356.

—— (1972) 'The role of affects in psychoanalytic theory', in *Physiology, Emotion and Psychosomatic Illness*, Ciba Found. Symp. 8, New series, Amsterdam: Elsevier-Excerpta Medica.

—— (1976) 'Countertransference and role-responsiveness', *Int. Rev. Psycho-anal.* 3: 43-47.

Sandler, J., Dare, C., and Holder, A. (1973) *The Patient and The Analyst: The Basis of the Psychoanalytic Process*, London: Allen and Unwin.

Sandler, J., Holder, A., Kawenoka, M., Kennedy, H.E., and Neurath,

L., (1969) 'Notes on some theoretical and clinical aspects of transference', *Int. J. Psycho-Anal.* 50: 633-645.

Schafer, R. (1976) *A New Language for Psycho-Analysis*, London: Yale University Press.

—— (1983) *The Analytic Attitude*, London: The Hogarth Press.

Scharfman, M.A. (1980) 'Further reflections on Dora', in M. Kanzer and J. Glenn (eds) *Freud and his Patients*, New York: Jason Aronson.

Schmale, A.H. Jr., (1962) 'Needs, gratifications and the vicissitudes of the self-representation', in *The Psycho-Analytic Study of Society, II*, New York: Int. Univ. Press.

Schmideberg, M. (1971) 'A contribution to the history of the psychoanalytic movement in Britain', *Brit. J. Psychiat.* 118: 61-68.

Schneiderman, S. (ed) (1980) *Returning to Freud: Clinical Psychoanalysis in the School of Lacan*, New Haven: Yale Univ. Press.

Schur, M. (1959) 'The ego and the id in anxiety', *Int. J. Psycho-Anal.* 41: 650-651. (Abstract.)

Searles, H.F. (1959) 'The effort to drive the other person crazy', in Searles (1965).

—— (1960) *The Nonhuman Environment*, New York: Int. Univ. Press.

—— (1962) 'Scorn, disillusionment and adoration in the psychotherapy of schizophrenia', in Searles (1965).

—— (1965) *Collected Papers on Schizophrenia and Related Subjects.* London: The Hogarth Press, New York: Int. Univ. Press.

Séchéhaye, M.A. (1951) *Symbolic Realization*, New York: Int. Univ. Press.

Segal, H. (1964) *Introduction to the Work of Melanie Klein*, London: Heinemann.

—— (1979) *Klein*, London: Fontana/Collins.

Sharpe, E. (1930) 'The technique of psycho-analysis' in *Collected Papers on Psycho-Analysis*, London: Hogarth Press, 1958.

—— (1940) 'Psycho-physical problems revealed in language: an examination of metaphor', in *Collected Papers on Psycho-Analysis*, London: The Hogarth Press, 1950.

—— (1947) 'The psycho-analyst', *Int. J. Psycho-Anal.* 28: 201-213.

Sherfey, M.J. (1966) 'The evolution and nature of female sexuality in relation to psychoanalytic theory', *J. Amer. Psychoanal. Assn.* 14: 28-128.

Sherman, M.H. (1983) 'Lytton and James Strachey: biography and

BIBLIOGRAPHY

psycho-analysis', in N. Kiell (ed.) *Blood Brothers – Siblings as Writers*, New York: Int. Univ. Press.

Shields, R.S. (1962) *A Cure of Delinquents*, London: Heinemann.

Slipp, S. (1977) 'Interpersonal factors in hysteria: Freud's seduction theory and the case of Dora', *J. Amer. Acad. Psychoanal.* 5: 359-376.

Smith, S. (1977) 'The golden fantasy: a regressive reaction to separation anxiety', *Int. J. Psycho-Anal.* 58: 311-324.

Smith, W.R. (1885) *Kinship and Marriage in Early Arabia*, Cambridge: Cambridge Univ. Press.

Sperling, M. (1950) 'Children's interpretation and reaction to the unconscious of their mothers', *Int. J. Psycho-Anal.* 31: 36-41.

Spiegel, L.A. (1951) 'A review of contributions to the psychoanalytic theory of adolescence', *Psychoanal. Study Child* 6: 375-393.

Spitz, R.A. (1945) 'Hospitalism', *Psychoanal. Study Child* 1: 53-74.

—— (1951) 'The psychogenic diseases in infancy', *Psychoanal. Study Child* 6: 255-275.

—— (1959) *A Genetic Field Theory of Ego Formation*, New York: Int. Univ. Press.

—— (1962) 'Autoerotism re-examined', *Psychoanal. Study Child* 17: 283-315.

Steiner, (1985) 'Some thoughts about tradition and change arising from an examination of the British Psycho-Analytical Society's Controversial Discussions (1943-1944)', *Int. Rev. Psycho-Anal.* 12. 27-71.

Sterba, R. (1934) 'The fate of the ego in analytic therapy', *Int J. Psycho-Anal.* 15: 117-126.

Stewart, H. (1966) 'On consciousness, negative hallucinations and the hypnotic state', *Int. J. Psycho-Anal.* 47: 50-53.

Stoller, R. (1968) *Sex and Gender*, New York: Science House.

Strachey, J. (1934) 'On the nature of the therapeutic action of psycho-analysis', *Int. J. Psycho-Anal.* 15: 127-159.

—— (1959) Editorial introduction to S. Freud (1926b) *Inhibitions, Symptoms and Anxiety*.

—— (1963a) 'Jubilee dinner speech. The British Psycho-Analytical Society: fiftieth anniversary', London: The British Psycho-Analytical Society.

—— (1963b) 'Joan Rivière: Obituary', *Int. J. Psycho-Anal.* 44: 228-230.

Strouse, J. (1980) *Alice James: A Biography*, London: Jonathan Cape, 1981.

Sutherland, D. (1980) 'The British object relations theorists: Balint, Winnicott, Fairbairn, Guntrip', *J. Amer. Psychoanal. Assn.* 28: 829-860.

Temperley, J. (1975) 'The marriages of female hysterics', Conference paper, Group for the Advancement of Psychotherapy in Social Work, November 1975.

Tower, L.E. (1956) 'Countertransference', *J. Amer. Psychoanal. Assn.* 4. 224-255.

Trombley, S. (1981) *All that Summer She was Mad – Virginia Woolf and her Doctors*, London: Junction Books.

Tustin, F. (1972) *Autism and Childhood Psychosis*, London: The Hogarth Press.

—— (1981) *Autistic States in Children*, London: Routledge and Kegan Paul.

Veith, I. (1975) *Hysteria. The History of a Disease*, Chicago: Univ. Chicago Press.

Winnicott, D.W. (1940) 'Children in war', in Winnicott (1958).

—— (1945a) 'Primitive emotional development', in Winnicott (1958).

—— (1945b) 'The evacuated child. The return of the evacuated child', in Winnicott (1957).

—— (1948a) 'Reparation in respect of mother's organized defence against depression', in Winnicott (1958).

—— (1948b) 'Paediatrics and psychiatry', in Winnicott (1958).

—— (1949a) 'Mind and its relation to the psyche-soma', in Winnicott (1958).

—— (1949b) 'Birth memories, birth trauma and anxiety', in Winnicott (1958).

—— (1949c) 'Hate in the countertransference', in Winnicott (1958).

—— (1951) 'Transitional objects and transitional phenomena', in Winnicott (1958).

—— (1952) 'Psychoses and child care', in Winnicott (1958).

—— (1954a) 'Withdrawal and regression', in Winnicott (1958).

—— (1954b) 'Metapsychological and clinical aspects of regression within the psycho-analytical set-up', in Winnicott (1958).

—— (1956a) 'The antisocial tendency', in Winnicott (1958).

—— (1956b) 'Primary maternal preoccupation', in Winnicott (1958).

—— (1957) *The Child and the Outside World*, London: Tavistock Publications.

—— (1958) *Collected Papers. Through Paediatrics to Psycho-Analysis*, London: Tavistock Publications.

BIBLIOGRAPHY

—— (1959) 'Classification', in Winnicott (1965).

—— (1960a) 'Ego distortion in terms of true and false self', in Winnicott (1965).

—— (1960b) 'The theory of the parent-infant relationship', in Winnicott (1965).

—— (1960c) 'Countertransference', *Brit. J. Med. Psych.* 33: 17-21.

—— (1962) 'Ego integration in child development', in Winnicott (1965).

—— (1963a) 'Psychiatric disorder in terms of infantile maturational processes', in Winnicott (1965).

—— (1963b) 'Dependence in infant-care, in child-care, and in the psycho-analytical setting', in Winnicott (1965).

—— (1963c) 'The capacity for concern', in Winnicott (1965).

—— (1965) *The Maturational Processes and the Facilitating Environment*, London: The Hogarth Press.

- —— (1971) *Playing and Reality*, London: Tavistock Publications.

Winnicott, D.W., Green, A., Mannoni, O., *et al.* (1978) *Donald W. Winnicott*, Buenos Aires: Editorial Trieb.

Zetzel, E. (1968) 'The so-called good hysteric', *Int. J. Psycho-Anal.* 49: 256-260.

INDEX

Abraham, K. 39, 42, 80 fn.5
acting out 85, 96, 99, 202, 224, 231,
    274, 277, 313, 326, 335, 342
action: 'deferred' 42-3, 347;
    -language 166
Adler, A. 390
affect 111, 201; and analytic
    situation 214-36; communication
    of 219, 232, 241, 244; theory of
    227, 252, 259-60; unconscious
    214, 225, 226
aggression 22, 118, 126, 197,
    209-10, 231, 315, 397
agony, primitive 176, 177, 231
ambivalence 151, 204, 207, 210,
    221, 230, 231, 250, 313, 355, 377,
    378-9
analyst 66, 99, 187-92, 194-5,
    273-81; and therapeutic change
    253-70; gift-giving to 138;
    identification with 94, 202-4;
    identity with 137-9, 144, 150-51,
    153; physical contact with 77,
    140, 145, 219, 282-94, 297, 313
analytic relationship 58, 99, 200-13
analytic situation 53, 55, 57, 66;
    affects and 214-36; words in 219,
    228-9, 237-52; 'x-phenomenon' in

66-7, 256, 259, 260, 262, 264, 269
Anna O. case 389
annihilation 139, 151, 152, 226
anorexia nervosa 148
anxiety 44, 103, 152, 221, 226,
    227-32, 315, 352; and aggression
    209; and defence 42, 239;
    automatic 119; castration- 118,
    227; depressive 227, 278;
    paranoid/persecutory 218, 227;
    revised concept of 119; separation-
    22, 118, 227; signal- 119, 226-8
Archimedes 172
Aristotle 158
attachement 295-8
Attenborough, D. 356
autism 102-3, 104, 176

basic fault 76, 88, 93, 114, 136, 139,
    140, 273, 275, 277, 279, 297
basic unity 76, 136-53, 308
Bacon Francis 317
Balint, A. 21, 53
Balint, E. 55, 57-60, 65, 67, 77, 331
Balint, M. 19, 21, 22, 50, 53, 54, 74,
    76, 88, 93, 101, 114, 156, 164,
    215, 242, 273, 282, 295-308

INDEX

INDEX

[426]

Mill, J. S. 25
Milner, M. 19, 170, 316
mirroring 59-61, 168, 212, 262
Mitchell, J. 77, 371 fn., 373, 381
Moi, T. 374 fn.
mother 43, 60-1, 90-2, 311, 319,
336, 338, 341, 343, 363, 374, 376,
378, 395; absence of 256; and
identification 84-5, 151, 159-61,
332; as auxiliary ego 83, 107, 122,
175, 177, 181; as instinct
barrier/protective shield 106-7,
120-7, 167, 226; attachment to
331-3, 340, 354-5, 379; death of
138, 337; depression in 77, 89,
337, 339, 340; hysterogenic 327;
pathogenic 132; phallic 313-5;
psychopathology in 122, 127;
separation from 127, 222, 269,
300
mother-child relation 76, 83, 85, 97,
115-6, 123, 132-4, 160, 338, 372
Myers, F. W. H. 25, 26, 46

Nacht, S. 201
Nagera, H. 378
narcissism 60, 103, 142, 156, 375;
primary 44, 104, 107, 118, 125,
159, 176
narcissistic disorder 92-4, 98, 214,
219
negative therapeutic reaction 221-2,
225-6, 386
neural patterning 103-5, 112
neurosis 135, 177-9, 194, 348, 359,
372, 374 fn., 381, 386, 388;
narcissistic 244; obsessional 26,
113, 117, 363, 375; transference-
132, 244, 257, 310, 375

Oberndorf, C. P. 32
object 21, 108, 134, 172, 203, 209,
214, 298, 372; choice of 159, 302;
loss of 119, 203, 207, 210; love-
126, 155, 338; primary 22, 60, 71,
96, 279-80, 378; self and 103, 126,
142, 165, 238-9; sexual 336-7,
346; transformational 66, 76,
83-100; transitional 59, 85-6, 105,
167-8
object relations 22, 43-4, 77, 85, 88,
92-3, 149, 172, 201, 208, 210,
215, 227, 241, 243, 273, 341;
internalization of 134, 160-2,
164; theory 20-1, 76, 394
obsessionality 26, 93, 95, 113, 117,
254, 255, 363, 375, 378
Oedipus complex 38, 43, 102, 118,
151, 334, 351, 354, 371-5, 388
orgasm 316, 349, 350, 357, 361

Padel, J. 76, 154
painting 138
Palombo, S. R. 168-9
paralysis, hysterical 385
paranoid-schizoid position 119, 233,
377
Parsons, T. 262-3
passivity 89, 96, 347, 387
Payne, S. 19, 27, 39, 41, 44, 218
Pedder, J. R. 55, 77, 295
perversion 104, 130, 228, 375
Pichon-Rivière, E. 377
pleasure principle 121, 141, 156, 318
Pontalis, J.-B. 42-3, 58, 154, 220
Pound, Ezra 392
primal scene 118, 325, 375
primary/secondary process 112, 117,
237, 264
projection 56, 58, 72, 102, 118, 142,
150, 164, 171, 219, 226, 242-3,
315, 323, 383, 392, 395
protective shield 120-27, 167, 226;
see also instinct, barrier against
Provence, S. 127, 131
psychic apparatus; see mental
apparatus
psychoanalysis 23, 74-5, 78, 185-99;
in Great Britain 24-52; see also

child analysis; lay analysis; self-analysis; 'wild' analysis
psychoanalytic technique 52, 144-7, 190, 212, 260, 273-7, 297, 333, 342
psychoanalytic theory 39, 77-8, 155, 214-5, 373-4, 381-8
psychoanalytic training 44-5, 51, 295
psychoanalytic treatment 44, 52, abstinence in 282, 297; fees for 253-4, 313; laughter in 196-7; of hysteria 309-27; of women, by woman analyst 331-43; silence in 193-4, 212, 232, 276, 278-9, 290; termination of 71, 210, 369
psychosis 104, 127, 129, 135, 176, 178, 194, 229, 260-1, 268, 375, 381; hallucinatory 256; transference- 140, 147, 151
psychosomatic symptoms 103, 104, 138, 197-9, 216
psychotherapy 23, 29, 138, 173, 187, 197, 206

Racker, H. 292
Radó, S. 58
Ramzy, I. 122, 151
Rangell, L. 155, 156, 169 fn., 214, 215
Rapaport, D. 214, 252
'Rat Man' case 26, 165
Read, Stanford 27
reality principle 156, 375
reality testing 106, 110, 113, 116, 140, 145
reconstruction 232-3, 235, 394
regression 77, 93, 95-6, 110-3, 128, 144-6, 150, 205, 256, 277-8, 282, 307, 375; benign and malignant 273, 295, 297
Reich, A. 52
Reich, W. 201
religion 152-3

repetition compulsion 118, 232, 278, 394
repression 66, 118, 141, 165, 223, 243, 347-8, 356, 390-2
resistance 52, 64, 79 fn.5, 93, 95-6, 99, 201, 239, 264, 269, 386
Rich, Adrienne 397
Rickman, J. 19, 27, 32, 47, 49, 156
Ricoeur, P. 156, 170
Riesenburg, Malcom R. 56
Rigall, R. M. 27
Ritvo, S. 132, 134
Rivière, J. 27, 39, 40, 46, 377, 394
Rose, J. 371 fn., 373, 374 fn.
Rosenfeld, H. 198
Russell, Bertrand 46
Rycroft, C. F. 19, 47, 53, 73, 167, 170, 237

Sachs, H. 32
sadism 257, 316
Sandler, J. 56, 72, 125, 220, 292, 293
Schafer, R. 165, 166
Schizoid disorder 92-4, 98, 133, 150, 214, 250
schizophrenia 122, 127, 175, 176, 180, 250
Schmideberg, M. 40
Schreber case 383
Schur, M. 103, 155, 170
Searl, N. 39
Searles, H. F. 127
Séchéhaye, M. 145
seduction 117-8, 359, 366, 375, 385, 388
self 22, 76, 92, 96, 155-6, 159, 182; alteration of 84-5, 88, 100; and object 103, 126, 142, 165, 238-39; splitting of 88; true/false 78, 128, 168, 193, 298-9, 303, 305-7
self-analysis 70, 100, 204, 388, 390
self-psychology 169 fn.
sexual development 44, 118, 123, 134, 353, 355